PENGUIN

CW00516529

THOMAS CARLYLE: SE

THOMAS CARLYLE was born in Dumfriesshire, Scotland, in 1795. Intended by his family to become a Presbyterian minister, he was influenced by the 'Scottish Enlightenment' while at the University of Edinburgh and became a teacher instead. He later turned to literary work, publishing a life of Schiller and translations of Goethe in the 1820s. He married Jane Welsh in 1826; for a while they were forced to live in her remote farm to save money, but he began to publish his long series of major works with *Signs of the Times* in 1829 and *Sartor Resartus* in 1833–4. By the time his first truly successful book, *The French Revolution*, was published in 1837 (completely rewritten after John Stuart Mill had accidentally burnt the only copy of the manuscript), the Carlyles lived in Cheyne Walk, Chelsea, and he became known as 'the Sage of Chelsea'. Later important works included *Chartism* (1839), *On Heroes, Hero-Worship and the Heroic in History* (1841) and *Past and Present* (1843). Carlyle was greatly admired by Ruskin and William Morris at this time, but his increasingly authoritarian and anti-democratic views also attracted a good deal of criticism. He published an edition of Cromwell's letters and speeches, and biographies of his friend William Sterling and Frederick the Great. In 1866 he was heartbroken by his wife's death and, in his guilt that he had been a far from perfect husband, got his friend J. A. Froude to publish a very frank account of their life together which broke all the conventions of Victorian biography. He died in 1881.

ALAN SHELSTON was Senior Lecturer in English Literature at the University of Manchester until retirement in 2002. He has edited a number of Gaskell's works including *The Life of Charlotte Brontë* (1975) and *North and South* (2005), and was joint editor with John Chapple of *The Further Letters of Mrs Gaskell*. He has published a selection of Hardy's poetry and written on a number of nineteenth-century authors including Dickens and Henry James.

THOMAS CARLYLE

Selected Writings

Edited and with an Introduction and Notes by
ALAN SHELSTON

PENGUIN BOOKS

For my Mother and Father

PENGUIN CLASSICS

UK | USA | Canada | Ireland | Australia
India | New Zealand | South Africa

Penguin Books is part of the Penguin Random House group of companies
whose addresses can be found at global.penguinrandomhouse.com.

Penguin
Random House
UK

This collection first published in the Penguin English Library 1971
Published in Penguin Classics 1980
Reprinted in Penguin Classics 2015

003

Introduction and Notes copyright © Alan Shelston, 1971
All rights reserved

Set in 10.25/12.25 pt Adobe Sabon
Typeset by Jouve (UK), Milton Keynes
Printed in Great Britain by Clays Ltd, Elcograf S.p.A.

ISBN: 978-0-141-39676-7

Contents

Introduction

In his biography of Carlyle, published only a year after the death of its hero, J. A. Froude reprinted a letter written to Carlyle by an unknown fellow-countryman in 1870. After making the usual apologies for intruding upon greatness, the writer goes on to justify himself:

> You know that in this country, when people are perplexed or in doubt, they go to their minister for counsel; you are my minister, my honoured and trusted teacher, and to you I, having for more than a year back ceased to believe as my fathers believed in matters of religion, and being now an enquirer in that field, come for light on the subject of prayer.
>
> *(Thomas Carlyle: A History of the First Forty Years of His Life*, London, 1882, Vol. II, Ch. 1.)

The writer was one of the 'millions' of Carlyle's readers who, according to Froude, 'have looked and look to him not for amusement but for moral guidance', and his letter confirms Froude's emphasis on this aspect of Carlyle's reputation when he wrote that –

> ... Amidst the controversies, the arguments, the doubts, the crowding uncertainties of forty years ago, Carlyle's voice was to the young generation of Englishmen like the sound of 'ten thousand trumpets' in their ears.
>
> *(Thomas Carlyle: A History of His Life in London*, London, 1884, Vol. I, Ch. 11.)

For his own generation Carlyle was not simply a contributor to the Victorian social and intellectual debate, and not simply a particularly dramatic historian, he was a prophetic voice crying out with clarity and conviction amidst the apparent confusion of an age of change. John Stuart Mill, for example, while he became increasingly disenchanted with that Carlylean voice, nevertheless paid tribute to its force in words that emphasize its visionary quality:

> I felt that he was a poet, and that I was not; and that as such, he not only saw many things long before me, which I could only when they were pointed out to me, hobble after and prove, but that it was highly probable he could see many things which were not visible to me even after they were pointed out.
>
> (*Autobiography*, London, 1873, Ch. 5.)

There is a subconscious irony in the last part of that judgement, and Mill is very careful to distinguish between the kind of Carlyle's appeal, and its actual content, but it comes with particular force from the inheritor of utilitarianism, the creed that Carlyle most detested. Almost all of Carlyle's contemporaries seem to have acknowledged his significance: Alton Locke, the hero of Kingsley's novel, pays tribute to 'the general effect which his works had on me . . . the same as they have had, thank God, on thousands of my class and of every other'; Dickens described him as a man who 'knows everything', while George Meredith, with rather more discrimination, referred to him as 'the greatest of the Britons of his time . . . Titanic not Olympian: a heaver of rocks, not a shaper'. The more fastidious of the Victorians tended to hedge their bets – thus Hopkins called him 'morally an imposter', and a 'false prophet', before conceding that 'I find it difficult to think there is imposture in his genius itself', while Matthew Arnold went so far as to describe him as a 'moral desperado' – but they were never able to ignore the message that was uttered with increasing urgency from his Chelsea retreat.

Initially Carlyle's reputation survived his death in 1881: in 1900 alone nine separate editions of *Sartor Resartus* were published, and when cheap reprints of the classics became popular at the beginning of this century his works figured prominently amongst them. Much of his appeal, like that of Ruskin, was to the self-educated: there is an interesting testimony to this effect from Yeats, who in his *Autobiographies* refers to him as 'the chief inspirer of self-educated men in the 'eighties and early 'nineties'. *Sartor Resartus* was one of the works recommended to Wells's Mr Kipps. But the shelves of any second-hand bookseller now testify to a vanished reputation, for when reaction did set in it was complete and unqualified. An age which had justifiable grounds to be suspicious of the rhetorical expression of inspirational ideas found Carlyle's work unacceptable on the grounds of both style and content. His prose, which even his admiring contemporaries had sometimes found confusing, came to be regarded as completely unreadable, while the tendency of his political ideas towards an undiscriminating adulation of authority rendered him objectionable to a generation with practical experience of the evils of fascism. In the rehabilitation of the Victorians that has been a major development of recent literary scholarship the case of Carlyle has been left largely in abeyance. Despite the efforts of Professor Basil Willey and Raymond Williams, for example, to draw attention to the positive aspects of Carlyle's insight into his age, and of American scholars like George Levine and Albert LaValley to redefine the nature of his significance, he remains, if less reviled, to a large extent unread. As a contemporary reviewer remarked, however,

> with regard to Mr Carlyle ... his influence on his own age, if nothing else, must always make him an object of interest to every other.
>
> (*Spectator*, 2 October 1858.)

and it is clear that any attempt to understand the nineteenth century which would ignore him altogether is bound to remain incomplete. Moreover if we can no longer accept that valuation of Carlyle which saw him as an inspired prophet, we should not neglect those qualities in his work which have more lasting relevance: we may not care to accept his prescriptions, but his diagnoses were often penetrating and valid.

Thomas Carlyle was born on 4 December 1795 at the village of Ecclefechan, almost one hundred miles from Edinburgh. His parents were poor, industrious, and above all devout, and from them Carlyle imbibed a sense of moral purpose that was never to leave him. Throughout his lifetime he acknowledged the influence over him of parents who believed literally in the prospect of hellfire for the damned: as he wrote in his *Reminiscences*, 'An inflexible element of Authority encircled us all.' In 1809 he was sent to the University of Edinburgh, where he afterwards claimed that he learnt very little. His only pleasure there seems to have been in the study of mathematics and on leaving the university he became a teacher of that subject at Annan Academy. By now his enthusiasm for orthodox Christianity, which had encouraged his parents to hope that he might become a Presbyterian minister, was more tenuous, although through no want of application on the part of his mother, who corresponded with him regularly. 'Have you got through the Bible yet? If you have, read it again', she wrote, but by this time Carlyle was exploring wider fields. Writing to his mother he announces his intention 'to stay a while with you, accompanied with a cargo of books, Italian, German and others' and in spite of her worried remonstrance – 'I pray for a blessing on your learning ... Do make religion your great study, Tom' – the books had their effect. Carlyle's interests at this time included both native and foreign literature in fact, and his desire for a sense of purpose in what he read led to an overwhelming enthusiasm for the German Romantics, and in particular for Goethe.

Carlyle's earliest published work, which consisted largely of commissioned essays and reviews, reflects these developments in his intellectual interests. In 1822, for example, he published an essay on Goethe's *Faust* in the *New Edinburgh Review*, from 1823 to 1824 a biography of Schiller in instalments in the *London Magazine*, and again in 1824 a translation of Goethe's novel *Wilhelm Meister's Apprenticeship*. To Schiller and Goethe

were later added Jean Paul Richter, Heine and Novalis, while
essays on Burns and on Boswell's *Life of Johnson*, as well as on
Diderot and Voltaire, reveal a range of interest perhaps only
possible in a reader who through force of circumstance was
independent of the literary world of his day. Meanwhile, however, Carlyle had revealed a new kind of interest when in 1829
the *Edinburgh Review* published his long essay *Signs of the
Times*, a radical attack on prevailing utilitarian social philosophy.
The essay was first published anonymously, but its authorship
was scarcely a secret and Carlyle's career as social commentator had begun.

Signs of the Times did not pass unnoticed; Carlyle's next major
work was very nearly never published at all. Still living in Edinburgh, he wrote the involved mystico-philosophical fantasy
Sartor Resartus in which, under the pretence of having been
asked to review an obscure German publication, he charted the
experiences of an imaginary transcendentalist philosopher, lost
in a world of materialism and superficiality. The philosopher,
of course, thinly disguised, is a projection of Carlyle himself,
but the elaboration of the fantasy is such that it is hardly surprising that Carlyle could not find a publisher for it. By now
he was married, and indeed approaching middle age: if he was
to succeed in a literary career it had to be quickly. Eventually,
in 1833, *Sartor Resartus* was taken by *Fraser's Magazine*, to
be published in instalments: its author was to be paid at a specially reduced rate. If the editor of *Fraser's* was afterwards able
to claim that his judgement had been vindicated by the reactions of his readers however, Carlyle, who by now had set up a
permanent home in London, was at work on a far more substantial undertaking. *The French Revolution: A History* was
published in three volumes in 1837 and it met with a very different response. Overnight, almost, Carlyle was famous, for
the work attracted the attention not only of a wide reading
public, but of the leading literary figures of the day. From an
unknown author in search of a publisher Carlyle was suddenly
transformed into a literary giant.

The French Revolution is as much a work of social prophecy
as of history, and the particular appeal of its subject-matter for

Carlyle lay in the opportunity that it gave him to describe a society in turmoil. It is hardly surprising therefore that two years later he should turn his attention again to the condition of society at home, and in *Chartism* (1839) he readily related social unrest in Britain to the conflagration that had been the subject of his history. Carlyle the historian is in fact inseparable from Carlyle the social prophet: the emotional and moral urgency of his utterance in either role is that of the Calvinist who looked for truth amongst the German philosophers and poets. Carlyle was now set upon a literary career in which, whatever he wrote, the prophetic tone would dominate and, like all prophets, he cared little for the susceptibilities of his audience. *Heroes, Hero-Worship and the Heroic in History* (1841) is devoted to his theory of the 'Great Man' which was later to find expression in *Oliver Cromwell's Letters and Speeches* (1845) and ultimately in the monumental *History of Friedrich II of Prussia, called Frederick the Great* (1858–65). In *Past and Present* (1843) he compares the world around him, to its considerable disadvantage, with that of a twelfth-century monastic community, while in *Latter-Day Pamphlets* (1850), which was preceded by his notorious essay *The Nigger Question*, he berates what he saw as the social paralysis of mid-Victorian England, excoriating contemporary philanthropic panaceas with a virulence bordering on the insane. What was wanted, Carlyle cried, was not material assistance but spiritual regeneration:

These days of universal death must be days of universal rebirth, if the ruin is not to be total and final.

(*Latter-Day Pamphlets*, No. I)

As Carlyle aged he became steadily more withdrawn, despite the increasing violence of his utterance. The more extravagant developments in his thinking disturbed even his greatest admirers and he became convinced, not without reason, that his apocalyptic warnings were being ignored. After the death, in 1866, of his wife Jane Welsh, who had endured and sustained him for forty years, he wrote very little for publication: a final pamphlet,

Shooting Niagara: and After?, occasioned by the prospect of the Second Reform Bill of 1867, is the saddest of all literary reactions to that symbolic event. Froude records that in 1870 Carlyle lost the use of his right hand: this too has its own unhappy appropriateness. And yet, if Carlyle contended both in public and in private with the demons of anarchy and chaos, he remained a man who never lost the sympathy of his friends. Browning, for one, protested on his death that he was the most tender-hearted of men. Something of this quality is found in his biography of his friend John Sterling (1851), and finally in his *Reminiscences*, autobiographical fragments which he gathered together after the death of his wife. These memoirs, rambling and sometimes confused, nevertheless give a moving demonstration of Carlyle's feelings towards people he had loved and admired in his early life – his father, his wife, his friend Edward Irving, and his first patron, Lord Jeffrey. Froude's decision to publish them shortly after Carlyle's death led to considerable controversy at the time but it has proved to our advantage, for they reveal a little-known aspect of Carlyle, the private communings of the public voice. For almost fifteen years that voice had been virtually silent when he died in 1881: born in the same year as Keats, he had lived on, albeit unknowingly, into the age of Hardy and Henry James.

The awe, mingled sometimes with suspicion, which Carlyle inspired in his contemporaries can to some extent be explained in terms of his very strangeness to them. His unshakeable moral conviction, born of his Calvinist upbringing, is markedly different from the humanistic and ultimately literary attitudes of writers like Coleridge and Matthew Arnold; less discriminating, it was more self-convinced, and Carlyle himself was uncompromising about the literary scene on his first visit to London. Writing to Jane Welsh he complains:

> Coleridge is sunk inextricably in the depths of putrescent indolence. Southey and Wordsworth have retired far from the din of this monstrous city: so has Thomas Moore. Whom have we left? . . . Poor De Quincey . . . Vanity and opium have brought

him to the state of 'dog distract or monkey sick' ... Hazlitt is writing his way through France and Italy. The ginshops and pawnbrokers bewail his absence ... 'Good heavens!' I often inwardly exclaim, 'and is this the literary world?' This rascal rout, this dirty rabble, destitute not only of high feeling and knowledge or intellect, but even of common honesty ... They are only things for writing articles.

(Froude, *Carlyle's Early Life*, Vol. I, Ch. 15)

To the end of his life Carlyle referred constantly back to the Scots peasant tradition which he insisted had made him what he was, and undoubtedly that tradition provided him with a distinctive kind of insight into the industrial and metropolitan world in which he chose to live.

If Carlyle's background makes for distinctiveness from the Victorian literary world he is distinctive in another, and perhaps more telling way. As Professor Willey has pointed out, he was the Romantic who lived on, and to understand his thinking we have to set it not against that of Victorian social commentators like Arnold and Ruskin, but against that of the great Romantic figures of the earlier part of the century. His strictures on intellectual sophistication, on what he calls 'dilletantism', compare with those of Wordsworth on 'this degrading thirst after outrageous stimulation' in the Preface to the *Lyrical Ballads*; his opposition to the over-valuation of the rational with not only Wordsworth, but also Blake. Like Wordsworth and Blake he mistrusted the claims of Newtonian science and the 'enlightenment' of the eighteenth century, and to the end of his career he never ceased to inveigh against a time 'so steeped in falsity' that 'a French Revolution had to end it'. In the opening chapter of *Frederick the Great* Carlyle defines his own chronological perspectives when, after attacking the eighteenth century as a 'Century spendthrift; fraudulent-bankrupt; gone at length utterly insolvent,' he continues:

'And yet it is the Century of our own Grandfathers?' cries the reader. Yes, reader! truly. It is the grand out of which we ourselves have sprung; whereon now we have our immediate

footing; – and, alas, in large sections of the practical world,
it . . . still continues flourishing all round us! To forget it quite is
not yet possible, nor would be profitable.

Carlyle never did 'forget it quite', and this perhaps accounts for
the way in which his career became, in many ways, a continuous
process of decline. His attacks on utilitarianism, for example, in
Signs of the Times, and on laissez-faire economics in *Chartism*, are
effective because he is attacking genuine manifestations of the
rationalist ethic; the further he gets in time from the century which
he detested the more difficult the enemy is for him to define.

The Romantic must needs find his own religion. If, like his
fellow Romantics, Carlyle posits a distinction between the spe-
cious realities of the material world and the ultimate truths that
lie behind them, he also discovered a personal philosophical
structure through which those truths could be expressed. 'Close
thy *Byron*; open thy *Goethe*' he exclaims in *Sartor Resartus*;
the transcendentalism of the great German idealist poets and
philosophers whom he read as a young man – Schiller, Jean
Paul Richter, Goethe, Fichte, Kant, Novalis – provided him
with both a source of inspiration and a mode of expression.

Carlyle began the study of German in 1819 and by 1824 he
had become sufficiently proficient to have published his translation of *Wilhelm Meister*. In his various translations, in his
biography of Schiller and in the essays for the reviews which he
wrote at this formative stage of his career Carlyle can justly
claim to be considered as the first serious interpreter to British
audiences of what until then had been very much a coterie
interest. For Carlyle, German literature was far more than a
passing enthusiasm and the influence that it had upon him was
to be a major factor throughout his literary career. The explica-
tion of this influence has had an almost fatal attraction for
Carlyle scholars, both in this country and abroad, but it must
never be underestimated. Its finer points are extremely complex, not to say confusing – Mill's comment that Carlyle's
writings 'seemed a haze of poetry and German metaphysics'
is very apt – but the central attraction for Carlyle of German
Romanticism is clear enough: he responded above all to the

emphasis which it places on the uniqueness of the individual experience set against the eternal and limitless perspectives of Time and Space. In the opening lecture of *Heroes and Hero-Worship* he defines the idea and attributes it to its source:

'There is but one Temple in the Universe,' says the devout Novalis, 'and that is the Body of Man. Nothing is holier than that high form . . .' This sounds like a mere flourish of rhetoric; but it is not so . . . We are the miracle of miracles, – the great inscrutable mystery of God.

At a period in Carlyle's life when he was finding the religious literalism of his upbringing untenable he had thus discovered an authoritative mysticism that absolved him from the problems posed by explicitly Christian belief. On the title-page of *Sartor Resartus* he quotes a favourite couplet from Goethe:

> Mein Vermächtnis, wie herrlich weit und breit
> Die Zeit ist mein Vermächtnis, mein Acker ist die Zeit
>
> (My inheritance, how lordly wide and fair,
> Time is my estate; to Time I'm heir)

and while *Sartor Resartus*, that whimsical case-history of a tortured and triumphant soul, is the most obvious example of Carlyle's debt to German Romanticism, the recurrence of this couplet at the conclusion of *Chartism* serves as a reminder of its effect on all aspects of Carlyle's work. His reformulation of German thought was highly selective – he seems for instance to have been able to ignore the humanizing aspect of the mature Goethe's concept of *Bildung*, and in particular its emphasis on the peaceful integration of the individual with society – and it was often sentimentalized and over-simplified, leading to excesses in his later years that can only be described as disastrous. At the outset of his career, however, Carlyle's reading of German literature provided him with the opportunity to transform the morality of his Calvinist childhood, and gave him a unique insight into the limitations of that utilitarian self-assurance which, in intellectual circles at least, seemed at one time likely to dominate his age.

The transcendental element in Carlyle is clear in the opening pages of *Signs of the Times*, his first sustained essay on social issues:

> The poorest Day that passes over us is the conflux of two Eternities; it is made up of currents that issue from the remotest Past and flow onwards into the remotest Future.

This emphasis on the infinite perspectives of the human situation gives point to the critique of Benthamite utilitarianism which is the main purpose of the essay: Carlyle is concerned not simply with a theoretical disquisition but with the affirmation of a faith which is not to be proscribed by a materialistic social philosophy. Written at a time when the effects of the industrial revolution were becoming clear, the essay gains also from Carlyle's sense of the special nature of this point in time, and in particular from his acknowledgement of the possibilities inherent in technological change. There is nothing Luddite about Carlyle's definition of the age as an 'Age of Machinery': having so categorized it he is quick to stress the positive side of the progress of technology:

> What wonderful accessions have thus been made, and are still making, to the physical power of mankind; how much better fed, clothed, lodged and, in all outward respects, accommodated men now are, or might be, by a given quantity of labour, is a grateful reflection which forces itself on every one.

Whatever else may be said about Carlyle, in the early stages of his career, at least, he was not afraid to confront the realities of the world around him, and his positive response to change here is in courageous contrast to the alienation which was to become the standard response of so many of his artistic contemporaries. The advantages of 'machinery' however can only be achieved if man is master of the machine and not its servant, and Carlyle's great complaint against the 'Age of Machinery' in

Signs of the Times is that the machine has taken comprehensive control:

> Not the external and physical alone is now managed by machinery, but the internal and spiritual also ... Men are grown mechanical in head and in heart, as well as in hand. They have lost faith in individual endeavour, and in natural force, of any kind. Not for internal perfection, but for external combinations and arrangements, for institutions, constitutions, – for Mechanism of one sort or other, do they hope and struggle. Their whole efforts, attachments, opinions, turn on mechanism, and are of a mechanical character.

'Not for internal perfection' – the phrase reminds us of Matthew Arnold's definition of the true source of culture in *Culture and Anarchy* almost forty years later, and there is much in both the spirit and the content of *Signs of the Times* that anticipates Arnold's more famous essay. *Signs of the Times*, like *Culture and Anarchy*, was inspired by a period of agitation leading to a Reform Bill, and much of its quality comes from its re-creation of the tensions of that period. Social unrest and political instability are cited as symptomatic of what Carlyle recognizes as

> ... a deep-lying struggle in the whole fabric of society; a boundless grinding collision of the New with the Old ...

and here again it is to Carlyle's credit that he aligns himself positively, but not uncritically, with the modern:

> Doubtless this age also is advancing. Its very unrest, its ceaseless activity, its discontent contain matter of promise. Knowledge, education are opening the eyes of the humblest; are increasing the number of thinking minds without limit. This is as it should be; for not in turning back, not in resisting, but only in resolutely struggling forward, does our life consist.

Signs of the Times, as well as being the first of Carlyle's social essays, is in many ways the most effective of them, showing an open-mindedness that its author was rarely to achieve again. Stylistically too it is a success; the clear and confident prose of its concluding paragraphs is a measure of the quality of its arguments and gives no hint of the mystifying rhetoric which has come to be regarded as the characteristic Carlylean mode of expression. By the time of *Chartism*, written ten years later, the hints of hysteria are clear to see; in *Latter-Day Pamphlets*, written at the end of a further decade, hysteria is the predominant tone.

In *Chartism*, at least, the honesty of Carlyle's confrontation with social realities still survives. It was part of Carlyle's creed that the cataclysmic events of history were both predestined and an inevitable consequence of human self-deception, hence his life-long obsession with the French Revolution as the archetypal historical exemplum. In *Chartism* he argues that

> . . . These Chartisms, Radicalisms, Reform Bill, Tithe Bill, and infinite other discrepancy, and acrid argument and jargon that there is yet to be, are *our* French Revolution: God grant that we, with our better methods, may be able to transact it by argument alone.

The sense of historical perspective is reinforced throughout the essay by the kind of humanitarian feeling that was to inspire *Past and Present*, and that is an essential part of the Carlylean paradox. In *Chartism* Carlyle's observations on the operation of the New Poor Law, for example, and on the state of affairs in Ireland, give substance to his famous 'Condition of England' question in the opening chapter:

> Is the condition of the English working people wrong; so wrong that rational working men cannot, will not, and even should not rest quiet under it?

The force of that 'rational' is considerable: put in this way the question clearly assumes an affirmative answer and here, and in his comments, for example, on the way in which, as a consequence of laissez-faire economics, 'Cash payment' has come to be 'the universal sole nexus of man to man', Carlyle shows an insight that is valuably reinforced by this emotional involvement.

I have referred, however, to the 'Carlylean paradox', and in *Chartism* Carlyle's emotional involvement is in fact of a very ambiguous kind. At its best it suggests a genuinely humanitarian commitment, but when it is combined with speculations on the proper basis of human relationships which owe much to the less fortunate aspects of Carlyle's debt to German philosophy its dangers become apparent. When Carlyle writes, for example, that, in the past 'it was something other than money that the high expected from the low, and could not live without getting from the low' he invites tentative agreement: when he writes of social disturbances that they are

> ... Bellowings, inarticulate cries as of a dumb creature in rage and pain ... inarticulate prayers: 'Guide me, govern me! I am mad and miserable, and cannot guide myself!'

and continues:

> Surely of all 'rights of man,' this right of the ignorant man to be guided by the wiser, to be, *gently or forcibly* [my italics] held in the true course by him, is the indisputablest ...

it is clear that he is already on the road to the brutalistic authoritarianism of *The Nigger Question* and *Latter-Day Pamphlets*. *Chartism* is a particularly interesting essay in that it demonstrates so clearly the best and worst of Carlyle, both in its content and in its style: after the powerful opening chapters analyzing the condition of England on the eve of the 'hungry forties' it deteriorates into speculative and often fanciful rant. Even the two solutions of Education and Emigration which Carlyle suggests in his final chapter are indicative of his social schizophrenia. The first is a valid response to a genuine social need, the second an extension of a spurious racial interpretation of history outlined in an earlier chapter.

In *Chartism* we have for the first time in Carlyle a sustained attack on the ideal of democracy:

Democracy is, by the nature of it, a self-cancelling business; and gives in the long-run a net result of *zero* ... Democracy never yet, that we heard of, was able to accomplish much work, beyond that same cancelling of itself ... it abrogates the old arrangement of things; and leaves, as we say, *zero* and vacuity for the institution of a new arrangement ... The relation of the taught to their teacher, of the loyal subject to his guiding king, is, under one shape or another, the vital element of human Society; indispensable to it, perennial in it; without which, as a body reft of its soul, it falls down into death, and with horrid noisome dissolution passes away and disappears.

Carlyle's theory of the pre-eminence of the Hero, a legacy of transcendentalism that he could well have done without, recurs in one form or another in all of his work from this date. It is defined in its most explicit form at the beginning of *Heroes and Hero-Worship*:

I liken common languid Times, with their unbelief, distress, perplexity, with their languid doubting characters and embarrassed circumstances, impotently crumbling-down into ever worse distress towards final ruin; – all this I liken to dry dead fuel, waiting for the lightning out of Heaven that shall kindle it. The great man, with his free force direct out of God's own hand, is the lightning.

The 'heroes' of *Heroes and Hero-Worship* are in fact a demonstration of the enduring strength of Carlyle's Calvinism: Luther and John Knox are his examples of the 'Hero as Priest', while Cromwell, to whom he was to return at length in *Oliver Cromwell's Letters and Speeches*, precedes Napoleon as 'Hero as King'. The most tactful, one might almost say persuasive, embodiment of the idea is the figure of Abbot Sampson in *Past and Present*; by the time of *Latter-Day Pamphlets* it has become so obsessive that specific reference, with the exception of a parenthetical apostrophe to Sir Robert Peel, seems to have been considered unnecessary. Ironically Carlyle was eventually caught in his own trap: in *Frederick the Great* he was to choose a hero so unsuitable for the role that he was to spend the seven worst years of his life trying to make him presentable.

Carlyle's theory of the hero can obviously be traced to the influence upon him of German thought, and in particular that of Fichte, but his application of the theory to the problems posed by the limitations of democracy is a direct consequence of his relentless opposition to utilitarianism in any form. In an early passage in *Chartism* he derides the science of statistics:

> . . . With what serene conclusiveness a member of some Useful-Knowledge Society stops your mouth with a figure of arithmetic!

The derision is echoed in his strictures on bureaucracy in *Latter-Day Pamphlets*, which anticipates the Circumlocution Office in Dickens's *Little Dorrit* by some seven years. We are familiar enough in our own day with complaints of this kind, and indeed it is easy to see why they attract a sympathetic response. But the weakness of Carlyle's case here is that 'statistical enquiry', painfully slow a process though it may be, and much as its results may disturb our preconceptions, is an essential means towards social enlightenment – indeed this has perhaps never been more effectively demonstrated than at the very time when Carlyle was deriding its pretensions – while an elected legislature, and a specialist Civil Service, are essential instruments of government. They are imperfect instruments indeed, but the only alternatives, as Carlyle so clearly, if not always wittingly, demonstrates, are anarchy or, ultimately, dictatorship. If Carlyle is to be attacked, however, on the grounds of his adulation of authority, it must be remembered that this aspect of his development is a direct consequence of his rejection of the powers of reason. If his case has a particular relevance for us today it is because it demonstrates so clearly the dangers to which utopian anti-rationalism is prone. Carlyle's dismissal of democracy throughout *Latter-Day Pamphlets*, and indeed his singling out of universal suffrage for especial parody as the representative aspect of nineteenth-century constitutional aspirations, is in fact a turning away from the complexity of issues whose difficulties he himself had done so much to define.

The issue of Carlyle's 'fascism' is one that has been rendered inescapable by the events of the twentieth century. Certainly guilt by association is easily demonstrated: Carlyle undoubtedly appealed to fascist ideologists in Europe in the 1920s and 1930s, and both in Italy and in Germany he was heralded as a prophet of their cause. More dramatically we know that Hitler himself took *Frederick the Great* with him into the Berlin bunker, but one might reasonably claim that it was the subject as much as the author of the work which attracted him. At a more serious level there is plenty in the work of Carlyle to have attracted this following: to his obsession with the hero and his offensive dismissal of philanthropic humanitarianism in, for example, the second of the *Latter-Day Pamphlets*, can be added his amateurish dabbling in racial theory, with his elevation of the 'Teutonic' races and his contempt for the Irish, the Negroes, and Jews. The case is a damning one and, in that his more intelligent contemporaries, like Mill and Arnold, give evidence of having sensed it, it can hardly be evaded by the rather easy apology that Carlyle had not seen fascism in action. What can be said, I think, is that the obsessive recurrence of these elements in Carlyle's work, particularly in the later stages of his literary career, suggests not ideological belief but rather psychological disturbance and intellectual deterioration. Nothing is more remarkable in Carlyle than the way in which he simply stopped thinking: it is indicated by the way in which certain examples, and indeed phrases and sentences, recur throughout his work. When one first reads Carlyle the impression is of a wonderfully, in every sense of the word, stocked mind. The more of him one reads, the more one realizes that his arsenal of bizarre allusions is in fact deceptive, for the same references are used time and again to the point of cliché: Carlyle in fact is talking to himself in a language which he invented and which ultimately only he understands.

I have concentrated so far in this Introduction on Carlyle the social theorist rather than on Carlyle the historian, since it is in that role, I suspect, that his most immediate interest lies for us today. Carlyle himself, of course, would scarcely have acknowledged the distinction and, as I have suggested, the two aspects of his career, properly speaking, are inseparable. To his contemporaries, however, he was first and foremost the author of *The French Revolution* – 'Mr Carlyle's wonderful book', as Dickens described it – and in so far as his work can be categorized his most substantial undertakings, *The French Revolution*, *Oliver Cromwell's Letters and Speeches* and *Frederick the Great*, are all the consequence of his belief, stated in his essay *On History Again*, that: 'History is not only the fittest study but the only study, and includes all others whatsoever.'

Historiographically, Carlyle is a freak. The late Professor Cobban, in a judgement that bears repeating, has commented:

> The examiners of a modern doctoral thesis, confronted with a
> history on Carlyle's pattern, would greet the phenomenon with
> consternation; while Gibbon, if he could have read it, might
> have recanted his faith that the days of the Goths and Vandals
> could not come again.
>
> ('Carlyle's *French Revolution*', History, 48, 1963)

More specifically, at a time when the study of history, conforming with the general intellectual trends of the nineteenth century, was becoming increasingly scientific and aiming above all at academic objectivity, Carlyle, in accordance with his own transcendentalist priorities, believed in a philosophy of history that was inspirational rather than rational, subjective rather than objective, impressionistic rather than precise. For the scrupulously scientific historian he had a simple term of contempt – 'Dryasdust' – and he dismisses his activities in a memorable passage in *Past and Present*:

> Alas, what mountains of dead ashes, wreck and burnt bones,
> does assiduous Pedantry dig up from the Past Time, and name
> it History, and Philosophy of History; till, as we say, the human
> soul sinks wearied and bewildered; till the Past Time seems all
> one infinite incredible gray void, without sun, stars, hearth-fires,
> or candle-light; dim offensive dust-whirlwinds filling universal

> Nature; and over your Historical Library, it is as if all the Titans
> had written for themselves: DRY RUBBISH SHOT HERE!
>
> (Book Two, Ch. 2)

The anomalous nature of Carlyle's historiographical position
can be explained by the fact that his own conception of history
was such as to take it out of the region of history altogether.
History, for Carlyle, was the pre-eminent study because it was
nothing less, in transcendental terms, than the revelation in this
world of the Divine Purpose, while the agents of the Divine
Purpose are the individual lives of which history is composed.
The two ideas are combined in a passage in *Sartor Resartus*:

> Great Men are the inspired (speaking and acting) Texts of
> that divine BOOK OF REVELATIONS, whereof a Chapter
> is completed from epoch to epoch, and by some named HIS-
> TORY; to which inspired Texts your numerous talented men,
> and your innumerable untalented men, are the better or worse
> exegetic Commentaries, and wagonload of too-stupid, heretical
> or orthodox, weekly Sermons. For my study, the inspired Texts
> themselves!
>
> (Book Two, Ch. 8)

The concept, of course, is yet another consequence of Carlyle's involvement with German philosophy, but it is interesting
to see how it allows, for a lapsed Calvinist, belief both in
predestination – 'Time already waits, unseen, yet definitely
shaped, predetermined and inevitable in the Time come', as
Carlyle writes in his essay *On History* – and in individual
responsibility. The 'Great Men' of history are both an inspiration in themselves, and a reminder of the failings of others, a
constant object-lesson for the mortal reader. As Longfellow
was to put it in a verse beloved of Victorian schoolmasters:

> Lives of great men all remind us
> We can make our lives sublime,
> And, in passing, leave behind us
> Footprints on the sands of time.

Carlyle's belief in the especial significance of history meant quite clearly the abandonment of any pretence of comprehensive objectivity. What matters above all in history is the message which history has for the here and now: all else is irrelevant. Since, as Carlyle says in *On History Again*, history is 'the only *articulate* communication . . . which the Past can have with the Present', the task of the historian, and it is an extremely urgent one, must be to isolate the message from the irrelevant matter by which it is obscured:

> . . . To distinguish well what does still reach to the surface, and is alive and frondent for us; and what no longer reaches to the surface, but moulders safe underground, never to send forth leaves or fruit for mankind any more.
>
> (*Oliver Cromwell*, Introduction, Ch. 1)

History, then, must be relevant, and history must concern itself with the lives of men, since these are the ultimate reality. First and foremost, of course, it must concern itself with the lives of Heroes, but it does not deal with them in isolation since

> . . . Social Life is the aggregate of all the individual men's Lives who constitute society; History is the essence of innumerable biographies.
>
> (*On History*)

It is understandable that Carlyle's obsession with the Hero should have received so much attention, but in that it had a radical effect on his historical technique it is perhaps this emphasis on 'innumerable biographies' that is the most interesting aspect of Carlyle's approach to history to us today. Certainly the great central characters of his dramas remain in our memory – Mirabeau, Marat, Robespierre and Danton in *The French Revolution*; Frederick, and his father, Frederick Wilhelm, in *Frederick the Great* – but they play out their parts against the ceaseless activity of the multitudinous extras in the cast, and it is this ceaseless activity that remains as our most durable impression.

Carlyle was aware from the first of the methodological problems which his conception of history involved. In a letter to Mill in 1833 he insisted, discussing the art of history, that 'the first indispensable condition of conditions is that we *see* the things transacted', but the problem of translating that vision to the reader is no simple one since, as he points out in *On History*, the actual process of recording events destroys their vitality:

> The most gifted man can observe, still more can record, only the *series* of his own impressions: his observation, therefore, to say nothing of its other imperfections, must be *successive*, while the things done were often *simultaneous* . . . It is not in acted, as it is in written History: actual events are nowise so simply related to each other as parent and offspring are; every single event is the offspring not of one, but of all other events, prior or contemporaneous, and will in its turn combine with all others to give birth to new: it is an ever living, ever working Chaos of Being, wherein shape after shape bodies itself forth from innumerable elements,

and finally, in a McLuhanesque flourish:

> Narrative is *linear*, Action is *solid*.

For all his contempt for 'Dryasdust', Carlyle was an assiduous researcher where his own projects were concerned and for each of his three major historical works he undertook substantial preparation. To cope with the problems of recapturing the actual texture of events themselves he devised a unique method of deploying the labours of his research, converting the actual sources which he consulted into a reconstituted and revitalized artistic medium. In *The Letters and Speeches of Oliver Cromwell* the method is fairly straightforward, if original at the time: the story of the English Civil War and the Commonwealth is told in Cromwell's own words with the assistance of interspersed editorial comment. In *The French Revolution*, however, and in *Frederick the Great*, the method is far more complex. In each of these works Carlyle creates from his sources a vast historical collage, all the time quoting from them either directly or obliquely, and indeed if necessary quoting himself in an attempt to avoid the impersonality of the authorial voice. At its worst the technique is disjointed, confusing and ultimately tedious: this is most obviously the case in long sections of *Frederick the Great*, where Carlyle, disillusioned both by the work in hand and by the consciousness of failure in the prophetic role in which he had cast himself, was unable to summon up the reserves of energy and concentration that his method demands. In *The French Revolution*, however, written when Carlyle was at the height of his powers, the method is a triumphant success; inspired by Carlyle's conviction of the significance of his theme and underpinned by a firmly held narrative line, it vindicates as far as anything can his inspirational concept of history.

A distinguished Professor, now long since retired, was reputed to indicate the impending conclusion of his lectures with the words, 'now for a few poetic touches'. No discussion of Carlyle can evade the problem of his style, but if it is introduced at this point as a phenomenon on its own that is not because it is felt that it can be treated in any way as an afterthought. Carlyle's style is part and parcel of his apocalyptic message, as he himself indicated when he observed to Sterling that he saw 'the whole structure of Johnsonian English breaking up from its foundations, revolutions there as visible as anywhere else!' The peculiar feverishness of Carlyle's mode of expression, the sense which the reader gets of the ink not having been given time to dry on the page, is a direct consequence of his relentless emphasis on the need to be constantly active:

> I too could now say to myself: Be no longer a Chaos, but a World, or even Worldkin. Produce! Produce! Were it but the pitifullest infinitesmal fraction of a Product, produce it in God's name! 'Tis the utmost thou hast in thee: out with it then. Up, Up! Whatsoever thy hand findeth to do, do it with thy whole might. Work while it is called To-day; for the Night cometh, wherein no man can work.

That passage comes at the conclusion of the climactic chapter on 'The Everlasting Yea' in *Sartor Resartus*; the man who wrote it can scarcely have seen literary style as a conscious adornment of the content of his work.

Nevertheless Carlyle's style – what critics have come to call 'Carlylese' – is so remarkably unlike anything else in English literature that it has seemed impenetrable to many readers. Indeed the difficulties which it poses, one suspects, contributed much at one time to his appeal as 'literature' (one remembers Leonard Bast, in *Howards End*, attempting to form his prose style on the model of Ruskin: 'he understood him to be the greatest master of English prose'). The chief characteristic of the style, however, is rhetorical rather than literary, a direct consequence of that impulse which led to his parents' aspirations that Carlyle might one day occupy a Presbyterian pulpit.

Carlyle's prose aims above all at involving, and indeed implicating, the reader in the unending battle against the false gods of nineteenth-century England. It is declamatory, gymnastically aggressive, and cares little for the nuances of reason and sensitivity. Its devices are legion, but one can, I think, distinguish three particular features which contribute to its hortatory effect: in the first place there is a deliberate distortion of conventional sentence structure which attracts the reader by its very virtuosity; secondly there is the repetition of particularly distinctive phrases, sometimes coinages of Carlyle's own making; and finally there is the extensive deployment of a range of allusions, the impact of which lies as much in their general rhetorical suggestiveness as in their specific meaning. At a fairly elementary level all three techniques can be seen in the following paragraph from *Chartism*:

> Another thing, which the British reader often reads and hears in this time, is worth his meditating for a moment: That Society 'exists for the protection of property.' To which it is added, that the poor man also has property, namely, his 'labour,' and the fifteen-pence or three-and-six-pence a-day he can get for that. True enough, O friends, 'for protecting *property*;' most true: and indeed, if you will once sufficiently enforce that Eighth

Commandment, the whole 'rights of man' are well cared for; I know no better definition of the rights of man. *Thou shalt not steal, thou shalt not be stolen from*: what a Society were that; Plato's Republic, More's Utopia mere emblems of it! Give every man what is his, the accurate price of what he has done and been, no man shall any more complain, neither shall the earth suffer any more. For the protection of property, in very truth, and for that alone!

Here we have an explicit approach to the reader at the start of the paragraph, reinforced later by the apostrophe 'O friends', which includes in fact both the reader and all those who accept the commonplace which is about to be redefined. The sentence structure is deliberately manipulated to emphasize the key phrase of the passage, 'protection of property', and this is repeated, with deliberate adjustments, and set against the other repeated catchphrase 'rights of man' in a way which suggests unseen implications in the supposedly conventional equation. Finally we have the references to the Bible, supported by the semi-biblical rhythms of the passage itself, and to 'Plato's Republic, More's Utopia', all of which suggest the scale against which the 'rights of man' should really be measured. By the end of the paragraph the phrase 'protection of property', which Carlyle originally instanced as a cliché, has a weight of implication as yet undefined.

The basic movement of the prose in this instance is one of accumulation and progress: read in context (this edition p. 164) the paragraph can be seen to prepare for Carlyle's own definition of 'property' in the paragraph which follows. In Carlyle's later work the movement of his prose tends to be circular and self-enclosed, more often than not leading the reader back to the point from which he started, and it is tempting to detect in the development of Carlyle's style a deterioration corresponding with the increasing repugnance of his ideas. Such an argument, while perhaps supportable in general terms, involves a selective approach to the evidence, however, and in an essay entitled 'The Use and Abuse of Carlylese' (reprinted in *The Art of Victorian Prose*, ed. G. Levine and W. Madden, London,

1968) George Levine has argued against the over-simplification which it involves. In a very stimulating discussion of the issue Levine prefers to argue that what is missing from Carlyle's later prose is that energetic optimism embodied in *Signs of the Times*, in *The French Revolution* and in *Chartism*, which allows Carlyle to envisage even the most cataclysmic events in terms of the potential offered for renewal and rebirth. This, he argues, counteracts the negative implications of Carlyle's critique of the world around him; once it has disappeared, the balance of the prose, and indeed its tension, disappear also.

In a letter to Emerson, written in 1842, Carlyle rebuked the American idealist for the escapist tendencies of his ideas: 'A man has no right to say to his own generation, turning quite away from it, "Be Damned!" It is the whole Past and the whole Future, this same cotton-spinning, dollar-hunting, canting and shrieking, very wretched generation of ours. Come back into it I tell you.' Carlyle himself never needed such a warning, and all of his major works can be said to have been written in response to social disturbance and the possibility of change. If this is most obviously true of *Signs of the Times*, *Chartism*, *The French Revolution* and *Oliver Cromwell*, it is none the less the case, implicitly, with *Past and Present* and *Latter-Day Pamphlets*, with their concern with forming order out of apparent chaos, and with *Frederick the Great*, whose hero is seen as the one true man in an age whose falsehood has brought it to the brink of anarchy. *Sartor Resartus* explores the theme in terms of the inner life of man, whose struggles are resolved by his assertion of the 'Everlasting Yea'. There is no clearer indication of the difference between the best and the worst of Carlyle than that embodied in his reaction to change: at his prime he sees it in terms of opportunity, but ultimately he can only think in terms of disruption. His historical method and his prose style reflect this development: in *The French Revolution* he confronts the new with the new in a way which can genuinely be said to liberate the imagination, whereas in *Frederick the Great* he exhausts not only himself but also, in the end, his reader. More than any other author in our literature Carlyle requires a degree of apologetics that will induce suspicion in the most uncommitted reader, and his decline is a consequence of weaknesses which are endemic in his viewpoint from the start. To see him simply in terms of that decline, however, is to do him an injustice which we would not inflict upon authors who do less violence to our sensibilities.

This volume aims at a selection of Carlyle's work that is representative of all stages of his career, rather than at a hypothetical 'Best of Carlyle', or even 'Essential Carlyle'. I have tried to follow the principle of representing individual works by substantial passages, and where possible complete sections or chapters from them, for it seems to me that such a policy offers less opportunity for editorial misrepresentation than the alternative of selecting a wider variety of shorter pieces. Inevitably this has occasionally meant the inclusion of material which a more active editor might have omitted, but experience has shown that Carlyle does not lend himself easily to editorial surgery. I am conscious of two serious omissions: *Oliver Cromwell's Letters and Speeches* and *The Nigger Question* are both unrepresented. In the case of the former it seemed to me clear that no selection could indicate the nature of the work satisfactorily and I have no qualms about its omission. *The Nigger Question* is a more difficult case, since it has achieved such a degree of notoriety, but I decided ultimately that it could only be represented in full, or not at all, and reasons of space dictated the latter course. I should perhaps add that similar factors were involved in the case of the late essay, *Shooting Niagara: and After?*, although here the omission has caused me less concern.

ACKNOWLEDGEMENTS

I have pestered so many of my colleagues at the University of Manchester with inquiries relating to Carlyle that it seems invidious to mention individuals. I feel however that I must acknowledge particular indebtedness to Mr John Chapple, of the Department of English, who has always been helpful when I have turned to him for advice, and to Dr Lilian Furst,

Dr Michael Rose and Dr Alan Wilson, whose specialized knowledge in their respective fields has been of considerable assistance. In acknowledging debts, of course, I in no way wish to imply responsibility for the inadequacies which undoubtedly remain: they are all my own.

ALAN SHELSTON

University of Manchester
September 1970

Selected Bibliography

In preparing this selection I have used the text of the 'Library Edition' of Carlyle's *Collected Works*, 30 vols, London, 1870–1. This edition was published by Chapman and Hall and was made up of individual volumes published during Carlyle's lifetime and for which Carlyle himself had prepared summaries and indexes. I have also consulted the 'Centenary Edition' of the *Collected Works*, 30 vols, ed. H. D. Traill, London, 1896–9. This was also published by Chapman and Hall and was based on the earlier edition, retaining Carlyle's notes and indexes. It contains a certain amount of additional minor material, but its chief distinction from the earlier edition lies in the brief essays with which Traill introduces each volume. Neither edition contains the *Reminiscences*; in this case I have used the text of the first edition, ed. J. A. Froude, 2 vols, London, 1881. The edition by Charles Eliot Norton, 2 vols, London, 1887, should also be consulted.

The best biography of Carlyle is still that by Froude, which appeared in four volumes, 1882–4 (*Thomas Carlyle: A History of the First Forty Years of His Life*, 2 vols, London, 1882; *Thomas Carlyle: A History of His Life in London*, 2 vols, London, 1884). Froude's frankness, which caused such controversy when his work first appeared, has given it a lasting quality which is scarcely matched by the six volumes of D. A. Wilson, published with separate titles from 1923 to 1934. There is an excellent critical biography in one volume by Emery Neff, *Carlyle*, London, 1932, and a more recent study by Julian Symons, *Thomas Carlyle*, London, 1952.

There is a considerable amount of Carlyle criticism, and for a detailed list the reader is referred to the *New Cambridge Bibliography of English Literature*, Vol. III, ed. G. Watson, and to the critical bibliography by C. Moore in *The English Romantic Poets and Essayists*, ed. C. W. and L. H. Houtchens, rev. ed., New York, 1966. I have found the following works particularly valuable:

E. Neff, *Carlyle and Mill*, New York, 1924.

C. F. Harrold, *Carlyle and German Thought, 1819–34*, New Haven, 1934.

L. M. Young, *Carlyle and the Art of History*, Philadelphia, 1939.

B. Willey, *Nineteenth Century Studies*, London, 1949.

J. Holloway, *The Victorian Sage*, London, 1953.

R. Williams, *Culture and Society*, London, 1961.

G. B. Tennyson, *Sartor Called Resartus*, Princeton, 1965.

H. Ben-Israel, *English Historians on the French Revolution*, London, 1968.

G. Levine, *The Boundaries of Fiction*, Princeton, 1968.

G. Levine and W. Madden, eds, *The Art of Victorian Prose*, New York, 1968.

A. J. LaValley, *Carlyle and the Idea of the Modern*, New Haven, 1968.

H. L. Sussman, *Victorians and the Machine*, Cambridge, Mass., 1968.

Where Carlyle's footnotes have been retained they are indicated in the text by asterisks, etc., and appear at the foot of the page.

Three dots ... at the beginning or end of a passage in the selection indicates that it is an incomplete part of the chapter or section of the work from which it has been taken.

SELECTED WRITINGS

SELECTED WRITINGS

Early Essays

In a sense it is misleading to talk of the 'early' stages of Carlyle's career since, while *Signs of the Times* attracted favourable notice in 1829, he had been writing for almost twenty years before *The French Revolution* established him as a public figure. Much of the work produced during this period consisted of reviews and essays written for the journals, most notably Lord Jeffrey's *Edinburgh Review* and, in the 1830s, *Fraser's Magazine*. At the same time Carlyle was translating German literature: in 1824 his translation of *Wilhelm Meister* was published in Edinburgh, and this was followed in 1827 by *German Romance: Specimens of its Chief Authors*, which included translations of Jean Paul Richter and Goethe.

Four extracts from Carlyle's work during this stage of his career are reprinted here. That on Goethe is taken from the Introduction to the fourth volume of *German Romance*. The essay on Burns was published in the *Edinburgh Review* in December 1828; that on Voltaire in the *Foreign Review* in 1829. *On History* appeared in *Fraser's Magazine* in November 1830.

from Goethe

... Of a nature so rare and complex it is difficult to form a true comprehension; difficult even to express what comprehension one has formed. In Goethe's mind, the first aspect that strikes us is its calmness, then its beauty; a deeper inspection reveals to us its vastness and unmeasured strength. This man rules, and is not ruled. The stern and fiery energies of a most passionate soul lie silent in the centre of his being; a trembling sensibility has been inured to stand, without flinching or murmur, the sharpest trials. Nothing outward, nothing inward, shall agitate or control him. The brightest and most capricious fancy, the most piercing and inquisitive intellect, the wildest and deepest imagination; the highest thrills of joy, the bitterest pangs of sorrow: all these are his, he is not theirs. While he moves every heart from its steadfastness, his own is firm and still: the words that search into the inmost recesses of our nature, he pronounces with a tone of coldness and equanimity; in the deepest pathos he weeps not, or his tears are like water trickling from a rock of adamant. He is king of himself and of his world; nor does he rule it like a vulgar great man, like a Napoleon or Charles Twelfth, by the mere brute exertion of his will, grounded on no principle, or on a false one: his faculties and feelings are not fettered or prostrated under the iron sway of Passion, but led and guided in kindly union under the mild sway of Reason; as the fierce primeval elements of Nature were stilled at the coming of Light, and bound together, under its soft vesture, into a glorious and beneficent Creation.

This is the true Rest of man; no stunted unbelieving callousness, no reckless surrender to blind Force, no opiate delusion; but the harmonious adjustment of Necessity and Accident, of what is changeable and what is unchangeable in our destiny; the calm supremacy of the spirit over its circumstances; the dim aim of every human soul, the full attainment of only a chosen few. It comes not unsought to any; but the wise are wise because they think no price too high for it. Goethe's inward home has been reared by slow and laborious efforts; but it stands on no hollow or deceitful basis: for his peace is not from blindness, but from clear vision; not from uncertain hope of alteration, but from sure insight into what cannot alter. His world seems once to have been desolate and baleful as that of the darkest sceptic: but he has covered it anew with beauty and solemnity, derived from deeper sources, over which Doubt can have no sway. He has inquired fearlessly, and fearlessly searched out and denied the False; but he has not forgotten, what is equally essential and infinitely harder, to search out and admit the True. His heart is still full of warmth, though his head is clear and cold; the world for him is still full of grandeur, though he clothes it with no false colours; his fellow-creatures are still objects of reverence and love, though their basenesses are plainer to no eye than to his. To reconcile these contradictions is the task of all good men, each for himself, in his own way and manner; a task which, in our age, is encompassed with difficulties peculiar to the time; and which Goethe seems to have accomplished with a success that few can rival. A mind so in unity with itself, even though it were a poor and small one, would arrest our attention, and win some kind regard from us; but when this mind ranks among the strongest and most complicated of the species, it becomes a sight full of interest, a study full of deep instruction.

Such a mind as Goethe's is the fruit not only of a royal endowment by nature, but also of a culture proportionate to her bounty. In Goethe's original form of spirit we discern the highest gifts of manhood, without any deficiency of the lower: he has an eye and a heart equally for the sublime, the common, and the ridiculous; the elements at once of a poet, a thinker, and a wit. Of his culture we have often spoken already; and it deserves again to be held up to praise and imitation. This, as he himself unostentatiously confesses, has been the soul of all his conduct, the great enterprise of his life; and few that understand him will be apt to deny that he has prospered. As a writer, his resources have been accumulated from nearly all the provinces of human intellect and activity; and he has trained himself to use these complicated instruments with a light expertness which we might have admired in the professor of a solitary department. Freedom, and grace, and smiling earnestness are the characteristics of his works: the matter of them flows along in chaste abundance, in the softest combination; and their style is referred to by native critics as the highest specimen of the German tongue. On this latter point the vote of a stranger may well be deemed unavailing; but the charms of Goethe's style lie deeper than the mere words; for language, in the hands of a master, is the express image of thought, or rather it is the body of which thought is the soul; the former rises into being together with the latter, and the graces of the one are shadowed forth in the movements of the other. Goethe's language, even to a foreigner, is full of character and secondary meanings; polished, yet vernacular and cordial, it sounds like the dialect of wise, ancient, and true-hearted men: in poetry, brief, sharp, simple and expressive; in prose, perhaps still more pleasing; for it is at once concise and full, rich, clear, unpretending and melodious; and the sense, not presented in alternating flashes, piece after piece revealed and withdrawn, rises before us as in continuous dawning, and stands at last simultaneously complete, and bathed in the mellowest and ruddiest sunshine. It brings to mind what the prose of Hooker, Bacon, Milton, Browne, would have been, had they written under the good, without the bad influences, of that French precision, which has polished and attenuated, trimmed and impoverished, all modern languages; made our meaning clear, and too often shallow as well as clear.

But Goethe's culture as a writer is perhaps less remarkable than his culture as a man. He has learned not in head only, but

also in heart; not from Art and Literature, but also by action
and passion, in the rugged school of Experience. If asked what
was the grand characteristic of his writings, we should not say
knowledge, but wisdom. A mind that has seen, and suffered,
and done, speaks to us of what it has tried and conquered. A
gay delineation will give us notice of dark and toilsome experiences, of business done in the great deep of the spirit; a maxim,
trivial to the careless eye, will rise with light and solution over
long perplexed periods of our own history. It is thus that heart
speaks to heart, that the life of one man becomes a possession
to all. Here is a mind of the most subtle and tumultuous elements; but it is governed in peaceful diligence, and its impetuous
and ethereal faculties work softly together for good and noble
ends. Goethe may be called a Philosopher; for he loves and has
practised as a man the wisdom which, as a poet, he inculcates.
Composure and cheerful seriousness seem to breathe over all
his character. There is no whining over human woes: it is understood that we must simply all strive to alleviate or remove
them. There is no noisy battling for opinions; but a persevering
effort to make Truth lovely, and recommend her, by a thousand
avenues, to the hearts of all men. Of his personal manners we
can easily believe the universal report, as often given in the way
of censure as of praise, that he is a man of consummate breed-
ing and the stateliest presence: for an air of polished tolerance,
of courtly, we might almost say majestic repose, and serene
humanity, is visible throughout his works. In no line of them
does he speak with asperity of any man; scarcely ever even of a
thing. He knows the good, and loves it; he knows the bad and
hateful, and rejects it; but in neither case with violence: his love
is calm and active; his rejection is implied, rather than pro-
nounced; meek and gentle, though we see that it is thorough,
and never to be revoked. The noblest and the basest he not only
seems to comprehend, but to personate and body forth in their
most secret lineaments: hence actions and opinions appear to
him as they are, with all the circumstances which extenuate or
endear them to the hearts where they originated and are entertained. This also is the spirit of our Shakspeare, and perhaps of

every great dramatic poet. Shakspeare is no sectarian; to all he deals with equity and mercy; because he knows all, and his heart is wide enough for all. In his mind the world is a whole; he figures it as Providence governs it; and to him it is not strange that the sun should be caused to shine on the evil and the good, and the rain to fall on the just and the unjust . . .

from Burns

... To the ill-starred Burns was given the power of making man's life more venerable, but that of wisely guiding his own life was not given. Destiny, – for so in our ignorance we must speak, – his faults, the faults of others, proved too hard for him; and that spirit, which might have soared could it but have walked, soon sank to the dust, its glorious faculties trodden under foot in the blossom; and died, we may almost say, without ever having lived. And so kind and warm a soul; so full of inborn riches, of love to all living and lifeless things! How his heart flows out in sympathy over universal Nature; and in her bleakest provinces discerns a beauty and a meaning! The 'Daisy' falls not unheeded under his ploughshare; nor the ruined nest of that 'wee, cowering, timorous beastie,' cast forth, after all its provident pains, to 'thole the sleety dribble and cranreuch cauld.' The 'hoar visage' of Winter delights him; he dwells with a sad and oft-returning fondness in these scenes of solemn desolation; but the voice of the tempest becomes an anthem to his ears; he loves to walk in the sounding woods, for 'it raises his thoughts to *Him that walketh on the wings of the wind*.' A true Poet-soul, for it needs but to be struck and the sound it yields will be music! But observe him chiefly as he mingles with his brother men. What warm, all comprehending fellow-feeling; what trustful, boundless love; what generous exaggeration of the object loved! His rustic friend, his nut-brown maiden, are no longer mean and homely, but a hero and a queen, whom he prizes as the paragons of Earth. The rough scenes of Scottish life, not seen by him in any Arcadian illusion, but in the rude contradiction, in the smoke and soil of a too

harsh reality, are still lovely to him: Poverty is indeed his companion, but Love also, and Courage; the simple feelings, the
worth, the nobleness, that dwell under the straw roof, are dear
and venerable to his heart: and thus over the lowest provinces
of man's existence he pours the glory of his own soul; and they
rise, in shadow and sunshine, softened and brightened into a
beauty which other eyes discern not in the highest. He has a
just self-consciousness, which too often degenerates into pride;
yet it is a noble pride, for defence, not for offence; no cold suspicious feeling, but a frank and social one. The Peasant Poet
bears himself, we might say, like a King in exile: he is cast
among the low, and feels himself equal to the highest; yet he
claims no rank, that none may be disputed to him. The forward
he can repel, the supercilious he can subdue; pretensions of
wealth or ancestry are of no avail with him; there is a fire in
that dark eye, under which the 'insolence of condescension'
cannot thrive. In his abasement, in his extreme need, he forgets
not for a moment the majesty of Poetry and Manhood. And
yet, far as he feels himself above common men, he wanders not
apart from them, but mixes warmly in their interests; nay
throws himself into their arms, and, as it were, entreats them to
love him. It is moving to see how, in his darkest despondency,
this proud being still seeks relief from friendship; unbosoms
himself, often to the unworthy; and, amid tears, strains to his
glowing heart a heart that knows only the name of friendship.
And yet he was 'quick to learn;' a man of keen vision, before
whom common disguises afforded no concealment. His understanding saw through the hollowness even of accomplished
deceivers; but there was a generous credulity in his heart. And
so did our Peasant show himself among us; 'a soul like an
Æolian harp,[1] in whose strings the vulgar wind, as it passed
through them, changed itself into articulate melody.' And this
was he for whom the world found no fitter business than quarrelling with smugglers and vintners, computing excise-dues
upon tallow, and gauging alebarrels![2] In such toils was that
mighty Spirit sorrowfully wasted: and a hundred years may
pass on, before another such is given us to waste.

*

All that remains of Burns, the Writings he has left, seem to us, as we hinted above, no more than a poor mutilated fraction of what was in him; brief, broken glimpses of a genius that could never show itself complete; that wanted all things for completeness: culture, leisure, true effort, nay even length of life. His poems are, with scarcely any exception, mere occasional effusions; poured forth with little premeditation; expressing, by such means as offered, the passion, opinion, or humour of the hour. Never in one instance was it permitted him to grapple with any subject with the full collection of his strength, to fuse and mould it in the concentrated fire of his genius. To try by the strict rules of Art such imperfect fragments, would be at once unprofitable and unfair. Nevertheless, there is something in these poems, marred and defective as they are, which forbids the most fastidious student of poetry to pass them by. Some sort of enduring quality they must have: for after fifty years of the wildest vicissitudes in poetic taste, they still continue to be read; nay, are read more and more eagerly, more and more extensively; and this not only by literary virtuosos, and that class upon whom transitory causes operate most strongly, but by all classes, down to the most hard unlettered and truly natural class, who read little, and especially no poetry, except because they find pleasure in it. The grounds of so singular and wide a popularity, which extends, in a literal sense, from the palace to the hut, and over all regions where the English tongue is spoken, are well worth inquiring into. After every just deduction, it seems to imply some rare excellence in these works. What is that excellence?

To answer this question will not lead us far. The excellence of Burns is, indeed, among the rarest, whether in poetry or prose; but, at the same time, it is plain and easily recognized: his *Sincerity*, his indisputable air of Truth. Here are no fabulous woes or joys; no hollow fantastic sentimentalities; no wiredrawn refinings, either in thought or feeling: the passion that is traced before us has glowed in a living heart; the opinion he utters has risen in his own understanding, and been a light to his own steps. He does not write from hearsay, but from sight and experience; it is the scenes that he has lived and laboured amidst, that he describes: those scenes, rude and humble as they are, have kindled beautiful emotions in his soul, noble thoughts, and definite resolves; and he speaks forth what is in him, not from any outward call of vanity or interest, but because his heart is too full to be silent. He speaks it with such melody and modulation as he can; 'in homely rustic jingle'; but it is his own, and genuine. This is the grand secret for finding readers and retaining them: let him who would move and convince others, be first moved and convinced himself. Horace's rule, *Si vis me flere*,[3] is applicable in a wider sense than the literal one. To every poet, to every writer, we might say: Be true, if you would be believed. Let a man but speak forth with genuine earnestness the thought, the emotion, the actual condition of his own heart; and other men, so strangely are we all knit together by the tie of sympathy, must and will give heed to him. In culture, in extent of view, we may stand above the speaker, or below him; but in either case, his words, if they are earnest and sincere, will find some response within us; for in spite of all casual varieties in outward rank or inward, as face answers to face, so does the heart of man to man.

This may appear a very simple principle, and one which Burns had little merit in discovering. True, the discovery is easy enough: but the practical appliance is not easy; is indeed the fundamental difficulty which all poets have to strive with, and which scarcely one in the hundred ever fairly surmounts. A head too dull to discriminate the true from the false; a heart too dull to love the one at all risks, and to hate the other in spite of all temptations, are alike fatal to a writer. With either, or, as more commonly happens, with both of these deficiencies combine a love of distinction, a wish to be original, which is seldom wanting, and we have Affectation, the bane of literature, as Cant, its elder brother, is of morals. How often does the one and the other front us, in poetry, as in life! Great poets themselves are not always free of this vice; nay, it is precisely on a certain sort of degree of greatness that it is most commonly ingrafted. A strong effort after excellence will sometimes solace itself with a mere shadow of success; he who has much to unfold, will sometimes unfold it imperfectly. Byron, for instance, was no common man: yet if we examine his poetry with this view, we shall find it far enough from faultless. Generally speaking, we should say that it is not true. He refreshes us, not with the divine fountain, but too often with vulgar strong waters, stimulating indeed to the taste, but soon ending in dislike, or even nausea. Are his Harolds and Giaours,[4] we would ask, real men; we mean, poetically consistent and conceivable men? Do not these characters, does not the character of their author, which more or less shines through them all, rather appear a thing put on for the occasion; no natural or possible mode of being, but something intended to look much grander than nature? Surely, all these stormful agonies, this volcanic heroism, superhuman contempt and moody desperation, with so much scowling, and teeth-gnashing, and other sulphurous humour, is more like the brawling of a player in some paltry tragedy, which is to last three hours, than the bearing of a man in the business of life, which is to last threescore and ten years. To our minds there is a taint of this sort, something which we should call theatrical, false, affected, in every one of these otherwise so powerful pieces. Perhaps *Don Juan*, especially the latter parts of it, is the only thing approaching to a *sincere* work, he ever wrote; the only work where he showed himself, in any measure, as he was; and seemed so intent on his subject as, for moments, to forget himself. Yet Byron hated this vice; we believe, heartily detested it: nay he had declared formal war against it in words. So difficult is it even for the strongest to make this primary attainment, which might seem the simplest of all: to *read its own consciousness without mistakes*, without errors involuntary or wilful. We recollect no poet of Burns's susceptibility who comes before us from the first, and abides with us to the last, with such a total want of affectation. He is an honest man, and an honest writer. In his successes and his failures, in his greatness and his littleness, he is ever clear, simple, true, and glitters with no lustre but his own. We reckon this to be a great virtue; to be, in fact, the root of most other virtues, literary as well as moral . . .

from Voltaire

. . . Voltaire's intellectual endowment and acquirement, his talent or genius as literary man, lies opened to us in a series of Writings, unexampled, as we believe, in two respects, – their extent, and their diversity. Perhaps there is no writer, not a mere compiler, but writing from his own invention or elaboration, who has left so many volumes behind him; and if to the merely arithmetical, we add a critical estimate, the singularity is still greater; for these volumes are not written without an appearance of due care and preparation; perhaps there is not one altogether feeble and confused treatise, nay one feeble and confused sentence, to be found in them. As to variety, again, they range nearly over all human subjects; from Theology down to Domestic Economy; from the Familiar Letter to the Political History; from the Pasquinade[5] to the Epic Poem. Some strange gift, or union of gifts, must have been at work here; for the result is, at least, in the highest degree uncommon, and to be wondered at, if not to be admired.

If, through all this many-coloured versatility, we try to decipher the essential, distinctive features of Voltaire's intellect, it seems to us that we find there a counterpart to our theory of his moral character; as, indeed, if that theory was accurate, we must do: for the thinking and the moral nature, distinguished by the necessities of speech, have no such distinction in themselves; but, rightly examined, exhibit in every case the strictest sympathy and correspondence, are, indeed, but different phases of the same indissoluble unity, – a living mind. In life, Voltaire was found to be without good claim to the title of philosopher; and now, in literature, and for similar reasons, we find in him

the same deficiencies. Here too it is not greatness, but the very
extreme of expertness, that we recognize; not strength, so much
as agility; not depth, but superficial extent. That truly surprising ability seems rather the unparalleled combination of many
common talents, than the exercise of any finer or higher one:
for here too the want of earnestness, of intense continuance, is
fatal to him. He has the eye of a lynx; sees deeper, at the first
glance, than any other man; but no second glance is given.
Thus Truth, which to the philosopher, has from of old been
said to live in a well, remains for the most part hidden from
him; we may say forever hidden, if we take the highest, and
only philosophical species of Truth; for this does not reveal
itself to any mortal, without quite another sort of meditation
than Voltaire ever seems to have bestowed on it. In fact, his
deductions are uniformly of a forensic, argumentative, immediately practical nature; often true, we will admit, so far as they
go; but not the whole truth; and false, when taken for the
whole. In regard to feeling, it is the same with him: he is, in
general, humane, mildly affectionate, not without touches of
nobleness; but light, fitful, discontinuous; 'a smart freethinker,
all things in an hour.' He is no Poet and Philosopher, but a
popular sweet Singer and Haranguer: in all senses, and in all
styles, a *Concionator*,[6] which, for the most part, will turn out
to be an altogether different character. It is true, in this last
province he stands unrivalled; for such an audience, the most
fit and perfectly persuasive of all preachers: but in many far
higher provinces, he is neither perfect nor unrivalled; has been
often surpassed; was surpassed even in his own age and nation.
For a decisive, thorough-going, in any measure gigantic force
of thought, he is far inferior to Diderot: with all the liveliness
he has not the soft elegance, with more than the wit he has but
a small portion of the wisdom, that belonged to Fontenelle: as
in real sensibility, so in the delineation of it, in pathos, loftiness
and earnest eloquence, he cannot, making all fair abatements,
and there are many, be compared with Rousseau.

Doubtless, an astonishing fertility, quickness, address; an
openness also, and universal susceptibility of mind, must have
belonged to him. As little can we deny that he manifests an

assiduous perseverance, a capability of long-continued exertion, strange in so volatile a man; and consummate skill in
husbanding and wisely directing his exertion. The very knowledge he had amassed, granting, which is but partly true, that it
was superficial remembered knowledge, might have distinguished him as a mere Dutch commentator.[7] From Newton's
Principia to the *Shaster* and *Vedam*,[8] nothing has escaped him:
he has glanced into all literatures and all sciences; nay studied
in them, for he can speak a rational word on all. It is known,
for instance, that he understood Newton when no other man in
France understood him: indeed, his countrymen may call Voltaire their discoverer of intellectual England; – a discovery, it is
true, rather of the Curtis than of the Columbus sort,[9] yet one
which in his day still remained to be made. Nay from all sides
he brings new light into his country: now, for the first time, to
the upturned wondering eyes of Frenchmen in general, does it
become clear that Thought has actually a kind of existence in
other kingdoms; that some glimmerings of civilization had
dawned here and there on the human species, prior to the *Siècle
de Louis Quatorze*. Of Voltaire's acquaintance with History,
at least with what he called History, be it civil, religious, or
literary; of his innumerable, indescribable collection of facts,
gathered from all sources, – from European Chronicles and
State Papers, from eastern *Zends* and *Jewish Talmuds*,[10] we
need not remind any reader. It has been objected that his information was often borrowed at second-hand; that he had his
plodders and pioneers, whom, as living dictionaries, he skilfully consulted in time of need. This also seems to be partly
true, but deducts little from our estimate of him: for the skill
so to borrow is even rarer than the power to lend. Voltaire's
knowledge is not a mere showroom of curiosities, but truly a
museum for purposes of teaching; every object is in its place,
and there for its uses: nowhere do we find confusion or vain
display; everywhere intention, instructiveness and the clearest
order.

  Perhaps it is this very power of Order, of rapid, perspicuous
Arrangement, that lies at the root of Voltaire's best gifts; or
rather, we should say, it is that keen, accurate intellectual

vision, from which, to a mind of any intensity, Order naturally arises. The clear quick vision, and the methodic arrangement which springs from it, are looked upon as peculiarly French qualities; and Voltaire, at all times, manifests them in a more than French degree. Let him but cast his eye over any subject, in a moment he sees, though indeed only to a short depth, yet with instinctive decision, where the main bearings of it for that short depth lie; what is, or appears to be, its logical coherence; how causes connect themselves with effects; how the whole is to be seized, and in lucid sequence represented to his own or to other minds. In this respect, moreover, it is happy for him that, below the short depth alluded to, his view does not properly grow dim, but altogether terminates: thus there is nothing farther to occasion him misgivings; has he not already sounded into that basis of bottomless Darkness on which all things firmly rest? What lies below is delusion, imagination, some form of Superstition or Folly; which he, nothing doubting, altogether casts away. Accordingly, he is the most intelligible of writers; everywhere transparent at a glance. There is no delineation or disquisition of his, that has not its whole purport written on its forehead; all is precise, all is rightly adjusted; that keen spirit of Order shows itself in the whole, and in every line of the whole.

If we say that this power of Arrangement, as applied both to the acquisition and to the communication of ideas, is Voltaire's most serviceable faculty in all his enterprises, we say nothing singular: for take the word in its largest acceptation, and it comprehends the whole office of Understanding, logically so called; is the means whereby man accomplishes whatever, in the way of outward force, has been made possible for him; conquers all practical obstacles, and rises to be the 'king of this lower world.' It is the organ of all that Knowledge which can properly be reckoned synonymous with Power; for hereby man strikes with wise aim, into the infinite agencies of Nature, and multiplies his own small strength to unlimited degrees. It has been said also that man may rise to be the 'god of this lower world;' but that is a far loftier height, not attainable by such

power-knowledge, but by quite another sort, for which Voltaire
in particular shows hardly any aptitude.

In truth, readily as we have recognised his spirit of Method,
with its many uses, we are far from ascribing to him any
perceptible portion of that greatest praise in thinking, or in
writing, the praise of philosophic, still less of poetic Method;
which, especially the latter, must be the fruit of deep feeling as
well as of clear vision, – of genius as well as talent; and is much
more likely to be found in the compositions of a Hooker or
a Shakspeare than of a Voltaire. The Method discernible in
Voltaire, and this on all subjects whatever, is a purely business
Method. The order that arises from it is not Beauty, but, at
best, Regularity. His objects do not lie round him in pictorial,
not always in scientific grouping; but rather in commodious
rows, where each may be seen and come at, like goods in a
well-kept warehouse. We might say, there is not the deep natural symmetry of a forest oak, but the simple artificial symmetry
of a parlour chandelier. Compare, for example, the plan of the
Henriade to that of our so barbarous *Hamlet*. The plan of the
former is a geometrical diagram by Fermat;[11] that of the latter
a cartoon by Raphael. The *Henriade*, as we see it completed, is
a polished, square-built Tuileries: *Hamlet* is a mysterious star-
paved Valhalla and dwelling of the gods . . .

from On History

... A talent for History may be said to be born with us, as our
chief inheritance. In a certain sense all men are historians. Is
not every memory written quite full with Annals, wherein joy
and mourning, conquest and loss manifoldly alternate; and,
with or without philosophy, the whole fortunes of one little
inward Kingdom, and all its politics, foreign and domestic,
stand ineffaceably recorded? Our very speech is curiously historical. Most men, you may observe, speak only to narrate; not
in imparting what they have thought, which indeed were often
a very small matter, but in exhibiting what they have undergone
or seen, which is a quite unlimited one, do talkers dilate. Cut us
off from Narrative, how would the stream of conversation,
even among the wisest, languish into detached handfuls, and
among the foolish utterly evaporate! Thus, as we do nothing
but enact History, we say little but recite it: nay rather, in
that widest sense, our whole spiritual life is built thereon. For,
strictly considered, what is all Knowledge too but recorded
Experience, and a product of History; of which, therefore, Rea-
soning and Belief, no less than Action and Passion, are essential
materials?

Under a limited, and the only practicable shape, History
proper, that part of History which treats of remarkable action,
has, in all modern as well as ancient times, ranked among the
highest arts, and perhaps never stood higher than in these times
of ours. For whereas, of old, the charm of History lay chiefly
in gratifying our common appetite for the wonderful, for the
unknown; and her office was but as that of a Minstrel and
Story-teller, she has now farther become a Schoolmistress, and

professes to instruct in gratifying. Whether, with the stateliness
of that venerable character, she may not have taken up something of its austerity and frigidity; whether, in the logical
terseness of a Hume or Robertson, the graceful ease and gay
pictorial heartiness of a Herodotus or Froissart[12] may not be
wanting, is not the question for us here. Enough that all learners, all inquiring minds of every order, are gathered round her
footstool, and reverently pondering her lessons, as the true
basis of Wisdom. Poetry, Divinity, Politics, Physics, have each
their adherents and adversaries; each little guild supporting a
defensive and offensive war for its own special domain; while
the domain of History is as a Free Emporium, where all these
belligerents peaceably meet and furnish themselves; and Senti-
mentalist and Utilitarian, Sceptic and Theologian, with one
voice advise us: Examine History, for it is 'Philosophy teaching
by Experience.'

Far be it from us to disparage such teaching, the very attempt
at which must be precious. Neither shall we too rigidly inquire:
How much it has hitherto profited? Whether most of what
little practical wisdom men have, has come from study of professed History, or from other less boasted sources, whereby, as
matters now stand, a Marlborough may become great in the
world's business, with no History save what he derives from
Shakspeare's Plays? Nay, whether in that same teaching by
Experience, historical Philosophy has yet properly deciphered
the first element of all science in this kind: What the aim and
significance of that wondrous changeful Life it investigates and
paints may be? Whence the course of man's destinies in this
Earth originated, and whither they are tending? Or, indeed, if
they have any course and tendency, are really guided forward
by an unseen mysterious Wisdom, or only circle in blind mazes
without recognisable guidance? Which questions, altogether
fundamental, one might think, in any Philosophy of History,
have, since the era when Monkish Annalists were wont to
answer them by the long-ago extinguished light of their Mis-
sal and Breviary, been by most philosophical Historians only
glanced at dubiously and from afar; by many, not so much as
glanced at.

The truth is, two difficulties, never wholly surmountable, lie in the way. Before Philosophy can teach by Experience, the Philosophy has to be in readiness, the Experience must be gathered and intelligibly recorded. Now, overlooking the former consideration, and with regard only to the latter, let any one who has examined the current of human affairs, and how intricate, perplexed, unfathomable, even when seen into with our own eyes, are their thousandfold blending movements, say whether the true representing of it is easy or impossible. Social Life is the aggregate of all the individual men's Lives who constitute society; History is the essence of innumerable Biographies. But if one Biography, nay our own Biography, study and recapitulate it as we may, remains in so many points unintelligible to us; how much more must these million, the very facts of which, to say nothing of the purport of them, we know not, and cannot know!

Neither will it adequately avail us to assert that the general inward condition of Life is the same in all ages; and that only the remarkable deviations from the common endowment and common lot, and the more important variations which the outward figure of Life has from time to time undergone, deserve memory and record. The inward condition of Life, it may rather be affirmed, the conscious or half-conscious aim of mankind, so far as men are not mere digesting-machines, is the same in no two ages; neither are the more important outward variations easy to fix on, or always well capable of representation. Which was the greatest innovator, which was the more important personage in man's history, he who first led armies over the Alps, and gained the victories of Cannæ and Thrasymene;[13] or the nameless boor who first hammered out for himself an iron spade? When the oak-tree is felled, the whole forest echoes with it; but a hundred acorns are planted silently by some unnoticed breeze. Battles and war-tumults, which for the time din every ear, and with joy or terror intoxicate every heart, pass away like tavern-brawls; and, except some few Marathons and Morgartens,[14] are remembered by accident, not by desert. Laws themselves, political Constitutions, are not our Life; but only the house wherein our Life is led: nay they are but the bare walls of the house; all whose essential furniture, the inventions and traditions, and daily habits that regulate and support our existence, are the work not of Dracos and Hampdens, but of Phoenician mariners, of Italian masons and Saxon metallurgists, of philosophers, alchymists, prophets, and all the long-forgotten train of artists and artisans; who from the first have been jointly teaching us how to think and how to act, how to rule over spiritual and over physical Nature. Well may we say that of our History the more important part is lost without recovery; and, – as thanksgivings were once wont to be offered 'for unrecognised mercies,' – look with reverence into the dark untenanted places of the Past, where, in formless oblivion, our chief benefactors, with all their sedulous endeavours, but not with the fruit of these, lie entombed.

So imperfect is that same Experience, by which Philosophy is to teach. Nay, even with regard to those occurrences which do stand recorded, which, at their origin have seemed worthy of record, and the summary of which constitutes what we now call History, is not our understanding of them altogether incomplete; is it even possible to represent them as they were? The old story of Sir Walter Raleigh's looking from his prison-window, on some street tumult, which afterwards three witnesses reported in three different ways, himself differing from them all, is still a true lesson for us. Consider how it is that historical documents and records originate; even honest records, where the reporters were unbiased by personal regard; a case which, were nothing more wanted, must ever be among the rarest. The real leading features of a historical Transaction, those movements that essentially characterise it, and alone deserve to be recorded, are nowise the foremost to be noted. At first, among the various witnesses, who are also parties interested, there is only vague wonder, and fear or hope, and the noise of Rumour's thousand tongues; till, after a season, the conflict of testimonies has subsided into some general issue; and then it is settled, by majority of votes, that such and such a 'Crossing of the Rubicon,' an 'Impeachment of Strafford,' a 'Convocation of the Notables,'[15] are epochs in the world's history, cardinal points on which grand world-revolutions have hinged. Suppose, however, that the majority of votes was all wrong; that the real cardinal points lay far deeper; and had been passed over unnoticed, because no Seer, but only mere Onlookers, chanced to be there! Our clock strikes when there is a change from hour to hour; but no hammer in the Horologe of Time peals through the universe when there is a change from Era to Era. Men understand not what is among their hands: as calmness is the characteristic of strength, so the weightiest causes may be most silent. It is, in no case, the real historical Transaction, but only some more or less plausible scheme and theory of the Transaction, or the harmonised result of many such schemes, each varying from the other and all varying from truth, that we can ever hope to behold.

Nay, were our faculty of insight into passing things never so complete, there is still a fatal discrepancy between our manner of observing these, and their manner of occurring. The most gifted man can observe, still more can record, only the *series* of his own impressions: his observation, therefore, to say nothing of its other imperfections, must be *successive*, while the things done were often *simultaneous*; the things done were not a series, but a group. It is not in acted, as it is in written History: actual events are nowise so simply related to each other as parent and offspring are; every single event is the offspring not of one, but of all other events, prior or contemporaneous, and will in its turn combine with all others to give birth to new: it is an everliving, everworking Chaos of Being, wherein shape after shape bodies itself forth from innumerable elements. And this Chaos, boundless as the habitation and duration of man, unfathomable as the soul and destiny of man, is what the historian will depict, and scientifically gauge, we may say, by threading it with single lines of a few ells in length! For as all Action is, by its nature, to be figured as extended in breadth and in depth, as well as in length; that is to say, is based on Passion and Mystery, if we investigate its origin; and spreads abroad on all hands, modifying and modified; as well as advances towards completion, – so all Narrative is, by its nature, of only one dimension; only travels forward towards one, or towards successive points: Narrative is *linear*, Action is *solid*. Alas for

our 'chains,' or chainlets, of 'causes and effects,' which we so
assiduously track through certain handbreadths of years and
square miles, when the whole is a broad, deep Immensity, and
each atom is 'chained' and complected with all! Truly, if History is Philosophy teaching by Experience, the writer fitted to
compose History is hitherto an unknown man. The Experience
itself would require All-knowledge to record it, – were the
All-wisdom needful for such Philosophy as would interpret it,
to be had for asking. Better were it that mere earthly Historians
should lower such pretensions, more suitable for Omniscience
than for human science; and aiming only at some picture of the
things acted, which picture itself will at best be a poor approximation, leave the inscrutable purport of them an acknowledged
secret; or at most, in reverent Faith, far different from that
teaching of Philosophy, pause over the mysterious vestiges of
Him, whose path is in the great deep of Time, whom History
indeed reveals, but only all History, and in Eternity, will clearly
reveal.

Such considerations truly were of small profit, did they,
instead of teaching us vigilance and reverent humility in our
inquiries into History, abate our esteem for them, or discourage
us from unweariedly prosecuting them. Let us search more and
more into the Past; let all men explore it, as the true fountain of
knowledge; by whose light alone, consciously or unconsciously
employed, can the Present and the Future be interpreted or
guessed at. For though the whole meaning lies far beyond our
ken; yet in that complex Manuscript, covered over with formless inextricably-entangled unknown characters, – nay which is
a *Palimpsest*,[16] and had once prophetic writing, still dimly
legible there, – some letters, some words, may be deciphered;
and if no complete Philosophy, here and there an intelligible
precept, available in practice, be gathered: well understanding,
in the mean while, that it is only a little portion we have deciphered; that much still remains to be interpreted; that History
is a real Prophetic Manuscript, and can be fully interpreted by
no man.

But the Artist in History may be distinguished from the Artisan in History; for here, as in all other provinces, there are

Artists and Artisans; men who labour mechanically in a department, without eye for the Whole, not feeling that there is a
Whole; and men who inform and ennoble the humblest department with an Idea of the Whole, and habitually know that only
in the Whole is the Partial to be truly discerned. The proceed-
ings and the duties of these two, in regard to History, must
be altogether different. Not, indeed, that each has not a real
worth, in his several degree. The simple husbandman can till
his field, and by knowledge he has gained of its soil, sow it
with the fit grain, though the deep rocks and central fires are
unknown to him: his little crop hangs under and over the firma-
ment of stars, and sails through whole untracked celestial
spaces, between Aries and Libra;[17] nevertheless, it ripens for
him in due season, and he gathers it safe into his barn. As a
husbandman he is blameless in disregarding those higher wonders; but as a thinker, and faithful inquirer into Nature, he
were wrong. So likewise is it with the Historian, who examines
some special aspect of History; and from this or that combination of circumstances, political, moral, economical, and the
issues it has led to, infers that such and such properties belong
to human society, and that the like circumstances will produce
the like issue; which inference, if other trials confirm it, must be
held true and practically valuable. He is wrong only, and an
artisan, when he fancies that these properties, discovered or
discoverable, exhaust the matter; and sees not, at every step,
that it is inexhaustible.

However, that class of cause-and-effect speculators, with
whom no wonder would remain wonderful, but all things in
Heaven and Earth must be computed and 'accounted for:' and
even the Unknown, the Infinite in man's Life, had under the
words *enthusiasm*, *superstition*, *spirit of the age* and so forth,
obtained, as it were, an algebraical symbol and given value, –
have now well-nigh played their part in European culture; and
may be considered, as in most countries, even in England itself
where they linger the latest, verging towards extinction. He
who reads the inscrutable Book of Nature as if it were a Merchant's Ledger, is justly suspected of having never seen that

Book, but only some school Synopsis thereof; from which, if taken for the real Book, more error than insight is to be derived.

Doubtless also, it is with a growing feeling of the infinite nature of History, that in these times, the old principle, division of labour, has been so widely applied to it. The Political Historian, once almost the sole cultivator of History, has now found various associates, who strive to elucidate other phases of human Life; of which, as hinted above, the political conditions it is passed under are but one, and though the primary, perhaps not the most important of the many outward arrangements. Of this Historian himself, moreover, in his own special department, new and higher things are beginning to be expected. From of old, it was too often to be reproachfully observed of him, that he dwelt with disproportionate fondness in Senate-houses, in Battlefields, nay even in Kings' Antechambers; forgetting, that far away from such scenes, the mighty tide of Thought and Action was still rolling on its wondrous course, in gloom and brightness; and in its thousand remote valleys, a whole world of Existence, with or without an earthly sun of Happiness to warm it, with or without a heavenly sun of Holiness to purify and sanctify it, was blossoming and fading, whether the 'famous victory' were won or lost. The time seems coming when much of this must be amended; and he who sees no world but that of courts and camps; and writes only how soldiers were drilled and shot, and how this ministerial conjuror out-conjured that other, and then guided, or at least held, something which he called the rudder of Government, but which was rather the spigot of Taxation, wherewith, in place of steering, he could tap, and the more cunningly the nearer the lees, – will pass for a more or less instructive Gazetteer, but will no longer be called a Historian . . .

Signs of the Times

Signs of the Times was written in 1829 and appeared anonymously in the *Edinburgh Review* for June of that year. It is the first of Carlyle's essays on social themes, and although he himself referred to it as, 'Bad in general, but the best I could make it', it is in fact a remarkably effective attack on the acceptance of utilitarian values by many of his contemporaries. Although *Signs of the Times* was not publicly acknowledged as Carlyle's until ten years later, his responsibility for it was known at the time of its publication. The essay can be regarded as the first great protest against attitudes that were to provide a dogma for Victorian materialism, anticipating works like Ruskin's *Unto This Last* and Matthew Arnold's *Culture and Anarchy*. It is reprinted here complete.

Signs of the Times

It is no very good symptom either of nations or individuals, that they deal much in vaticination.[1] Happy men are full of the present, for its bounty suffices them; and wise men also, for its duties engage them. Our grand business undoubtedly is, not to *see* what lies dimly at a distance, but to *do* what lies clearly at hand.

> Know'st thou *Yesterday*, its aim and reason;
> Work'st thou well *Today*, for worthy things?
> Calmly wait the *Morrow's* hidden season,
> Need'st not fear what hap soe'er it brings.[2]

But man's 'large discourse of reason' *will* look 'before and after;' and, impatient of the 'ignorant present time,' will indulge in anticipation far more than profits him. Seldom can the unhappy be persuaded that the evil of the day is sufficient for it; and the ambitious will not be content with present splendour, but paints yet more glorious triumphs, on the cloud-curtain of the future.

The case, however, is still worse with nations. For here the prophets are not one, but many; and each incites and confirms the other; so that the fatidical[3] fury spreads wider and wider, till at last even Saul must join in it. For there is still a real magic in the action and reaction of minds on one another. The casual deliration[4] of a few becomes, by this mysterious reverberation, the frenzy of many; men lose the use, not only of their understandings, but of their bodily senses; while the most obdurate unbelieving hearts melt, like the rest, in the furnace where all are cast as victims and as fuel. It is grievous to think, that this noble omnipotence of Sympathy has been so rarely the Aaron's-rod[5] of Truth and Virtue, and so often the Enchanter's-rod of Wickedness and Folly! No solitary miscreant, scarcely any solitary maniac, would venture on such actions and imaginations, as large communities of sane men have, in such circumstances, entertained as sound wisdom. Witness long scenes of the French Revolution, in these late times! Levity is no protection against such visitations, nor the utmost earnestness of character. The New-England Puritan burns witches, wrestles for months with the horrors of Satan's invisible world, and all ghastly phantasms, the daily and hourly precursors of the Last Day; then suddenly bethinks him that he is frantic, weeps bitterly, prays contritely, and the history of that gloomy season lies behind him like a frightful dream.

Old England too has had her share of such frenzies and panics; though happily, like other old maladies, they have grown milder of late: and since the days of Titus Oates have mostly passed without loss of men's lives; or indeed without much other loss than that of reason, for the time, in the sufferers. In this mitigated form, however, the distemper is of pretty regular recurrence; and may be reckoned on at intervals, like other natural visitations; so that reasonable men deal with it, as the Londoners do with their fogs, – go cautiously out into the groping crowd, and patiently carry lanterns at noon; knowing, by a well-grounded faith, that the sun is still in existence, and will one day reappear. How often have we heard, for the last fifty years, that the country was wrecked, and fast sinking; whereas, up to this date, the country is entire and afloat! The 'State in Danger' is a condition of things, which we have witnessed a hundred times; and as for the Church, it has seldom been out of 'danger' since we can remember it.

All men are aware that the present is a crisis of this sort; and why it has become so. The repeal of the Test Acts, and then of the Catholic disabilities,[6] has struck many of their admirers with an indescribable astonishment. Those things seemed fixed and immovable; deep as the foundations of the world; and lo, in a moment they have vanished, and their place knows them no more! Our worthy friends mistook the slumbering Leviathan for an island; often as they had been assured, that Intolerance was, and could be nothing but a Monster; and so, mooring under the lee, they had anchored comfortably in his scaly rind, thinking to take good cheer; as for some space they did. But now their Leviathan has suddenly dived under; and they can no longer be fastened in the stream of time; but must drift forward on it, even like the rest of the world: no very appalling fate, we think, could they but understand it; which, however, they will not yet, for a season. Their little island is gone; sunk deep amid confused eddies; and what is left worth caring for in the universe? What is it to them that the great continents of the earth are still standing; and the polestar and all our loadstars, in the heavens, still shining and eternal? Their cherished little haven is gone, and they will not be comforted! And therefore, day after day, in all manner of periodical or perennial publications, the most lugubrious predictions are sent forth. The King has virtually abdicated; the Church is a widow, without jointure; public principle is gone; private honesty is going; society, in short, is fast falling in pieces; and a time of unmixed evil is come on us.

At such a period, it was to be expected that the rage of prophecy should be more than usually excited. Accordingly, the Millennarians have come forth on the right hand, and the Millites on the left. The Fifth-monarchy men[7] prophesy from the Bible, and the Utilitarians from Bentham. The one announces that the last of the seals is to be opened, positively, in the year 1860; and the other assures us that 'the greatest-happiness principle' is to make a heaven of earth, in a still shorter time. We know these symptoms too well, to think it necessary or safe to interfere with them. Time and the hours will bring relief to all parties. The grand encourager of Delphic or other noises is – the Echo. Left to themselves, they will the sooner dissipate, and die away in space.

Meanwhile, we too admit that the present is an important time; as all present time necessarily is. The poorest Day that passes over us is the conflux of two Eternities; it is made up of currents that issue from the remotest Past, and flow onwards into the remotest Future. We were wise indeed, could we discern truly the signs of our own time; and by knowledge of its wants and advantages, wisely adjust our own position in it. Let us, instead of gazing idly into the obscure distance, look calmly around us, for a little, on the perplexed scene where we stand. Perhaps, on a more serious inspection, something of its perplexity will disappear, some of its distinctive characters and deeper tendencies more clearly reveal themselves; whereby our own relations to it, our own true aims and endeavours in it, may also become clearer.

Were we required to characterise this age of ours by any single epithet, we should be tempted to call it, not an Heroical, Devotional, Philosophical, or Moral Age, but, above all others, the Mechanical Age. It is the Age of Machinery, in every outward and inward sense of that word; the age which, with its whole undivided might, forwards, teaches and practises the great art of adapting means to ends. Nothing is now done directly, or by hand; all is by rule and calculated contrivance. For the simplest operation, some helps and accompaniments, some cunning abbreviating process is in readiness. Our old modes of exertion are all discredited, and thrown aside. On every hand, the living artisan is driven from his workshop, to make room for a speedier, inanimate one. The shuttle drops from the fingers of the weaver, and falls into iron fingers that ply it faster. The sailor furls his sail, and lays down his oar; and bids a strong, unwearied servant, on vaporous wings, bear him through the waters. Men have crossed oceans by steam; the Birmingham Fire-king has visited the fabulous East;[8] and the genius of the Cape, were there any Camoens[9] now to sing it, has again been alarmed, and with far stranger thunder than Gama's. There is no end to machinery. Even the horse is stripped of his harness, and finds a fleet fire-horse yoked in his stead. Nay, we have an artist that hatches chickens by steam; the very brood-hen is to be superseded! For all earthly, and for some unearthly purposes, we have machines and mechanic furtherances; for mincing our cabbages; for casting us into magnetic sleep. We remove mountains, and make seas our smooth highway; nothing can resist us. We war with rude Nature; and, by our resistless engines, come off always victorious, and loaded with spoils.

What wonderful accessions have thus been made, and are still making, to the physical power of mankind; how much better fed, clothed, lodged and, in all outward respects, accommodated men now are, or might be, by a given quantity of labour, is a grateful reflection which forces itself on every one. What changes, too, this addition of power is introducing into the Social System; how wealth has more and more increased, and at the same time gathered itself more and more into masses, strangely altering the old relations, and increasing the distance between the rich and the poor, will be a question for Political Economists, and a much more complex and important one than any they have yet engaged with.

But leaving these matters for the present, let us observe how the mechanical genius of our time has diffused itself into quite other provinces. Not the external and physical alone is now managed by machinery, but the internal and spiritual also. Here too nothing follows its spontaneous course, nothing is left to be accomplished by old natural methods. Everything has its cunningly devised implements, its pre-established apparatus, it is not done by hand, but by machinery. Thus we have machines for Education: Lancastrian machines; Hamiltonian machines;[10] monitors, maps and emblems. Instruction, that mysterious communing of Wisdom with Ignorance, is no longer an indefinable tentative process, requiring a study of individual aptitudes, and a perpetual variation of means and methods, to attain the same end; but a secure, universal, straightforward business, to be conducted in the gross, by proper mechanism, with such intellect as comes to hand. Then, we have Religious machines, of all imaginable varieties; the Bible-Society,[11] professing a far higher and heavenly structure, is found, on inquiry, to be altogether an earthly contrivance; supported by collection of moneys, by fomenting of vanities, by puffing, intrigue and chicane; a machine for converting the Heathen. It is the same in all other departments. Has any man, or any society of men, a truth to speak, a piece of spiritual work to do; they can nowise proceed at once and with the mere natural organs, but must first call a public meeting, appoint committees, issue prospectuses, eat a public dinner; in a word, construct or borrow machinery, wherewith to speak it and do it. Without machinery they were hopeless, helpless; a colony of Hindoo weavers squatting in the heart of Lancashire. Mark, too, how every machine must have its moving power, in some of the great currents of society; every little sect among us, Unitarians, Utilitarians, Anabaptists, Phrenologists, must have its Periodical, its monthly or quarterly Magazine; – hanging out, like its windmill, into the *popularis aura*,[12] to grind meal for the society.

With individuals, in like manner, natural strength avails little. No individual now hopes to accomplish the poorest enterprise single-handed and without mechanical aids; he must make interest with some existing corporation, and till his field with their oxen. In these days, more emphatically than ever, 'to live, signifies to unite with a party, or to make one.' Philosophy, Science, Art, Literature, all depend on machinery. No Newton, by silent meditation, now discovers the system of the world from the falling of an apple; but some quite other than Newton stands in his Museum, his Scientific Institution, and behind whole batteries of retorts, digesters and galvanic piles imperatively 'interrogates Nature,' – who, however, shows no haste to answer. In defect of Raphaels, and Angelos, and Mozarts, we have Royal Academies of Painting, Sculpture, Music; whereby the languishing spirit of Art may be strengthened, as by the more generous diet of a Public Kitchen. Literature, too, has its Paternoster-row mechanism, its Trade-dinners, its Editorial conclaves, and huge subterranean, puffing bellows; so that books are not only printed, but, in a great measure, written and sold, by machinery.

National culture, spiritual benefit of all sorts, is under the same management. No Queen Christina, in these times, needs to send for her Descartes; no King Frederick for his Voltaire, and painfully nourish him with pensions and flattery: any sovereign of taste, who wishes to enlighten his people, has only to impose a new tax, and with the proceeds establish Philosophic Institutes. Hence the Royal and Imperial Societies, the Bibliothèques, Glyptothèques, Technothèques, which front us in all capital cities;[13] like so many well-finished hives, to which it is expected the stray agencies of Wisdom will swarm of their own accord, and hive and make honey. In like manner, among ourselves, when it is thought that religion is declining, we have only to vote half-a-million's worth of bricks and mortar, and build new churches. In Ireland it seems they have gone still farther, having actually established a 'Penny-a-week Purgatory Society'![14] Thus does the Genius of Mechanism stand by to help us in all difficulties and emergencies, and with his iron back bears all our burdens.

These things, which we state lightly enough here, are yet of deep import, and indicate a mighty change in our whole manner of existence. For the same habit regulates not our modes of action alone, but our modes of thought and feeling. Men are grown mechanical in head and in heart, as well as in hand. They have lost faith in individual endeavour, and in natural force, of any kind. Not for internal perfection, but for external combinations and arrangements, for institutions, constitutions, – for Mechanism of one sort or other, do they hope and struggle. Their whole efforts, attachments, opinions, turn on mechanism, and are of a mechanical character.

We may trace this tendency in all the great manifestations of our time; in its intellectual aspect, the studies it most favours and its manner of conducting them; in its practical aspects, its politics, arts, religion, morals; in the whole sources, and throughout the whole currents, of its spiritual, no less than its material activity.

Consider, for example, the state of Science generally, in Europe, at this period. It is admitted, on all sides, that the Metaphysical and Moral Sciences are falling into decay, while the Physical are engrossing, every day, more respect and attention. In most of the European nations there is now no such thing as a Science of Mind; only more or less advancement in the general science, or the special sciences, of matter. The French were the first to desert Metaphysics; and though they have lately affected to revive their school, it has yet no signs of vitality. The land of Malebranche, Pascal, Descartes and Fénelon, has now only its Cousins and Villemains;[15] while, in the department of

Physics, it reckons far other names. Among ourselves, the Philosophy of Mind, after a rickety infancy, which never reached the vigour of manhood, fell suddenly into decay, languished and finally died out, with its last amiable cultivator, Professor Stewart.[16] In no nation but Germany has any decisive effort been made in psychological science; not to speak of any decisive result. The science of the age, in short, is physical, chemical, physiological; in all shapes mechanical. Our favourite Mathematics, the highly prized exponent of all these other sciences, has also become more and more mechanical. Excellence in what is called its higher departments depends less on natural genius than on acquired expertness in wielding its machinery. Without undervaluing the wonderful results which a Lagrange or Laplace[17] educes by means of it, we may remark, that their calculus, differential and integral, is little else than a more cunningly-constructed arithmetical mill; where the factors being put in, are, as it were, ground into the true product, under cover, and without other effort on our part than steady turning of the handle. We have more Mathematics than ever; but less Mathesis. Archimedes and Plato could not have read the *Mécanique Céleste*; but neither would the whole French Institute see aught in that saying, 'God geometrises!' but a sentimental rodomontade.

Nay, our whole Metaphysics itself, from Locke's time downwards, has been physical; not a spiritual philosophy, but a material one. The singular estimation in which his Essay[18] was so long held as a scientific work (an estimation grounded, indeed, on the estimable character of the man) will one day be thought a curious indication of the spirit of these times. His whole doctrine is mechanical, in its aim and origin, in its method and its results. It is not a philosophy of the mind: it is a mere discussion concerning the origin of our consciousness, or ideas, or whatever else they are called; a genetic history of what we see *in* the mind. The grand secrets of Necessity and Freewill, of the Mind's vital or non-vital dependence on Matter, of our mysterious relations to Time and Space, to God, to the Universe, are not, in the faintest degree, touched on in these inquiries; and seem not to have the smallest connexion with them.

The last class of our Scotch Metaphysicians had a dim notion that much of this was wrong; but they knew not how to right it. The school of Reid[19] had also from the first taken a mechanical course, not seeing any other. The singular conclusions at which Hume, setting out from their admitted premises, was arriving, brought this school into being; they let loose Instinct, as an undiscriminating bandog, to guard them against these conclusions; – they tugged lustily at the logical chain by which Hume was so coldly towing them and the world into bottomless abysses of Atheism and Fatalism. But the chain somehow snapped between them; and the issue has been that nobody now cares about either, – any more than about Hartley's, Darwin's, or Priestley's contemporaneous doings in England.[20] Hartley's vibrations and vibratiuncles, one would think, were material and mechanical enough; but our Continental neighbours have gone still farther. One of their philosophers has lately discovered, that 'as the liver secretes bile, so does the brain secrete thought;' which astonishing discovery Dr Cabanis,[21] more lately still, in his *Rapports du Physique et du Morale de l'Homme*, has pushed into its minutest developments.

The metaphysical philosophy of this last inquirer is certainly no shadowy or unsubstantial one. He fairly lays open our moral structure with his dissecting-knives and real metal probes; and exhibits it to the inspection of mankind, by Leuwenhoek microscopes,[22] and inflation with the anatomical blow-pipe. Thought, he is inclined to hold, is still secreted by the brain; but then Poetry and Religion (and it is really worth knowing) are 'a product of the smaller intestines'! We have the greatest admiration for this learned doctor: with what scientific stoicism he walks through the land of wonders, unwondering; like a wise man through some huge, gaudy, imposing Vauxhall,[23] whose fireworks, cascades and symphonies, the vulgar may enjoy and believe in, – but where he finds nothing real but the saltpetre, pasteboard and catgut. His book may be regarded as the ultimatum of mechanical metaphysics in our time; a remarkable realisation of what in Martinus Scriblerus was still only an idea, that 'as the jack had a meat-roasting quality, so had the body a thinking quality,' – upon the strength of which the

Nurembergers were to build a wood-and-leather man, 'who should reason as well as most country parsons.' Vaucanson did indeed make a wooden duck,[24] that seemed to eat and digest; but that bold scheme of the Nurembergers remained for a more modern virtuoso.

This condition of the two great departments of knowledge, – the outward, cultivated exclusively on mechanical principles; the inward, finally abandoned, because, cultivated on such principles, it is found to yield no result, – sufficiently indicates the intellectual bias of our time, its all-pervading disposition towards that line of inquiry. In fact, an inward persuasion has long been diffusing itself, and now and then even comes to utterance, That, except the external, there are no true sciences; that to the inward world (if there be any) our only conceivable road is through the outward; that, in short, what cannot be investigated and understood mechanically, cannot be investigated and understood at all. We advert the more particularly to these intellectual propensities, as to prominent symptoms of our age, because Opinion is at all times doubly related to Action, first as cause, then as effect; and the speculative tendency of any age will therefore give us, on the whole, the best indications of its practical tendency.

Nowhere, for example, is the deep, almost exclusive faith we have in Mechanism more visible than in the Politics of this time. Civil government does by its nature include much that is mechanical, and must be treated accordingly. We term it indeed, in ordinary language, the Machine of Society, and talk of it as the grand working wheel from which all private machines must derive, or to which they must adapt, their movements. Considered merely as a metaphor, all this is well enough; but here, as in so many other cases, the 'foam hardens itself into a shell,' and the shadow we have wantonly evoked stands terrible before us and will not depart at our bidding. Government includes much also that is not mechanical, and cannot be treated mechanically; of which latter truth, as appears to us, the political speculations and exertions of our time are taking less and less cognisance.

Nay, in the very outset, we might note the mighty interest taken in *mere political arrangements*, as itself the sign of a

mechanical age. The whole discontent of Europe takes this direction. The deep, strong cry of all civilised nations, – a cry
which, every one now sees, must and will be answered, – is:
Give us a reform of Government! A good structure of legislation, a proper check upon the executive, a wise arrangement of
the judiciary, is *all* that is wanting for human happiness. The
Philosopher of this age is not a Socrates, a Plato, a Hooker, or
Taylor, who inculcates on men the necessity and infinite worth
of moral goodness, the great truth that our happiness depends
on the mind which is within us, and not on the circumstances
which are without us; but a Smith, a De Lolme, a Bentham,[25]
who chiefly inculcates the reverse of this, – that our happiness
depends entirely on external circumstances; nay, that the
strength and dignity of the mind within us is itself the creature
and consequence of these. Were the laws, the government, in
good order, all were well with us; the rest would care for itself!
Dissentients from this opinion, expressed or implied, are now
rarely to be met with; widely and angrily as men differ in its
application, the principle is admitted by all.

Equally mechanical, and of equal simplicity, are the methods
proposed by both parties for completing or securing this all-
sufficient perfection of arrangement. It is no longer the moral,
religious, spiritual condition of the people that is our concern,
but their physical, practical, economical condition, as regulated by public laws. Thus is the Body-politic more than ever
worshipped and tended; but the Soul-politic less than ever.
Love of country, in any high or generous sense, in any other
than an almost animal sense, or mere habit, has little importance attached to it in such reforms, or in the opposition shown
them. Men are to be guided only by their self-interests. Good
government is a good balancing of these; and, except a keen
eye and appetite for self-interest, requires no virtue in any quarter. To both parties it is emphatically a machine: to the
discontented, a 'taxing-machine;' to the contented, a 'machine
for securing property.' Its duties and its faults are not those of
a father, but of an active parish-constable.

Thus it is by the mere condition of the machine, by preserving it untouched, or else by reconstructing it, and oiling it anew,

that man's salvation as a social being is to be insured and indefinitely promoted. Contrive the fabric of law aright, and without farther effort on your part, that divine spirit of Freedom, which all hearts venerate and long for, will of herself come to inhabit it; and under her healing wings every noxious influence will wither, every good and salutary one more and more expand. Nay, so devoted are we to this principle, and at the same time so curiously mechanical, that a new trade, specially grounded on it, has arisen among us, under the name of 'Codification,' or code-making in the abstract; whereby any people, for a reasonable consideration, may be accommodated with a patent code; – more easily than curious individuals with patent breeches, for the people does *not* need to be measured first.

To us who live in the midst of all this, and see continually the faith, hope and practice of every one founded on Mechanism of one kind or other, it is apt to seem quite natural, and as if it could never have been otherwise. Nevertheless, if we recollect or reflect a little, we shall find both that it has been, and might again be otherwise. The domain of Mechanism, – meaning thereby political, ecclesiastical or other outward establishments, – was once considered as embracing, and we are persuaded can at any time embrace, but a limited portion of man's interests, and by no means the highest portion.

To speak a little pedantically, there is a science of *Dynamics* in man's fortunes and nature, as well as of *Mechanics*. There is a science which treats of, and practically addresses, the primary, unmodified forces and energies of man, the mysterious springs of Love, and Fear, and Wonder, of Enthusiasm, Poetry, Religion, all which have a truly vital and *infinite* character; as well as a science which practically addresses the finite, modified developments of these, when they take the shape of immediate 'motives,' as hope of reward, or as fear of punishment.

Now it is certain, that in former times the wise men, the enlightened lovers of their kind, who appeared generally as Moralists, Poets or Priests, did, without neglecting the Mechanical province, deal chiefly with the Dynamical; applying themselves chiefly to regulate, increase and purify the inward primary powers of man; and fancying that herein lay the main difficulty, and the best service they could undertake. But a wide difference is manifest in our age. For the wise men, who now appear as Political Philosophers, deal exclusively with the Mechanical province; and occupying themselves in counting-up and estimating men's motives, strive by curious checking and balancing, and other adjustments of Profit and Loss, to guide them to their true advantage: while, unfortunately, those same 'motives' are so innumerable, and so variable in every individual, that no really useful conclusion can ever be drawn from their enumeration. But though Mechanism, wisely contrived, has done much for man in a social and moral point of view, we cannot be persuaded that it has ever been the chief source of his worth or happiness. Consider the great elements of human enjoyment, the attainments and possessions that exalt man's life to its present height, and see what part of these he owes to institutions, to Mechanism of any kind; and what to the instinctive, unbounded force, which Nature herself lent him, and still continues to him. Shall we say, for example, that Science and Art are indebted principally to the founders of Schools and Universities? Did not Science originate rather, and gain advancement, in the obscure closets of the Roger Bacons, Keplers, Newtons; in the workshops of the Fausts and the Watts; wherever, and in what guise soever Nature, from the first times downwards, had sent a gifted spirit upon the earth? Again, were Homer and Shakspeare members of any beneficed guild, or made Poets by means of it? Were Painting and Sculpture created by forethought, brought into the world by institutions for that end? No; Science and Art have, from first to last, been the free gift of Nature; an unsolicited, unexpected gift; often even a fatal one. These things rose up, as it were, by spontaneous growth, in the free soil and sunshine of Nature. They were not planted or grafted, nor even greatly multiplied or improved by the culture or manuring of institutions. Generally speaking, they have derived only partial help from these; often enough have suffered damage. They made constitutions for themselves. They originated in the Dynamical nature of man, not in his Mechanical nature.

Or, to take an infinitely higher instance, that of the Christian Religion, which, under every theory of it, in the believing or unbelieving mind, must ever be regarded as the crowning glory, or rather the life and soul, of our whole modern culture: How did Christianity arise and spread abroad among men? Was it by institutions, and establishments and well-arranged systems of mechanism? Not so; on the contrary, in all past and existing institutions for those ends, its divine spirit has invariably been found to languish and decay. It arose in the mystic deeps of man's soul; and was spread abroad by the 'preaching of the word,' by simple, altogether natural and individual efforts; and flew, like hallowed fire, from heart to heart, till all were purified and illuminated by it; and its heavenly light shone, as it still shines, and (as sun or star) will ever shine, through the whole dark destinies of man. Here again was no Mechanism; man's highest attainment was accomplished Dynamically, not Mechanically.

Nay, we will venture to say, that no high attainment, not even any far-extending movement among men, was ever accomplished otherwise. Strange as it may seem, if we read History with any degree of thoughtfulness, we shall find that the checks and balances of Profit and Loss have never been the grand agents with men; that they have never been roused into deep, thorough, all-pervading efforts by any computable prospect of Profit and Loss, for any visible, finite object; but always for some invisible and infinite one. The Crusades took their rise in Religion; their visible object was, commercially speaking, worth nothing. It was the boundless Invisible world that was laid bare in the imaginations of those men; and in its burning light, the visible shrunk as a scroll. Not mechanical, nor produced by mechanical means, was this vast movement. No dining at Freemasons' Tavern,[26] with the other long train of modern machinery; no cunning reconciliation of 'vested interests,' was required here: only the passionate voice of one man, the rapt soul looking through the eyes of one man; and rugged, steel-clad Europe trembled beneath his words, and followed him whither he listed. In later ages it was still the same. The Reformation had an invisible, mystic and ideal aim; the result was indeed to be embodied in external things; but its spirit, its worth, was internal, invisible, infinite. Our English Revolution too originated in Religion. Men did battle, in those old days, not for Purse-sake, but for Conscience-sake. Nay, in our own days it is no way different. The French Revolution itself had something higher in it than cheap bread and a Habeas-corpus act.[27] Here too was an Idea; a Dynamic, not a Mechanic force. It was a struggle, though a blind and at last an insane one, for the infinite, divine nature of Right, of Freedom, of Country.

Thus does man, in every age, vindicate, consciously or unconsciously, his celestial birthright. Thus does Nature hold on her wondrous, unquestionable course; and all our systems and theories are but so many froth-eddies or sand-banks, which from time to time she casts up, and washes away. When we can drain the Ocean into mill-ponds, and bottle-up the Force of Gravity, to be sold by retail, in gas-jars; then may we hope to comprehend the infinitudes of man's soul under formulas of Profit and Loss; and rule over this too, as over a patent engine, by checks, and valves, and balances.

Nay, even with regard to Government itself, can it be necessary to remind any one that Freedom, without which indeed all spiritual life is impossible, depends on infinitely more complex influences than either the extension or the curtailment of the 'democratic interest'? Who is there that, 'taking the high *priori* road,'[28] shall point out what these influences are; what deep, subtle, inextricably entangled influences they have been and may be? For man is not the creature and product of Mechanism; but, in a far truer sense, its creator and producer: it is the noble People that makes the noble Government; rather than conversely. On the whole, Institutions are much; but they are not all. The freest and highest spirits of the world have often been found under strange outward circumstances: Saint Paul and his brother Apostles were politically slaves; Epictetus was personally one.[29] Again, forget the influences of Chivalry and Religion, and ask: What countries produced Columbus and Las Casas? Or, descending from virtue and heroism to mere energy and spiritual talent: Cortes, Pizarro, Alba, Ximenes?[30] The Spaniards of the sixteenth century were indisputably the noblest nation of Europe; yet they had the Inquisition and Philip II. They have the same government at this day; and are the lowest nation. The Dutch too have retained their old constitution; but no Siege of Leyden, no William the Silent, not even an Egmont or De Witt any longer appears among them. With ourselves also, where much has changed, effect has nowise followed cause as it should have done: two centuries ago, the Commons Speaker addressed Queen Elizabeth on bended knees, happy that the virago's foot did not even smite him; yet the people were then governed, not by a Castlereagh, but by a Burghley; they had their Shakspeare and Philip Sidney, where we have our Sheridan Knowles and Beau Brummel.[31]

These and the like facts are so familiar, the truths which they preach so obvious, and have in all past times been so universally believed and acted on, that we should almost feel ashamed for repeating them; were it not that, on every hand, the memory of them seems to have passed away, or at best died into a faint tradition, of no value as a practical principle. To judge by the loud clamour of our Constitution-builders, Statists, Economists, directors, creators, reformers of Public Societies; in a word, all manner of Mechanists, from the Cartwright up to the Code-maker; and by the nearly total silence of all Preachers and Teachers who should give a voice to Poetry, Religion and Morality, we might fancy either that man's Dynamical nature was, to all spiritual intents, extinct, or else so perfected that nothing more was to be made of it by the old means; and henceforth only in his Mechanical contrivances did any hope exist for him.

To define the limits of these two departments of man's activity, which work one into another, and by means of one another, so intricately and inseparably, were by its nature an impossible attempt. Their relative importance, even to the wisest mind, will vary in different times, according to the special wants and dispositions of those times. Meanwhile, it seems clear enough that only in the right coordination of the two, and the vigorous forwarding of *both*, does our true line of action lie. Undue cultivation of the inward or Dynamical province leads to idle, visionary, impracticable courses, and, especially in rude eras, to Superstition and Fanaticism, with their long train of baleful and well-known evils. Undue cultivation of the outward, again, though less immediately prejudicial, and even for the time productive of many palpable benefits, must, in the long-run, by destroying Moral Force, which is the parent of all other Force, prove not less certainly, and perhaps still more hopelessly, pernicious. This, we take it, is the grand characteristic of our age. By our skill in Mechanism, it has come to pass, that in the management of external things we excel all other ages; while in whatever respects the pure moral nature, in true dignity of soul and character, we are perhaps inferior to most civilised ages.

In fact, if we look deeper, we shall find that this faith in Mechanism has now struck its roots down into man's most intimate, primary sources of conviction; and is thence sending up, over his whole life and activity, innumerable stems, – fruit-bearing and poison-bearing. The truth is, men have lost their belief in the Invisible, and believe, and hope, and work only in the Visible; or, to speak it in other words: This is not a Religious age. Only the material, the immediately practical, not the divine and spiritual, is important to us. The infinite, absolute character of Virtue has passed into a finite, conditional one; it is no longer a worship of the Beautiful and Good; but a calculation of the Profitable. Worship, indeed, in any sense, is not recognised among us, or is mechanically explained into Fear of pain, or Hope of pleasure. Our true Deity is Mechanism. It has subdued external Nature for us, and we think it will do all other things. We are Giants in physical power: in a deeper than metaphorical sense, was are Titans, that strive, by heaping mountain on mountain, to conquer Heaven also.

The strong Mechanical character, so visible in the spiritual pursuits and methods of this age, may be traced much farther into the condition and prevailing disposition of our spiritual nature itself. Consider, for example, the general fashion of Intellect in this era. Intellect, the power man has of knowing and believing, is now nearly synonymous with Logic, or the mere power of arranging and communicating. Its implement is not Meditation, but Argument. 'Cause and effect' is almost the

only category under which we look at, and work with, all
Nature. Our first question with regard to any object is not,
What is it? but, How is it? We are no longer instinctively driven
to apprehend, and lay to heart, what is Good and Lovely, but
rather to inquire, as onlookers, how it is produced, whence it
comes, whither it goes. Our favourite Philosophers have no
love and no hatred; they stand among us not to do, nor to create anything, but as a sort of Logic-mills to grind out the true
causes and effects of all that is done and created. To the eye of
a Smith, a Hume or a Constant,[32] all is well that works quietly.
An Order of Ignatius Loyola, a Presbyterianism of John Knox,
a Wickliffe or a Henry the Eighth, are simply so many mechanical phenomena, caused or causing.

The *Euphuist* of our day[33] differs much from his pleasant
predecessors. An intellectual dapperling of these times boasts
chiefly of his irresistible perspicacity, his 'dwelling in the daylight of truth,' and so forth; which, on examination, turns out
to be a dwelling in the *rush*-light of 'closet-logic,' and a deep
unconsciousness that there is any other light to dwell in or any
other objects to survey with it. Wonder, indeed, is, on all hands,
dying out: it is the sign of uncultivation to wonder. Speak to
any small man of a high, majestic Reformation, of a high,
majestic Luther; and forthwith he sets about 'accounting' for it;
how the 'circumstances of the time' called for such a character,
and found him, we suppose, standing girt and road-ready, to
do its errand; how the 'circumstances of the time' created, fashioned, floated him quietly along into the result; how, in short,
this small man, had he been there, could have performed the
like himself! For it is the 'force of circumstances' that does
everything; the force of one man can do nothing. Now all this
is grounded on little more than a metaphor. We figure Society
as a 'Machine,' and that mind is opposed to mind, as body is to
body; whereby two, or at most ten, little minds must be stronger
than one great mind. Notable absurdity! For the plain truth,
very plain, we think, is, that minds are opposed to minds in
quite a different way; and *one* man that has a higher Wisdom,
a hitherto unknown spiritual Truth in him, is stronger, not than
ten men that have it not, or than ten thousand, but than *all* men

that have it not; and stands among them with a quite ethereal, angelic power, as with a sword out of Heaven's own armory, sky-tempered, which no buckler, and no tower of brass, will finally withstand.

But to us, in these times, such considerations rarely occur. We enjoy, we see nothing by direct vision; but only by reflection, and in anatomical dismemberment. Like Sir Hudibras, for every Why we must have a Wherefore.[34] We have our little *theory* on all human and divine things. Poetry, the working of genius itself, which in all times, with one or another meaning, has been called Inspiration, and held to be mysterious and inscrutable, is no longer without its scientific exposition. The building of the lofty rhyme is like any other masonry or bricklaying: we have theories of its rise, height, decline and fall, – which latter, it would seem, is now near, among all people. Of our 'Theories of Taste,' as they are called, wherein the deep, infinite, unspeakable Love of Wisdom and Beauty, which dwells in all men, is 'explained,' made mechanically visible, from 'Association' and the like, why should we say anything? Hume has written us a 'Natural History of Religion;'[35] in which one Natural History all the rest are included. Strangely too does the general feeling coincide with Hume's in this wonderful problem; for whether his 'Natural History' be the right one or not, that Religion must have a Natural History, all of us, cleric and laic, seem to be agreed. He indeed regards it as a Disease, we again as Health; so far there is a difference; but in our first principle we are at one.

To what extent theological Unbelief, we mean intellectual dissent from the Church, in its view of Holy Writ, prevails at this day, would be a highly important, were it not, under any circumstances, an almost impossible inquiry. But the Unbelief, which is of a still more fundamental character, every man may see prevailing, with scarcely any but the faintest contradiction, all around him; even in the Pulpit itself. Religion in most countries, more or less in every country, is no longer what it was, and should be, – a thousand-voiced psalm from the heart of Man to his invisible Father, the fountain of all Goodness, Beauty, Truth, and revealed in every revelation of these; but for

the most part, a wise prudential feeling grounded on mere calculation; a matter, as all others now are, of Expediency and
Utility; whereby some smaller quantum of earthly enjoyment
may be exchanged for a far larger quantum of celestial enjoyment. Thus Religion too is Profit, a working for wages; not
Reverence, but vulgar Hope or Fear. Many, we know, very
many we hope, are still religious in a far different sense; were it
not so, our case were too desperate: but to witness that such is
the temper of the times, we take any calm observant man, who
agrees or disagrees in our feeling on the matter, and ask him
whether our *view* of it is not in general well-founded.

   Literature too, if we consider it, gives similar testimony. At
no former era has Literature, the printed communication of
Thought, been of such importance as it is now. We often hear
that the Church is in danger; and truly so it is, – in a danger it
seems not to know of: for, with its tithes in the most perfect
safety, its functions are becoming more and more superseded.
The true Church of England, at this moment, lies in the Editors
of its Newspapers. These preach to the people daily, weekly;
admonishing kings themselves; advising peace or war, with an
authority which only the first Reformers, and a long-past class
of Popes, were possessed of; inflicting moral censure; imparting
moral encouragement, consolation, edification; in all ways diligently 'administering the Discipline of the Church.' It may be
said too, that in private disposition the new Preachers somewhat resemble the Mendicant Friars of old times: outwardly
full of holy zeal; inwardly not without stratagem, and hunger
for terrestrial things. But omitting this class, and the boundless
host of watery personages who pipe, as they are able, on so
many scrannel straws, let us look at the higher regions of Literature, where, if anywhere, the pure melodies of Poesy and
Wisdom should be heard. Of natural talent there is no deficiency: one or two richly-endowed individuals even give us a
superiority in this respect. But what is the song they sing? Is it
a tone of the Memnon Statue,[36] breathing music as the *light*
first touches it? A 'liquid wisdom,' disclosing to our sense the
deep, infinite harmonies of Nature and man's soul? Alas, no! It
is not a matin or vesper hymn to the Spirit of Beauty, but a

fierce clashing of cymbals, and shouting of multitudes, as children pass through the fire to Moloch![37] Poetry itself has no eye for the Invisible. Beauty is no longer the god it worships, but some brute image of Strength; which we may well call an idol, for true Strength is one and the same with Beauty, and its worship also is a hymn. The meek, silent Light can mould, create and purify all Nature; but the loud Whirlwind, the sign and product of Disunion, of Weakness, passes on, and is forgotten. How widely this veneration for the physically Strongest has spread itself through Literature, any one may judge who reads either criticism or poem. We praise a work, not as 'true,' but as 'strong;' our highest praise is that it has 'affected' us, has 'terrified' us. All this, it has been well observed, is the 'maximum of the Barbarous,' the symptom, not of vigorous refinement, but of luxurious corruption. It speaks much, too, for men's indestructible love of truth, that nothing of this kind will abide with them; that even the talent of a Byron cannot permanently seduce us into idol-worship; that he too, with all his wild siren charming, already begins to be disregarded and forgotten.

Again, with respect to our Moral condition: here also, he who runs may read that the same physical, mechanical influences are everywhere busy. For the 'superior morality,' of which we hear so much, we too would desire to be thankful: at the same time, it were but blindness to deny that this 'superior morality' is properly rather an 'inferior criminality,' produced not by greater love of Virtue, but by greater perfection of Police; and of that far subtler and stronger Police, called Public Opinion. This last watches over us with its Argus eyes[38] more keenly than ever; but the 'inward eye' seems heavy with sleep. Of any belief in invisible, divine things, we find as few traces in our Morality as elsewhere. It is by tangible, material considerations that we are guided, not by inward and spiritual. Self-denial, the parent of all virtue, in any true sense of that word, has perhaps seldom been rarer: so rare is it, that the most, even in their abstract speculations, regard its existence as a chimera. Virtue is Pleasure, is Profit; no celestial, but an earthly thing. Virtuous men, Philanthropists, Martyrs are happy accidents; their 'taste' lies the right way! In all senses, we worship and follow after

Power; which may be called a physical pursuit. No man now loves Truth, as Truth must be loved, with an infinite love; but only with a finite love, and as it were *par amours*. Nay, properly speaking, he does not *believe* and know it, but only '*thinks*' it, and that 'there is every probability'! He preaches it aloud, and rushes courageously forth with it, – if there is a multitude huzzaing at his back; yet ever keeps looking over his shoulder, and the instant the huzzaing languishes, he too stops short.

In fact, what morality we have takes the shape of Ambition, of 'Honour;' beyond money and money's worth, our only rational blessedness is Popularity. It were but a fool's trick to die for conscience. Only for 'character,' by duel, or, in case of extremity, by suicide, is the wise man bound to die. By arguing on the 'force of circumstances,' we have argued away all force from ourselves; and stand leashed together, uniform in dress and movement, like the rowers of some boundless galley. This and that may be right and true; *but* we must not do it. Wonderful 'Force of Public Opinion'! We must act and walk in all points as it prescribes; follow the traffic it bids us, realise the sum of money, the degree of 'influence' it expects of us, *or* we shall be lightly esteemed; certain mouthfuls of articulate wind will be blown at us, and this what mortal courage can front? Thus, while civil liberty is more and more secured to us, our moral liberty is all but lost. Practically considered, our creed is Fatalism; and, free in hand and foot, we are shackled in heart and soul with far straiter than feudal chains. Truly may we say, with the Philosopher, 'the deep meaning of the Laws of Mechanism lies heavy on us'; and in the closet, in the marketplace, in the temple, by the social hearth, encumbers the whole movements of our mind, and over our noblest faculties is spreading a nightmare sleep.

These dark features, we are aware, belong more or less to other ages, as well as to ours. This faith in Mechanism, in the all-importance of physical things, is in every age the common refuge of Weakness and blind Discontent; of all who believe, as many will ever do, that man's true good lies without him, not within. We are aware also, that, as applied to ourselves in all their aggravation, they form but half a picture; that in the whole picture there are bright lights as well as gloomy shadows. If we here dwell chiefly on the latter, let us not be blamed: it is in general more profitable to reckon up our defects than to boast of our attainments.

Neither, with all these evils more or less clearly before us, have we at any time despaired of the fortunes of society. Despair, or even despondency, in that respect, appears to us, in all cases, a groundless feeling. We have a faith in the imperishable dignity of man; in the high vocation to which, throughout this his earthly history, he has been appointed. However it may be with individual nations, whatever melancholic speculators may assert, it seems a well-ascertained fact, that in all times, reckoning even from those of the Heraclides and Pelasgi,[39] the happiness and greatness of mankind at large have been continually progressive. Doubtless this age also is advancing. Its very unrest, its ceaseless activity, its discontent contains matter of promise. Knowledge, education are opening the eyes of the humblest; are increasing the number of thinking minds without limit. This is as it should be; for not in turning back, not in resisting, but only in resolutely struggling forward, does our life consist.

Nay, after all, our spiritual maladies are but of Opinion; we are but fettered by chains of our own forging, and which ourselves also can rend asunder. This deep, paralysed subjection to physical objects comes not from Nature, but from our own unwise mode of *viewing* Nature. Neither can we understand that man wants, at this hour, any faculty of heart, soul or body, that ever belonged to him. 'He, who has been born, has been a First Man;' has had lying before his young eyes, and as yet unhardened into scientific shapes, a world as plastic, infinite, divine, as lay before the eyes of Adam himself. If Mechanism, like some glass bell, encircles and imprisons us; if the soul looks forth on a fair heavenly country which it cannot reach, and pines, and in its scanty atmosphere is ready to perish, – yet the bell is but of glass; 'one bold stroke to break the bell in pieces, and thou are delivered!' Not the invisible world is wanting, for it dwells in man's soul, and this last is still here. Are the solemn temples, in which the Divinity was once visibly revealed among us, crumbling away? We can repair them, we can rebuild them. The wisdom, the heroic worth of our forefathers, which we have lost, we can recover. That admiration of old nobleness, which now so often shows itself as a faint *dilettantism*, will one day become a generous emulation, and man may again be all that he has been, and more than he has been. Nor are these the mere daydreams of fancy; they are clear possibilities; nay, in this time they are even assuming the character of hopes. Indications we do see in other countries and in our own, signs infinitely cheering to us, that Mechanism is not always to be our hard taskmaster, but one day to be our pliant, all-ministering servant; that a new and brighter spiritual era is slowly evolving itself for all men. But on these things our present course forbids us to enter.

Meanwhile, that great outward changes are in progress can be doubtful to no one. The time is sick and out of joint. Many things have reached their height; and it is a wise adage that tells us, 'the darkest hour is nearest the dawn.' Wherever we can gather indication of the public thought, whether from printed books, as in France or Germany, or from Carbonari rebellions[40] and other political tumults, as in Spain, Portugal, Italy and Greece, the voice it utters is the same. The thinking minds of all nations call for change. There is a deep-lying struggle in the whole fabric of society; a boundless grinding collision of the New with the Old. The French Revolution, as is now visible enough, was not the parent of this mighty movement, but its offspring. Those two hostile influences, which always exist in human things, and on the constant intercommunion of which depends their health and safety, had lain in separate masses, accumulating through generations, and France was the scene of their fiercest explosion; but the final issue was not unfolded in that country; nay it is not yet anywhere unfolded. Political freedom is hitherto the object of these efforts; but they will not and cannot stop there. It is towards a higher freedom than mere freedom from oppression by his fellow-mortal, that man dimly aims. Of this higher, heavenly freedom, which is 'man's reasonable service,' all his noble institutions, his faithful endeavours and loftiest attainments, are but the body, and more and more approximated emblem.

On the whole, as this wondrous planet, Earth, is journeying with its fellows through infinite Space, so are the wondrous destinies embarked on it journeying through infinite Time, under a higher guidance than ours. For the present, as our astronomy informs us, its path lies towards *Hercules*, the constellation of *Physical Power*; but that is not our most pressing concern. Go where it will, the deep HEAVEN will be around it. Therein let us have hope and sure faith. To reform a world, to reform a nation, no wise man will undertake; and all but foolish men know, that the only solid, though a far slower reformation, is what each begins and perfects on *himself*.

Sartor Resartus

Sartor Resartus – literally 'The Tailor Re-Patched' – was written in 1830–31; in a letter to his brother John, Carlyle wrote: 'What I am writing at is the strangest of all things. A very singular piece, I assure you. It glances from heaven to earth and back again, in a strange satirical frenzy, whether fine or not remains to be seen.' The book purports to describe the life and opinions of a mystical German philosopher, Diogenes Teufelsdröckh of Weissnichtwo, which are presented to the public by an equally imaginary editor who has received for review a copy of Teufelsdröckh's treatise on the 'Philosophy of Clothes'. The key to Teufelsdröckh's philosophy lies in its assertion that finite circumstances are accidental and ultimately irrelevant: reality is only embodied within infinite and spiritual perspectives. Carlyle's adoption of the double persona of Teufelsdröckh and his editor for the expression of these views, however, is a device which enables him to put forward the more extreme ideas of transcendentalist philosophy without seeming to commit himself personally, and this ambiguity is reinforced by the elaborately whimsical tone of the work. If the source of the ideas in *Sartor Resartus* is German transcendentalism, the most obvious influence on its style is Sterne's *Tristram Shandy*, which is in fact referred to on several occasions during the course of the work.

Sartor Resartus may have lost the classic status that was accorded to it when Carlyle's reputation was at its height, but it remains an astonishing tour de force, and many of the ideas embodied in it are central to an understanding of Carlyle as a whole. It is divided into three books; the concluding chapters of Book One are reprinted here.

The World Out of Clothes*

If in the Descriptive-Historical portion of this Volume, Teufels-dröckh, discussing merely the *Werden* (Origin and successive Improvement) of Clothes, has astonished many a reader, much more will he in the Speculative-Philosophical portion, which treats of their *Wirken*, of Influences. It is here that the present Editor first feels the pressure of his task; for here properly the higher and new Philosophy of Clothes commences: an untried, almost inconceivable region, or chaos; in venturing upon which, how difficult, yet how unspeakably important is it to know what course, of survey and conquest, is the true one; where the footing is firm substance and will bear us, where it is hollow, or mere cloud, and may engulf us. Teufelsdröckh undertakes no less than to expound the moral, political, even religious Influences of Clothes; he undertakes to make manifest, in its thousand-fold bearings, this grand Proposition, that Man's earthly interests 'are all hooked and buttoned together, and held up, by Clothes.' He says in so many words, 'Society is founded upon Cloth;' and again, 'Society sails through the Infinitude on Cloth, as on a Faust's Mantle, or rather like the Sheet of clean and unclean beasts in the Apostle's Dream;[1] and without such Sheet or Mantle, would sink to endless depths, or mount to inane limboes, and in either case be no more.'

By what chains, or indeed infinitely complected tissues, of Meditation this grand Theorem is here unfolded, and innumerable practical Corollaries are drawn therefrom, it were perhaps a mad ambition to attempt exhibiting. Our Professor's method

* Book One, Chapter 8.

is not, in any case, that of common school Logic, where the truths all stand in a row, each holding by the skirts of the other; but at best that of practical Reason, proceeding by large Intuition over whole systematic groups and kingdoms; whereby, we might say, a noble complexity, almost like that of Nature, reigns in his Philosophy, or spiritual Picture of Nature: a mighty maze, yet, as faith whispers, not without a plan. Nay we complained above, that a certain ignoble complexity, what we must call mere confusion, was also discernible. Often, also, we have to exclaim: Would to Heaven those same Biographical Documents were come! For it seems as if the demonstration lay much in the Author's individuality; as if it were not Argument that had taught him, but Experience. At present it is only in local glimpses, and by significant fragments, picked often at wide-enough intervals from the original Volume, and carefully collated, that we can hope to impart some outline or foreshadow of this Doctrine. Readers of any intelligence are once more invited to favour us with their most concentrated attention: let these, after intense consideration, and not till then, pronounce, Whether on the utmost verge of our actual horizon there is not a looming as of Land; a promise of new Fortunate Islands,[2] perhaps whole undiscovered Americas, for such as have canvas to sail thither? – As exordium to the whole, stand here the following long citation:

'With men of a speculative turn,' writes Teufelsdröckh, 'there come seasons, meditative, sweet, yet awful hours, when in wonder and fear you ask yourself that unanswerable question: Who am I; the thing that can say "I" (*das Wesen das sich* ICH *nennt*)? The world, with its loud trafficking, retires into the distance; and, through the paper-hangings, and stone-walls, and thick-plied tissues of Commerce and Polity, and all the living and lifeless integuments (of Society and a Body), wherewith your Existence sits surrounded, – the sight reaches forth into the void Deep, and you are alone with the Universe, and silently commune with it, as one mysterious Presence with another.

'Who am I; what is this ME? A Voice, a Motion, an Appearance; – some embodied, visualised Idea in the Eternal

Mind? *Cogito, ergo sum.*[3] Alas, poor Cogitator, this takes us but a little way. Sure enough, I am; and lately was not: but Whence? How? Whereto? The answer lies around, written in all colours and motions, uttered in all tones of jubilee and wail, in thousand-figured, thousand-voiced, harmonious Nature: but where is the cunning eye and ear to whom that God-written Apocalypse will yield articulate meaning? We sit as in a boundless Phantasmagoria and Dream-grotto; boundless, for the faintest star, the remotest century, lies not even nearer the verge thereof: sounds and many-coloured visions flit round our sense; but Him, the Unslumbering, whose work both Dream and Dreamer are, we see not; except in rare half-waking moments, suspect not. Creation, says one, lies before us, like a glorious Rainbow; but the Sun that made it lies behind us, hidden from us. Then, in that strange Dream, how we clutch at shadows as if they were substances; and sleep deepest while fancying ourselves most awake! Which of your Philosophical Systems is other than a dream-theorem; a net quotient, confidently given out, where divisor and dividend are both unknown? What are all your national Wars, with their Moscow Retreats, and sanguinary hate-filled Revolutions, but the Somnambulism of uneasy Sleepers? This Dreaming, this Somnambulism is what we on Earth call Life; wherein the most indeed undoubtingly wander, as if they knew right hand from left; yet they only are wise who know that they know nothing.

Pity that all Metaphysics had hitherto proved so inexpressibly unproductive! The secret of Man's Being is still like the Sphinx's secret: a riddle that he cannot rede; and for ignorance of which he suffers death, the worst death, a spiritual. What are your Axioms, and Categories, and Systems, and Aphorisms? Words, words. High Air-castles are cunningly built of Words, the Words well bedded also in good Logic-mortar; wherein, however, no Knowledge will come to lodge. *The whole is greater than the part*: how exceedingly true! *Nature abhors a vacuum*: how exceedingly false and calumnious! Again, *Nothing can act but where it is*: with all my heart; only, WHERE is it? Be not the slave of Words: is not the Distant, the Dead,

while I love it, and long for it, and mourn for it, Here, in the
genuine sense, as truly as the floor I stand on? But that same
WHERE, with its brother WHEN, are from the first the master-
colours of our Dream-grotto; say rather, the Canvas (the warp
and woof thereof) whereon all our Dreams and Life-visions are
painted. Nevertheless, has not a deeper meditation taught certain of every climate and age, that the WHERE and WHEN, so
mysteriously inseparable from all our thoughts, are but superficial terrestrial adhesions to thought; that the Seer may discern
them where they mount up out of the celestial EVERYWHERE
and FOREVER: have not all nations conceived their God as
Omnipresent and Eternal; as existing in a universal HERE, an
everlasting Now? Think well, thou too wilt find that Space is
but a mode of our human Sense, so likewise Time; there is no
Space and no Time: WE are – we know not what; – light-spar-
kles floating in the æther of Deity!

'So that this so solid-seeming World, after all, were but
an air-image, our ME the only reality: and Nature, with its
thousand-fold production and destruction, but the reflex of
our own inward Force, the "phantasy of our Dream;" or what
the Earth-Spirit in *Faust* names it, *the living visible Garment
of God*:

> "In Being's floods, in Action's storm,
> I walk and work, above, beneath,
> Work and weave in endless motion!
> Birth and Death,
> An infinite ocean;
> A seizing and giving
> The fire of Living:
> 'Tis thus at the roaring Loom of Time I ply,
> And weave for God the Garment thou seest Him by."[4]

'Of twenty millions that have read and spouted this thunder–
speech of the *Erdgeist*, are there yet twenty units of us that have
learned the meaning thereof?

'It was in some such mood, when wearied and fordone with
these high speculations, that I first came upon the question of

Clothes. Strange enough, it strikes me, is this same fact of there being Tailors and Tailored. The Horse I ride has his own whole fell: strip him of the girths and flaps and extraneous tags I have fastened round him, and the noble creature is his own sempster and weaver and spinner; nay his own bootmaker, jeweller, and man-milliner; he bounds free through the valleys, with a perennial rainproof court-suit on his body; wherein warmth and easiness of fit have reached perfection; nay, the graces also have been considered, and frills and fringes, with gay variety of colour, featly appended, and ever in the right place, are not wanting. While I – good Heaven! – have thatched myself over with the dead fleeces of sheep, the bark of vegetables, the entrails of worms, the hides of oxen or seals, the felt of furred beasts; and walk abroad a moving Rag-screen, overheaped with shreds and tatters raked from the Charnel-house of Nature, where they would have rotted, to rot on me more slowly! Day after day, I must thatch myself anew; day after day, this despicable thatch must lose some film of its thickness; some film of it, frayed away by tear and wear, must be brushed-off into the Ashpit, into the Laystall; till by degrees the whole has been brushed thither, and I, the dust-making, patent Rag-grinder, get new material to grind down. O subter-brutish! vile! most vile! For have not I too a compact all-enclosing Skin, whiter or dingier? Am I a botched mass of tailors' and cobblers' shreds, then; or a tightly-articulated, homogeneous little Figure, automatic, nay alive?

'Strange enough how creatures of the human-kind shut their eyes to plainest facts; and by the mere inertia of Oblivion and Stupidity, live at ease in the midst of Wonders and Terrors. But indeed man is, and was always, a blockhead and dullard; much readier to feel and digest, than to think and consider. Prejudice, which he pretends to hate, is his absolute lawgiver; mere use-and-wont everywhere leads him by the nose; thus let but a Rising of the Sun, let but a Creation of the World happen *twice*, and it ceases to be marvellous, to be noteworthy, or noticeable. Perhaps not once in a lifetime does it occur to your ordinary biped, of any country or generation, be he gold-mantled Prince or russet-jerkined Peasant, that his

Vestments and his Self are not one and indivisible; that *he* is naked, without vestments, till he buy or steal such, and by forethought sew and button them.

'For my own part, these considerations of our Clothes-thatch, and how, reaching inwards even to our heart of hearts, it tailorises and demoralises us, fill me with a certain horror at myself and mankind; almost as one feels at those Dutch Cows, which, during the wet season, you see grazing deliberately with jackets and petticoats (of striped sacking), in the meadows of Gouda.[5] Nevertheless there is something great in the moment when a man first strips himself of adventitious wrappages; and sees indeed that he is naked, and, as Swift has it, "a forked straddling animal with bandy legs;"[6] yet also a Spirit, and unutterable Mystery of Mysteries.'

Adamitism*

Let no courteous reader take offence at the opinions broached in the conclusion of the last Chapter. The Editor himself, on first glancing over that singular passage, was inclined to exclaim: What, have we got not only a Sansculottist, but an enemy to Clothes in the abstract? A new Adamite,[7] in this century, which flatters itself that it is the Nineteenth, and destructive both to Superstition and Enthusiasm?

Consider, thou foolish Teufelsdröckh, what benefits unspeakable all ages and sexes derive from Clothes. For example, when thou thyself, a watery, pulpy, slobbery freshman and new-comer in this Planet, sattest muling and puking in thy nurse's arms; sucking thy coral, and looking forth into the world in the blankest manner, what hadst thou been without thy blankets, and bibs, and other nameless hulls? A terror to thyself and mankind! Or hast thou forgotten the day when thou first receivedst breeches, and thy long clothes became short? The village where thou livedst was all apprised of the fact; and neighbour after neighbour kissed thy pudding-cheek, and gave thee, as handsel, silver or copper coins, on that the first gala-day of thy existence. Again, wert not thou, at one period of life, a Buck, or Blood, or Macaroni, or Incroyable, or Dandy, or by whatever name, according to year and place, such phenomenon is distinguished? In that one word lie included mysterious volumes. Nay, now when the reign of folly is over, or altered, and thy clothes are not for triumph but for defence, hast thou always worn them perforce, and as a consequence of Man's

* Book One, Chapter 9.

Fall; never rejoiced in them as in a warm movable House, a Body round thy Body, wherein that strange THEE of thine sat snug, defying all variations of Climate? Girt with thick double-milled kerseys; half-buried under shawls and broadbrims, and overalls and mud-boots, thy very fingers cased in doeskin and mittens, thou hast bestrode that 'Horse I ride;' and, though it were in wild winter, dashed through the world, glorying in it as if thou wert its lord. In vain did the sleet beat round thy temples; it lighted only on thy impenetrable, felted or woven, case of wool. In vain did the winds howl, – forests sounding and creaking, deep calling unto deep, – and the storms heap themselves together into one huge Arctic whirlpool: thou flewest through the middle thereof, striking fire from the highway; wild music hummed in thy ears, thou too wert as a 'sailor of the air;' the wreck of matter and the crash of worlds was thy element and propitiously wafting tide. Without Clothes, without bit or saddle, what hadst thou been; what had thy fleet quadruped been? – Nature is good, but she is not the best: here truly was the victory of Art over Nature. A thunderbolt indeed might have pierced thee; all short of this thou couldst defy.

Or, cries the courteous reader, has your Teufelsdröckh forgotten what he said lately about 'Aboriginal Savages,'[8] and their 'condition miserable indeed'? Would he have all this unsaid; and us betake ourselves again to the 'matted cloak,' and go sheeted in a 'thick natural fell'?

Nowise, courteous reader! The Professor knows full well what he is saying; and both thou and we, in our haste, do him wrong. If Clothes, in these times, 'so tailorise and demoralise us,' have they no redeeming value; can they not be altered to serve better; must they of necessity be thrown to the dogs? The truth is, Teufelsdröckh, though a Sansculottist, is no Adamite; and much perhaps as he might wish to go forth before this degenerate age 'as a Sign,' would nowise wish to do it, as those old Adamites did, in a state of Nakedness. The utility of Clothes is altogether apparent to him: nay perhaps he has an insight into their more recondite, and almost mystic qualities, what we might call the omnipotent virtue of Clothes, such as was never before vouchsafed to any man. For example:

'You see two individuals,' he writes, 'one dressed in fine Red, the other in coarse threadbare Blue: Red says to Blue, "Be hanged and anatomised;" Blue hears with a shudder, and (O wonder of wonders!) marches sorrowfully to the gallows; is there noosed-up, vibrates his hour, and the surgeons dissect him, and fit his bones into a skeleton for medical purposes. How is this; or what make ye of your *Nothing can act but where it is?* Red has no physical hold of Blue, no *clutch* of him, is nowise in *contact* with him: neither are those ministering Sheriffs and Lord-Lieutenants and Hangmen and Tipstaves so related to commanding Red, that he can tug them hither and thither; but each stands distinct within his own skin. Nevertheless, as it is spoken, so is it done: the articulated Word sets all hands in Action; and Rope and Improved-drop perform their work.

'Thinking reader, the reason seems to me twofold: First, that *Man is a Spirit*, and bound by invisible bonds to *All Men*; secondly, that *he wears Clothes*, which are the visible emblems of that fact. Has not your Red hanging-individual a horsehair wig, squirrel-skins, and a plush-gown; whereby all mortals know that he is a JUDGE? – Society, which the more I think of it astonishes me the more, is founded upon Cloth.

'Often in my atrabiliar moods, when I read of pompous ceremonials, Frankfort Coronations,[9] Royal Drawing-rooms, Levees, Couchees; and how the ushers and macers and pursuivants are all in waiting; how Duke this is presented by Archduke that, and Colonel A by General B, and innumerable Bishops, Admirals, and miscellaneous Functionaries, are advancing gallantly to the Anointed Presence; and I strive, in my remote privacy, to form a clear picture of that solemnity, – on a sudden, as by some enchanter's wand, the – shall I speak it? – the Clothes fly-off the whole dramatic corps; and Dukes, Grandees, Bishops, Generals, Anointed Presence itself, every mother's son of them, stand straddling there, not a shirt on them; and I know not whether to laugh or weep. This physical or psychical infirmity, in which perhaps I am not singular, I have, after hesitation, thought right to publish, for the solace of those afflicted with the like.'

Would to Heaven, say we, thou hadst thought right to keep it secret! Who is there now that can read the five columns of Presentations in his Morning Newspaper without a shudder? Hypochondriac men, and all men are to a certain extent hypochondriac, should be more gently treated. With what readiness our fancy, in this shattered state of the nerves, follows out the consequences which Teufelsdröckh, with a devilish coolness, goes on to draw:

'What would Majesty do, could such an accident befall in reality; should the buttons all simultaneously start, and the solid wool evaporate, in very Deed, as here in Dream? *Ach Gott!* How each skulks into the nearest hiding-place; their high State Tragedy (*Haupt- und Staats-Action*) becomes a Pickle-herring-Farce[10] to weep at, which is the worst kind of Farce; *the tables* (according to Horace), and with them, the whole fabric of Government, Legislation, Property, Police, and Civilised Society, *are dissolved*,[11] in wails and howls.'

Lives the man that can figure a naked Duke of Windlestraw addressing a naked House of Lords? Imagination, choked as in mephitic air, recoils on itself, and will not forward with the picture. The Woolsack, the Ministerial, the Opposition Benches – *infandum! infandum!*[12] And yet why is the thing impossible? Was not every soul, or rather every body, of these Guardians of our Liberties, naked, or nearly so, last night; 'a forked Radish with a head fantastically carved'?[13] And why might he not, did our stern fate so order it, walk out to St Stephen's,[14] as well as into bed, in that no-fashion; and there, with other similar Radishes, hold a Bed of Justice?[15] 'Solace of those afflicted with the like!' Unhappy Teufelsdröckh, had man ever such a 'physical or psychical infirmity' before? And now how many, perhaps, may thy unparalleled confession (which we, even to the sounder British world, and goaded-on by Critical and Biographical duty, grudge to reimpart) incurably infect therewith! Art thou the malignest of Sansculottists, or only the maddest?

'It will remain to be examined,' adds the inexorable Teufelsdröckh, 'in how far the SCARECROW, as a Clothed Person, is not also entitled to benefit of clergy, and English trial by jury: nay perhaps, considering his high function (for is not he too a

Defender of Property, and Sovereign armed with the *terrors* of the Law?), to a certain royal Immunity and Inviolability; which, however, misers and the meaner class of persons are not always voluntarily disposed to grant him.'

'O my Friends, we are (in Yorick Sterne's words)[16] but as "turkeys driven, with a stick and red clout, to the market:" or if some drivers, as they do in Norfolk, take a dried bladder and 'put peas in it, the rattle thereof terrifies the boldest!'

Pure Reason*

It must now be apparent enough that our Professor, as above hinted, is a speculative Radical, and of the very darkest tinge; acknowledging, for most part, in the solemnities and paraphernalia of civilised Life, which we make so much of, nothing but so many Cloth-rags, turkey-poles, and 'bladders with dried peas.' To linger among such speculations, longer than mere Science requires, a discerning public can have no wish. For our purposes the simple fact that such a *Naked World* is possible, nay actually exists (under the Clothed one), will be sufficient. Much, therefore, we omit about 'Kings wrestling naked on the green with Carmen,' and the Kings being thrown: 'dissect them with scalpels,' says Teufelsdröckh; 'the same viscera, tissues, livers, lights, and other life-tackle, are there: examine their spiritual mechanism; the same great Need, great Greed, and little Faculty; nay ten to one but the Carman, who understands draught-cattle, the rimming of wheels, something of the laws of unstable and stable equilibrium, with other branches of wagon-science, and has actually put forth his hand and operated on Nature, is the more cunningly gifted of the two. Whence, then, their so unspeakable difference? From Clothes.' Much also we shall omit about confusion of Ranks, and Joan and My Lady, and how it would be everywhere 'Hail fellow well met,' and Chaos were come again: all which to any one that has once fairly pictured-out the grand mother-idea, *Society in a state of Nakedness*, will spontaneously suggest itself. Should some sceptical individual still entertain doubts whether

* Book One, Chapter 10.

in a world without Clothes, the smallest Politeness, Polity, or even Police, could exist, let him turn to the original Volume, and view there the boundless Serbonian Bog of Sansculottism, stretching sour and pestilential: over which we have lightly flown; where not only whole armies but whole nations might sink![17] If indeed the following argument, in its brief riveting emphasis, be not of itself incontrovertible and final:

'Are we Opossums; have we natural Pouches, like the Kangaroo? Or how, without Clothes, could we possess the master-organ, soul's seat, and true pineal gland of the Body Social: I mean, a PURSE?'

Nevertheless it is impossible to hate Professor Teufelsdröckh; at worst, one knows not whether to hate or to love him. For though, in looking at the fair tapestry of human Life, with its royal and even sacred figures, he dwells not on the obverse alone, but here chiefly on the reverse; and indeed turns out the rough seams, tatters, and manifold thrums of that unsightly wrong-side, with an almost diabolic patience and indifference, which must have sunk him in the estimation of most readers, – there is that within which unspeakably distinguishes him from all other past and present Sansculottists. The grand unparalleled peculiarity of Teufelsdröckh is, that with all this Descendental-ism, he combines a Transcendentalism, no less superlative; whereby if on the one hand he degrade man below most ani-mals, except those jacketed Gouda Cows, he, on the other, exalts him beyond the visible Heavens, almost to an equality with the Gods.

'To the eye of vulgar Logic,' says he, 'what is man? An omnivorous Biped that wears Breeches. To the eye of Pure Rea-son what is he? A Soul, a Spirit, and divine Apparition. Round his mysterious ME, there lies, under all those wool-rags, a Gar-ment of Flesh (or of Senses), contextured in the Loom of Heaven; whereby he is revealed to his like, and dwells with them in UNION and DIVISION; and sees and fashions for him-self a Universe, with azure Starry Spaces, and long Thousands of Years. Deep-hidden is he under that strange Garment; amid Sounds and Colours and Forms, as it were, swathed-in, and inextricably over-shrouded: yet it is skywoven, and worthy of a

God. Stands he not thereby in the centre of Immensities, in the conflux of Eternities? He feels; power has been given him to know, to believe; nay does not the spirit of Love, free in its celestial primeval brightness, even here, though but for moments, look through? Well said Saint Chrysostom, with his lips of gold, "the true SHEKINAH is Man:"[18] where else is the GOD'S-PRESENCE manifested not to our eyes only, but to our hearts, as in our fellow-man?'

In such passages, unhappily too rare, the high Platonic Mysticism of our Author, which is perhaps the fundamental element of his nature, bursts forth, as it were, in full flood: and, through all the vapour and tarnish of what is often so perverse, so mean in his exterior and environment, we seem to look into a whole inward Sea of Light and Love; – though, alas, the grim coppery clouds soon roll together again, and hide it from view.

Such tendency to Mysticism is everywhere traceable in this man; and indeed, to attentive readers, must have been long ago apparent. Nothing that he sees but has more than a common meaning, but has two meanings: thus, if in the highest Imperial Sceptre and Charlemagne-Mantle, as well as in the poorest Ox-goad and Gipsy-Blanket, he finds Prose, Decay, Contemptibility; there is in each sort Poetry also, and a reverend Worth. For Matter, were it never so despicable, is Spirit, the manifestation of Spirit: were it never so honourable, can it be more? The thing Visible, nay the thing Imagined, the thing in any way conceived as Visible, what is it but a Garment, a Clothing of the higher, celestial Invisible, 'unimaginable, formless, dark with excess of bright'? Under which point of view the following passage, so strange in purport, so strange in phrase, seems characteristic enough:

'The beginning of all Wisdom is to look fixedly on Clothes, or even with armed eyesight, till they become *transparent*. "The Philosopher," says the wisest of this age,[19] "must station himself in the middle:" how true! The Philosopher is he to whom the Highest has descended, and the Lowest has mounted up; who is the equal and kindly brother of all.

'Shall we tremble before clothwebs and cobwebs, whether woven in Arkwright looms, or by the silent Arachnes[20] that weave unrestingly in our Imagination? Or, on the other hand, what is there that we cannot love; since all was created by God?

'Happy he who can look through the Clothes of a Man (the woollen, and fleshly, and official Bank-paper and State-paper Clothes) into the Man himself; and discern, it may be, in this or the other Dread Potentate, a more or less incompetent Digestive apparatus; yet also an inscrutable venerable Mystery, in the meanest Tinker that sees with eyes!'

For the rest, as is natural to a man of this kind, he deals much in the feeling of Wonder; insists on the necessity and high worth of universal Wonder; which he holds to be the only reasonable temper for the denizen of so singular a Planet as ours. 'Wonder,' says he, 'is the basis of Worship: the reign of wonder is perennial, indestructible in Man; only at certain stages (as the present), it is, for some short season, a reign *in partibus infidelium*.'[21] That progress of Science, which is to destroy Wonder, and in its stead substitute Mensuration and Numeration, finds small favour with Teufelsdröckh, much as he otherwise venerates these two latter processes.

'Shall your Science,' exclaims he, 'proceed in the small chink-lighted, or even oil-lighted, underground workshop of Logic alone; and man's mind become an Arithmetical Mill, whereof Memory is the Hopper, and mere Tables of Sines and Tangents, Codification and Treatises of what you call Political Economy, are the Meal? And what is that Science, which the scientific head alone, were it screwed off, and (like the Doctor's in the Arabian Tale)[22] set in a basin to keep it alive, could prosecute without shadow of a heart, – but one other of the mechanical and menial handicrafts, for which the Scientific Head (having a Soul in it) is too noble an organ? I mean that Thought without Reverence is barren, perhaps poisonous; at best, dies like cookery with the day that called it forth; does not live, like sowing, in successive tilths and wider-spreading harvests, bringing food and plenteous increase to all Time.'

In such wise does Teufelsdröckh deal hits, harder or softer, according to ability; yet ever, as we would fain persuade ourselves, with charitable intent. Above all, that class of 'Logic-choppers, and treble-pipe Scoffers, and Professed Enemies to

Wonder; who, in these days, so numerously patrol as night-constables about the Mechanics' Institute of Science,[23] and cackle, like true Old-Roman geese and goslings round their Capitol,[24] on any alarm, or on none; nay who often, as illuminated Sceptics, walk abroad into peaceable society, in full daylight, with rattle and lantern, and insist on guiding you and guarding you therewith, though the Sun is shining, and the street populous with mere justice-loving men:' that whole class is inexpressibly wearisome to him. Hear with what uncommon animation he perorates:

'The man who cannot wonder, who does not habitually wonder (and worship), were he President of innumerable Royal Societies, and carried the whole *Mécanique Céleste* and *Hegel's Philosophy*,[25] and the epitome of all Laboratories and Observatories with their results, in his single head, – is but a Pair of Spectacles behind which there is no Eye. Let those who have Eyes look through him, then he may be useful.

'Thou wilt have no Mystery and Mysticism; wilt walk through thy world by the sunshine of what thou callest Truth, or even by the hand-lamp of what I call Attorney-Logic; and "explain" all, "account" for all, or believe nothing of it? Nay, thou wilt attempt laughter; whoso recognises the unfathomable, all-pervading domain of Mystery, which is everywhere under our feet and among our hands; to whom the Universe is an Oracle and Temple, as well as a Kitchen and Cattle-stall, – he shall be a delirious Mystic; to him thou, with sniffing charity, wilt protrusively proffer thy hand-lamp, and shriek, as one injured, when he kicks his foot through it? – *Armer Teufel!*[26] Doth not thy cow calve, doth not thy bull gender? Thou thyself, wert thou not born, wilt thou not die? "Explain" me all this, or do one of two things: Retire into private places with thy foolish cackle; or, what were better, give it up, and weep, not that the reign of wonder is done, and God's world all disembellished and prosaic, but that thou hitherto art a Dilettante and sandblind Pedant.'

Prospective*

The Philosophy of Clothes is now to all readers, as we predicted it would do, unfolding itself into new boundless
expansions, of a cloudcapt, almost chimerical aspect, yet not
without azure loomings in the far distance, and streaks as of an
Elysian brightness; the highly questionable purport and promise of which it is becoming more and more important for us
to ascertain. Is that a real Elysian brightness, cries many a
timid wayfarer, or the reflex of Pandemonian lava? Is it of a
truth leading us into beatific Asphodel meadows, or the yellow-
burning marl of a Hell-on-Earth?[27]

Our Professor, like other Mystics, whether delirious or inspired,
gives an Editor enough to do. Even higher and dizzier are the
heights he leads us to; more piercing, all-comprehending, all
confounding are his views and glances. For example, this of
Nature being not an Aggregate but a Whole:

'Well sang the Hebrew Psalmist:[28] "If I take the wings of the
morning and dwell in the uttermost parts of the universe, God
is there." Thou thyself, O cultivated reader, who too probably
art no Psalmist, but a Prosaist, knowing GOD only by tradition, knowest thou any corner of the world where at least
FORCE is not? The drop which thou shakest from thy wet
hand, rests not where it falls, but tomorrow thou findest it
swept away; already on the wings of the Northwind, it is near-
ing the Tropic of Cancer. How came it to evaporate, and not lie

* Book One, Chapter 11.

motionless? Thinkest thou there is aught motionless; without Force, and utterly dead?

'As I rode through the Schwarzwald,[29] I said to myself: That little fire which glows star-like across the dark-growing (*nach-ende*) moor, where the sooty smith bends over his anvil, and thou hopest to replace thy lost horse-shoe, – is it a detached, separated speck, cut-off from the whole Universe; or indissolubly joined to the whole? Thou fool, that smithy-fire was (primarily) kindled at the Sun; is fed by air that circulates from before Noah's Deluge, from beyond the Dogstar; therein, with Iron Force, and Coal Force, and the far stranger Force of Man, are cunning affinities and battles and victories of Force brought about; it is a little ganglion, or nervous centre, in the great vital system of Im mensity. Call it, if thou wilt, an unconscious Altar, kindled on the bosom of the All; whose iron sacrifice, whose iron smoke and influence reach quite through the All; whose dingy Priest, not by word, yet by brain and sinew, preaches forth the mystery of Force; nay preaches forth (exoterically enough) one little textlet from the Gospel of Freedom, the Gospel of Man's Force, com manding, and one day to be all-commanding.

'Detached, separated! I say there is no such separation: nothing hitherto was ever stranded, cast aside; but all, were it only a withered leaf, works together with all; is borne forward on the bottomless, shoreless flood of Action, and lives through perpetual metamorphoses. The withered leaf is not dead and lost, there are Forces in it and around it, though working in inverse order; else how could it *rot*? Despise not the rag from which man makes Paper, or the litter from which the earth makes Corn. Rightly viewed no meanest object is insignificant; all objects are as windows, through which the philosophic eye looks into Infinitude itself.'

Again, leaving that wondrous Schwarzwald Smithy-Altar, what vacant, high-sailing air-ships are these, and whither will they sail with us?

'All visible things are emblems; what thou seest is not there on its own account; strictly taken, is not there at all: Matter exists only spiritually, and to represent some Idea, and *body* it

forth. Hence Clothes, as despicable as we think them, are so
un speakably significant. Clothes, from the King's mantle down
wards, are emblematic, not of want only, but of a manifold cunning Victory over Want. On the other hand, all Emblematic
things are properly Clothes, thought-woven or hand-woven:
must not the Imagination weave Garments, visible Bodies,
wherein the else invisible creations and inspirations of our Reason are, like Spirits, revealed, and first become all-powerful; – the
rather if, as we often see, the Hand too aid her, and (by wool
Clothes or otherwise) reveal such even to the outward eye?

'Men are properly said to be clothed with Authority, clothed
with Beauty, with Curses, and the like. Nay, if you consider it,
what is Man himself, and his whole terrestrial Life, but an
Em blem; a Clothing or visible Garment for that divine ME of
his, cast hither, like a light-particle, down from Heaven? Thus
is he said also to be clothed with a Body.

'Language is called the Garment of Thought: however, it
should rather be, Language is the Flesh-Garment, the Body, of
Thought. I said that Imagination wove this Flesh-Garment;
and does not she? Metaphors are her stuff: examine Language;
what, if you except some few primitive elements (of natural
sound), what is it all but Metaphors, recognised as such, or no
longer recognised; still fluid and florid, or now solid-grown
and colourless? If those same primitive elements are the osseous fixtures in the Flesh – Garment, Language, – then are
Metaphors its muscles and tissues and living integuments. An
unmetaphorical style you shall in vain seek for: is not your
very *Attention a Stretching-to*? The difference lies here: some
styles are lean, adust, wiry, the muscle itself seems osseous;
some are even quite pallid, hunger-bitten and dead-looking;
while others again glow in the flush of health and vigorous
self-growth, sometimes (as in my own case) not without an
apoplectic tendency. Moreover, there are sham Meta phors,
which overhanging that same Thought's-Body (best naked),
and deceptively bedizening, or bolstering it out, may be called
its false stuffings, superfluous show-cloaks (*Putz-Mäntel*), and
tawdry woollen rags: whereof he that runs and reads may
gather whole hampers, – and burn them.'

Than which paragraph on Metaphors did the reader ever chance to see a more surprisingly metaphorical? However, that is not our chief grievance; the Professor continues:

'Why multiply instances? It is written, the Heavens and the Earth shall fade away like a Vesture;[30] which indeed they are; the Time-vesture of the Eternal. Whatsoever sensibly exists, whatsoever represents Spirit to Spirit, is properly a Clothing, a suit of Raiment, put on for a season, and to be laid off. Thus in this one pregnant subject of CLOTHES, rightly understood, is included all that men have thought, dreamed, done, and been: the whole External Universe and what it holds is but Clothing; and the essence of all Science lies in the PHILOSOPHY OF CLOTHES.'

Towards these dim infinitely-expanded regions, close-bordering on the impalpable Inane, it is not without apprehension, and perpetual difficulties, that the Editor sees himself journeying and struggling. Till lately a cheerful daystar of hope hung before him, in the expected Aid of Hofrath Heuschrecke;[31] which daystar, however, melts now, not into the red of morning, but into a vague, gray half-light, uncertain whether dawn of day or dusk of utter darkness. For the last week, these so-called Biographical Documents are in his hand. By the kindness of a Scottish Hamburg Merchant, whose name, known to the whole mercantile world, he must not mention; but whose honourable courtesy, now and often before spontaneously manifested to him, a mere literary stranger, he cannot soon forget, – the bulky Weissnichtwo Packet, with all its Customhouse seals, foreign hieroglyphs, and miscellaneous tokens of Travel, arrived here in perfect safety, and free of cost. The reader shall now fancy with what hot haste it was broken up, with what breathless expectation glanced over; and, alas, with what unquiet disappointment it has, since then, been often thrown down, and again taken up.

Hofrath Heuschrecke, in a too long-winded Letter, full of compliments, Weissnichtwo politics, dinners, dining repartees, and other ephemeral trivialities; proceeds to remind us of what we knew well already: that however it may be with Metaphysics, and other abstract Science originating in the Head

(*Verstand*) alone, no Life-Philosophy (*Lebensphilosophie*), such as this of Clothes pretends to be, which originates equally in the Character (*Gemüth*), and equally speaks thereto, can attain its significance till the Character itself is known and seen; 'till the Author's View of the World (*Weltansicht*), and how he actively and passively came by such a view, are clear: in short till a Biography of him has been philosophico-poetically written, and philosophico-poetically read.' 'Nay,' adds he, 'were the speculative scientific Truth even known, you still, in this inquiring age, ask yourself, Whence came it, and Why, and How? – and rest not, till, if no better may be, Fancy have shaped-out an answer; and either in the authentic lineaments of Fact, or the forged ones of Fiction, a complete picture and Genetical History of the Man and his spiritual Endeavour lies before you. But why,' says the Hofrath, and indeed say we, 'do I dilate on the uses of our Teufelsdröckh's Biography? The great Herr Minister von Goethe has penetratingly remarked[32] that "Man is properly the *only* object that interests man:" thus I too have noted, that in Weissnichtwo our whole conversation is little or nothing else but Biography or AutoBiography; ever humano-anecdotical (*menschlich-anekdotisch*). Biography is by nature the most universally profitable, universally pleasant of all things: especially Biography of distinguished 'individuals.

'By this time, *mein Verehrtester* (my Most Esteemed),' continues he, with an eloquence which, unless the words be purloined from Teufelsdröckh, or some trick of his, as we suspect, is well-nigh unaccountable, 'by this time you are fairly plunged (*vertieft*) in that mighty forest of Clothes-Philosophy; and looking round, as all readers do, with astonishment enough. Such portions and passages as you have already mastered, and brought to paper, could not but awaken a strange curiosity touching the mind they issued from; the perhaps unparalleled physical mechanism, which manufactured such matter, and emitted it to the light of day. Had Teufelsdröckh also a father and mother; did he, at one time, wear drivel-bibs, and live on spoon-meat? Did he ever, in rapture and tears, clasp a friend's bosom to his; looks he also wistfully into the long burial-aisle of the Past, where only winds, and their low harsh moan, give

inarticulate answer? Has he fought duels; – good Heaven! how
did he comport himself when in Love? By what singular stair-
steps, in short, and subterranean passages, and sloughs of
Despair, and steep Pisgah hills, has he reached this wonderful
prophetic Hebron[33] (a true Old-Clothes Jewry) where he now
dwells?

'To all these natural questions the voice of public History is
as yet silent. Certain only that he has been, and is, a Pilgrim,
and Traveller from a far Country; more or less footsore and
travel-soiled; has parted with road-companions; fallen among
thieves; been poisoned by bad cookery, blistered with bugbites;
nevertheless, at every stage (for they have let him pass), has had
the Bill to discharge. But the whole particulars of his Route,
his Weather-observations, the picturesque Sketches he took,
though all regularly jotted down (in indelible sympathetic-ink
by an invisible interior Penman), are these nowhere forthcom-
ing? Perhaps quite lost: one other leaf of that mighty Volume
(of human Memory) left to fly abroad, unprinted, unpublished,
unbound up, as waste paper; and to rot, the sport of rainy
winds?

'No, *verehrtester Herr Herausgeber*,[34] in no wise! I here, by
the unexampled favour you stand in with our Sage, send not a
Biography only, but an Autobiography: at least the materials
for such; wherefrom, if I misreckon not, your perspicacity
will draw fullest insight: and so the whole Philosophy and
Philosopher of Clothes will stand clear to the wondering eyes
of England, nay thence, through America, through Hindostan,
and the antipodal New Holland, finally conquer (*einnehmen*)
great part of this terrestrial Planet!'

And now let the sympathising reader judge of our feeling
when, in place of this same Autobiography with 'fullest insight,'
we find – Six considerable PAPER-BAGS, carefully sealed, and
marked successively, in gilt China-ink, with the symbols of the
Six southern Zodiacal Signs, beginning at Libra; in the inside of
which sealed Bags lie miscellaneous masses of Sheets, and
oftener Shreds and Snips, written in Professor Teufelsdröckh's
scarce legible *cursiv-schrift*;[35] and treating of all imaginable
things under the Zodiac and above it, but of his own personal

history only at rare intervals, and then in the most enigmatic manner.

Whole fascicles there are, wherein the Professor, or, as he here, speaking in the third person, calls himself, 'the Wanderer,' is not once named. Then again, amidst what seems to be a Metaphysico-theological Disquisition, 'Detached Thoughts on the Steam-engine,' or 'The continued Possibility of Prophecy,' we shall meet with some quite private, not unimportant Biographical fact. On certain sheets stand Dreams, authentic or not, while the circumjacent waking Actions are omitted. Anecdotes, oftenest without date of place or time, fly loosely on separate slips, like Sibylline leaves.[36] Interspersed also are long purely Autobiographical delineations; yet without connexion, without recognisable coherence; so unimportant, so superfluously minute, they almost remind us of 'P. P. Clerk of this Parish.' Thus does famine of intelligence alternate with waste. Selection, order, appears to be unknown to the Professor. In all Bags the same imbroglio; only perhaps in the Bag *Capricorn*, and those near it, the confusion a little worse confounded. Close by a rather eloquent Oration, 'On receiving the Doctor's-Hat,' lie wash-bills, marked *bezahlt* (settled). His Travels are indicated by the Street-Advertisements of the various cities he has visited; of which Street-Advertisements, in most living tongues, here is perhaps the completest collection extant.

So that if the Clothes-Volume itself was too like a Chaos, we have now instead of the solar Luminary that should still it, the airy Limbo which by intermixture will farther volatilise and discompose it! As we shall perhaps see it our duty ultimately to deposit these Six Paper-Bags in the British Museum, farther description, and all vituperation of them, may be spared. Biography or Autobiography of Teufelsdröckh there is, clearly enough, none to be gleaned here: at most some sketchy, shadowy fugitive likeness of him may, by unheard-of efforts, partly of intellect, partly of imagination, on the side of Editor and of Reader, rise up between them. Only as a gaseous-chaotic Appendix to that aqueous-chaotic Volume can the contents of the Six Bags hover round us, and portions thereof be incorporated with our delineation of it.

Daily and nightly does the Editor sit (with green spectacles) deciphering these unimaginable Documents from their perplexed *cursiv-schrift*; collating them with the almost equally unimaginable Volume, which stands in legible print. Over such a universal medley of high and low, of hot, cold, moist and dry, is he here struggling (by union of like with like, which is Method) to build a firm Bridge for British travellers. Never perhaps since our first Bridge-builders, Sin and Death,[37] built that stupendous Arch from Hell-gate to the Earth, did any Pontifex, or Pontiff, undertake such a task as the present Editor. For in this Arch too, leading, as we humbly presume, far otherwards than that grand primeval one, the materials are to be fished-up from the weltering deep, and down from the simmering air, here one mass, there another, and cunningly cemented, while the elements boil beneath: nor is there any supernatural force to do it with; but simply the Diligence and feeble thinking Faculty of an English Editor, endeavouring to evolve printed Creation out of a German printed and written Chaos, wherein, as he shoots to and fro in it, gathering, clutching, piecing the Why to the far-distant Wherefore, his whole Faculty and Self are like to be swallowed up.

Patiently, under these incessant toils and agitations, does the Editor, dismissing all anger, see his otherwise robust health declining; some fraction of his allotted natural sleep nightly leaving him, and little but an inflamed nervous-system to be looked for. What is the use of health, or of life, if not to do some work therewith? And what work nobler than transplanting foreign Thought into the barren domestic soil; except indeed planting Thought of your own, which the fewest are privileged to do? Wild as it looks, this Philosophy of Clothes, can we ever reach its real meaning, promises to reveal newcoming Eras, the first dim rudiments and already-budding germs of a nobler Era, in Universal History. Is not such a prize worth some striving? Forward with us, courageous reader; be it towards failure, or towards success! The latter thou sharest with us; the former also is not all our own.

The French Revolution

The French Revolution fascinated Carlyle throughout his career. It appealed to him both as an embodiment of his deterministic views about the processes of history and as a dramatic warning to his own age. He began work on his history as such in 1833, reading extensively in the various volumes of memoirs that had appeared since the revolution itself and consulting, in particular, John Stuart Mill, who at one time had considered such a project himself. Carlyle began writing in September 1834; the work was finally completed in January 1837 and published six months later, when it transformed Carlyle's literary reputation.

As a work of history *The French Revolution* clearly has its limitations, but they should not be exaggerated. Carlyle's reliance on recollections and memoirs, rather than on what a modern historian would regard as genuinely primary sources, has in fact led the work to be regarded as more impressionistic than is really the case; for so determinedly rhetorical an account it is remarkably accurate in its basic information. More serious is Carlyle's failure to consider his subject against the wider perspectives of European political history; his compulsive interest in the revolution as such mitigates against a more objective focus. Furthermore his own brand of determinism prevents him from taking sufficiently into account the economic and constitutional factors that contributed to the events which he describes. This being said, however, the merits of *The French Revolution* are considerable. Its great set scenes are skilfully balanced by a feeling for the significant minutiae of history, while the work as a whole is given coherence by Carlyle's exercise of a controlling sense of literary structure, and by his manipulation of the ironies implicit in his material. Above all it has a compelling narrative power, and an immediacy and vividness born of its author's capacity to immerse himself totally in his subject-matter.

The French Revolution is divided into three volumes. The first, entitled 'The Bastille', opens with the death of Louis XV in 1774, analyses the situation leading up to the assembling of the States General in May 1789, and concludes with the insurrection at Versailles in October of that year. The second volume, 'The Constitution', describes the unsuccessful attempts of the moderates to establish a constitutional form of government. The third volume, 'The Guillotine', deals predominantly with the collapse of moderation, and the consequent Reign of Terror. Four passages have been selected for inclusion here.

Carlyle's historical method involved extensive reference to incidents and personalities about which he had read in his sources. To avoid an unnecessary proliferation of detail I have only identified in the notes those personalities, institutions and events a knowledge of which is necessary for the understanding of the passages themselves. I have also omitted from the text Carlyle's own footnotes giving reference to his sources, since these are of limited value outside the work as a whole, in most editions of which they may be consulted.

Astraea Redux*[1]

(The French Revolution *opens with the death of Louis XV in* 1774 *and presents the first years of the reign of Louis XVI as a period of uneasy calm, terminated by the summoning of the States General in May* 1789, *the first major concession to popular opinion made by the court.*)

A paradoxical philosopher, carrying to the uttermost length that aphorism of Montesquieu's, 'Happy the people whose annals are tiresome,' has said, 'Happy the people whose annals are vacant.' In which saying, mad as it looks, may there not still be found some grain of reason? For truly, as it has been written, 'Silence is divine,' and of Heaven; so in all earthly things too there is a silence which is better than any speech. Consider it well, the Event, the thing which can be spoken of and recorded, is it not, in all cases, some disruption, some solution of continuity? Were it even a glad Event, it involves change, involves loss (of active Force); and so far, either in the past or in the present, is an irregularity, a disease. Stillest perseverance were our blessedness; not dislocation and alteration, – could they be avoided.

The oak grows silently, in the forest, a thousand years; only in the thousandth year, when the woodman arrives with his axe, is there heard an echoing through the solitudes; and the oak announces itself when, with far-sounding crash, it *falls*. How silent too was the planting of the acorn; scattered from the lap of some wandering wind! Nay, when our oak flowered,

* I, Book Two, Chapter 1.

or put on its leaves (its glad Events), what shout of proclamation could there be? Hardly from the most observant a word of
recognition. These things *befell* not, they were slowly *done*; not
in an hour, but through the flight of days: what was to be said
of it? This hour seemed altogether as the last was, as the next
would be.

It is thus everywhere that foolish Rumour babbles not of
what was done, but of what was misdone or undone; and foolish History (ever, more or less, the written epitomised synopsis
of Rumour) knows so little that were not as well unknown.
Attila Invasions, Walter-the-Penniless Crusades, Sicilian Vespers, Thirty-Years Wars: mere sin and misery; not work, but
hindrance of work! For the Earth, all this while, was yearly
green and yellow with her kind harvests; the hand of the craftsman, the mind of the thinker rested not: and so, after all, and
in spite of all, we have this so glorious high-domed blossoming
World; concerning which, poor History may well ask, with
wonder, Whence it came? She knows so little of it, knows so
much of what obstructed it, what would have rendered it
impossible. Such, nevertheless, by necessity or foolish choice, is
her rule and practice; whereby that paradox, 'Happy the people
whose annals are vacant,' is not without its true side.

And yet, what seems more pertinent to note here, there is a
stillness, not of unobstructed growth, but of passive inertness,
the symptom of imminent downfall. As victory is silent, so is
defeat. Of the opposing forces the weaker has resigned itself;
the stronger marches on, noiseless now, but rapid, inevitable:
the fall and overturn will not be noiseless. How all grows, and
has its period, even as the herbs of the fields, be it annual,
centennial, millennial! All grows and dies, each by its own
wondrous laws, in wondrous fashion of its own; spiritual
things most wondrously of all. Inscrutable, to the wisest, are
these latter; not to be prophesied of, or understood. If when the
oak stands proudliest flourishing to the eye, you know that its
heart is sound, it is not so with the man; how much less with
the Society, with the Nation of men! Of such it may be affirmed
even that the superficial aspect, that the inward feeling of full

health, is generally ominous. For indeed it is of apoplexy, so to speak, and a plethoric lazy habit of body, that Churches, King-ships, Social Institutions, oftenest die. Sad, when such Institution plethorically says to itself, Take thy ease, thou hast goods laid up; – like the fool of the Gospel, to whom it was answered, Fool *this night* thy life shall be required of thee!

Is it the healthy peace, or the ominous unhealthy, that rests on France, for these next Ten Years?[2] Over which the Historian can pass lightly, without call to linger: for as yet events are not, much less performances. Time of sunniest stillness; – shall we call it, what all men thought it, the new Age of Gold? Call it at least, of Paper; which in many ways is the succedaneum of Gold. Bank-paper, wherewith you can still buy when there is no gold left; Book-paper, splendent with Theories, Philosophies, Sensibilities, – beautiful art, not only of revealing Thought, but also of so beautifully hiding from us the want of Thought! Paper is made from the *rags* of things that did once exist; there are endless excellences in Paper. – What wisest Philosophe, in this halcyon uneventful period, could prophesy that there was approaching, big with darkness and confusion, the event of events?[3] Hope ushers in a Revolution, – as earthquakes are pre-ceded by bright weather. On the Fifth of May, fifteen years hence, old Louis will not be sending for the Sacraments; but a new Louis, his grandson, with the whole pomp of astonished intoxicated France, will be opening the States-General . . .[4]

Storm and Victory*

(The assembling of the States General led to the establishment of the
National Assembly, and raised hopes for reform which were quickly
to be denied. In particular it was believed that the court party aimed
to counter progress along constitutional lines by a coup de force.
When military installations around Paris and Versailles were reinforced in June 1789 the citizens demanded arms with which to defend
themselves. The sacking of the Bastille on 14 July 1789 was a consequence of the search for arms rather than a deliberate attempt to
release its prisoners, of whom in fact there were very few, but it was
as a libertarian gesture that the incident achieved its symbolic significance in the history of the revolution.)

But, to the living and the struggling, a new, Fourteenth morning dawns. Under all roofs of this distracted City is the nodus
of a drama, not untragical, crowding towards solution. The
bustlings and preparings, the tremors and menaces; the tears
that fell from old eyes! This day, my sons, ye shall quit you like
men. By the memory of your fathers' wrongs, by the hope of
your children's rights! Tyranny impends in red wrath: help for
you is none, if not in your own right hands. This day ye must
do or die.

From earliest light, a sleepless Permanent Committee[5] has
heard the old cry, now waxing almost frantic, mutinous: Arms!
Arms! Provost Flesselles, or what traitors there are among you,
may think of those Charleville Boxes.[6] A hundred-and-fifty-
thousand of us; and but the third man furnished with so much

* I, Book Five, Chapter 6.

as a pike! Arms are the one thing needful: with arms we are an unconquerable man-defying National Guard;[7] without arms, a rabble to be whiffed with grapeshot.

Happily the word has arisen, for no secret can be kept, – that there lie muskets at the *Hôtel des Invalides*. Thither will we: King's Procureur M. Ethys de Corny, and whatsoever of authority a Permanent Committee can lend, shall go with us. Besenval's Camp is there;[8] perhaps he will not fire on us; if he kill us, we shall but die.

Alas, poor Besenval, with his troops melting away in that manner, has not the smallest humour to fire! At five o'clock this morning, as he lay dreaming, oblivious in the *Ecole Militaire,* a 'figure' stood suddenly at his bedside; 'with face rather handsome; eyes inflamed, speech rapid and curt, air audacious:' such a figure drew Priam's curtains![9] The message and monition of the figure was, that resistance would be hopeless; that if blood flowed, wo to him who shed it. Thus spoke the figure: and vanished. 'Withal there was a kind of eloquence that struck one.' Besenval admits that he should have arrested him, but did not. Who this figure with inflamed eyes, with speech rapid and curt, might be? Besenval knows, but mentions not. Camille Desmoulins? Pythagorean Marquis Valadi, inflamed with 'violent motions all night at the Palais Royal'? Fame names him 'Young M. Meillar;' then shuts her lips about him forever.

In any case, behold, about nine in the morning, our National Volunteers rolling in long wide flood south-westward to the *Hôtel des Invalides;* in search of the one thing needful. King's Procureur M. Ethys de Corny and officials are there; the Curé of Saint-Etienne du Mont marches unpacific at the head of his militant Parish; the Clerks of the Basoche in red coats we see marching, now Volunteers of the Basoche; the Volunteers of the Palais Royal: – National Volunteers, numerable by tens of thousands; of one heart and mind. The King's muskets are the Nation's; think, old M. de Sombreuil, how, in this extremity, thou wilt refuse them! Old M. de Sombreuil would fain hold parley, send couriers; but it skills not: the walls are scaled, no Invalide firing a shot; the gates must be flung open. Patriotism rushes in, tumultuous, from grunsel up to ridge-tile, through all

rooms and passages; rummaging distractedly for arms. What
cellar, or what cranny can escape it? The arms are found; all
safe there; lying packed in straw, – apparently with a view to
being burnt! More ravenous than famishing lions over dead
prey, the multitude, with clangour and vociferation, pounces
on them; struggling, dashing, clutching: – to the jamming-up,
to the pressure, fracture and probable extinction of the weaker
Patriot. And so, with such protracted crash of deafening, most
discordant Orchestra-music, the Scene is changed; and eight-
and-twenty thousand sufficient firelocks are on the shoulders
of as many National Guards, lifted thereby out of darkness
into fiery light.

Let Besenval look at the glitter of these muskets, as they flash
by! Gardes Françaises,[10] it is said, have cannon levelled on
him; ready to open, if need were, from the other side of the
River. Motionless sits he; 'astonished,' one may flatter oneself,
'at the proud bearing (*fière contenance*) of the Parisians.' –
And now, to the Bastille, ye intrepid Parisians! There grapeshot
still threatens: thither all men's thoughts and steps are now
tending.

   Old De Launay,[11] as we hinted, withdrew 'into his interior'
soon after midnight of Sunday. He remains there ever since,
hampered, as all military gentlemen now are, in the saddest
conflict of uncertainties. The Hôtel-de-Ville 'invites' him to
admit National Soldiers, which is a soft name for surrendering.
On the other hand, His Majesty's orders were precise. His garrison is but eighty-two old Invalides, reinforced by thirty-two
young Swiss; his walls indeed are nine feet thick, he has cannon
and powder; but, alas, only one day's provision of victuals. The
city too is French, the poor garrison mostly French. Rigorous
old De Launay, think what thou wilt do!

   All morning, since nine, there has been a cry everywhere: To
the Bastille! Repeated 'deputations of citizens' have been here,
passionate for arms; whom De Launay has got dismissed by
soft speeches through portholes. Towards noon, Elector Thuriot de la Rosière gains admittance; finds De Launay indisposed
for surrender; nay disposed for blowing up the place rather.

Thuriot mounts with him to the battlements: heaps of paving-stones, old iron and missiles lie piled; cannon all duly levelled; in every embrasure a cannon, – only drawn back a little! But outwards, behold, O Thuriot, how the multitude flows on, welling through every street: tocsin furiously pealing, all drums beating the *générale*: the Suburb Saint-Antoine rolling hither-ward wholly, as one man! Such vision (spectral yet real) thou, O Thuriot, as from thy Mount of Vision, beholdest in this moment: prophetic of what other Phantasmagories, and loud-gibbering Spectral Realities, which thou yet beholdest not, but shalt! '*Que voulez-vous?*' said De Launay, turning pale at the sight, with an air of reproach, almost of menace. 'Monsieur,' said Thuriot, rising into the moral-sublime, 'what mean *you*? Consider if I could not precipitate *both* of us from this height,' – say only a hundred feet, exclusive of the walled ditch! Whereupon De Launay fell silent. Thuriot shows himself from some pinnacle, to comfort the multitude becoming suspicious, fremescent: then descends; departs with protest; with warning addressed also to the Invalides, – on whom, however, it pro-duces but a mixed indistinct impression. The old heads are none of the clearest; besides, it is said, De Launay has been profuse of beverages (*prodigua des buissons*). They think, they will not fire, – if not fired on, if they can help it; but must, on the whole, be ruled considerably by circumstances.

Wo to thee, De Launay, in such an hour, if thou canst not, taking some one firm decision, *rule* circumstances! Soft speeches will not serve; hard grapeshot is questionable; but hovering between the two is *un*questionable. Ever wilder swells the tide of men; their infinite hum waxing ever louder, into impreca-tions, perhaps into crackle of stray musketry, – which latter, on walls nine feet thick, cannot do execution. The Outer Draw-bridge has been lowered for Thuriot; new *deputation of citizens* (it is the third, and noisiest of all) penetrates that way into the Outer Court: soft speeches producing no clearance of these, De Launay gives fire; pulls up his Drawbridge. A slight sputter; – which has *kindled* the too combustible chaos; made it a roaring fire-chaos! Bursts forth Insurrection, at sight of its own blood (for there were deaths by that sputter of fire), into endless

rolling explosion of musketry, distraction, execration; – and
over head, from the Fortress, let one great gun, with its grapeshot, go booming, to show what we *could* do. The Bastille is
besieged!

On, then, all Frenchmen, that have hearts in your bodies!
Roar with all your throats, of cartilage and metal, ye Sons of
Liberty; stir spasmodically whatsoever of utmost faculty is in
you, soul, body, or spirit; for it is the hour! Smite, thou Louis
Tournay, cartwright of the Marais, old-soldier of the Regiment
Dauphiné; smite at that Outer Drawbridge chain, though the
fiery hail whistles round thee! Never, over nave or felloe, did
thy axe strike such a stroke. Down with it, man; down with it
to Orcus:[12] let the whole accursed Edifice sink thither, and Tyranny be swallowed up forever! Mounted, some say, on the roof
of the guard-room, some 'on bayonets stuck into joints of the
wall,' Louis Tournay smites, brave Aubin Bonnemère (also an
old soldier) seconding him: the chain yields, breaks; the huge
Drawbridge slams down, thundering (*avec fracas*). Glorious:
and yet, alas, it is still but the outworks. The Eight grim Towers, with their Invalide musketry, their paving-stones and
cannon-mouths, still soar aloft intact; – Ditch yawning impassable, stone-faced; the inner Drawbridge with its *back* towards
us: the Bastille is still to take!

To describe this Siege of the Bastille (thought to be one of the
most important in History) perhaps transcends the talent of
mortals. Could one but, after infinite reading, get to understand
so much as the plan of the building! But there is open Esplanade,
at the end of the Rue Saint-Antoine; there are such Forecourts,
Cour Avancé, *Cour de l'Orme*, arched Gateway (where Louis
Tournay now fights); then new drawbridges, dormant-bridges,
rampart-bastions, and the grim Eight Towers: a labyrinthic
Mass, high-frowning there, of all ages from twenty years to
four hundred and twenty; – beleaguered, in this its last hour, as
we said, by mere Chaos come again! Ordnance of all calibres;
throats of all capacities; men of all plans, every man his own
engineer: seldom since the war of Pygmies and Cranes[13] was
there seen so anomalous a thing. Half-pay Elie is home for a

suit of regimentals; no one would heed him in coloured clothes: half-pay Hulin is haranguing Gardes Françaises in the Place de Grève. Frantic Patriots pick up the grapeshots; bear them, still hot (or seemingly so), to the Hôtel-de-Ville: – Paris, you perceive, is to be burnt! Flesselles is 'pale to the very lips;' for the roar of the multitude grows deep. Paris wholly has got to the acme of its frenzy; whirled, all ways, by panic madness. At every street-barricade, there whirls simmering a minor whirlpool, – strengthening the barricade, since God knows what is coming; and all minor whirlpools play distractedly into that grand Fire-Mahlstrom which is lashing round the Bastille.

And so it lashes and it roars. Cholat the wine-merchant has become an impromptu cannoneer. See Georget, of the Marine Service, fresh from Brest, ply the King of Siam's cannon.[14] Singular (if we were not used to the like): Georget lay, last night, taking his ease at his inn; the King of Siam's cannon also lay, knowing nothing of *him,* for a hundred years. Yet now, at the right instant, they have got together, and discourse eloquent music. For, hearing what was toward, Georget sprang from the Brest Diligence,[15] and ran. Gardes Françaises also will be here, with real artillery: were not the walls so thick! – Upwards from the Esplanade, horizontally from all neighbouring roofs and windows, flashes one irregular deluge of musketry, without effect. The Invalides lie flat, firing comparatively at their ease from behind stone; hardly through portholes show the tip of a nose. We fall, shot; and make no impression!

Let conflagration rage; of whatsoever is combustible! Guard-rooms are burnt, Invalides mess-rooms. A distracted 'Peruke-maker with two fiery torches' is for burning 'the saltpetres of the Arsenal;' – had not a woman run screaming; had not a Patriot, with some tincture of Natural Philosophy, instantly struck the wind out of him (butt of musket on pit of stomach), overturned barrels, and stayed the devouring element. A young beautiful lady, seized escaping in these Outer Courts, and thought falsely to be De Launay's daughter, shall be burnt in De Launay's sight; she lies swooned on a paillasse: but again a Patriot, it is brave Aubin Bonnemère the old soldier, dashes in, and rescues her. Straw is burnt; three cartloads of it, hauled thither, go up in white smoke: almost to the choking of Patriotism itself; so that Elie had, with singed brows, to drag back one cart; and Réole the 'gigantic haberdasher' another. Smoke as of Tophet;[16] confusion as of Babel; noise as of the Crack of Doom!

Blood flows; the aliment of new madness. The wounded are carried into houses of the Rue Cerisaie; the dying leave their last mandate not to yield till the accursed Stronghold fall. And yet, alas, how fall? The walls are so thick! Deputations, three in number, arrive from the Hôtel-de-Ville; Abbé Fauchet (who was of one) can say, with what almost superhuman courage of benevolence. These wave their Town-flag in the arched Gateway; and stand, rolling their drum; but to no purpose. In such Crack of Doom, De Launay cannot hear them, dare not believe them: they return, with justified rage, the whew of lead still singing in their ears. What to do? The Firemen are here, squirting with their fire-pumps on the Invalides cannon, to wet the touchholes; they unfortunately cannot squirt so high; but produce only clouds of spray. Individuals of classical knowledge propose *catapults*. Santerre, the sonorous Brewer of the Suburb Saint-Antoine, advises rather that the place be fired, by a 'mixture of phosphorus and oil-of-turpentine spouted up through forcing-pumps:' O Spinola-Santerre, hast thou the mixture *ready*? Every man his own engineer! And still the fire-deluge abates not: even women are firing, and Turks; at least one woman (with her sweetheart), and one Turk. Gardes Françaises have come: real cannon, real cannoneers. Usher Maillard is busy; half-pay Elie, half-pay Hulin rage in the midst of thousands.

How the great Bastille Clock ticks (inaudible) in its Inner Court there, at its ease, hour after hour; as if nothing special, for it or the world, were passing! It tolled One when the firing began; and is now pointing towards Five, and still the firing slakes not. – Far down, in their vaults, the seven Prisoners hear muffled din as of earthquakes; their Turnkeys answer vaguely.

Wo to thee, De Launay, with thy poor hundred Invalides! Broglie is distant,[17] and his ears heavy: Besenval hears, but can send no help. One poor troop of Hussars has crept, reconnoitering, cautiously along the Quais, as far as the Pont Neuf.

'We are come to join you,' said the Captain; for the crowd seems shoreless. A large-headed dwarfish individual, of smoke-bleared aspect, shambles forward, opening his blue lips, for there is sense in him; and croaks: 'Alight then, and give up your arms!' The Hussar-Captain is too happy to be escorted to the Barriers, and dismissed on parole. Who the squat individual was? Men answer, It is M. Marat,[18] author of the excellent pacific *Avis au Peuple!* Great truly, O thou remarkable Dogleech, is this thy day of emergence and new-birth: and yet this same day come four years – ! – But let the curtains of the Future hang.

What shall De Launay do? One thing only De Launay could have done: what he said he would do. Fancy him sitting, from the first, with lighted taper, within arm's length of the Powder-Magazine; motionless, like old Roman Senator, or Bronze Lamp-holder; coldly apprising Thuriot, and all men, by a slight motion of his eye, what his resolution was: – Harmless he sat there, while unharmed; but the King's Fortress, meanwhile, could, might, would or should in nowise be surrendered, save to the King's Messenger: one old man's life is worthless, so it be lost with honour; but think, ye brawling *canaille*, how will it be when a whole Bastille springs skyward! – In such statuesque, taper-holding attitude, one fancies De Launay might have left Thuriot, the red Clerks of the Basoche, Curé of Saint-Stephen and all the tagrag-and-bobtail of the world, to work their will.

And yet, withal, he could not do it. Hast thou considered how each man's heart is so tremulously responsive to the hearts of all men; hast thou noted how omnipotent is the very sound of many men? How their shriek of indignation palsies the strong soul; their howl of contumely withers with unfelt pangs? The Ritter Gluck[19] confessed that the ground-tone of the noblest passage, in one of his noblest Operas, was the voice of the Populace he had heard at Vienna, crying to their Kaiser: Bread! Bread! Great is the combined voice of men; the utterance of their *instincts*, which are truer than their *thoughts*: it is the greatest a man encounters, among the sounds and shadows which make up this World of Time. He who can resist that, has his footing somewhere *beyond* Time. De Launay could not do it. Distracted, he hovers between two; hopes in the middle of despair; surrenders not his Fortress; declares that he will blow it up, seizes torches to blow it up, and does not blow it. Unhappy old De Launay, it is the death-agony of thy Bastille and thee! Jail, Jailoring and Jailor, all three, such as they may have been, must finish.

For four hours now has the World-Bedlam roared: call it the World-Chimæra, blowing fire! The poor Invalides have sunk under their battlements, or rise only with reversed muskets: they have made a white flag of napkins; go beating the *cham-ade*,[20] or seeming to beat, for one can hear nothing. The very Swiss at the Portcullis look weary of firing; disheartened in the fire-deluge: a porthole at the drawbridge is opened, as by one that would speak. See Huissier Maillard, the shifty man! On his plank, swinging over the abyss of that stone Ditch; plank resting on parapet, balanced by weight of Patriots, – he hovers perilous: such a Dove towards such an Ark! Deftly, thou shifty Usher: one man already fell; and lies smashed, far down there, against the masonry! Usher Maillard falls not: deftly, unerring he walks, with outspread palm. The Swiss holds a paper through his porthole; the shifty Usher snatches it, and returns. Terms of surrender: Pardon, immunity to all! Are they accepted? – '*Foi d' officier*, On the word of an officer,' answers half-pay Hulin, – or half-pay Elie, for men do not agree on it, – 'they are!' Sinks the drawbridge, – Usher Maillard bolting it when down; rushes-in the living deluge: the Bastille is fallen! *Victoire! La Bastille est prise!*

Not a Revolt*

Why dwell on what follows? Hulin's *foi d'officier* should have been kept, but could not. The Swiss stand drawn up, disguised in white canvas smocks; the Invalides without disguise; their arms all piled against the wall. The first rush of victors, in ecstasy that the death-peril is passed, 'leaps joyfully on their necks;' but new victors rush, and ever new, also in ecstasy not wholly of joy. As we said, it was a living deluge, plunging headlong: had not the Gardes Françaises, in their cool military way, 'wheeled round with arms levelled,' it would have plunged suicidally, by the hundred or the thousand, into the Bastille-ditch.

And so it goes plunging through court and corridor; billowing uncontrollable, firing from windows – on itself; in hot frenzy of triumph, of grief and vengeance for its slain. The poor Invalides will fare ill; one Swiss, running off in his white smock, is driven back, with a death-thrust. Let all Prisoners be marched to the Townhall, to be judged! – Alas, already one poor Invalide has his right hand slashed off him; his maimed body dragged to the Place de Grève, and hanged there. This same right hand, it is said, turned back De Launay from the Powder-Magazine, and saved Paris.

De Launay, 'discovered in gray frock with poppy-coloured riband,' is for killing himself with the sword of his cane. He shall to the Hôtel-de-Ville; Hulin, Maillard and others escorting him; Elie marching foremost 'with the capitulation-paper on his sword's point.' Through roarings and cursings; through hustlings, clutchings, and at last through strokes! Your escort is

* I, Book Five, Chapter 7.

hustled aside, felled down; Hulin sinks exhausted on a heap of
stones. Miserable De Launay! He shall never enter the
Hôtel-de-Ville: only his 'bloody hair-queue, held up in a bloody
hand;' that shall enter, for a sign. The bleeding trunk lies on the
steps there; the head is off through the streets; ghastly, aloft on
a pike.

Rigorous De Launay has died; crying out, 'O friends, kill
me fast!' Merciful De Losme must die; though Gratitude
embraces him, in this fearful hour, and will die for him; it avails
not. Brothers, your wrath is cruel! Your Place de Grève is
become a Throat of the Tiger; full of mere fierce bellowings,
and thirst of blood. One other officer is massacred; one other
Invalide is hanged on the Lamp-iron; with difficulty, with generous perseverance, the Gardes Françaises will save the rest.
Provost Flesselles, stricken long since with the paleness of
death, must descend from his seat, 'to be judged at the Palais
Royal:' – alas, to be shot dead, by an unknown hand, at the
turning of the first street! –

O evening sun of July, how, at this hour, thy beams fall
slant on reapers amid peaceful woody fields; on old women
spinning in cottages; on ships far out in the silent main; on
Balls at the Orangerie of Versailles, where high-rouged Dames
of the Palace are even now dancing with double-jacketed
Hussar-Officers; – and also on this roaring Hell-porch of a
Hôtel-de-Ville! Babel Tower, with the confusion of tongues,
were not Bedlam added with the conflagration of thoughts, was
no type of it. One forest of distracted steel bristles, endless, in
front of an Electoral Committee;[21] points itself, in horid radii,
against this and the other accused breast. It was the Titans warring with Olympus;[22] and they, scarcely crediting it, have
conquered: prodigy of prodigies; delirious, – as it could not but
be. Denunciation, vengeance; blaze of triumph on a dark
ground of terror; all outward, all inward things fallen into one
general wreck of madness!

Electoral Committee? Had it a thousand throats of brass, it
would not suffice. Abbé Lefevre, in the Vaults down below, is
black as Vulcan, distributing that 'five thousand-weight of
Powder;' with what perils, these eight-and-forty hours! Last

night, a Patriot, in liquor, insisted on sitting to smoke on the edge of one of the Powder-barrels: there smoked he, independent of the world, – till the Abbé 'purchased his pipe for three francs,' and pitched it far.

Elie, in the grand Hall, Electoral Committee looking on, sits 'with drawn sword bent in three places;' with battered helm, for he was of the Queen's Regiment, Cavalry; with torn regimentals, face singed and soiled; comparable, some think, to 'an antique warrior;' – judging the people; forming a list of Bastille Heroes. O Friends, stain not with blood the greenest laurels ever gained in this world: such is the burden of Elie's song: could it but be listened to. Courage, Elie! Courage, ye Municipal Electors! A declining sun; the need of victuals, and of telling news, will bring assuagement, dispersion: all earthly things must end.

Along the streets of Paris circulate Seven Bastille Prisoners, borne shoulder-high; seven Heads on pikes; the Keys of the Bastille; and much else. See also the Gardes Françaises, in their steadfast military way, marching home to their barracks, with the Invalides and Swiss kindly enclosed in hollow square. It is one year and two months since these same men stood unparticipating, with Brennus d'Agoust at the Palais de Justice, when Fate overtook D'Espréménil;[23] and now they have participated; and will participate. Not Gardes Françaises henceforth, but *Centre Grenadiers of the National Guard*: men of iron discipline and humour, – not without a kind of thought in them!

Likewise ashlar stones of the Bastille continue thundering through the dusk; its paper archives shall fly white. Old secrets come to view; and long-buried Despair finds voice. Read this portion of an old Letter: 'If for my consolation Monseigneur would grant me, for the sake of God and the Most Blessed Trinity, that I could have news of my dear wife; were it only her name on a card, to show that she is alive! It were the greatest consolation I could receive; and I should forever bless the greatness of Monseigneur.' Poor Prisoner, who namest thyself *Quéret-Démery*, and hast no other history, – she is *dead*, that dear wife of thine, and thou art dead! 'Tis fifty years since thy breaking heart put this question; to be heard now first, and long heard, in the hearts of men.

But so does the July twilight thicken; so must Paris, as sick children, and all distracted creatures do, brawl itself finally into a kind of sleep. Municipal Electors, astonished to find their heads still uppermost, are home; only Moreau de Saint-Méry, of tropical birth and heart, of coolest judgment; he, with two others, shall sit permanent at the Townhall. Paris sleeps; gleams upward the illuminated City: patrols go clashing, without common watchword; there go rumours; alarms of war, to the extent of 'fifteen thousand men marching through the Suburb Saint-Antoine,' – who never got it marched through. Of the day's distraction judge by this of the night: Moreau de Saint-Méry, 'before rising from his seat, gave upwards of three thousand orders.' What a head; comparable to Friar Bacon's Brass Head![24] Within it lies all Paris. Prompt must the answer be, right or wrong; in Paris is no other Authority extant. Seriously, a most cool clear head; – for which also thou, O brave Saint-Méry, in many capacities, from august Senator to Merchant's-Clerk, Book-dealer, Vice-King; in many places, from Virginia to Sardinia, shalt, ever as a brave man, find employment.

Besenval has decamped, under cloud of dusk, 'amid a great affluence of people,' who did not harm him; he marches, with faint-growing tread, down the left bank of the Seine, all night, – towards infinite space. Re-summoned shall Besenval himself be; for trial, for difficult acquittal. His King's troops, his Royal-Allemand, are gone hence forever.

The Versailles Ball and lemonade is done; the Orangerie is silent except for nightbirds. Over in the Salle des Menus Vice-President Lafayette,[25] with unsnuffed lights, 'with some Hundred or so of Members, stretched on tables round him,' sits erect; outwatching the Bear. This day, a second solemn Deputation went to his Majesty; a second, and then a third: with no effect. What will the end of these things be?

In the Court, all is mystery, not without whisperings of terror; though ye dream of lemonade and epaulettes, ye foolish women! His Majesty, kept in happy ignorance, perhaps dreams of double-barrels and the Woods of Meudon.[26] Late at night, the Duke de Liancourt, having official right of entrance, gains access to the Royal Apartments; unfolds, with earnest clearness, in his constitutional way, the Job's-news. '*Mais*,' said poor Louis, '*c'est une révolte*, Why, that is a revolt!' – 'Sire,' answered Liancourt, 'it is not a revolt, – it is a revolution.'

Epimenides*

How true, that there is nothing dead in this Universe; that what we call dead is only changed, its forces working in inverse order! 'The leaf that lies rotting in moist winds,' says one, 'has still force; else how could it *rot*?' Our whole Universe is but an infinite Complex of Forces; thousandfold, from Gravitation up to Thought and Will; man's Freedom environed with Necessity of Nature: in all which nothing at any moment slumbers, but all is forever awake and busy. The thing that lies isolated inactive thou shalt nowhere discover; seek everywhere, from the granite mountain, slow-mouldering since Creation, to the passing cloud-vapour, to the living man; to the action, to the

* II, Book Three, Chapter 1.

spoken word of man. The word that is spoken, as we know,
flies irrevocable: not less, but more, the action that is done.
'The gods themselves,' sings Pindar, 'cannot annihilate the
action that is done.'[27] No: this, once done, is done always; cast
forth into endless Time; and, long conspicuous or soon hidden,
must verily work and grow forever there, an indestructible new
element in the Infinite of Things. Or, indeed, what *is* this Infinite
of Things itself, which men name Universe, but an Action, a sum-
total of Actions and Activities? The living ready-made sum-total
of these three, – which Calculation cannot add, cannot bring on
its tablets; yet the sum, we say, is written visible: All that has been
done. All that is doing. All that will be done! Understand it well,
the Thing thou beholdest, that Thing is an Action, the product
and expression of exerted Force: the All of Things is an infinite
conjugation of the verb *To do*. Shoreless Fountain-Ocean of
Force, of power to *do*; wherein Force rolls and circles, billowing,
many-streamed, harmonious; wide as Immensity, deep as Eternity; beautiful and terrible, not to be comprehended: this is what
man names Existence and Universe; this thousand-tinted Flame-
image, at once veil and revelation, reflex such as he, in his poor
brain and heart, can paint, of One Unnameable, dwelling in
inaccessible light! From beyond the Star-galaxies, from before the
Beginning of Days, it billows and rolls, – round *thee*, nay thyself
art of it, in this point of Space where thou now standest, in this
moment which thy clock measures.

Or, apart from all Transcendentalism, is it not a plain truth
of sense, which the duller mind can even consider as a truism,
that human things wholly are in continual movement, and
action and reaction; working continually forward, phasis after
phasis, by unalterable laws, towards prescribed issues? How
often must we say, and yet not rightly lay to heart: The seed
that is sown, it will spring! Given the summer's blossoming,
then there is also given the autumnal withering; so it is ordered
not with seedfields only, but with transactions, arrangements,
philosophies, societies, French Revolutions, whatsoever man
works with in this lower world. The Beginning holds in it
the End, and all that leads thereto; as the acorn does the oak
and its fortunes. Solemn enough, did we think of it, – which

unhappily, and also happily, we do not very much! Thou there
canst begin; the Beginning is for thee, and there: but where, and
of what sort, and for whom will the End be? All grows, and seeks
and endures its destinies: consider likewise how much grows, as
the trees do, whether *we* think of it or not. So that when your
Epimenides, your somnolent Peter Klaus, since named Rip Van
Winkle,[28] awakens again, he finds it a changed world. In that
seven-years sleep of his, so much has changed! All that is without
us will change while we think not of it; much even that is within
us. The truth that was yesterday a restless Problem, has today
grown a Belief burning to be uttered: on the morrow, contradiction has exasperated it into mad Fanaticism; obstruction has
dulled it into sick Inertness; it is sinking towards silence, of satisfaction or of resignation. Today is not Yesterday, for man or for
thing. Yesterday there was the oath of Love; today has come the
curse of Hate. Not willingly: ah, no; but it could not help coming.
The golden radiance of youth, would it willingly have tarnished
itself into the dimness of old age? – Fearful: how we stand
enveloped, deep-sunk, in that Mystery of TIME; and are Sons of
Time; fashioned and woven out of Time; and on us, and on all
that we have, or see, or do, is written: Rest not, Continue not,
Forward to thy doom!

But in seasons of Revolution, which indeed distinguish themselves from common seasons by their *velocity* mainly, your
miraculous Seven-sleeper[29] might, with miracle enough, awake
sooner: not by the century, or seven years, need he sleep; often
not by the seven months. Fancy, for example, some new Peter
Klaus, sated with the jubilee of that Federation day, had lain
down, say directly after the Blessing of Talleyrand; and, reckoning it all safe *now*, had fallen composedly asleep under the
timberwork of the Fatherland's Altar; to sleep there, not twenty-
one years, but as it were year and day. The cannonading of
Nanci,[30] so far off, does not disturb him; nor does the black mort-
cloth, close at hand, nor the requiems chanted, and minute-guns,
incense-pans and concourse right over his head: none of these;
but Peter sleeps through them all. Through one circling year, as
we say; from July the 14th of 1790, till July the 17th of 1791: but

on that latter day, no Klaus, nor most leaden Epimenides, only the Dead could continue sleeping: and so our miraculous Peter Klaus awakens. With what eyes, O Peter! Earth and sky have still their joyous July look, and the Champ-de-Mars is multitudinous with men: but the jubilee-huzzahing has become Bedlam-shrieking, of terror and revenge; not blessing of Talleyrand, or any blessing, but cursing, imprecation and shrill wail; our cannon-salvoes are turned to sharp shot; for swinging of incense-pans and Eighty-three Departmental Banners, we have waving of the one sanguineous *Drapeau Rouge*.[31] – Thou foolish Klaus! The one lay in the other, the one *was* the other *minus* Time; even as Hannibal's rock-rending vinegar lay in the sweet new wine.[32] That sweet Federation was of last year; this sour Divulsion is the selfsame substance, only older by the appointed days.

No miraculous Klaus or Epimenides sleeps in these times; and yet, may not many a man, if of due opacity and levity, act the same miracle in a natural way; we mean, with his eyes open? Eyes has he, but he sees not, except what is under his nose. With a sparkling briskness of glance, as if he not only saw but saw through, such a one goes whisking, assiduous, in his circle of officialities; not dreaming but that *it* is the whole world: as indeed, where your vision terminates, does not inanity begin *there*, and the world's end clearly disclose itself – to you? Whereby our brisk-sparkling assiduous official person (call him, for instance, Lafayette),[33] suddenly startled, after year and day, by huge grapeshot tumult, stares not less astonished at it than Peter Klaus would have done. Such natural-miracle can Lafayette perform; and indeed not he only but most other offi-cials, non-officials, and generally the whole French People can perform it; and do bounce up, ever and anon, like amazed Seven-sleepers awakening; awakening amazed at the noise they themselves *make*. So strangely is Freedom, as we say, environed in Necessity; such a singular Somnambulism, of Conscious and Unconscious, of Voluntary and Involuntary, is this life of man. If anywhere in the world there was astonishment that the Federation Oath went into grapeshot, surely of all per-sons the French, first swearers and then shooters, felt astonished the most.

Alas, offences must come. The sublime Feast of Pikes with its effulgence of brotherly love, unknown since the Age of Gold, has changed nothing. That prurient heat in Twenty-five millions of hearts is not cooled thereby; but is still hot, nay hotter. Lift off the pressure of command from so many millions; all pressure or binding rule, except such melodramatic Federation Oath as they have bound *themselves* with! For *Thou shalt* was from of old the condition of man's being, and his weal and blessedness was in obeying that. Wo for him when, were it on the hest of the clearest necessity, rebellion, disloyal isolation, and mere *I will*, becomes his rule! But the Gospel of Jean-Jacques[34] has come, and the first Sacrament of it has been celebrated: all things, as we say, are got into hot and hotter prurience; and must go on pruriently fermenting, in continual change noted or unnoted.

'Worn out with disgusts,' Captain after Captain, in Royalist mustachioes, mounts his war-horse, or his Rozinante wargarron,[35] and rides minatory across the Rhine; till all have ridden. Neither does civic Emigration cease; Seigneur after Seigneur must, in like manner, ride or roll; impelled to it, and even compelled. For the very Peasants despise him, in that he dare not join his order and fight. Can he bear to have a Distaff, a *Quenouille* sent to him: say in copper-plate shadow, by post; or fixed up in wooden reality over his gate-lintel: as if he were no Hercules, but an Omphale?[36] Such scutcheon they forward to him diligently from beyond the Rhine; till he too bestir himself and march, and in sour humour another Lord of Land is gone, *not* taking the Land with him. Nay, what of Captains and emigrating Seigneurs? There is not an angry word on any of those Twenty-five million French tongues, and indeed not an angry thought in their hearts, but is some fraction of the great Battle. Add many successions of angry words together, you have the manual brawl; add brawls together, with the festering sorrows they leave, and they rise to riots and revolts. One reverend thing after another ceases to meet reverence: in visible material combustion, château after château mounts up; in spiritual invisible combustion, one authority after another. With noise and glare, or noiselessly and unnoted, a whole Old System of things is vanishing piecemeal: the morrow thou shalt look, and it is not.

The Three Votings*

(*In September 1792 the National Convention superseded the Legislative Assembly as the executive government of France. Its first act was the declaration of a Republic and it then made arrangements for the trial of Louis XVI on a charge of treason. There was considerable debate in the Convention on both the advisability of the trial and the nature of the possible sentence. Eventually it was decided to try Louis before the Convention itself, the extremist Jacobins pressing for the death penalty while the more moderate Girondins attempted to save the King by proposing that the matter of his punishment should be decided by a referendum. The trial of Louis XVI began on 16 January 1793, he was sentenced to death on 19 January, and guillotined on 21 January.*)

Is Louis Capet[37] guilty of conspiring against Liberty? Shall our Sentence be itself final, or need ratifying by Appeal to the People? If guilty, what Punishment? This is the form agreed to, after uproar and 'several hours of tumultuous indecision:' these are the Three successive Questions, whereon the Convention shall now pronounce. Paris floods round their Hall; multitudinous, many-sounding. Europe and all Nations listen for their answer. Deputy after Deputy shall answer to his name: Guilty or Not guilty?

As to the Guilt, there is, as above hinted, no doubt in the mind of Patriot men. Overwhelming majority pronounces Guilt; the unanimous Convention votes for Guilt, only some feeble twenty-eight voting not Innocence, but refusing to vote at all. Neither does the Second Question prove doubtful, whatever the Girondins[38] might calculate. Would not Appeal to the People be another name for civil war? Majority of two to one answers that there shall be no Appeal: this also is settled. Loud Patriotism, now at ten o'clock, may hush itself for the night; and retire to its bed not without hope. Tuesday has gone well. On the morrow comes, What Punishment? On the morrow is the tug of war.

Consider therefore if, on this Wednesday morning, there is an affluence of Patriotism; if Paris stands a-tiptoe, and all Deputies are at their post! Seven-hundred and Forty-nine honourable Deputies; only some twenty absent on mission, Duchâtel and some seven others absent by sickness. Meanwhile expectant Patriotism and Paris standing a-tiptoe have need of patience. For this Wednesday again passes in debate and effervescence; Girondins proposing that a 'majority of three-fourths' shall be required; Patriots fiercely resisting them. Danton, who has just got back from mission in the Netherlands,[39] does obtain 'order of the day' on this Girondin proposal; nay he obtains farther that we decide *sans désemparer*, in Permanent-session, till we have done.

And so, finally, at eight in the evening this Third stupendous Voting, by roll-call or *appel nominal,* does begin. What Punishment? Girondins undecided, Patriots decided, men afraid of Royalty, men afraid of Anarchy, must answer here and now. Infinite Patriotism, dusky in the lamp-light, floods all corridors, crowds all galleries; sternly waiting to hear. Shrill-sounding Ushers summon you by Name and Department; you must rise to the Tribune, and say.

Eye-witnesses have represented this scene of the Third Voting, and of the votings that grew out of it, – a scene protracted, like to be endless, lasting, with few brief intervals, from Wednesday till Sunday morning, – as one of the strangest seen in the Revolution. Long night wears itself into day, morning's paleness is spread over all faces; and again the wintry shadows sink, and the dim lamps are lit: but through day and night and the vicissitudes of hours, Member after Member is mounting

continually those Tribune-steps; pausing aloft there, in the clearer
upper light, to speak his Fate-word; then diving down into the
dusk and throng again. Like Phantoms in the hour of midnight;
most spectral, pandemonial! Never did President Vergniaud,
or any terrestrial President, superintend the like. A King's Life,
and so much else that depends thereon, hangs trembling in
the balance. Man after man mounts; the buzz hushes itself till
he have spoken: Death; Banishment; Imprisonment till the Peace.
Many say, Death; with what cautious well-studied phrases and
paragraphs they could devise, of explanation, of enforcement,
of faint recommendation to mercy. Many too say, Banishment;
something short of Death. The balance trembles, none can yet
guess whitherward. Whereat anxious Patriotism bellows; irre-
pressible by Ushers.

The poor Girondins, many of them, under such fierce bellowing of Patriotism, say Death; justifying, *motivant*, that most
miserable word of theirs by some brief casuistry and jesuitry.
Vergniaud himself says, Death; justifying by jesuitry. Rich
Lepelletier Saint-Fargeau had been of the Noblesse, and then of
the Patriot Left Side, in the Constituent; and had argued and
reported, there and elsewhere, not a little, *against* Capital Punishment: nevertheless he now says, Death; a word which may
cost him dear. Manuel did surely rank with the Decided in
August last; but he has been sinking and backsliding ever since
September and the scenes of September. In this Convention,
above all, no word he could speak would find favour; he says
now, Banishment; and in mute wrath quits the place forever, –
much hustled in the corridors. Philippe Egalité[40] votes, in his
soul and conscience, Death: at the sound of which and of
whom, even Patriotism shakes its head; and there runs a groan
and shudder through this Hall of Doom. Robespierre's vote
cannot be doubtful; his speech is long. Men see the figure of
shrill Sieyes ascend; hardly pausing, passing merely, this figure
says, '*La Mort sans phrase*, Death without phrases;' and fares
onward and downward. Most spectral, pandemonial!

And yet if the Reader fancy it of a funeral, sorrowful or even
grave character, he is far mistaken: 'the Ushers in the Mountain
quarter,' says Mercier, 'had become as Box-keepers at the

Opera;' opening and shutting of Galleries for privileged persons, for 'D'Orléans Egalité's mistresses,' or other high-dizened women of condition, rustling with laces and tricolor. Gallant Deputies pass and repass thitherward, treating them with ices, refreshments and small-talk; the high-dizened heads beck responsive; some have their card and pin, pricking down the Ayes and Noes, as at a game of *Rouge-et-Noir*. Farther aloft reigns Mère Duchesse[41] with her unrouged Amazons; she cannot be prevented making long *Hahas*, when the vote is not *La Mort*. In these Galleries there is refection, drinking of wine and brandy 'as in open tavern, *en pleine tabagie*.' Betting goes on in all coffee-houses of the neighbourhood. But within doors, fatigue, impatience, uttermost weariness sit now on all visages; lighted up only from time to time by turns of the game. Members have fallen asleep; Ushers come and awaken them to vote: other Members calculate whether they shall not have time to run and dine. Figures rise, like phantoms, pale in the dusky lamp-light; utter from this Tribune, only one word: Death. '*Tout est optique*,' says Mercier, 'The world is all an optical shadow.' Deep in the Thursday night, when the Voting is done, and Secretaries are summing it up, sick Duchâtel, more spectral than another, comes borne on a chair, wrapt in blankets, in 'nightgown and nightcap,' to vote for Mercy: one vote it is thought may turn the scale.

Ah no! In profoundest silence, President Vergniaud, with a voice full of sorrow, has to say: 'I declare, in the name of the Convention, that the punishment it pronounces on Louis Capet is that of Death.' Death by a small majority of Fifty-three. Nay, if we deduct from the one side, and add to the other, a certain Twenty-six, who said Death but coupled some faintest ineffectual surmise of mercy with it, the majority will be but *One*.

Death is the sentence: but its execution? It is not executed yet! Scarcely is the vote declared when Louis's Three Advocates enter; with Protest in his name, with demand for Delay, for Appeal to the People. For this do Desèze and Tronchet plead, with brief eloquence: brave old Malesherbes pleads for it with

eloquent want of eloquence, in broken sentences, in embarrass-
ment and sobs; that brave time-honoured face, with its gray
strength, its broad sagacity and honesty, is mastered with emotion, melts into dumb tears. – They reject the Appeal to the
People; that having been already settled. But as to the Delay,
what they call *Sursis*, it *shall* be considered; shall be voted for
tomorrow: at present we adjourn. Whereupon Patriotism
'hisses' from the Mountain: but a 'tyrannical majority' has so
decided, and adjourns.

There is still this *fourth* Vote, then, growls indignant
Patriotism: – this vote, and who knows what other votes, and
adjournments of voting; and the whole matter still hovering
hypothetical! And at every new vote those Jesuit Girondins,
even they who voted for Death, would so fain find a loophole!
Patriotism must watch and rage. Tyrannical adjournments
there have been; one, and now another at midnight on plea of
fatigue, – all Friday wasted in hesitation and higgling; in
re-counting of the votes, which are found correct as they stood!
Patriotism bays fiercer than ever; Patriotism, by long watching,
has become red-eyed, almost rabid.

'Delay: yes or no?' men do vote it finally, all Saturday, all
day and night. Men's nerves are worn out, men's hearts are desperate; now it shall end. Vergniaud, spite of the baying, ventures
to say Yes, Delay; though he had voted Death. Philippe Egalité
says, in his soul and conscience, No. The next Member mounting: 'Since Philippe says No, I for my part say Yes, *moi je dis
Oui.*' The balance still trembles. Till finally, at three o'clock on
Sunday morning, we have: *No Delay*, by a majority of Seventy;
Death within four-and-twenty hours!

Garat, Minister of Justice, has to go to the Temple with this
stern message: he ejaculates repeatedly, '*Quelle commission
affreuse*, What a frightful function!' Louis begs for a Confessor; for yet three days of life, to prepare himself to die. The
Confessor is granted; the three days and all respite are refused.

There is no deliverance, then? Thick stone walls answer, None.
Has King Louis no friends? Men of action, of courage grown
desperate, in this his extreme need? King Louis's friends are

feeble and far. Not even a voice in the coffee-houses rises for him. At Méot the Restaurateur's no Captain Dampmartin now dines;[42] or sees death-doing whiskerandoes on furlough exhibit daggers of improved structure. Méot's gallant Royalists on furlough are far across the marches; they are wandering distracted over the world: or their bones lie whitening Argonne Wood.[43] Only some weak Priests, leave Pamphlets on all the bourne-stones, this night, calling for a rescue: calling for the pious women to rise; or are taken distributing Pamphlets, and sent to prison.

Nay there is one death-doer, of the ancient Méot sort, who, with effort, has done even less and worse: slain a Deputy, and set all the Patriotism of Paris on edge! It was five on Saturday evening when Lepelletier Saint-Fargeau, having given his vote, *No Delay*, ran over to Février's in the Palais Royal to snatch a morsel of dinner. He had dined, and was paying. A thickset man 'with black hair and blue beard,' in a loose kind of frock, stept up to him; it was, as Février and the bystanders bethought them, one Pâris of the old King's-Guard. 'Are you Lepelletier?' asks he. – 'Yes.' – 'You voted in the King's Business – ?' – 'I voted Death.' – '*Scélérat*, take that!' cries Pâris, flashing out a sabre from under his frock, and plunging it deep in Lepelletier's side. Février clutches him: but he breaks off; is gone.

The voter Lepelletier lies dead; he has expired in great pain, at one in the morning; – two hours before that Vote of *No Delay* was fully summed up. Guardsman Pâris is flying over France; cannot be taken; will be found some months after, self-shot in a remote inn. – Robespierre sees reason to think that Prince d'Artois himself is privately in Town; that the Convention will be butchered in the lump. Patriotism sounds mere wail and vengeance: Santerre doubles and trebles all his patrols. Pity is lost in rage and fear; the Convention has refused the three days of life and all respite.

Place de la Révolution*

To this conclusion, then, hast thou come, O hapless Louis! The Son of Sixty Kings is to die on the Scaffold by form of Law. Under Sixty Kings this same form of Law, form of Society, has been fashioning itself together these thousand years; and has become, one way and other, a most strange Machine. Surely, if needful, it is also frightful, this Machine; dead, blind; not what it should be; which, with swift stroke, or by cold slow torture, has wasted the lives and souls of innumerable men. And behold now a King himself, or say rather Kinghood in his person, is to expire here in cruel tortures; – like a Phalaris shut in the belly of his own red-heated Brazen Bull![44] It is ever so; and thou shouldst know it, O haughty tyrannous man: injustice breeds injustice; curses and falsehoods do verily return *always home,* wide as they may wander. Innocent Louis bears the sins of many generations: he too experiences that man's tribunal is not in this Earth; that if he had no Higher one, it were not well with him.

A King dying by such violence appeals impressively to the imagination; as the like must do, and ought to do. And yet at bottom it is not the King dying, but the man! Kingship is a coat: the grand loss is of the skin. The man from whom you take his Life, to him can the whole combined world do *more*? Lally went on his hurdle; his mouth filled with a gag.[45] Miserablest mortals, doomed for picking pockets, have a whole five-act Tragedy in them, in that dumb pain, as they go to the gallows, unregarded; they consume the cup of trembling down to the lees. For Kings and for Beggars, for the justly doomed

* III, Book Two, Chapter 8.

and the unjustly, it is a hard thing to die. Pity them all: thy utmost pity, with all aids and appliances and throne-and-scaffold contrasts, how far short is it of the thing pitied!

A Confessor has come; Abbé Edgeworth, of Irish extraction, whom the King knew by good report, has come promptly on this solemn mission. Leave the Earth alone, then, thou hapless King; it with its malice will go its way, thou also canst go thine. A hard scene yet remains: the parting with our loved ones. Kind hearts, environed in the same grim peril with us; to be left *here*! Let the Reader look with the eyes of Valet Cléry[46] through these glass-doors, where also the Municipality watches; and see the cruelest of scenes:

'At half-past eight, the door of the ante-room opened: the Queen appeared first, leading her Son by the hand; then Madame Royale and Madame Elizabeth: they all flung themselves into the arms of the King. Silence reigned for some minutes; interrupted only by sobs. The Queen made a movement to lead his Majesty towards the inner room, where M. Edgeworth was waiting unknown to them: "No," said the King, "let us go into the dining-room; it is there only that I can see you." They entered there; I shut the door of it, which was of glass. The King sat down, the Queen on his left hand, Madame Elizabeth on his right, Madame Royale almost in front; the young Prince remained standing between his Father's legs. They all leaned towards him, and often held him embraced. This scene of wo lasted an hour and three quarters; during which we could hear nothing; we could see only that always when the King spoke, the sobbings of the Princesses redoubled, continued for some minutes; and that then the King began again to speak.' – And so our meetings and our partings do now end! The sorrows we gave each other; the poor joys we faithfully shared, and all our lovings and our sufferings, and confused toilings under the earthly Sun, are over. Thou good soul, I shall never, never through all ages of Time, see thee any more! – NEVER! O Reader, knowest thou that hard word?

For nearly two hours this agony lasts; then they tear themselves asunder. 'Promise that you will see us on the morrow.' He promises: – Ah yes, yes; yet once; and go now, ye loved ones; cry to God for yourselves and me! – It was a hard scene, but it is over. He will not see them on the morrow. The Queen, in passing through the ante-room, glanced at the Cerberus Municipals;[47] and, with woman's vehemence, said through her tears, '*Vous êtes tous des scélérats*.'

King Louis slept sound, till five in the morning, when Cléry, as he had been ordered, awoke him. Cléry dressed his hair: while this went forward, Louis took a ring from his watch, and kept trying it on his finger; it was his wedding-ring, which he is now to return to the Queen as a mute farewell. At half-past six, he took the Sacrament; and continued in devotion, and conference with Abbé Edgeworth. He will not see his Family: it were too hard to bear.

At eight, the Municipals enter: the King gives them his Will, and messages and effects; which they, at first, brutally refuse to take charge of: he gives them a roll of gold pieces, a hundred and twenty-five louis; these are to be returned to Malesherbes, who had lent them. At nine, Santerre says the hour is come. The King begs yet to retire for three minutes. At the end of three minutes, Santerre again says the hour is come. 'Stamping on the ground with his right-foot, Louis answers: "*Partons*, Let us go."' – How the rolling of those drums comes in, through the Temple bastions and bulwarks, on the heart of a queenly wife; soon to be a widow! He is gone, then, and has not seen us? A Queen weeps bitterly; a King's Sister and Children. Over all these Four does Death also hover: all shall perish miserably save one; she, as Duchesse d'Angoulême, will live, – not happily.

At the Temple Gate were some faint cries, perhaps from voices of pitiful women: '*Grâce! Grâce!*' Through the rest of the streets there is silence as of the grave. No man not armed is allowed to be there: the armed, did any even pity, dare not express it, each man overawed by all his neighbours. All windows are down, none seen looking through them. All shops are shut. No wheel-carriage rolls, this morning, in these streets but one only. Eighty-thousand armed men stand ranked, like armed statues of men; cannons bristle, cannoneers with match burning, but no word or movement: it is as a city enchanted into silence and stone: one carriage with its escort, slowly rumbling, is the only sound. Louis reads, in his Book of Devotion, the Prayers of the Dying: clatter of this death-march falls sharp on the ear, in the great silence; but the thought would fain struggle heavenward, and forget the Earth.

As the clocks strike ten, behold the Place de la Révolution, once Place de Louis Quinze: the Guillotine, mounted near the old Pedestal where once stood the Statue of that Louis! Far round, all bristles with cannons and armed men: spectators crowding in the rear; D'Orléans Egalité there in cabriolet. Swift messengers, *hoquetons*, speed to the Townhall, every three minutes: near by is the Convention sitting – vengeful for Lepelletier. Heedless of all, Louis reads his Prayers of the Dying; not till five minutes yet has he finished; then the Carriage opens. What temper he is in? Ten different witnesses will give ten different accounts of it. He is in the collision of all tempers; arrived now at the black Mahlstrom and descent of Death: in sorrow, in indignation, in resignation struggling to be resigned. 'Take care of M. Edgeworth,' he straitly charges the Lieutenant who is sitting with them: then they two descend.

The drums are beating: '*Taisez-vous*, Silence!' he cries 'in a terrible voice, *d'une voix terrible*.' He mounts the scaffold, not without delay; he is in puce coat, breeches of gray, white stockings. He strips off the coat; stands disclosed in a sleeve-waistcoat of white flannel. The Executioners approach to bind him: he spurns, resists; Abbé Edgeworth has to remind him how the Saviour, in whom men trust, submitted to be bound. His hands are tied, his head bare; the fatal moment is come. He advances to the edge of the Scaffold, 'his face very red,' and says: 'Frenchmen, I die innocent: it is from the Scaffold and near appearing before God that I tell you so. I pardon my enemies; I desire that France—' A General on horseback, Santerre or another, prances out, with uplifted hand: '*Tambours!*' The drums drown the voice. 'Executioners, do your duty!' The Executioners, desperate lest themselves be murdered (for Santerre and his Armed Ranks will strike, if they do not), seize the hapless Louis: six of them desperate, him singly desperate, struggling there; and bind him to their plank. Abbé Edgeworth, stooping, bespeaks him: 'Son of Saint Louis, ascend to Heaven.' The Axe clanks down; a King's Life is shorn away. It is Monday the 21st of January 1793. He was aged Thirty-eight years four months and twenty-eight days.

Executioner Samson shows the Head: fierce shout of *Vive la République* rises, and swells; caps raised on bayonets, hats waving: students of the College of Four Nations take it up, on the far Quais; fling it over Paris. D'Orléans drives off in his cabriolet: the Townhall Councillors rub their hands, saying, 'It is done, It is done.' There is dipping of handkerchiefs, of pike-points in the blood. Headsman Samson, though he afterwards denied it, sells locks of the hair: fractions of the puce coat are long after worn in rings. – And so, in some half-hour it is done; and the multitude has all departed. Pastry-cooks, coffee-sellers, milkmen sing out their trivial quotidian cries: the world wags on, as if this were a common day. In the coffee-houses that evening, says Prudhomme, Patriot shook hands with Patriot in a more cordial manner than usual. Not till some days after, according to Mercier, did public men see what a grave thing it was.

A grave thing it indisputably is; and will have consequences. On the morrow morning, Roland, so long steeped to the lips in disgust and chagrin, sends in his demission.[48] His accounts lie all ready, correct in black-on-white to the uttermost farthing: these he wants but to have audited, that he might retire to remote obscurity, to the country and his books. They will never be audited, those accounts; he will never get retired thither.

It was on Tuesday that Roland demitted. On Thursday comes Lepelletier St-Fargeau's Funeral, and passage to the Pantheon of Great Men. Notable as the wild pageant of a winter day. The Body is borne aloft, half-bare; the winding-sheet disclosing the death-wound: sabre and bloody clothes parade themselves; a 'lugubrious music' wailing harsh *nœniæ*.[49] Oak-crowns shower down from windows; President Vergniaud walks there, with Convention, with Jacobin Society, and all Patriots of every colour, all mourning brotherlike.

Notable also for another thing this Burial of Lepelletier: it was the last act these men ever did with concert! All Parties and figures of Opinion, that agitate this distracted France and its

Convention, now stand, as it were, face to face, and dagger to dagger; the King's Life, round which they all struck and battled, being hurled down. Dumouriez, conquering Holland, growls ominous discontent,[50] at the head of Armies. Men say Dumouriez will have a King; that young D'Orléans Egalité shall be his King. Deputy Fauchet,[51] in the *Journal des Amis*, curses his day, more bitterly than Job did; invokes the poniards of Regicides, of 'Arras Vipers' or Robespierres, of Pluto Dantons, of horrid Butchers Legendre and Simulacra d'Herbois, to send him swiftly to another world than *theirs*. This is *Te-Deum* Fauchet, of the Bastille Victory, of the *Cercle Social*. Sharp was the death-hail rattling round one's Flag-of-truce, on that Bastille day: but it was soft to such wreckage of high Hope as this; one's New Golden Era going down in leaden dross, and sulphurous black of the Everlasting Darkness!

At home this Killing of a King has divided all friends; and abroad it has united all enemies. Fraternity of Peoples, Revolutionary Propagandism; Atheism, Regicide; total destruction of social order in this world! All Kings, and lovers of Kings, and haters of Anarchy, rank in coalition; as in a war for life. England signifies to Citizen Chauvelin, the Ambassador or rather Ambassador's-Cloak, that he must quit the country in eight days. Ambassador's-Cloak and Ambassador, Chauvelin and Talleyrand, depart accordingly. Talleyrand, implicated in that Iron Press of the Tuileries,[52] thinks it safest to make for America.

England has cast out the Embassy: England declares war, – being shocked principally, it would seem, at the condition of the River Scheldt.[53] Spain declares war; being shocked principally at some other thing; which doubtless the Manifesto indicates. Nay we find it was not England that declared war first, or Spain first; but that France herself declared war first on both of them; – a point of immense Parliamentary and Journalistic interest in those days, but which has become of no interest whatever in these. They all declare war. The sword is drawn, the scabbard thrown away. It is even as Danton said, in one of his all-too gigantic figures: 'The coalised Kings threaten us; we hurl at their feet, as gage of battle, the Head of a King.'

Chartism

Chartism was written in 1839, at a time when there had been considerable public agitation in support of the various aims of the Charter, the most important of which was the principle of universal suffrage. Carlyle's decision to write on the topic was his own; he first offered his projected essay to Mill, then editor of the *Westminster Review*, but when Mill turned it down he began negotiations with Lockhart's *Quarterly Review*, the leading Tory journal. Carlyle predicted at the time that 'Such an article, equally astonishing to Girondins, Radicals, do-nothing Aristocrats, Conservatives, and unbelieving dilettante Whigs, can hope for no harbour in any Review', and he was proved right when Lockhart, having seen the finished essay, also rejected it. *Chartism* eventually appeared as a work in its own right in December 1839 (dated 1840).

Even by Carlyle's standard *Chartism* is a very uneven work. Deeply felt sympathy for the condition of working men is mixed with a detestation of utilitarian theory and an incipient authoritarianism; the quality of the essay itself falls away very noticeably as it moves from analysis to suggested remedies. Since it shows so clearly the credit and debit side of Carlyle's emotive response to the problems of his time, *Chartism* is reprinted here complete, in spite of its occasional longeurs.

1. Condition-of-England Question

'It never smokes but there is fire.' – *Old Proverb*

A feeling very generally exists that the condition and disposition of the Working Classes is a rather ominous matter at
present; that something ought to be said, something ought to
be done, in regard to it. And surely, at an epoch of history when
the 'National Petition' carts itself in wagons along the streets,[1]
and is presented 'bound with iron hoops, four men bearing it,'
to a Reformed House of Commons; and Chartism numbered
by the million and half, taking nothing by its iron-hooped Petition, breaks out into brickbats, cheap pikes, and even into
sputterings of conflagration, such very general feeling cannot
be considered unnatural! To us individually this matter appears,
and has for many years appeared, to be the most ominous of all
practical matters whatever; a matter in regard to which if something be not done, something will *do* itself one day, and in a
fashion that will please nobody. The time is verily come for
acting in it; how much more for consultation about acting in it,
for speech and articulate inquiry about it!

We are aware that, according to the newspapers, Chartism is
extinct; that a Reform Ministry[2] has 'put down the chimera of
Chartism' in the most felicitous effectual manner. So say the
newspapers; – and yet, alas, most readers of newspapers know
withal that it is indeed the 'chimera' of Chartism, not the reality, which has been put down. The distracted incoherent
embodiment of Chartism, whereby in late months it took shape
and became visible, this has been put down; or rather has fallen
down and gone asunder by gravitation and law of nature: but

the living essence of Chartism has not been put down. Chartism means the bitter discontent grown fierce and mad, the wrong condition therefore or the wrong disposition, of the Working Classes of England. It is a new name for a thing which has had many names, which will yet have many. The matter of Chartism is weighty, deep-rooted, far-extending; did not begin yesterday; will by no means end this day or tomorrow. Reform Ministry, constabulary rural police, new levy of soldiers, grants of money to Birmingham; all this is well, or is not well; all this will put down only the embodiment or 'chimera' of Chartism. The essence continuing, new and ever new embodiments, chimeras madder or less mad, have to continue. The melancholy fact remains, that this thing known at present by the name Chartism does exist; has existed; and, either 'put down' into secret treason, with rusty pistols, vitriol-bottle and match box, or openly brandishing pike and torch (one knows not in which case *more* fatal-looking), is like to exist till quite other methods have been tried with it. What means this bitter discontent of the Working Classes? Whence comes it, whither goes it? Above all, at what price, on what terms, will it probably consent to depart from us and die into rest? These are questions.

To say that it is mad, incendiary, nefarious, is no answer. To say all this, in never so many dialects, is saying little. 'Glasgow Thuggery',[3] 'Glasgow Thugs;' it is a witty nickname: the practice of 'Number 60' entering his dark room, to contract for and settle the price of blood with operative assassins, in a Christian city, once distinguished by its rigorous Christianity, is doubtless a fact worthy of all horror: but what will horror do for it? What will execration; nay at bottom, what will condemnation and banishment to Botany Bay do for it? Glasgow Thuggery, Chartist torch-meetings, Birmingham riots, Swing conflagrations,[4] are so many symptoms on the surface; you abolish the symptom to no purpose, if the disease is left untouched. Boils on the surface are curable or incurable, – small matter which, while the virulent humour festers deep within; poisoning the sources of life; and certain enough to find for itself ever new boils and sore issues; ways of announcing that it continues there, that it would fain not continue there.

Delirious Chartism will not have raged entirely to no purpose, as indeed no earthly thing does so, if it have forced all
thinking men of the community to think of this vital matter,
too apt to be overlooked otherwise. Is the condition of the English working people wrong; so wrong that rational working
men cannot, will not, and even should not rest quiet under it?
A most grave case, complex beyond all others in the world; a
case wherein Botany Bay, constabulary rural police, and suchlike, will avail but little. Or is the discontent itself mad, like the
shape it took? Not the condition of the working people that is
wrong; but their disposition, their own thoughts, beliefs and
feelings that are wrong? This too were a most grave case, little
less alarming, little less complex than the former one. In this
case too, where constabulary police and mere rigour of coercion seems more at home, coercion will by no means do all,
coercion by itself will not even do much. If there do exist general madness of discontent, then sanity and some measure of
content must be brought about again, – not by constabulary
police alone. When the thoughts of a people, in the great mass
of it, have grown mad, the combined issue of that people's
workings will be a madness, an incoherency and ruin! Sanity
will have to be recovered for the general mass; coercion itself
will otherwise cease to be able to coerce.

We have heard it asked, Why Parliament throws no light on
this question of the Working Classes, and the condition or disposition they are in? Truly to a remote observer of Parliamentary
procedure it seems surprising, especially in late Reformed
times, to see what space this question occupies in the Debates
of the Nation. Can any other business whatsoever be so pressing on legislators? A Reformed Parliament, one would think,
should inquire into popular discontents *before* they get the
length of pikes and torches! For what end at all are men, Honourable Members and Reform Members, sent to St Stephen's,
with clamour and effort; kept talking, struggling, motioning
and counter-motioning? The condition of the great body of
people in a country is the condition of the country itself: this
you would say is a truism in all times; a truism rather pressing
to get recognised as a truth now, and be acted upon, in these

times. Yet read Hansard's Debates, or the Morning Papers, if you have nothing to do! The old grand question, whether A is to be in office or B, with the innumerable subsidiary questions growing out of that, courting paragraphs and suffrages for a blessed solution of that: Canada question, Irish Appropriation question, West-India question, Queen's Bedchamber question; Game Laws, Usury Laws; African Blacks, Hill Coolies, Smithfield cattle, and Dog-carts, – all manner of questions and subjects, except simply this the alpha and omega of all! Surely Honourable Members ought to speak of the Condition-of-England question too. Radical Members, above all; friends of the people; chosen with effort, by the people, to interpret and articulate the dumb deep want of the people! To a remote observer they seem oblivious of their duty. Are they not there, by trade, mission, and express appointment of themselves and others, to speak for the good of the British Nation? Whatsoever great British interest can the least speak for itself, for that beyond all they are called to speak. They are either speakers for that great dumb toiling class which cannot speak, or they are nothing that one can well specify.

Alas, the remote observer knows not the nature of Parliaments: how Parliaments, extant there for the British Nation's sake, find that they are extant withal for their own sake; how Parliaments travel so naturally in their deep-rutted routine, commonplace worn into ruts axle-deep, from which only strength, insight and courageous generous exertion can lift any Parliament or vehicle; how in Parliaments, Reformed or Unreformed, there may chance to be a strong man, an original, clear-sighted, great-hearted, patient and valiant man, or to be none such; – how, on the whole, Parliaments, lumbering along in their deep ruts of commonplace, find, as so many of us otherwise do, that the ruts *are* axle-deep, and the travelling very toilsome of itself, and for the day the evil thereof sufficient! What Parliaments ought to have done in this business, what they will, can or cannot yet do, and where the limits of their faculty and culpability may lie, in regard to it, were a long investigation; into which we need not enter at this moment. What they have done is unhappily plain enough. Hitherto, on this most national of questions, the Collective Wisdom of the Nation has availed us as good as nothing whatever.

And yet, as we say, it is a question which cannot be left to the Collective Folly of the Nation! In or out of Parliament, darkness, neglect, hallucination must contrive to cease in regard to it; true insight into it must be had. How inexpressibly useful were true insight into it; a genuine understanding by the upper classes of society what it is that the under classes intrinsically mean; a clear interpretation of the thought which at heart torments these wild inarticulate souls, struggling there, with inarticulate uproar, like dumb creatures in pain, unable to speak what is in them! Something they do mean; some true thing withal, in the centre of their confused hearts, – for they are hearts created by Heaven too: to the Heaven it is clear what thing; to us not clear. Would that it were! Perfect clearness on it were equivalent to remedy of it. For, as is well said, all battle is misunderstanding; did the parties know one another, the battle would cease. No man at bottom means injustice; it is always for some obscure distorted image of a right that he contends: an obscure image diffracted, exaggerated, in the wonderfulest way, by natural dimness and selfishness; getting tenfold more diffracted by exasperation of contest, till at length it become all but irrecognisable; yet still the image of a right. Could a man own to himself that the thing he fought for was wrong, contrary to fairness and the law of reason, he would own also that it thereby stood condemned and hopeless; he could fight for it no longer. Nay independently of right, could the contending parties get but accurately to discern one another's might and strength to contend, the one would peaceably yield to the other and to Necessity; the contest in this case too were over. No African expedition now, as in the days of Herodotus, is fitted out *against the South-wind*.[5] One expedition was satisfactory in that department. The South-wind Simoom continues blowing occasionally, hateful as ever, maddening as ever; but one expedition was enough. Do we not all submit to Death? The highest sentence of the law, sentence of death, is passed on all of us by the fact of birth; yet we live patiently under it, patiently undergo it when the hour comes. Clear undeniable right, clear

undeniable might: either of these once ascertained puts an end
to battle. All battle is a confused experiment to ascertain one
and both of these.

What are the rights, what are the mights of the discontented
Working Classes in England at this epoch? He were an Œdipus,
and deliverer from sad social pestilence,[6] who could resolve us
fully! For we may say beforehand, The struggle that divides the
upper and lower in society over Europe, and more painfully
and notably in England than elsewhere, this too is a struggle
which will end and adjust itself as all other struggles do and
have done, by making the right clear and the might clear; not
otherwise than by that. Meantime, the questions, Why are the
Working Classes discontented; what is their condition, economical, moral, in their houses and their hearts, as it is in
reality and as they figure it to themselves to be; what do they
complain of; what ought they, and ought they not to complain
of? – these are measurable questions; on some of these any
common mortal, did he but turn his eyes to them, might throw
some light. Certain researches and considerations of ours on
the matter, since no one else will undertake it, are now to be
made public. The researches have yielded us little, almost nothing; but the considerations are of old date, and press to have
utterance. We are not without hope that our general notion of
the business, if we can get it uttered at all, will meet some assent
from many candid men.

2. Statistics

A witty statesman said, you might prove anything by figures. We have looked into various statistic works, Statistic-Society Reports, Poor-Law Reports, Reports and Pamphlets not a few, with a sedulous eye to this question of the Working Classes and their general condition in England; we grieve to say, with as good as no result whatever. Assertion swallows assertion; according to the old Proverb, 'as the *statist* thinks, the bell clinks'![7] Tables are like cobwebs, like the sieve of the Danaides;[8] beautifully reticulated, orderly to look upon, but which will hold no conclusion. Tables are abstractions, and the object a most concrete one, so difficult to read the essence of. There are innumerable circumstances; and one circumstance left out may be the vital one on which all turned. Statistics is a science which ought to be honourable, the basis of many most important sciences; but it is not to be carried on by steam, this science, any more than others are; a wise head is requisite for carrying it on. Conclusive facts are inseparable from inconclusive except by a head that already understands and knows. Vain to send the purblind and blind to the shore of a Pactolus[9] never so golden: these find only gravel; the seer and finder alone picks up gold grains there. And now the purblind offering you, with asseveration and protrusive importunity, his basket of gravel as gold, what steps are to be taken with him? – Statistics, one may hope, will improve gradually, and become good for something. Meanwhile, it is to be feared the crabbed satirist was partly right, as things go: 'A judicious man,' says he, 'looks at Statistics, not to get knowledge, but to save himself from having ignorance foisted on him.' With what serene conclusiveness a

member of some Useful-Knowledge Society stops your mouth
with a figure of arithmetic! To him it seems he has there
extracted the elixir of the matter, on which now nothing more
can be said. It is needful that you look into his said extracted
elixir; and ascertain, alas, too probably, not without a sigh,
that it is wash and vapidity, good only for the gutters.

Twice or three times have we heard the lamentations and
prophecies of a humane Jeremiah, mourner for the poor, cut
short by a statistic fact of the most decisive nature: How can
the condition of the poor be other than good, be other than
better; has not the average duration of life in England, and
therefore among the most numerous class in England, been
proved to have increased? Our Jeremiah had to admit that, if
so, it was an astounding fact, whereby all that ever he, for his
part, had observed on other sides of the matter, was overset
without remedy. If life last longer, life must be less worn upon,
by outward suffering, by inward discontent, by hardship of any
kind; the general condition of the poor must be bettering
instead of worsening. So was our Jeremiah cut short. And now
for the 'proof'? Readers who are curious in statistic proofs may
see it drawn out with all solemnity, in a Pamphlet 'published by
Charles Knight and Company,' – and perhaps himself draw
inferences from it. Northampton Tables, compiled by Dr Price
'from registers of the Parish of All Saints from 1735 to 1780;'
Carlisle Tables collected by Dr Heysham[10] from observation of
Carlisle City for eight years, 'the calculations founded on
them' conducted by another Doctor; incredible 'document
considered satisfactory by men of science in France;' – alas, is
it not as if some zealous scientific son of Adam had proved the
deepening of the Ocean, by survey, accurate or cursory, of two
mud-splashes on the coast of the Isle of Dogs? 'Not to get
knowledge, but to save yourself from having ignorance foisted
on you'!

The condition of the working-man in this country, what it is
and has been, whether it is improving or retrograding, – is a
question to which from statistics hitherto no solution can be
got. Hitherto, after many tables and statements, one is still left
mainly to what he can ascertain by his own eyes, looking at the

concrete phenomenon for himself. There is no other method; and yet it is a most imperfect method. Each man expands his own hand-breadth of observation to the limits of the general whole; more or less, each man must take what he himself has seen and ascertained for a sample of all that is seeable and ascertainable. Hence discrepancies, controversies, wide-spread, long-continued; which there is at present no means or hope of satisfactorily ending. When Parliament takes up 'the Condition-of-England question,' as it will have to do one day, then indeed much may be amended! Inquiries wisely gone into, even on this most complex matter, will yield results worth something, not nothing. But it is a most complex matter; on which, whether for the past or the present, Statistic Inquiry, with its limited means, with its short vision and headlong extensive dogmatism, as yet too often throws not light, but error worse than darkness.

What constitutes the well-being of a man? Many things; of which the wages he gets, and the bread he buys with them, are but one preliminary item. Grant, however, that the wages were the whole; that once knowing the wages and the price of bread, we know all; then what are the wages? Statistic Inquiry, in its present unguided condition, cannot tell. The average rate of day's wages is not correctly ascertained for any portion of this country; not only not for half-centuries, it is not even ascertained anywhere for decades or years: far from instituting comparisons with the past, the present itself is unknown to us. And then, given the average of wages, what is the constancy of employment; what is the difficulty of finding employment; the fluctuation from season to season, from year to year? Is it constant, calculable wages; or fluctuating, incalculable, more or less of the nature of gambling? This secondary circumstance, of quality in wages, is perhaps even more important than the primary one of quantity. Farther we ask, Can the labourer, by thrift and industry, hope to rise to mastership; or is such hope cut off from him? How is he related to his employer; by bonds of friendliness and mutual help; or by hostility, opposition, and chains of mutual necessity alone? In a word, what degree of contentment can a human creature be supposed to enjoy in that

position? With hunger preying on him, his contentment is likely
to be small! But even with abundance, his discontent, his real
misery may be great. The labourer's feelings, his notion of
being justly dealt with or unjustly; his wholesome composure,
frugality, prosperity in the one case, his acrid unrest, reckless-
ness, gin-drinking, and gradual ruin in the other, – how shall
figures of arithmetic represent all this? So much is still to be
ascertained; much of it by no means easy to ascertain! Till,
among the 'Hill Cooly' and 'Dog-cart' questions, there arise in
Parliament and extensively out of it a 'Condition-of-England
question' and quite a new set of inquirers and methods, little of
it is likely to be ascertained.

One fact on this subject, a fact which arithmetic *is* capable
of representing, we have often considered would be worth all
the rest: Whether the labourer, whatever his wages are, is saving
money? Laying up money, he proves that his condition, painful
as it may be without and within, is not yet desperate; that he
looks forward to a better day coming, and is still resolutely
steering towards the same; that all the lights and darknesses
of his lot are united under a blessed radiance of hope, – the
last, first, nay one may say the sole blessedness of man. Is
the habit of saving increased and increasing, or the contrary?
Where the present writer has been able to look with his own
eyes, it is decreasing, and in many quarters all but disappear-
ing. Statistic science turns up her Savings-Bank Accounts, and
answers, 'Increasing rapidly.' Would that one could believe it!
But the Danaides'-sieve character of such statistic reticulated
documents is too manifest. A few years ago, in regions where
thrift, to one's own knowledge, still was, Savings-Banks were
not; the labourer lent his money to some farmer, of capital, or
supposed to be of capital, – and has too often lost it since; or he
bought a cow with it, bought a cottage with it; nay hid it under
his thatch: the Savings-Banks books then exhibited mere blank
and zero. That they swell yearly now, if such be the fact, indicates that what thrift exists does gradually resort more and
more thither rather than elsewhither; but the question, Is thrift
increasing? runs through the reticulation, and is as water spilt
on the ground, not to be gathered here.

These are inquiries on which, had there been a proper 'Condition-of-England question,' some light would have been thrown, before 'torch-meetings' arose to illustrate them! Far as they lie out of the course of Parliamentary routine, they should have been gone into, should have been glanced at, in one or the other fashion. A Legislature making laws for the Working Classes, in total uncertainty as to these things, is legislating in the dark; not wisely, nor to good issues. The simple fundamental question, Can the labouring man in this England of ours, who is willing to labour, find work, and subsistence by his work? is matter of mere conjecture and assertion hitherto; not ascertainable by authentic evidence: the Legislature, satisfied to legislate in the dark, has not yet sought any evidence on it. They pass their New Poor-Law Bill,[11] without evidence as to all this. Perhaps their New Poor-Law Bill is itself only intended as an *experimentum crucis* to ascertain all this? Chartism is an answer, seemingly not in the affirmative.

3. New Poor Law

To read the Reports of the Poor-Law Commissioners, if one had faith enough, would be a pleasure to the friend of humanity. One sole recipe seems to have been needful for the woes of England: 'refusal of out-door relief.' England lay in sick discontent, writhing powerless on its fever-bed, dark, nigh desperate, in wastefulness, want, improvidence, and eating care, till like Hyperion[12] down the eastern steeps, the Poor-Law Commissioners arose, and said, Let there be workhouses, and bread of affliction and water of affliction there! It was a simple invention; as all truly great inventions are. And see, in any quarter, instantly as the walls of the workhouse arise, misery and necessity fly away, out of sight, – out of being, as is fondly hoped, and dissolve into the inane; industry, frugality, fertility, rise of wages, peace on earth and goodwill towards men do, – in the Poor-Law Commissioners' Reports, – infallibly, rapidly or not so rapidly, to the joy of all parties, supervene. It was a consummation devoutly to be wished. We have looked over these four annual Poor-Law Reports with a variety of reflections; with no thought that our Poor-Law Commissioners are the inhuman men their enemies accuse them of being; with a feeling of thankfulness rather that there do exist men of that structure too; with a persuasion deeper and deeper that Nature, who makes nothing to no purpose, has not made either them or their Poor-Law Amendment Act in vain. We hope to prove that they and it were an indispensable element, harsh but salutary, in the progress of things.

That this Poor-Law Amendment Act meanwhile should be, as we sometimes hear it named, the 'chief glory' of a Reform

Cabinet, betokens, one would imagine, rather a scarcity of glory there. To say to the poor, Ye shall eat the bread of affliction and drink the water of affliction, and be very miserable while here, required not so much a stretch of heroic faculty in any sense, as due toughness of bowels. If paupers are made miserable, paupers will needs decline in multitude. It is a secret known to all rat-catchers: stop up the granary-crevices, afflict with continual mewing, alarm, and going-off of traps, your 'chargeable labourers' disappear, and cease from the establishment. A still briefer method is that of arsenic; perhaps even a milder, where otherwise permissible. Rats and paupers can be abolished; the human faculty was from of old adequate to grind them down, slowly or at once, and needed no ghost or Reform Ministry to teach it. Furthermore when one hears of 'all the labour of the country being absorbed into employment' by this new system of affliction, when labour complaining of want can find no audience, one cannot but pause. That misery and unemployed labour should 'disappear' in that case is natural enough; should go out of sight, – but out of existence? What we do know is, that 'the rates are diminished,' as they cannot well help being; that no statistic tables as yet report much increase of death by starvation: this we do know, and not very conclusively anything more than this. If this be absorption of all the labour of the country, then all the labour of the country is absorbed.

To believe practically that the poor and luckless are here only as a nuisance to be abraded and abated, and in some permissible manner made away with, and swept out of sight, is not an amiable faith. That the arrangements of good and ill success in this perplexed scramble of a world, which a blind goddess was always thought to preside over, are in fact the work of a seeing goddess or god, and require only not to be meddled with: what stretch of heroic faculty or inspiration of genius was needed to teach one that? To button your pockets and stand still, is no complex recipe. *Laissez-faire, laissez passer*! Whatever goes on, ought it not to go on; 'the widow picking nettles for her children's dinner; and the perfumed seigneur delicately lounging in the Œil-du-Boeuf,[13] who has an alchemy whereby he will extract from her the third nettle, and name it rent and law'? What is written and enacted, has it not black-on-white to show for itself? Justice is justice; but all attorney's parchment is of the nature of Targum[14] or sacred-parchment. In brief, ours is a world requiring only to be well let alone. Scramble along, thou insane scramble of a world, with thy pope's tiaras, king's mantles and beggar's gabardines, chivalry-ribbons and plebeian gallows-ropes, where a Paul shall die on the gibbet and a Nero sit fiddling as imperial Cæsar; thou art all right, and shalt scramble even so; and whoever in the press is trodden down, has only to lie there and be trampled broad: – Such at bottom seems to be the chief social principle, if principle it have, which the Poor-Law Amendment Act has the merit of courageously asserting, in opposition to many things. A chief social principle which this present writer, for one, will by no manner of means believe in, but pronounce at all fit times to be false, heretical and damnable, if ever aught was!

And yet, as we said, Nature makes nothing in vain; not even a Poor-Law Amendment Act. For withal we are far from joining in the outcry raised against these poor Poor-Law Commissioners, as if they were tigers in men's shape; as if their Amendment Act were a mere monstrosity and horror, deserving instant abrogation. They are not tigers; they are men filled with an idea of a theory: their Amendment Act, heretical and damnable as a whole truth, is orthodox, and laudable as a *half*-truth; and was imperatively required to be put in practice. To create men filled with a theory, that refusal of out-door relief was the one thing needful: Nature had no readier way of getting out-door relief refused. In fact, if we look at the old Poor-Law, in its assertion of the opposite social principle, that Fortune's awards are *not* those of Justice, we shall find it to have become still more unsupportable, demanding, if England was not destined for speedy anarchy, to be done away with.

Any law, however well meant as a law, which has become a bounty on unthrift, idleness, bastardy and beer-drinking, must be put an end to. In all ways it needs, especially in these times, to be proclaimed aloud that for the idle man there is no place in this England of ours. He that will not work, and save according to his means, let him go elsewhither; let him know that for *him* the Law has made no soft provision, but a hard and stern one; that by the Law of Nature, which the Law of England would vainly contend against in the long-run, *he* is doomed either to quit these habits, or miserably be extruded from this Earth, which is made on principles different from these. He that will not work according to his faculty, let him perish according to his necessity: there is no law juster than that. Would to Heaven one could preach it abroad into the hearts of all sons and daughters of Adam, for it is a law applicable to all; and bring it to bear, with practical obligation strict as the Poor-Law Bastille, on all! We had then, in good truth, a 'perfect constitution of society;' and 'God's fair Earth and Task-garden, where whosoever is not working must be begging or stealing,' were then actually what always, through so many changes and struggles, it is endeavouring to become.

That this law of 'No work no recompense' should first of all be enforced on the *manual* worker, and brought stringently home to him and his numerous class, while so many other classes and persons still go loose from it, was natural to the case. Let it be enforced there, and rigidly made good. It behoves to be enforced everywhere, and rigidly made good; – alas, not by such simple methods as 'refusal of out-door relief,' but by far other and costlier ones; which too, however, a bountiful Providence is not unfurnished with, nor, in these latter generations (if we will understand their convulsions and confusions), sparing to apply. Work is the mission of man in this Earth. A day is ever struggling forward, a day will arrive in some approximate degree, when he who has no work to do, by whatever name he may be named, will not find it good to show himself in our quarter of the Solar System; but may go and look out elsewhere, If there be any *Idle* Planet discoverable? – Let the honest working man rejoice that such law, the first of Nature, has been made good on him; and hope that, by and by, all else will be made good. It is the beginning of all. We define the harsh New Poor-Law to *be* withal a 'protection of the thrifty labourer against the thriftless and dissolute;' a thing inexpressibly important; a *half*-result, detestable, if you will,

when looked upon as the whole result; yet without which the
whole result is forever unattainable. Let wastefulness, idleness,
drunkenness, improvidence take the fate which God has
appointed them; that their opposites may also have a chance
for *their* fate. Let the Poor-Law Administrators be considered
as useful labourers whom Nature has furnished with a whole
theory of the universe, that they might accomplish an indispensable fractional practice there, and prosper in it in spite of
much contradiction.

We will praise the New Poor-Law, farther, as the probable
preliminary of *some* general charge to be taken of the lowest
classes by the higher. Any general charge whatsoever, rather than
a conflict of charges, varying from parish to parish; the emblem
of darkness, of unreadable confusion. Supervisal by the central
government, in what spirit soever executed, is supervisal from
a centre. By degrees the object will become clearer, as it is at
once made thereby universally conspicuous. By degrees true
vision of it will become attainable, will be universally attained;
whatsoever order regarding it is just and wise, as grounded on
the truth of it, will then be capable of being taken. Let us welcome the New Poor-Law as the harsh beginning of much, the
harsh ending of much! Most harsh and barren lies the new
ploughers' fallow-field, the crude subsoil all turned up, which
never saw the sun; which as yet grows no herb; which has 'out-
door relief' for no one. Yet patience: innumerable weeds and
corruptions lie safely turned down and extinguished under it;
this same crude subsoil is the first step of all true husbandry; by
Heaven's blessing and the skyey influences, fruits that are good
and blessed will yet come of it.

For, in truth, the claim of the poor labourer is something
quite other than that 'Statute of the Forty-third of Elizabeth'[15]
will ever fulfil for him. Not to be supported by roundsmen systems, by never so liberal parish doles, or lodged in free and easy
workhouses when distress overtakes him; not for this, however
in words he may clamour for it; not for this, but for something
far different does the heart of him struggle. It is 'for justice' that
he struggles; for 'just wages,' – not in money alone! An ever-
toiling inferior, he would fain (though as yet he knows it not)

find for himself a superior that should lovingly and wisely govern: is not that too the 'just wages' of his service done? It is for a manlike place and relation, in this world where he sees himself a man, that he struggles. At bottom, may we not say, it is even for this, That guidance and government, which he cannot give himself, which in our so complex world he can no longer do without, might be afforded him? The thing he struggles for is one which no Forty-third of Elizabeth is in any condition to furnish him, to put him on the road towards getting. Let him quit the Forty-third of Elizabeth altogether; and rejoice that the Poor-Law Amendment Act has, even by harsh methods and against his own will, forced him away from it. That was a broken reed to lean on, if there ever was one; and did but run into his lamed right-hand. Let him cast it far from him, that broken reed, and look to quite the opposite point of the heavens for help. His unlamed right-hand, with the cunning industry that lies in it, is not this defined to be 'the sceptre of our Planet'? He that can work is a born king of something; is in communion with Nature, is master of a thing or things, is a priest and king of Nature so far. He that can work at nothing is but a usurping king, be his trappings what they may; he is the born slave of all things. Let a man honour his craftmanship, his *can-do*; and know that his rights of man have no concern at all with the Forty-third of Elizabeth.

4. Finest Peasantry in the World

The New Poor-Law is an announcement, sufficiently distinct, that whosoever will not work ought not to live. Can the poor man that is willing to work, always find work, and live by his work? Statistic Inquiry, as we saw, has no answer to give. Legislation presupposes the answer – to be in the affirmative. A large postulate; which should have been made a proposition of; which should have been demonstrated, made indubitable to all persons! A man willing to work, and unable to find work, is perhaps the saddest sight that Fortune's inequality exhibits under this sun. Burns expresses feelingly what thoughts it gave him:[16] a poor man seeking *work*; seeking leave to toil that he might be fed and sheltered! That he might but be put on a level with the four-footed workers of the Planet which is his! There is not a horse willing to work but can get food and shelter in requital; a thing this two-footed worker has to seek for, to solicit occasionally in vain. He is nobody's two-footed worker; he is not even anybody's slave. And yet he is a *two*-footed worker; it is currently reported there is an immortal soul in him, sent down out of Heaven into the Earth; and one beholds him *seeking* for this! – Nay what will a wise Legislature say, if it turn out that he cannot find it; that the answer to their postulate proposition is not affirmative but negative?

There is one fact which Statistic Science has communicated, and a most astonishing one; the inference from which is pregnant as to this matter. Ireland has near seven millions of working people, the third unit of whom, it appears by Statistic Science, has not for thirty weeks each year as many third-rate potatoes as will suffice him. It is a fact perhaps the most

eloquent that was ever written down in any language,[17] at any
date of the world's history. Was change and reformation needed
in Ireland? Has Ireland been governed and guided in a 'wise
and loving' manner? A government and guidance of white
European men which has issued in perennial hunger of potatoes
to the third man extant, – ought to drop a veil over its face, and
walk out of court under conduct of proper officers; saying no
word; expecting now of a surety sentence either to change or
die. All men, we must repeat, were made by God, and have
immortal souls in them. The Sanspotato is of the selfsame stuff
as the superfinest Lord Lieutenant. Not an individual Sanspotato human scarecrow but had a Life given him out of
Heaven, with Eternities depending on it; for once and no second
time. With Immensities in him, over him and round him;
with feelings which a Shakspeare's speech would not utter;
with desires illimitable as the Autocrat's of all the Russias! Him
various thrice-honoured persons, things and institutions have
long been teaching, long been guiding, governing: and it is to
perpetual scarcity of third-rate potatoes, and to what depends
thereon, that he has been taught and guided. Figure thyself,
O high-minded, clear-headed, clean-burnished reader, clapt by
enchantment into the torn coat and waste hunger-lair of that
same root-devouring brother man! –

Social anomalies are things to be defended, things to be
amended; and in all places and things, short of the Pit itself,
there is some admixture of worth and good. Room for extenu-
ation, for pity, for patience! And yet when the general result
has come to the length of perennial starvation, argument,
extenuating logic, pity and patience on that subject may be
considered as drawing to a close. It may be considered that
such arrangement of things will have to terminate. That it has
all just men for its natural enemies. That all just men, of what
outward colour soever in Politics or otherwise, will say: This
cannot last, Heaven disowns it, Earth is against it; Ireland will
be burnt into a black unpeopled field of ashes rather than this
should last. – The woes of Ireland, or 'justice to Ireland,' is not
the chapter we have to write at present. It is a deep matter, an
abysmal one, which no plummet of ours will sound. For the

oppression has gone far farther than into the economics of Ireland; inwards to her very heart and soul. The Irish National character is degraded, disordered; till this recover itself, nothing is yet recovered. Immethodic, headlong, violent, mendacious: what can you make of the wretched Irishman? 'A finer people never lived,' as the Irish lady said to us; 'only they have two faults, they do generally lie and steal: barring these' – ! A people that knows not to speak the truth, and to act the truth, such people has departed from even the possibility of well-being. Such people works no longer on Nature and Reality; works now on Phantasm, Simulation, Nonentity; the result it arrives at is naturally not a thing but no-thing, – defect even of potatoes. Scarcity, futility, confusion, distraction must be perennial there. Such a people circulates not order but disorder, through every vein of it; – and the cure, if it is to be a cure, must begin at the heart: not in his condition only but in himself must the Patient be all changed. Poor Ireland! And yet let no true Irishman, who believes and sees all this, despair by reason of it. Cannot he too do something to withstand the unproductive falsehood, there as it lies accursed around him, and change it into truth, which is fruitful and blessed? Every mortal can and shall himself be a true man: it is a great thing, and the parent of great things; – as from a single acorn the whole earth might in the end be peopled with oaks! Every mortal can do something: this let him faithfully do, and leave with assured heart the issue to a Higher Power!

We English pay, even now, the bitter smart of long centuries of injustice to our neighbour Island. Injustice, doubt it not, abounds; or Ireland would not be miserable. The Earth is good, bountifully sends food and increase; if man's unwisdom did not intervene and forbid. It was an evil day when Strigul[18] first meddled with that people. He could not extirpate them: could they but have agreed together, and extirpated him! Violent men there have been, and merciful; unjust rulers, and just; conflicting in a great element of violence, these five wild centuries now; and the violent and unjust have carried it, and we are come to *this*. England is guilty towards Ireland; and reaps at last, in full measure, the fruit of fifteen generations of wrong-doing.

But the thing we had to state here was our inference from that mournful fact of the third Sanspotato, – coupled with this other well-known fact that the Irish speak a partially intelligible dialect of English, and their fare across by steam is four-pence sterling! Crowds of miserable Irish darken all our towns.[19] The wild Milesian features, looking false ingenuity, restlessness, unreason, misery and mockery, salute you on all highways and byways. The English coachman, as he whirls past, lashes the Milesian with his whip, curses him with his tongue; the Milesian is holding out his hat to beg. He is the sorest evil this country has to strive with. In his rags and laughing savagery, he is there to undertake all work that can be done by mere strength of hand and back; for wages that will purchase him potatoes. He needs only salt for condiment; he lodges to his mind in any pighutch or doghutch, roosts in outhouses; and wears a suit of tatters, the getting off and on of which is said to be a difficult operation, transacted only in festivals and the hightides of the calendar. The Saxon man if he cannot work on these terms, finds no work. He too may be ignorant; but he has not sunk from decent manhood to squalid apehood: he cannot continue there. American forests lie untilled across the ocean; the uncivilised Irishman, not by his strength, but by the opposite of strength, drives out the Saxon native, takes possession in his room. There abides he, in his squalor and unreason, in his falsity and drunken violence, as the ready-made nucleus of degradation and disorder. Whosoever struggles, swimming with difficulty, may now find an example how the human being can exist not swimming but sunk. Let him sink; he is not the worst of men; not worse than this man. We have quarantines against pestilence; but there is no pestilence like that; and against it what quarantine is possible? It is lamentable to look upon. This soil of Britain, these Saxon men have cleared it, made it arable, fertile and a home for them; they and their fathers have done that. Under the sky there exists no force of men who with arms in their hands could drive them out of it; all force of men with arms these Saxons would seize, in their grim way, and fling (Heaven's justice and their own Saxon humour aiding them) swiftly into the sea. But behold, a force of men armed only with rags, ignorance and nakedness; and the Saxon owners, paralysed by invisible magic of paper formula, have to fly far, and hide themselves in Transatlantic forests. 'Irish repeal'? 'Would to God,' as Dutch William[20] said, *you* were King of Ireland, and could take yourself and it three thousand miles off, – there to repeal it!

And yet these poor Celtiberian Irish brothers, what can *they* help it? They cannot stay at home, and starve. It is just and natural that they come hither as a curse to us. Alas, for them too it is not a luxury. It is not a straight or joyful way of avenging their sore wrongs this; but a most sad circuitous one. Yet a way it is, and an effectual way. The time has come when the Irish population must either be improved a little, or else exterminated. Plausible management, adapted to this hollow outcry or to that, will no longer do; it must be management grounded on sincerity and fact, to which the truth of things will respond – by an actual beginning of improvement to these wretched brothermen. In a state of perennial ultra-savage famine, in the midst of civilisation, they cannot continue. For that the Saxon British will ever submit to sink along with them to such a state, we assume as impossible. There is in these latter, thank God, an ingenuity which is not false; a methodic spirit, of insight, of perseverant well-doing; a rationality and veracity which Nature with her truth does *not* disown; – withal there is a 'Berserkir rage' in the heart of them, which will prefer all things, including destruction and self-destruction, to that. Let no man awaken it, this same Berserkir rage! Deep-hidden it lies, far down in the centre, like genial central-fire, with stratum after stratum of arrangement, traditionary method, composed productiveness, all built above it, vivified and rendered fertile by it: justice, clearness, silence, perseverance, unhasting unresting diligence, hatred of disorder, hatred of injustice, which is the worst disorder, characterise this people; their inward fire we say, as all such fire should be, is hidden at the centre. Deep-hidden; but awakenable, but immeasurable; – let no man awaken it! With this strong silent people have the noisy vehement Irish now at length got common cause made. Ireland, now for the first time, in such strange circuitous way, does find itself embarked in the same boat with England, to sail together, or to sink together; the wretchedness of Ireland, slowly but inevitably, has crept over to us, and become our own wretchedness. The Irish population must get itself redressed and saved, for the sake of the English if for nothing else. Alas, that it should, on both sides, be poor toiling men that pay the smart for unruly Striguls, Henrys, Macdermots, and O'Donoghues! The strong have eaten sour grapes, and the teeth of the weak are set on edge. 'Curses,' says the Proverb, 'are like chickens, they return always *home.*'

But now, on the whole, it seems to us, English Statistic Science, with floods of the finest peasantry in the world streaming in on us daily, may fold up her Danaides reticulations on this matter of the Working Classes; and conclude, what every man who will take the statistic spectacles off his nose, and look, may discern in town or country: That the condition of the lower multitude of English labourers approximates more and more to that of the Irish competing with them in all markets; that whatsoever labour, to which mere strength with little skill will suffice, is to be done, will be done not at the English price, but at an approximation to the Irish price: at a price superior as yet to the Irish, that is, superior to scarcity of third-rate potatoes for thirty weeks yearly; superior, yet hourly, with the arrival of every new steamboat, sinking nearer to an equality with that. Half-a-million handloom weavers, working fifteen hours a-day, in perpetual inability to procure thereby enough of the coarsest food; English farm-labourers at nine shillings and at seven shillings a-week; Scotch farm-labourers who, 'in districts the half of whose husbandry is that of cows, taste no milk, can procure no milk:' all these things are credible to us; several of them are known to us by the best evidence, by eyesight. With all this it is consistent that the wages of 'skilled labour,' as it is called, should in many cases be higher than they ever were: the giant Steamengine in a giant English Nation[21] will here create violent demand for labour, and will there annihilate demand. But, alas, the great portion of labour is not skilled: the millions are and must be skilless, where strength alone is wanted: ploughers, delvers, borers; hewers of wood and drawers of water; menials of the Steamengine, only the *chief* menials and immediate *body*-servants of which require skill. English Commerce stretches its fibres over the whole earth; sensitive literally, nay quivering in convulsion, to the farthest influences of the earth. The huge demon of Mechanism smokes and thunders, panting at his great task, in all sections of English land; changing his *shape* like a very Proteus;[22] and infallibly, at every change of shape, *oversetting* whole multitudes of workmen, and as if with the waving of his shadow from afar, hurling them asunder, this way and that, in their crowded march and course of work or traffic; so that the wisest no longer knows his where about. With an Ireland pouring daily in on us, in these circumstances; deluging us down to its own waste confusion, outward and inward, it seems a cruel mockery to tell poor drudges that *their* condition is improving.

New Poor-Law! *Laissez-faire, laissez passer!* The master of horses, when the summer labour is done, has to feed his horses through the winter. If he said to his horses: 'Quadrupeds, I have no longer work for you; but work exists abundantly over the world: are you ignorant (or must I read you Political-Economy Lectures) that the Steamengine always in the long-run creates additional work? Railways are forming in one quarter of this earth, canals in another, much cartage is wanted; somewhere in Europe, Asia, Africa or America, doubt it not, ye will find cartage: go and seek cartage, and good go with you!' They, with protrusive upper lip, snort dubious; signifying that Europe, Asia, Africa and America lie somewhat out of their beat; that what cartage may be wanted there is not too well known to them. *They* can find no cartage. They gallop distracted along highways, all fenced in to the right and to the left: finally, under pains of hunger, they take to leaping fences; eating foreign property, and – we know the rest. Ah, it is not a joyful mirth, it is sadder than tears, the laugh Humanity is forced to, at *Laissez-faire* applied to poor peasants, in a world like our Europe of the year 1839!

So much can observation altogether unstatistic, looking only at a Drogheda or Dublin steamboat, ascertain for itself. Another thing, likewise ascertainable on this vast obscure matter, excites a superficial surprise, but only a superficial one: That it is the best-paid workmen who, by Strikes, Trades-unions, Chartism, and the like, complain the most. No doubt of it! The best-paid workmen are they alone that *can* so complain! How shall he, the handloom weaver, who in the day that is passing over him has to find food for the day, strike work? If he strike work, he starves within the week. He is past complaint! – The fact itself, however, is one which, if we consider it, leads us into still deeper regions of the malady. Wages, it would appear, are no index of well-being to the working man: without proper wages there can be no well-being; but with them also there may be none. Wages of working men differ greatly in different quarters of this country; according to the researches or the guess of Mr Symmons,[23] an intelligent humane inquirer, they vary in the ratio of not less than three to one. Cotton-spinners, as we learn, are generally well paid, while employed; their wages, one week with another, wives and children all working, amount to sums which, if well laid out, were fully adequate to comfortable living. And yet, alas, there seems little question that comfort or reasonable well-being is as much a stranger in these households as in any. At the cold hearth of the ever-toiling ever-hungering weaver, dwells at least some equability, fixation as if in perennial ice: hope never comes; but also irregular impatience is absent. Of outward things these others have or might have enough, but of all inward things there is the fatalest lack. Economy does not exist among them; their trade now in plethoric prosperity, anon extenuated into inanition and 'short-time,' is of the nature of gambling; they live by it like gamblers, now in luxurious superfluity, now in starvation. Black mutinous discontent devours them; simply the miserablest feeling that can inhabit the heart of man. English Commerce with its world-wide convulsive fluctuations, with its immeasurable Proteus Steam-demon, makes all paths uncertain for them, all life a bewilderment; sobriety, steadfastness, peaceable continuance, the first blessings of man, are not theirs.

It is in Glasgow among that class of operatives that 'Number 60,' in his dark room, pays down the price of blood. Be it with reason or with unreason, too surely they do in verity find the

time all out of joint; this world for them no home, but a dingy
prison-house, of reckless unthrift, rebellion, rancour, indignation against themselves and against all men. Is it a green flowery
world, with azure everlasting sky stretched over it, the work
and government of a God; or a murky-simmering Tophet,[24] of
copperas-fumes, cotton-fuzz, gin-riot, wrath and toil, created
by a Demon, governed by a Demon? The sum of their wretchedness merited and unmerited welters, huge, dark and baleful,
like a Dantean Hell, visible there in the statistics of Gin: Gin
justly named the most authentic incarnation of the Infernal
Principle in our times, too indisputable an incarnation; Gin the
black throat into which wretchedness of every sort, consum-
mating itself by calling on delirium to help it, whirls down;
abdication of the power to think or resolve, as too painful now,
on the part of men whose lot of all others would require
thought and resolution; liquid Madness sold at ten-pence the
quartern, all the products of which are and must be, like its
origin, mad, miserable, ruinous, and that only! If from this
black unluminous unheeded *Inferno*, and Prisonhouse of souls
in pain, there do flash up from time to time, some dismal wide-
spread glare of Chartism or the like, notable to all, claiming
remedy from all, – are we to regard it as more baleful than the
quiet state, or rather as not so baleful? Ireland is in chronic
atrophy these five centuries; the disease of nobler England,
identified now with that of Ireland, becomes acute, has crises,
and will be cured or kill.

5. Rights and Mights

It is not what a man outwardly has or wants that constitutes the happiness or misery of him. Nakedness, hunger, distress of all kinds, death itself have been cheerfully suffered, when the heart was right. It is the feeling of *injustice* that is insupportable to all men. The brutalest black African cannot bear that he should be used unjustly. No man can bear it, or ought to bear it. A deeper law than any parchment-law whatsoever, a law written direct by the hand of God in the inmost being of man, incessantly protests against it. What is injustice? Another name for *dis*order, for unveracity, unreality; a thing which veracious created Nature, even because it is not Chaos and a waste-whirling baseless Phantasm, rejects and disowns. It is not the outward pain of injustice; that, were it even the flaying of the back with knotted scourges, the severing of the head with guillotines, is comparatively a small matter. The real smart is the soul's pain and stigma, the hurt inflicted on the moral self. The rudest clown must draw himself up into attitude of battle, and resistance to the death, if such be offered him. He cannot live under it; his own soul aloud, and all the Universe with silent continual beckonings, says, It cannot be. He must revenge himself; *revancher* himself, make himself good again, – that so *meum* may be mine, *tuum* thine, and each party standing clear on his own basis, order be restored. There is something infinitely respectable in this, and we may say universally respected; it is the common stamp of manhood vindicating itself in all of us, the basis of whatever is worthy in all of us, and through superficial diversities, the same in all.

As *dis*order, insane by the nature of it, is the hatefulest of
things to man, who lives by sanity and order, so injustice is the
worst evil, some call it the only evil, in this world. All men submit
to toil, to disappointment, to unhappiness; it is their lot here; but
in all hearts, inextinguishable by sceptic logic, by sorrow, perver-
sion or despair itself, there is a small still voice intimating that it
is not the final lot; that wild, waste, incoherent as it looks, a God
presides over it; that it is not an injustice but a justice. Force itself,
the hopelessness of resistance, has doubtless a composing effect; –
against inanimate *Simooms*,[25] and much other infliction of the
like sort, we have found it suffice to produce complete composure. Yet, one would say, a permanent Injustice even from an
Infinite Power would prove unendurable by men. If men had lost
belief in a God, their only resource against a blind No-God, of
Necessity and Mechanism, that held them like a hideous World-
Steamengine, like a hideous Phalaris' Bull,[26] imprisoned in its
own iron belly, would be, with or without hope, – *revolt*. They
could, as Novalis says, by a 'simultaneous universal act of suicide,'[27] *depart* out of the World-Steamengine; and end, if not in
victory, yet in invincibility, and unsubduable protest that such
World-Steamengine was a failure and a stupidity.

Conquest, indeed, is a fact often witnessed; conquest, which
seems mere wrong and force, everywhere asserts itself as a right
among men. Yet if we examine, we shall find that, in this world,
no conquest could ever become permanent, which did not
withal show itself beneficial to the conquered as well as to conquerors. Mithridates King of Pontus, come now to extremity,
'appealed to the patriotism of his people;' but, says the history,
'he had squeezed them, and fleeced and plundered them for
long years;' his requisitions, flying irregular, devastative, like
the whirlwind, were less supportable than Roman strictness
and method, regular though never so rigorous: he therefore
appealed to their patriotism in vain. The Romans conquered
Mithridates.[28] The Romans, having conquered the world, held
it conquered, *because* they could best govern the world; the
mass of men found it nowise pressing to revolt; their fancy
might be afflicted more or less, but in their solid interests they
were better off than before.

So too in this England long ago, the old Saxon Nobles, disunited among themselves, and in power too nearly equal, could
not have governed the country well; Harold being slain, their
last chance of governing it, except in anarchy and civil war, was
over: a new class of strong Norman Nobles, entering with a
strong man, with a succession of strong men at the head of
them, and not disunited, but united by many ties, by their very
community of language and interest, had there been no other,
were in a condition to govern it; and did govern it, we can
believe, in some rather tolerable manner, or they would not have
continued there. They acted, little conscious of such function
on their part, as an immense volunteer Police Force, stationed
everywhere, united, disciplined, feudally regimented, ready for
action; strong Teutonic men; who, on the whole, proved effective men, and drilled this wild Teutonic people[29] into unity and
peaceable cooperation better than others could have done! How
can-do, if we will well interpret it, unites itself with *shall-do*
among mortals; how strength acts ever as the right-arm of justice; how might and right, so frightfully discrepant at first, are ever
in the long-run one and the same, – is a cheering consideration,
which always in the black tempestuous vortices of this world's
history, will shine out on us, like an everlasting polar star.

Of conquest we may say that it never yet went by brute force
and compulsion; conquest of that kind does not endure. Conquest, along with power of compulsion, an essential universally
in human society, must bring benefit along with it, or men, of
the ordinary strength of men, will fling it out. The strong man,
what is he if we will consider? The wise man; the man with the
gift of method, of faithfulness and valour, all of which are of
the basis of wisdom; who has insight into what is what, into
what will follow out of what, the eye to see and the hand to do;
who is *fit* to administer, to direct, and guidingly command: he
is the strong man. His muscles and bones are no stronger than
ours; but his soul is stronger, his soul is wiser, clearer, – is better
and nobler, for that is, has been and ever will be the root of all
clearness worthy of such a name. Beautiful it is, and a gleam
from the same eternal pole-star visible amid the destinies of men,
that all talent, all intellect is in the first place moral; – what a

world were this otherwise! But it is the heart always that sees, before the head *can* see: let us know that; and know therefore that the Good alone is deathless and victorious, that Hope is sure and steadfast, in all phases of this 'Place of Hope.' – Shiftiness, quirk, attorney-cunning is a kind of thing that fancies itself, and is often fancied, to be talent; but it is luckily mistaken in that. Succeed truly it does, what is called succeeding; and even must in general succeed, if the dispensers of success be of due stupidity: men of due stupidity will needs say to it, '*Thou* art wisdom, rule thou!' Whereupon it rules. But Nature answers, 'No, this ruling of thine is not according to *my* laws; thy wisdom was not wise enough! Dost thou take me too for a Quackery? For a Conventionality and Attorneyism? This chaff that thou sowest into my bosom, though it pass at the pollbooth and elsewhere for seed-corn, *I* will not grow wheat out of it, for it is chaff!'

But to return. Injustice, infidelity to truth and fact and Nature's order, being properly the one evil under the sun, and the feeling of injustice the one intolerable pain under the sun, our grand question as to the condition of these working men would be: Is it just? And first of all, What belief have they themselves formed about the justice of it? The words they promulgate are notable by way of answer; their actions are still more notable. Chartism with its pikes, Swing with his tinderbox, speak a most loud though inarticulate language. Glasgow Thuggery speaks aloud too, in a language we may well call infernal. What kind of 'wild-justice' must it be in the hearts of these men that prompts them, with cold deliberation, in conclave assembled, to doom their brother workman, as the deserter of his order and his order's cause, to die as a traitor and deserter; and have him executed, since not by any public judge and hangman, then by a private one; – like your old Chivalry *Femgericht*,[30] and Secret-Tribunal, suddenly in this strange guise become new; suddenly rising once more on the astonished eye, dressed now not in mail-shirts but in fustian jackets, meeting not in Westphalian forests but in the paved Gallowgate of Glasgow! Not loyal loving obedience to those placed over them, but a far other temper, must animate these men! It is frightful enough. Such temper must be widespread, virulent among the many, when even in its worst acme it can take such a form in a few. But indeed decay of loyalty in all senses, disobedience, decay of religious faith, has long been noticeable and lamentable in this largest class, as in other smaller ones. Revolt, sullen revengeful humour of revolt against the upper classes, decreasing respect for what their temporal superiors command, decreasing faith for what their spiritual superiors teach, is more and more the universal spirit of the lower classes. Such spirit may be blamed, may be vindicated; but all men must recognise it as extant there, all may know that it is mournful, that unless altered it will be fatal. Of lower classes so related to upper, happy nations are not made! To whatever other griefs the lower classes labour under, this bitterest and sorest grief now superadds itself: the unendurable conviction that they are unfairly dealt with, that their lot in this world is not founded on right, not even on necessity and might, and is neither what it should be, nor what it shall be.

Or why do we ask of Chartism, Glasgow Trades-unions, and suchlike? Has not broad Europe heard the question put, and answered, on the great scale; has not a FRENCH REVOLUTION been? Since the year 1789, there is now half a century complete; and a French Revolution not yet complete! Whosoever will look at that enormous Phenomenon may find many meanings in it, but this meaning as the ground of all: That it was a revolt of the oppressed lower classes against the oppressing or neglecting upper classes: not a French revolt only; no, a European one; full of stern monition to all countries of Europe. These Chartisms, Radicalisms, Reform Bill, Tithe Bill, and infinite other discrepancy, and acrid argument and jargon that there is yet to be, are *our* French Revolution: God grant that we, with our better methods, may be able to transact it by argument alone!

The French Revolution, now that we have sufficiently execrated its horrors and crimes, is found to have had withal a great meaning in it. As indeed, what great thing ever happened in this world, a world understood always to be made and governed by a Providence and Wisdom, not by an Unwisdom, without meaning somewhat? It was a tolerably audible voice of proclamation, and universal *oyez*! to all people, this of three-and-twenty years' close fighting, sieging, conflagrating, with a million or two of men shot dead: the world ought to know by this time that it was verily meant in earnest, that same Phenomenon, and had its own reasons for appearing there! Which accordingly the world begins now to do. The French Revolution is seen, or begins everywhere to be seen, 'as the crowning phenomenon of our Modern Time;' 'the inevitable stern end of much; the fearful, but also wonderful indispensable and sternly beneficent beginning of much.' He who would understand the struggling convulsive unrest of European society, in any and every country, at this day, may read it in broad glaring lines there, in that the most convulsive phenomenon of the last thousand years. Europe lay pining, obstructed, moribund; quack-ridden, hag-ridden, – is there a hag, or spectre of the Pit, so baleful, hideous as your accredited quack, were he never so close-shaven, mild-spoken, plausible to himself and others? Quack-ridden: in that one word lies all misery whatsoever. Speciosity in all departments usurps the place of reality, thrusts reality away; instead of performance, there is appearance of performance. The quack is a Falsehood Incarnate; and speaks, and makes and does mere falsehoods, which Nature with her veracity has to disown. As chief priest, as chief governor, he stands there, intrusted with much. The husbandman of 'Time's Seedfield;' he is the world's hired sower, hired and solemnly appointed to sow the kind true earth with wheat this year, that next year all men may have bread. He, miserable mortal, deceiving and self-deceiving, sows it, as we said, not with corn but with chaff; the world nothing doubting, harrows it in, pays him his wages, dismisses him with blessing, and – next year there has no corn sprung. Nature has disowned the chaff, declined growing chaff, and behold now there is no bread! It becomes necessary, in such case, to do several things; not soft things some of them, but hard.

Nay we will add that the very circumstance of quacks in unusual quantity getting domination, indicates that the heart of the world is *already* wrong. The impostor is false; but neither are his dupes altogether true: is not his first grand dupe the falsest of all, – himself namely? Sincere men, of never so limited intellect, have an instinct for discriminating sincerity. The cunningest Mephistopheles cannot deceive a simple Margaret of honest heart;[31] 'it stands written on his brow.' Masses of people capable of being led away by quacks are themselves of partially untrue spirit. Alas, in such times it grows to be the universal belief, sole accredited knowingness, and the contrary of it accounted puerile enthusiasm, this sorrowfulest *dis*belief that there is properly speaking any truth in the world, that the world was, has been or ever can be guided, except by simulation, dissimulation, and the sufficiently dextrous practice of pretence. The faith of men is dead: in what has guineas in its pocket, beefeaters riding behind it, and cannons trundling before it, they can believe; in what has none of these things they cannot believe. Sense for the true and false is lost; there is properly no longer any true or false. It is the heyday of Imposture; of Semblance recognising itself, and getting itself recognised, for Substance. Gaping multitudes listen; unlistening multitudes see not but that it is all right, and in the order of Nature. Earnest men, one of a million, shut their lips; suppressing thoughts, which there are no words to utter. To them it is too visible that spiritual life has departed; that material life, in whatsoever figure of it, cannot long remain behind. To them it seems as if our Europe of the Eighteenth Century, long hag-ridden, vexed with foul enchanters, to the length now of gorgeous Domdaniel *Parcs-aux-cerfs* and 'Peasants living on meal-husks and boiled grass,'[32] had verily sunk down to die and dissolve; and were now, with its French Philosophisms, Hume Scepticisms, Diderot Atheisms,[33] maundering in the final deliration; writhing, with its Seven-years Silesian robber-wars,[34] in the final agony. Glory to God, our Europe was not to die but to live! Our Europe rose like a frenzied giant; shook all that poisonous magician trumpery to right and left, trampling it stormfully under foot; and declared aloud that there was strength in him, not for life only, but for new and infinitely wider life. Antæus-like[35] the giant had struck his foot once more upon Reality and the Earth; there only, if in this Universe at all, lay strength and healing for him.

Heaven knows, it was not a gentle process; no wonder that it was a fearful process, this same 'Phoenix fire-consummation'! But the alternative was it or death; the merciful Heavens, merciful in their severity, sent us it rather.

And so the 'rights of man' were to be written down on paper; and experimentally wrought upon towards elaboration, in huge battle and wrestle, element conflicting with element, from side to side of this earth, for three-and-twenty years. Rights of man, wrongs of man? It is a question which has swallowed whole nations and generations; a question – on which we will not enter here. Far be it from us! Logic has small business with this question at present; logic has no plummet that will sound it at any time. But indeed the rights of man, as has been not unaptly remarked, are little worth ascertaining in comparison to the *mights* of man, – to what portion of his rights he has any chance of being able to make good! The accurate final rights of man lie in the far deeps of the Ideal, where 'the Ideal weds itself to the Possible,' as the Philosophers say. The ascertainable temporary rights of man vary not a little, according to place and time. They are known to depend much on what a man's convictions of them are. The Highland wife, with her husband at the foot of the gallows, patted him on the shoulder (if there be historical truth in Joseph Miller),[36] and said amid her tears: 'Go up, Donald, my man; the Laird bids ye.' To her it seemed the rights of lairds were great, the rights of men small; and she acquiesced. Deputy Lapoule, in the *Salle des Menus* at Versailles,[37] on the 4th of August 1789, demanded (he did actually 'demand,' and by unanimous vote obtain) that the 'obsolete law' authorising a Seigneur, on his return from the chase or other needful fatigue, to slaughter not above two of his vassals, and refresh his feet in their warm blood and bowels, should be 'abrogated.' From such obsolete law, or mad tradition and phantasm of an obsolete law, down to any corn-law, game-law, rotten-borough law, or other law or practice clamoured of in this time of ours, the distance travelled over is great!

What are the rights of men? All men are justified in demanding and searching for their rights; moreover, justified or not, they will do it: by Chartisms, Radicalisms, French Revolutions,

or whatsoever methods they have. Rights surely are right: on
the other hand, this other saying is most true, 'Use every man
according to his *rights*, and who shall escape whipping?'[38] These
two things, we say, are both true; and both are essential to make
up the whole truth. All good men know always and feel, each
for himself, that the one is not less true than the other; and
act accordingly. The contradiction is of the surface only; as in
opposite sides of the same fact: universal in this *dualism* of a life
we have. Between these two extremes, Society and all human
things must fluctuatingly adjust themselves the best they can.

And yet that there is verily a 'rights of man' let no mortal
doubt. An ideal of right does dwell in all men, in all arrangements, pactions and procedures of men: it is to this ideal of
right, more and more developing itself as it is more and more
approximated to, that human Society forever tends and struggles. We say also that any given thing either is unjust or else
just; however obscure the arguings and strugglings on it be, the
thing in itself there as it lies, infallibly enough, *is* the one or the
other. To which let us add only this, the first, last article of
faith, the alpha and omega of all faith among men, That nothing which is unjust can hope to continue in this world. A faith
true in all times, more or less forgotten in most, but altogether
frightfully brought to remembrance again in ours! Lyons fusilladings, Nantes noyadings,[39] reigns of terror, and such other
universal battle-thunder and explosion; these, if we will understand them, were but a new irrefragable preaching abroad of
that. It would appear that Speciosities which are not Realities
cannot any longer inhabit this world. It would appear that the
unjust thing has no friend in the Heaven, and a majority against
it on the Earth; nay that *it* has at bottom all men for its enemies;
that it may take shelter in this fallacy and then in that, but will
be hunted from fallacy to fallacy till it find no fallacy to shelter
in any more, but must march and go elsewhither; – that, in a
word, it ought to prepare incessantly for decent departure,
before *in*decent departure, ignominious drumming out, nay
savage smiting out and burning out, overtake it!

Alas, was that such new tidings? Is it not from of old indubitable, that Untruth, Injustice which is but acted untruth, has

no power to continue in this true Universe of ours? The tidings was world-old, or older, as old as the Fall of Lucifer: and yet in that epoch unhappily it was new tidings, unexpected, incredible; and there had to be such earthquakes and shakings of the nations before it could be listened to, and laid to heart even slightly! Let us lay it to heart, let us know it well, that new shakings be not needed. Known and laid to heart it must everywhere be, before peace can pretend to come. This seems to us the secret of our convulsed era; this which is so easily written, which is and has been and will be so hard to bring to pass. All true men, high and low, each in his sphere, are consciously or unconsciously bringing it to pass; all false and half-true men are fruitlessly spending themselves to hinder it from coming to pass.

6. Laissez-Faire

From all which enormous events, with truths old and new
embodied in them, what innumerable practical inferences are
to be drawn! Events are written lessons, glaring in huge hiero-
glyphic picture-writing, that all may read and know them: the
terror and horror they inspire is but the note of preparation for
the truth they are to teach; a mere waste of terror if that be not
learned. Inferences enough; most didactic, practically applicable in all departments of English things! One inference, but
one inclusive of all, shall content us here; this namely: That
Laissez-faire has as good as done its part in a great many provinces; that in the province of the Working Classes, *Laissez-faire*
having passed its New Poor-Law, has reached the suicidal
point, and now, as *felo-de-se*, lies dying there, in torchlight
meetings and suchlike; that, in brief, a government of the under
classes by the upper on a principle of *Let-alone* is no longer
possible in England in these days. This is the one inference
inclusive of all. For there can be no acting or doing of any kind,
till it be recognised that there is a thing to be done; the thing
once recognised, doing in a thousand shapes becomes possible.
The Working Classes cannot any longer go on without government; without being *actually* guided and governed; England
cannot subsist in peace till, by some means or other, some guidance and government for them is found.

For, alas, on us too the rude truth has come home. Wrappages and speciosities all worn off, the haggard naked fact
speaks to us: Are these millions taught? Are these millions
guided? We have a Church, the venerable embodiment of an
idea which may well call itself divine; which our fathers for

long ages, feeling it to be divine, have been embodying as we
see: it is a Church well furnished with equipments and appurtenances; educated in universities; rich in money; set on high
places that it may be conspicuous to all, honoured of all. We
have an Aristocracy of landed wealth and commercial wealth,
in whose hands lie the law-making and the law-administering;
an Aristocracy rich, powerful, long secure in its place; an Aristocracy with more faculty put free into its hands than was ever
before, in any country or time, put into the hands of any class
of men. This Church answers: Yes, the people are taught. This
Aristocracy, astonishment in every feature, answers: Yes, surely
the people are guided! Do we not pass what Acts of Parliament
are needful; as many as thirty-nine for the shooting of the partridges alone? Are there not treadmills, gibbets; even hospitals,
poor-rates, New Poor-Law? So answers Church; so answers
Aristocracy, astonishment in every feature.

Fact, in the mean while, takes his lucifer-box, sets fire to
wheat-stacks; sheds an all-too dismal light on several things.
Fact searches for his third-rate potato, not in the meekest
humour, six-and-thirty weeks each year; and does not find it.
Fact passionately joins Messiah Thom of Canterbury, and has
himself shot for a new fifth-monarchy brought in by Bedlam.[40]
Fact holds his fustian-jacket *Femgericht* in Glasgow City. Fact
carts his Petition over London streets, begging that you would
simply have the goodness to grant him universal suffrage and
'the five points,'[41] by way of remedy. These are not symptoms
of teaching and guiding.

Nay, at bottom, is it not a singular thing this of *Laissez-faire*,
from the first origin of it? As good as an *abdication* on the part
of governors; an admission that they are henceforth incompetent to govern, that they are not there to govern at all, but to
do – one knows not what! The universal demand of *Laissez-
faire* by a people from its governors or upper classes, is a
soft-sounding demand; but it is only one step removed from the
fatalest. 'Laissez-faire,' exclaims a sardonic German writer,[42]
'What is this universal cry for *Laissez-faire*? Does it mean that
human affairs require no guidance; that wisdom and forethought cannot guide them better than folly and accident?

Alas, does it not mean: "*Such* guidance is worse than none! Leave us alone of *your* guidance; eat your wages, and sleep!"' And now if guidance have grown indispensable, and the sleep continue, what becomes of the sleep and its wages? – In those entirely surprising circumstances to which the Eighteenth Century had brought us, in the time of Adam Smith, *Laissez-faire* was a reasonable cry; – as indeed, in all circumstances, for a wise governor there will be meaning in the principle of it. To wise governors you will cry: 'See what you will, and will not, let alone.' To unwise governors, to hungry Greeks throttling down hungry Greeks on the floor of a St Stephen's,[43] you will cry: 'Let *all* things alone; for Heaven's sake, meddle ye with nothing!'

How *Laissez-faire* may adjust itself in other provinces we say not: but we do venture to say, and ask whether events everywhere, in world-history and parish-history, in all manner of dialects are not saying it, That in regard to the lower orders of society, and their governance and guidance, the principle of *Laissez-faire* has terminated, and is no longer applicable at all, in this Europe of ours, still less in this England of ours. Not misgovernment, nor yet no-government; only government will now serve. What is the meaning of the 'five points,' if we will understand them? What are all popular commotions and maddest bellowings, from Peterloo to the Place-de-Grève[44] itself? Bellowings, *in*articulate cries as of a dumb creature in rage and pain; to the ear of wisdom they are inarticulate prayers: 'Guide me, govern me! I am mad and miserable, and cannot guide myself!' Surely of all 'rights of man,' this right of the ignorant man to be guided by the wiser, to be, gently or forcibly, held in the true course by him, is the indisputablest. Nature herself ordains it from the first; Society struggles towards perfection by enforcing and accomplishing it more and more. If Freedom have any meaning, it means enjoyment of this right, wherein all other rights are enjoyed. It is a sacred right and duty, on both sides; and the summary of all social duties whatsoever between the two. Why does the one toil with his hands, if the other be not to toil, still more unweariedly, with heart and head? The brawny craftsman finds it no child's-play to mould his unpliant rugged masses; neither is guidance of men a dilettantism: what it becomes when treated as a dilettantism, we may see! The wild horse bounds homeless through the wilderness, is not led to stall and manger; but neither does he toil for you, but for himself only.

Democracy, we are well aware, what is called 'self-government' of the multitude by the multitude, is in words the thing everywhere passionately clamoured for at present. Democracy makes rapid progress in these latter times, and ever more rapid, in a perilous accelerative ratio; towards democracy, and that only, the progress of things is everywhere tending as to the final goal and winning-post. So think, so clamour the multitudes everywhere. And yet all men may see, whose sight is good for much, that in democracy can lie no finality; that with the completest winning of democracy there is nothing yet won, – except emptiness, and the free chance to win! Democracy is, by the nature of it, a self-cancelling business; and gives in the long-run a net result of *zero*. Where no government is wanted, save that of the parish-constable, as in America with its boundless soil, every man being able to find work and recompense for himself, democracy may subsist; not elsewhere, except briefly, as a swift transition towards something other and farther. Democracy never yet, that we heard of, was able to accomplish much work, beyond that same cancelling of itself. Rome and Athens are themes for the schools; unexceptionable for that purpose. In Rome and Athens, as elsewhere, if we look practically, we shall find that it was not by loud voting and debating of many, but by wise insight and ordering of a few that the work was done. So is it ever, so will it ever be.

The French Convention was a Parliament elected 'by the five points,' with ballot-boxes, universal suffrages, and what not, as perfectly as Parliament can hope to be in this world; and had indeed a pretty spell of work to do, and did it. The French Convention had to cease from being a free Parliament, and become more arbitrary than any Sultan Bajazet, before it could so much as subsist. It had to purge out its argumentative Girondins, elect its Supreme Committee of *Salut*, guillotine into silence and extinction all that gainsaid it,[45] and rule and work literally by the sternest despotism ever seen in Europe, before it could rule at all. Napoleon was not president of a republic; Cromwell tried hard to rule in that way, but found that he could not. These, 'the armed soldiers of democracy,' had to chain democracy under their feet, and become despots over it, before they could work out the earnest obscure purpose of democracy itself!

Democracy, take it where you will in our Europe, is found but as a regulated method of rebellion and abrogation; it abrogates the old arrangement of things; and leaves, as we say, *zero* and vacuity for the institution of a new arrangement. It is the consummation of No-government and *Laissez-faire*. It may be natural for our Europe at present; but cannot be the ultimatum of it. Not towards the impossibility, 'self-government' of a multitude by a multitude; but towards some possibility, government by the wisest, does bewildered Europe struggle. The blessedest possibility: not misgovernment, not *Laissez-faire*, but veritable government! Cannot one discern too, across all democratic turbulence, clattering of ballot-boxes and infinite sorrowful jangle, needful or not, that this at bottom is the wish and prayer of all human hearts, everywhere and at all times: 'Give me a leader; a true leader, not a false sham-leader; a true leader, that he may guide me on the true way, that I may be loyal to him, that I may swear fealty to him and follow him, and feel that it is well with me!' The relation of the taught to their teacher, of the loyal subject to his guiding king, is, under one shape or another, the vital element of human Society; indispensable to it, perennial in it; without which, as a body reft of its soul, it falls down into death, and with horrid noisome dissolution passes away and disappears.

But verily in these times, with their new stern Evangel, that Speciosities which are not Realities can no longer be, all Aristocracies, Priesthoods, Persons in Authority, are called upon to consider. What is an Aristocracy? A corporation of the Best, of the Bravest. To this joyfully, with heart-loyalty, do men pay the half of their substance, to equip and decorate their Best, to lodge them in palaces, set them high over all. For it is of the nature of men, in every time, to honour and love their Best; to know no limits in honouring them. Whatsoever Aristocracy *is* still a corporation of the Best, is safe from all peril, and the land it rules is a safe and blessed land. Whatsoever Aristocracy does not even attempt to be that, but only to wear the clothes of that, is not safe; neither is the land it rules in safe! For this now is our sad lot, that we must find a *real* Aristocracy, that an apparent Aristocracy, how plausible soever, has become inadequate for us. One way or other, the world will absolutely need to be governed; if not by this class of men, then by that. One can predict, without gift of prophecy, that the era of routine is nearly ended. Wisdom and faculty alone, faithful, valiant, everzealous, not pleasant but painful, continual effort will suffice. Cost what it may, by one means or another, the toiling multitudes of this perplexed, over-crowded Europe must and will find governors. '*Laissez-faire*, Leave them to do'? The thing they will *do*, if so left, is too frightful to think of! It has been *done* once, in sight of the whole earth, in these generations: can it need to be done a second time?

For a Priesthood, in like manner, whatsoever its titles, possessions, professions, there is but one question: Does it teach and spiritually guide this people, yea or no? If yea, then is all well. But if no, then let it strive earnestly to alter, for as yet there is nothing well! Nothing, we say: and indeed is not this that we call spiritual guidance properly the soul of the whole, the life and eyesight of the whole? The world asks of its Church in these times, more passionately than of any other Institution any question, 'Canst thou teach us or not?' – A Priesthood in France, when the world asked, 'What canst thou do for us?' answered only, aloud and ever louder, 'Are we not of God? Invested with all power?' – till at length France cut short this controversy too, in what frightful way we know. To all men who believed in the Church, to all men who believed in God and the soul of man, there was no issue of the French Revolution half so sorrowful as that. France cast out its benighted blind Priesthood into destruction; yet with what a loss to France also! A solution of continuity, what we may well call such; and this where continuity is so momentous: the New, whatever it may be, cannot now *grow* out of the Old, but is severed sheer asunder from the Old, – how much lies wasted in that gap! That one whole generation of thinkers should be without a religion to believe, or even to contradict; that Christianity, in thinking France, should as it were fade away so long into a remote extraneous tradition, was one of the saddest facts connected with the future of that country. Look at such Political and Moral Philosophies, St-Simonisms, Robert-Macairisms, and the 'Literature of Desperation'![46] Kingship was perhaps but a cheap waste, compared with this of the Priestship; under which France still, all but unconsciously, labours; and may long labour, remediless the while. Let others consider it, and take warning by it! France is a pregnant example in all ways. Aristocracies that do not govern, Priesthoods that do not teach; the misery of that, and the misery of altering that, – are written in Belshazzar fire-letters[47] on the history of France.

Or does the British reader, safe in the assurance that 'England is not France,' call all this unpleasant doctrine of ours ideology, perfectibility, and a vacant dream? Does the British reader, resting on the faith that what has been these two generations was from the beginning, and will be to the end, assert to himself that things are already as they can be, as they must be; that on the whole, no Upper Classes did ever 'govern' the Lower, in this sense of governing? Believe it not, O British reader! Man is man everywhere; dislikes to have 'sensible species' and 'ghosts of defunct bodies' foisted on him, in England even as in France.

How much the Upper Classes did actually, in any the most perfect Feudal time, return to the Under by way of recompense, in government, guidance, protection, we will not undertake to specify here. In Charity-Balls, Soup-Kitchens, in Quarter-Sessions, Prison-Discipline and Tread-mills, we can well believe the old Feudal Aristocracy not to have surpassed the new. Yet we do say that the old Aristocracy were the governors of the Lower Classes, the guides of the Lower Classes; and even, at bottom, that they existed as an Aristocracy because they were found adequate for that. Not by Charity-Balls and Soup-Kitchens; not so; far otherwise! But it was their happiness that, in struggling for their own objects, they *had* to govern the Lower Classes, even in this sense of governing. For, in one word, *Cash Payment* had not then grown to be the universal sole nexus of man to man; it was something other than money that the high then expected from the low, and could not live without getting from the low. Not as buyer and seller alone, of land or what else it might be, but in many senses still as soldier and captain, as clansman and head, as loyal subject and guiding king, was the low related to the high. With the supreme triumph of Cash, a changed time has entered; there must a changed Aristocracy enter. We invite the British reader to meditate earnestly on these things.

Another thing, which the British reader often reads and hears in this time, is worth his meditating for a moment: That Society 'exists for the protection of property.' To which it is added, that the poor man also has property, namely, his 'labour,' and the fifteen-pence or three-and-sixpence a-day he can get for that. True enough, O friends, 'for protecting *property*;' most true: and indeed, if you will once sufficiently enforce that Eighth Commandment, the whole 'rights of man' are well cared for; I know no better definition of the rights of man. *Thou shalt not steal, thou shalt not be stolen from:* what a Society were that; Plato's Republic, More's Utopia mere emblems of it! Give every man what is his, the accurate price of what he has done and been, no man shall any more complain, neither shall the earth suffer any more. For the protection of property, in very truth, and for that alone!

And now what is thy property? That parchment title-deed, that purse thou buttonest in thy breeches-pocket? Is that thy valuable property? Unhappy brother, most poor insolvent brother, I without parchment at all, with purse oftenest in the flaccid state, imponderous, which will not fling against the wind, have quite other property than that! I have the miraculous breath of Life in me, breathed into my nostrils by Almighty God. I have affections, thoughts, a god-given *capability* to be and do; rights, therefore, – the right for instance to thy love if I love thee, to thy guidance if I obey thee: the strangest rights, whereof in church-pulpits one still hears something, though almost unintelligible now; rights stretching high into Immensity, far into Eternity! Fifteen-pence a-day; three-and-sixpence a-day; eight hundred pounds and odd a-day, dost thou call that my property? I value that little; little all I could purchase with that. For truly, as is said, what matters it? In torn boots, in soft-hung carriages-and-four, a man gets always to his journey's end. Socrates walked barefoot, or in wooden shoes, and yet arrived happily. They never asked him, *What* shoes or conveyance? never, What wages hadst thou? but simply, What work didst thou? – Property, O brother? 'Of my very body I have but a life-rent.' As for this flaccid purse of mine, 'tis something, nothing; has been the slave of pickpockets, cutthroats, Jew-brokers, gold-dust robbers; 'twas his, 'tis mine; – 'tis thine, if thou care much to steal it. But my soul, breathed into me by God, my *Me* and what capability is there; that is mine, and I will resist the stealing of it. I call that mine and not thine; I will keep that, and do what work I can with it: God has given it me, the Devil shall not take it away! Alas, my friends, Society exists and has existed for a great many purposes, not so easy to specify!

Society, it is understood, does not in any age prevent a man from being what he *can* be. A sooty African *can* become a Toussaint L'Ouverture, a murderous Three-fingered Jack, let the yellow West Indies say to it what they will.[48] A Scottish Poet,[49] 'proud of his name and country,' *can* apply fervently to 'Gentlemen of the Caledonian Hunt,' and become a gauger of beer-barrels, and tragical immortal broken-hearted Singer; the stifled echo of his melody audible through long centuries; one other note in 'that sacred *Miserere*' that rises up to Heaven, out of all times and lands. What I *can be* thou decidedly will not hinder me from being. Nay even for being what I *could be*, I have the strangest claims on thee, – not convenient to adjust at present! Protection of breeches-pocket property? O reader, to what shifts is poor Society reduced, struggling to give still some account of herself, in epochs when Cash Payment has become the sole nexus of man to man! On the whole, we will advise Society not to talk at all about what she exists for; but rather with her whole industry to exist, to try how she can keep existing! That is her best plan. She may depend upon it, if she ever, by cruel chance, did come to exist only for protection of breeches-pocket property, she would lose very soon the gift of protecting even that, and find her career in our lower world on the point of terminating! –

For the rest, that in the most perfect Feudal Ages, the Ideal of Aristocracy nowhere lived in vacant serene purity as an Ideal, but always as a poor imperfect Actual, little heeding or not knowing at all that an Ideal lay in it, – this too we will cheerfully admit. Imperfection, it is known, cleaves to human things; far is the Ideal departed from, in most times; very far! And yet so long as an Ideal (any soul of Truth) does, in never so confused a manner, exist and work within the Actual, it is a tolerable business. Not so, when the Ideal has entirely departed, and the Actual owns to itself that it has no Idea, no soul of Truth any longer: at that degree of imperfection human things cannot continue living; they are obliged to alter or expire, when they attain to that. Blotches and diseases exist on the skin and deeper, the heart continuing whole; but it is another matter when the heart itself becomes diseased; when there is no heart, but a monstrous gangrene pretending to exist there as heart!

On the whole, O reader, thou wilt find everywhere that things which had had an existence among men have first of all had to have a truth and worth in them, and were not semblances but realities. Nothing not a reality ever yet got men to pay bed and board to it for long. Look at Mahometanism itself! Dalai-Lamaism, even Dalai-Lamaism, one rejoices to discover, may be worth its victuals in this world; not a quackery but a sincerity; not a nothing but a something! The mistake of those who believe that fraud, force, injustice, whatsoever untrue thing, howsoever cloaked and decorated, was ever or can ever be the principle of man's relations to man, is great and the greatest. It is the error of the infidel; in whom the truth as yet is *not*. It is an error pregnant with mere errors and miseries; an error fatal, lamentable, to be abandoned by all men.

7. Not Laissez-Faire

How an Aristocracy, in these present times and circumstances, could, if never so well disposed, set about governing the Under Class? What they should do; endeavour or attempt to do? That is even the question of questions: – the question which *they* have to solve; which it is our utmost function at present to tell them, lies there for solving, and must and will be solved.

Insoluble we cannot fancy it. One select class Society has furnished with wealth, intelligence, leisure, means outward and inward for governing; another huge class, furnished by Society with none of those things, declares that it must be governed: Negative stands fronting Positive; if Negative and Positive *cannot* unite, – it will be worse for both! Let the faculty and earnest constant effort of England combine round this matter; let it once be recognised as a vital matter. Innumerable things our Upper Classes and Lawgivers might 'do;' but the preliminary of all things, we must repeat, is to know that a thing must needs be done. We lead them here to the shore of a boundless continent; ask them, Whether they do not with their own eyes see it, the strange symptoms of it, lying huge, dark, unexplored, inevitable; full of hope, but also full of difficulty, savagery, almost of despair? Let them enter; they must enter; Time and Necessity have brought them hither; where they are is no continuing! Let them enter; the first step once taken, the next will have become clearer, all future steps will become possible. It is a great problem for all of us; but for themselves, we may say, more than for any. On them chiefly, as the expected solvers of it, will the failure of a solution first fall. One way or other there must and will be a solution.

True, these matters lie far, very far indeed, from the 'usual
habits of Parliament,' in late times; from the routine course of
any Legislative or Administrative body of men that exists
among us. Too true! And that is even the thing we complain of:
had the mischief been looked into as it gradually rose; it would
not have attained this magnitude. That self-cancelling Donoth-
ingism and *Laissez-faire* should have got so ingrained into our
Practice, is the source of all these miseries. It is too true that
Parliament, for the matter of near a century now, has been able
to undertake the adjustment of almost one thing alone, of itself
and its own interests; leaving other interests to rub along very
much as they could and would. True, this was the practice of
the whole Eighteenth Century; and struggles still to prolong
itself into the Nineteenth, – which, however, is no longer the
time for it!

Those Eighteenth-century Parliaments, one may hope, will
become a curious object one day. Are not these same '*Memoires*' of Horace Walpole,[50] to an unparliamentary eye, already
a curious object? One of the clearest-sighted men of the Eighteenth Century writes down his Parliamentary observation of it
there; a determined despiser and merciless dissector of cant;
a liberal withal, one who will go all lengths for the 'glorious
revolution,' and resist Tory principles to the death: he writes,
with an indignant elegiac feeling, how Mr This, who had voted
so and then voted so, and was the son of this and the brother
of that, and had such claims to the fat appointment, was nevertheless scandalously postponed to Mr That; – whereupon are
not the affairs of this nation in a bad way? How hungry Greek
meets hungry Greek on the floor of St Stephen's, and wrestles
him and throttles him till he has to cry, Hold! the office is
thine! – of this does Horace write. – One must say, the destinies
of nations do not always rest entirely on Parliament. One must
say, it is a wonderful affair that science of 'government' as
practised in the Eighteenth Century of the Christian era, and
still struggling to practise itself. One must say, it was a lucky
century that could get it so practised: a century which had
inherited richly from its predecessors; and also which did, not
unnaturally, bequeath to its successors a French Revolution,

general overturn, and reign of terror; – intimating, in most audible thunder, conflagration, guillotinement, cannonading and
universal war and earthquake, that such century with its practices had *ended*.

Ended; – for decidedly that course of procedure will no
longer serve. Parliament will absolutely, with whatever effort,
have to lift itself out of those deep ruts of donothing routine;
and learn to say, on all sides, something more edifying than
Laissez-faire. If Parliament cannot learn it, what is to become
of Parliament? The toiling millions of England ask of their English Parliament foremost of all, Canst thou govern us or not?
Parliament with its privileges is strong; but Necessity and the
Laws of Nature are stronger than it. If Parliament cannot do
this thing, Parliament we prophesy will do some other thing
and things which, in the strangest and not the happiest way,
will forward its being done, – not much to the advantage of
Parliament probably! Done, one way or other, the thing must
be. In these complicated times, with Cash Payment as the sole
nexus between man and man, the Toiling Classes of mankind
declare, in their confused but most emphatic way, to the Untoil-
ing, that they will be governed; that they must, – under penalty
of Chartisms, Thuggeries, Rick-burnings, and even blacker things
than those. Vain also is it to think that the misery of one class,
of the great universal under class, can be isolated, and kept
apart and peculiar, down in that class. By infallible contagion,
evident enough to reflection, evident even to Political Economy
that will reflect, the misery of the lowest spreads upwards and
upwards till it reaches the very highest; till all has grown miserable, palpably false and wrong; and poor drudges hungering
'on meal-husks and boiled grass' do, by circuitous but sure
methods, bring king's heads to the block!

Cash Payment the sole nexus; and there are so many things
which cash will not pay! Cash is a great miracle; yet it has not
all power in Heaven, nor even on Earth. 'Supply and demand'
we will honour also; and yet how many 'demands' are there,
entirely indispensable, which have to go elsewhere than to the
shops, and produce quite other than cash, before they can get
their supply! On the whole, what astonishing payments does

cash make in this world! Of your Samuel Johnson, furnished with 'fourpence-halfpenny a-day,'[51] and solid lodging at nights on the paved streets, as his payment, we do not speak; – not in the way of complaint: it is a world-old business for the like of him, that same arrangement or a worse; perhaps the man, for his own uses, had need even of that, and of no better. Nay is not Society, busy with its Talfourd Copyright Bill[52] and the like, struggling to do something effectual for that man; – enacting with all industry that his own creation be accounted his own manufacture, and continue unstolen, on his own market-stand, for so long as sixty years? Perhaps Society is right there; for discrepancies on that side too may become excessive. All men are not patient docile Johnsons; some of them are half-mad inflammable Rousseaus. Such, in peculiar times, you may drive too far. Society in France, for example, was not destitute of cash: Society contrived to pay Philippe d'Orléans not yet Egalité[53] three hundred thousand a-year and odd, for driving cabriolets through the streets of Paris and other work done; but in cash, encouragement, arrangement, recompense or recognition of any kind, it had nothing to give this same half-mad Rousseau for his work done; whose brain in consequence, *too* 'much enforced' for a weak brain, uttered hasty sparks, *Contrat Social* and the like, which proved not so quenchable again! In regard to that species of men too, who knows whether *Laissez-faire* itself (which is Sergeant Talfourd's Copyright Bill continued to eternity instead of sixty years) will not turn out insufficient, and have to cease, one day? –

Alas, in regard to so very many things, *Laissez-faire* ought partly to endeavour to cease! But in regard to poor Sanspotato peasants, Trades-Union craftsmen, Chartist cotton-spinners, the time has come when it must either cease or a worse thing straight-way begin, – a thing of tinderboxes, vitriol-bottles, secondhand pistols, a visibly insupportable thing in the eyes of all.

8. New Eras

For in very truth it is a 'new Era;' a new Practice has become indispensable in it. One has heard so often of new eras, new and newest eras, that the word has grown rather empty of late. Yet new eras do come; there is no fact surer than that they have come more than once. And always with a change of era, with a change of intrinsic conditions, there had to be a change of practice and outward relations brought about, – if not peaceably, then by violence; for brought about it had to be, there could no rest come till then. How many eras and epochs, not noted at the moment; – which indeed is the blessedest condition of epochs, that they come quietly, making no proclamation of themselves, and are only visible long after: a Cromwell Rebellion, a French Revolution, 'striking on the Horologe of Time,' to tell all mortals what o'clock it has become, are too expensive, if one could help it! –

In a strange rhapsodic 'History of the Teuton Kindred (*Geschichte der Teutschen Sippschaft*),'[54] not yet translated into our language, we have found a Chapter on the Eras of England, which, were there room for it, would be instructive in this place. We shall crave leave to excerpt some pages; partly as a relief from the too near vexations of our own rather sorrowful Era; partly as calculated to throw, more or less obliquely, some degree of light on the meanings of that. The Author is anonymous: but we have heard him called the Herr Professor Sauerteig, and indeed think we know him under that name:

'Who shall say what work and works this England has yet to do? For what purpose this land of Britain was created, set

like a jewel in the encircling blue of Ocean; and this Tribe of
Saxons, fashioned in the depths of Time, "on the shores of
the Black Sea" or elsewhere, "out of Harzgebirge rock"[55] or
whatever other material, was sent travelling hitherward? No
man can say: it was for a work, and for works, incapable of
announcement in words. Thou seest them there; part of them
stand done, and visible to the eye; even these thou canst not
name: how much less the others still matter of prophecy only! –
They live and labour there, these twenty million Saxon men;
they have been born into this mystery of life out of the darkness of Past Time: – how changed now since the first Father
and first Mother of them set forth, quitting the tribe of
Theuth,[56] with passionate farewell, under questionable aus-
pices; on scanty bullock-cart, if they had even bullocks and a
cart; with axe and hunting-spear, to subdue a portion of our
common Planet! This Nation now has cities and seedfields,
has spring-vans, dray-wagons, Long-Acre carriages, nay railway
trains; has coined-money, exchange-bills, laws, books, war-
fleets, spinning-jennies, warehouses and West-India Docks: see
what it has built and done, what it can and will yet build and
do! These umbrageous pleasure-woods, green meadows, shaven
stubble-fields, smooth-sweeping roads; these high-domed cities,
and what they hold and bear; this mild Good-morrow which
the stranger bids thee, equitable, nay forbearant if need were,
judicially calm and law-observing towards thee a stranger, what
work has it not cost? How many brawny arms, generation after
generation, sank down wearied; how many noble hearts, toiling while life lasted, and wise heads wore themselves dim with
scanning and discerning, before this waste *White-cliff*, Albion
so-called, with its other Cassiterides *Tin Islands,*[57] became a
BRITISH EMPIRE! The stream of World-History has altered its
complexion; Romans are dead out, English are come in. The red
broad mark of Romanhood, stamped ineffaceably on that
Chart of Time, has disappeared from the present, and belongs
only to the past. England plays its part; England too has a mark
to leave, and we will hope none of the least significant. Of a
truth, whosoever had, with the bodily eye, seen Hengst and
Horsa mooring on the mud-beach of Thanet, on that spring

morning of the Year 449; and then, with the spiritual eye, looked forward to New York, Calcutta, Sidney Cove, across the ages and the oceans; and thought what Wellingtons, Washingtons, Shakspeares, Miltons, Watts, Arkwrights, William Pitts and Davie Crocketts had to issue from that business, and do their several taskworks so, – *he* would have said, those leather-boats of Hengst's had a kind of cargo in them! A genealogic Mythus superior to any in the old Greek, to almost any in the old Hebrew itself; and not a Mythus either, but every fibre of it fact. An Epic Poem was there, and all manner of poems; except that the Poet has not yet made his appearance.

'Six centuries of obscure endeavour,' continues Sauerteig, 'which to read Historians, you would incline to call mere obscure slaughter, discord, and misendeavour; of which all that the human memory, after a thousand readings, can remember, is that it resembled, what Milton names it, the "flocking and fighting of kites and crows:" this, in brief, is the history of the Heptarchy or Seven Kingdoms.[58] Six centuries; a stormy springtime, if there ever was one, for a Nation. Obscure fighting of kites and crows, however, was not the History of it; but was only what the dim Historians of it saw good to record. Were not forests felled, bogs drained, fields made arable, towns built, laws made, and the Thought and Practice of men in many ways perfected? Venerable Bede had got a language which he could now not only speak, but spell and put on paper: think what lies in that. Bemurmured by the German sea-flood swinging slow with sullen roar against those hoarse Northumbrian rocks, the venerable man set down several things in a legible manner. Or was the smith idle, hammering only wartools? He had learned metallurgy, stithy-work in general; and made ploughshares withal, and adzes and mason-hammers. *Castra*, Caesters or Chesters, Dons, Tons (*Zauns*, Enclosures or *Towns*), not a few, did they not stand there; of burnt brick, of timber, of lath-and-clay; sending up the peaceable smoke of hearths? England had a History then too; though no Historian to write it. Those "flockings and fightings," sad inevitable necessities, were the expensive tentative steps towards some capability of living and working in concert: experiments they were, not always conclusive, to ascertain who had the might over whom, the right over whom.

'Mr Thierry has written an ingenious book,[59] celebrating with considerable pathos the fate of the Saxons fallen under that fierce-hearted *Conquaestor*, Acquirer or Conqueror, as he is named. M. Thierry professes to have a turn for looking at that side of things: the fate of the Welsh too moves him; of the Celts generally, whom a fiercer race swept before them into the mountainous nooks of the West, whither they were not worth following. Noble deeds, according to M. Thierry, were done by these unsuccessful men, heroic sufferings undergone; which it is a pious duty to rescue from forgetfulness. True, surely! A tear at least is due to the unhappy: it is right and fit that there should be a man to assert that lost cause too, and see what can still be made of it. Most right: – and yet, on the whole, taking matters on that great scale, what can we say but that the cause which pleased the gods has in the end to please Cato also? Cato cannot alter it; Cato will find that he cannot at bottom wish to alter it.

'Might and Right do differ frightfully from hour to hour; but give them centuries to try it in, they are found to be identical. Whose land *was* this of Britain? God's who made it, His and no other's it was and is. Who of God's creatures had right to live in it? The wolves and bisons? Yes they; till one with a better right showed himself. The Celt, "aboriginal savage of Europe," as a snarling antiquary names him, arrived, pretending to have a better right; and did accordingly, not without pain to the bisons, make good the same. He had a better right to that piece of God's land; namely a better might to turn it to use; – a might to settle himself there, at least, and try what use he could turn it to. The bisons disappeared; the Celts took possession, and tilled. Forever, was it to be? Alas, *Forever* is not a category that can establish itself in this world of Time. A world of Time, by the very definition of it, is a world of mortality and mutability, of Beginning and Ending. No property is eternal but God the Maker's: whom Heaven permits to take possession, his is the right; Heaven's sanction is such permission, – while it lasts: nothing more can be said. Why does that hyssop grow there, in the chink of the wall? Because the whole Universe, sufficiently occupied otherwise, could not hitherto prevent its growing! It has the might and the right. By the same great law do Roman Empires establish themselves, Christian Religions promulgate themselves, and all extant Powers bear rule. The strong thing is the just thing: this thou wilt find throughout in our world; – as indeed was God and Truth the Maker of our world, or was Satan and Falsehood?

'One proposition widely current as to this Norman Conquest is of a Physiologic sort: That the conquerors and conquered here were of different races; nay that the Nobility of England is still, to this hour, of a somewhat different blood from the commonalty, their fine Norman features contrasting so pleasantly with the coarse Saxon ones of the others. God knows, there are coarse enough features to be seen among the commonalty of that country; but if the Nobility's be finer, it is not their Normanhood that can be the reason. Does the above Physiologist reflect who those same Normans, Northmen, originally were? Baltic Saxons, and what other miscellany of Lurdanes, Jutes and Deutsch Pirates from the East-sea marshes would join them in plunder of France! If living three centuries longer in Heathenism, sea-robbery, and the unlucrative fishing of amber could ennoble them beyond the others, then were they ennobled. The Normans were Saxons who had learned to speak French. No: by Thor and Wodan, the Saxons were all as noble as needful; – shaped, says the Mythus, "from the rock of the Harzgebirge;" brother-tribes being made of clay, wood, water, or what other material might be going! A stubborn, taciturn, sulky, indomitable rock-made race of men; as the figure they cut in all quarters, in the cane-brake of Arkansas, in the Ghauts of the Himmalaya, no less than in London City, in Warwick or Lancaster County, does still abundantly manifest.'

'To this English People in World-History, there have been, shall I prophesy, two grand tasks assigned? Huge-looming through the dim tumult of the always incommensurable Present Time, outlines of two tasks disclose themselves: the grand Industrial

task of conquering some half or more of this Terraqueous
Planet for the use of man; then secondly, the grand Constitutional task of sharing, in some pacific endurable manner, the
fruit of said conquest, and showing all people how it might
be done. These I will call their two tasks, discernible hitherto
in World-History; in both of these they have made respectable though unequal progress. Steamengines, ploughshares,
pickaxes; what is meant by conquering this Planet, they partly
know. Elective franchise, ballot-box, representative assembly;
how to accomplish sharing of that conquest, they do not so
well know. Europe knows not; Europe vehemently asks in
these days, but receives no answer, no credible answer. For as
to the partial Delolmish, Benthamee, or other French or English
answers,[60] current in the proper quarters, and highly beneficial
and indispensable there, thy belief in them as final answers, I
take it, is complete.'

'Succession of rebellions? Successive clippings away of the
Supreme Authority; class after class rising in revolt to say,
"We will no more be governed so"? That is not the history of
the English Constitution; not altogether that. Rebellion is the
means, but it is not the motive cause. The motive cause, and
true secret of the matter, were always this: The necessity there
was for rebelling?

'Rights I will permit thee to call everywhere "correctly-
articulated *mights*." A dreadful business to articulate correctly!
Consider those Barons of Runnymede; consider all manner of
successfully revolting men! Your Great Charter has to be
experimented on, by battle and debate, for a hundred-and-fifty
years; is then found to *be* correct; and stands as true *Magna
Charta*, – nigh cut in pieces by a tailor, short of measures, in
later generations. Mights, I say, are a dreadful business to
articulate correctly! Yet articulated they have to be; the time
comes for it, the need comes for it, and with enormous difficulty and experimenting it is got done. Call it not succession of
rebellions; call it rather succession of expansions, of enlightenment, gift of articulate utterance descending ever lower. Class
after class acquires faculty of utterance. – Necessity teaching

and compelling; as the dumb man, seeing the knife at his father's throat, suddenly acquired speech! Consider too how class after class not only acquires faculty of articulating what its might is, but likewise grows in might, acquires might or loses might; so that always, after a space, there is not only new gift of articulating, but there is something new to articulate. Constitutional epochs will never cease among men.

'And so now, the Barons all settled and satisfied, a new class hitherto silent had begun to speak: the Middle Class, namely. In the time of James First, not only Knights of the Shire but Parliamentary Burgesses assemble, to assert, to complain and propose; a real House of Commons has come decisively into play, – much to the astonishment of James First. We call it a growth of mights, if also of necessities; a growth of power to articulate mights, and make rights of them.

'In those past silent centuries, among those silent classes, much had been going on. Not only had red-deer in the New and other Forests been got preserved and shot; and treacheries of Simon de Montfort, wars of Red and White Roses, Battles of Crecy, Battles of Bosworth, and many other battles been got transacted and adjusted; but England wholly, not without sore toil and aching bones to the millions of sires and the millions of sons these eighteen generations, had been got drained and tilled, covered with yellow harvests, beautiful and rich possessions; the mud-wooden Caesters and Chesters had become steepled tile-roofed compact Towns. Sheffield had taken to the manufacture of Sheffield whittles; Worstead could from wool spin yarn, and knit or weave the same into stockings or breeches for men. England had property valuable to the auctioneer; but the accumulate manufacturing, commercial, economic *skill* which lay impalpably warehoused in English hands and heads, what auctioneer could estimate?

'Hardly an Englishman to be met with but could *do* something; some cunninger thing than break his fellow-creature's head with battle-axes. The seven incorporated trades, with their million guild-brethren, with their hammers, their shuttles and tools, what an army; – fit to conquer that land of England, as we say, and to hold it conquered! Nay, strangest of all, the

English people had acquired the faculty and habit of thinking, – even of believing: individual conscience had unfolded
itself among them; Conscience, and Intelligence its handmaid.
Ideas of innumerable kinds were circulating among these men:
witness one Shakspeare, a wool-comber, poacher, or whatever
else at Stratford in Warwickshire, who happened to write
books! The finest human figure, as I apprehend, that Nature
has hitherto seen fit to make of our widely diffused Teutonic
clay. Saxon, Norman, Celt or Sarmat,[61] I find no human soul so
beautiful, these fifteen-hundred known years; – our supreme
modern European man. Him England had contrived to realise:
were there not ideas?

'Ideas poetic and also Puritanic, – that had to seek utterance
in the notablest way! England had got her Shakspeare; but was
now about to get her Milton and Oliver Cromwell. This too we
will call a new expansion, hard as it might be to articulate and
adjust; this, that a man could actually have a Conscience for his
own behoof, and not for his Priest's only; that his Priest, be
who he might, would henceforth have to take that fact along
with him. One of the hardest things to adjust! It is not adjusted
down to this hour. It lasts onwards to the time they call "Glorious Revolution," before so much as a reasonable truce can be
made, and the war proceed by logic mainly. And still it is war,
and no peace, unless we call waste vacancy peace. But it needed
to be adjusted, as the others had done, as still others will do.
Nobility at Runnymede cannot endure foul-play grown palpable; no more can Gentry in Long Parliament; no more can
Commonalty in Parliament they name Reformed. Prynne's
bloody ears[62] were as a testimony and question to all England:
"Englishmen, is this fair?" England, no longer continent of herself, answered, bellowing as with the voice of lions: "No, it is
not fair!" '

'But now on the Industrial side, while this great Constitutional
controversy, and revolt of the Middle Class had not ended, had
yet but begun, what a shoot was that that England, carelessly,
in quest of other objects, struck out across the Ocean, into the
waste land which it named *New* England! Hail to thee, poor

little ship Mayflower, of Delft-Haven: poor common-looking ship, hired by common charterparty for coined dollars; caulked with mere oakum and tar; provisioned with vulgarest biscuit and bacon; – yet what ship Argo, or miraculous epic ship built by the Sea-Gods, was other than a foolish bumbarge in comparison![63] Golden fleeces or the like these sailed for, with or without effect; thou little Mayflower hadst in thee a veritable Promethean spark; the life-spark of the largest Nation on our Earth, – so we may already name the Transatlantic Saxon Nation. They went seeking leave to hear sermon in their own method, these Mayflower Puritans; a most honest indispensable search: and yet, like Saul the son of Kish, seeking a small thing, they found this unexpected great thing![64] Honour to the brave and true; they verily, we say, carry fire from Heaven, and have a power that themselves dream not of. Let all men honour Puritanism, since God has so honoured it. Islam itself, with its wild heartfelt "*Allah akbar*, God is great," was it not honoured? There is but one thing without honour; smitten with eternal barrenness, inability to do or be: Insincerity, Unbelief. He who believes no *thing*, who believes only the shows of things, is not in relation with Nature and Fact at all. Nature denies him; orders him at his earliest convenience to disappear. Let him disappear from her domains, – into those of Chaos, Hypothesis and Simulacrum, or wherever else his parish may be.'

'As to the Third Constitutional controversy, that of the Working Classes, which now debates itself everywhere these fifty years, in France specifically since 1789, in England too since 1831,[65] it is doubtless the hardest of all to get articulated: finis of peace, or even reasonable truce on this, is a thing I have little prospect of for several generations. Dark, wild-weltering, dreary, boundless; nothing heard on it yet but ballot-boxes, Parliamentary arguing; not to speak of much far worse arguing, by steel and lead, from Valmy[66] to Waterloo, to Peterloo! –

'And yet of Representative Assemblies may not this good be said: That contending parties in a country do thereby ascertain one another's strength? They fight there, since fight they must, by petition, Parliamentary eloquence, not by sword, bayonet

and bursts of military cannon. Why do men fight at all, if it be
not that they are yet unacquainted with one another's strength,
and must fight and ascertain it? Knowing that thou art stronger
than I, that thou canst compel me, I will submit to thee: unless
I chance to prefer extermination, and slightly circuitous suicide, there is no other course for me. That in England, by public
meetings, by petitions, by elections, leading-articles, and other
jangling hubbub and tongue-fence which perpetually goes on
everywhere in that country, people ascertain one another's
strength, and the most obdurate House of Lords has to yield
and give-in before it come to cannonading and guillotinement:
this is a saving characteristic of England. Nay, at bottom, is not
this the celebrated English Constitution itself? This *un*spoken
Constitution, whereof Privilege of Parliament, Money-Bill,
Mutiny-Bill, and all that could be spoken and enacted hitherto,
is not the essence and body, but only the shape and skin? Such
Constitution is, in our times, verily invaluable.'

'Long stormy spring-time, wet contentious April, winter chill-
ing the lap of very May; but at length the season of summer
does come. So long the tree stood naked; angry wiry naked
boughs moaning and creaking in the wind: you would say, Cut
it down, why cumbereth it the ground? Not so; we must wait;
all things will have their time. – Of the man Shakspeare, and
his Elizabethan Era, with its Sydneys, Raleighs, Bacons, what
could we say? That it was a spiritual flower-time. Suddenly, as
with the breath of June, your rude naked tree is touched; bursts
into leaves and flowers, *such* leaves and flowers. The past long
ages of nakedness, and wintry fermentation and elaboration,
have done their part, though seeming to do nothing. The past
silence has got a voice, all the more significant the longer it had
continued silent. In trees, men, institutions, creeds, nations, in
all things extant and growing in this Universe, we may note
such vicissitudes and budding-times. Moreover there are spiritual budding-times; and then also there are physical, appointed
to nations.

'Thus in the middle of that poor calumniated Eighteenth Century, see once more! Long winter again past, the dead-seeming

tree proves to be living, to have been always living; after motionless times, every bough shoots forth on the sudden, very strangely: – it now turns out that this favoured England was not only to have had her Shakspeares, Bacons, Sydneys, but to have her Watts, Arkwrights, Brindleys! We will honour greatness in all kinds. The Prospero evoked the singing of Ariel, and took captive the world with those melodies:[67] the same Prospero can send his Fire-demons panting across all oceans; shooting with the speed of meteors, on cunning highways, from end to end of kingdoms; and make Iron his missionary, preaching *its* evangel to the brute Primeval Powers, which listen and obey: neither is this small. Manchester, with its cotton-fuzz, its smoke and dust, its tumult and contentious squalor, is hideous to thee? Think not so: a precious substance, beautiful as magic dreams, and yet no dream but a reality, lies hidden in that noisome wrappage; – a wrappage struggling indeed (look at Chartisms and suchlike) to cast itself off, and leave the beauty free and visible there! Hast thou heard, with sound ears, the awakening of a Manchester, on Monday morning, at half-past five by the clock; the rushing-off of its thousand mills, like the boom of an Atlantic tide, ten-thousand times ten-thousand spools and spindles all set humming there, – it is perhaps if thou knew it well, sublime as a Niagara, or more so. Cotton-spinning is the clothing of the naked in its result; the triumph of man over matter in its means. Soot and despair are not the essence of it; they are divisible from it, – at this hour, are they not crying fiercely to be divided? The great Goethe, looking at cotton Switzerland, declared it, I am told, to be of all things that he had seen in this world the most poetical. Whereat friend Kanzler von Müller, in search of the palpable picturesque, could not but stare wide-eyed. Nevertheless our World-Poet knew well what he was saying.'

'Richard Arkwright, it would seem, was not a beautiful man; no romance-hero with haughty eyes, Apollo-lip, and gesture like the herald Mercury; a plain almost gross, bag-cheeked, pot-bellied Lancashire man, with an air of painful reflection, yet also of copious free digestion; – a man stationed by the community to shave certain dusty beards, in the Northern parts of England, at a halfpenny each. To such end, we say, by forethought, oversight, accident and arrangement, had Richard Arkwright been, by the community of England and his own consent, set apart. Nevertheless, in strapping of razors, in lathering of dusty beards, and the contradictions and confusions attendant thereon, the man had notions in that rough head of his; spindles, shuttles, wheels and contrivances plying ideally within the same: rather hopeless-looking; which, however, he did at last bring to bear. Not without difficulty! His townsfolk rose in mob round him, for threatening to shorten labour, to shorten wages; so that he had to fly, with broken washpots, scattered household, and seek refuge elsewhere. Nay his wife too, as I learn, rebelled; burnt his wooden model of his spinning-wheel; resolute that he should stick to his razors rather; – for which, however, he decisively, as thou wilt rejoice to understand, packed her out of doors. O reader, what a Historical Phenomenon is that bag-cheeked, potbellied, much-enduring, much-inventing barber! French Revolutions were a-brewing: to resist the same in any measure, imperial Kaisers were impotent without the cotton and cloth of England; and it was this man that had to give England the power of cotton.

'Neither had Watt of the Steamengine a heroic origin, any kindred with the princes of this world. The princes of this world were shooting their partridges; noisily, in Parliament or elsewhere, solving the question, Head or tail? while this man with blackened fingers, with grim brow, was searching out, in his workshop, the Fire-secret; or, having found it, was painfully wending to and fro in quest of a "moneyed man," as indispensable man-midwife of the same. Reader, thou shalt admire what is admirable, not what is dressed in admirable; learn to know the British lion even when he is not throne-supporter, and also the British jackass in lion's skin even when he is. Ah, couldst thou always, what a world were it! But has the Berlin Royal Academy or any English Useful-Knowledge Society discovered, for instance, who it was that first scratched earth with a stick; and threw *corns*, the biggest he could find, into it; seedgrains of a certain grass, which he named *white* or *wheat*? Again, what is the whole Tees-water and other breeding-world to him who stole home from the forests the first bison-calf, and bred it up to be a tame bison, a milk-cow? No machine of all they showed me in Birmingham can be put in comparison for ingenuity with that figure of the wedge named *knife*, of the wedges named *saw*, of the lever called *hammer*: – nay is it not with the hammer-knife, named *sword*, that men fight, and maintain any semblance of constituted authority that yet survives among us? The steamengine I call fire-demon and great but it is nothing to the invention of *fire*. Prometheus, Tubalcain, Triptolemus![68] Are not our greatest men as good as lost? The men that walk daily among us, clothing us, warming us, feeding us, walk shrouded in darkness, mere mythic men.

'It is said, ideas produce revolutions; and truly so they do; not spiritual ideas only, but even mechanical. In this clanging clashing universal Sword-dance that the European world now dances for the last half-century, Voltaire is but one choragus,[69] where Richard Arkwright is another. Let it dance itself out. When Arkwright shall have become mythic like Arachne,[70] we shall still spin in peaceable profit by him; and the Sword-dance, with all its sorrowful shufflings, Waterloo waltzes, Moscow gallopades, how forgotten will that be!'

'On the whole, were not all these things most unexpected, unforeseen? As indeed what thing is foreseen; especially what man, the parent of things! Robert Clive in that same time went out, with a developed gift of penmanship, as writer or superior book-keeper to a trading factory established in the distant East. With gift of penmanship developed; with other gifts not yet developed, which the calls of the case did by and by develop. Not fit for book-keeping alone, the man was found fit for con- quering Nawaubs, founding kingdoms, Indian Empires! In a questionable manner. Indian Empire from the other hemisphere took up its abode in Leadenhall Street, in the City of London.

'Accidental all these things and persons look, unexpected every one of them to man. Yet inevitable every one of them; foreseen, not unexpected, by Supreme Power; prepared, appointed from afar. Advancing always through all centuries, in the middle of the eighteenth they *arrived*. The Saxon kindred burst forth into cotton-spinning, cloth-cropping, iron-forging steamengineing, railwaying, commercing and careering towards all the winds of Heaven, in this inexplicable noisy manner; the noise of which, in Power-mills, in progress-of-the-species Magazines, still deafens us somewhat. Most noisy, sudden! The Staffordshire coal-stratum and coal-strata lay side by side with iron-strata, quiet since the creation of the world. Water flowed in Lancashire and Lanarkshire; bituminous fire lay bedded in rocks there too, – over which how many fighting Stanleys, black Douglasses, and other the like contentious persons, had fought out their bickerings and broils, not without result, we will hope! But God said, Let the iron missionaries be; and they were. Coal and iron, so long close unregardful neighbours, are wedded together; Birmingham and Wolverhampton, and the hundred Stygian forges, with their fire-throats and never-resting sledge-hammers, rose into day. Wet Manconium stretched out her hand towards Carolina and the torrid zone, and plucked cotton there; who could forbid her, that had the skill to weave it? Fish fled thereupon from the Mersey River, vexed with innumerable keels. England, I say, dug out her bitumen-fire, and bade it work: towns rose, and steeple-chimneys; – Chartisms also, and Parliaments they name Reformed.'

Such, figuratively given, are some prominent points, chief mountain-summits, of our English History past and present, according to the Author of this strange untranslated Work, whom we think we recognise to be an old acquaintance.

9. Parliamentary Radicalism

To us, looking at these matters somewhat in the same light, Reform-Bills, French Revolutions, Louis-Philippes, Chartisms, Revolts of Three Days, and what not, are no longer inexplicable. Where the great mass of men is tolerably right, all is right; where they are not right, all is wrong. The speaking classes speak and debate, each for itself; the great dumb, deep-buried class lies like an Enceladus,[71] who in his pain, if he will complain of it, has to produce earthquakes! Everywhere, in these countries, in these times, the central fact worthy of all consideration forces itself on us in this shape: the claim of the Free Working-man to be raised to a level, we may say, with the Working Slave; his anger and cureless discontent till that be done. Food, shelter, due guidance, in return for his labour: candidly interpreted, Chartism and all such *isms* mean that; and the madder they are, do they not the more emphatically mean, 'See what guidance you have given us! What delirium we are brought to talk and project, guided by nobody;' *Laissez-faire* on the part of the Governing Classes, we repeat again and again, will, with whatever difficulty, have to cease; pacific mutual division of the spoil, and a world well let alone, will no longer suffice. A Do-nothing Guidance; and it is a Do-something World! Would to God our Ducal *Duces* would become Leaders indeed; our Aristocracies and Priesthoods discover in some suitable degree what the world expected of them, what the world could no longer do without getting of them! Nameless unmeasured confusions, misery to themselves and us, might so be spared. But that too will be as God has appointed. If they learn, it will be well and happy: if not they, then others instead of them will and must, and once more, though after a long sad circuit, it will be well and happy.

Neither is the history of Chartism mysterious in these times; especially if that of Radicalism be looked at. All along, for the last five-and-twenty years, it was curious to note how the internal discontent of England struggled to find vent for itself through *any* orifice: the poor patient, all sick from centre to surface, complains now of this member, now of that; – corn-laws, currency-laws, free-trade, protection, want of free-trade: the poor patient tossing from side to side, seeking a sound side to lie on, finds none. This Doctor says, it is the liver; that other, it is the lungs, the head, the heart, defective transpiration in the skin. A thoroughgoing Doctor of eminence said, it was rotten boroughs; the want of extended suffrage to destroy rotten boroughs. From of old, the English patient himself had a continually recurring notion that this was it. The English people are used to suffrage; it is their panacea for all that goes wrong with them; they have a fixed-idea of suffrage. Singular enough: one's right to vote for a Member of Parliament, to send one's 'twenty-thousandth part of a master of tongue-fence to National Palaver,' – the Doctors asserted that this was Freedom, this and no other. It seemed credible to many men, of high degree and of low. The persuasion of remedy grew, the evil was pressing; Swing's ricks were on fire. Some nine years ago, a State-surgeon rose, and in peculiar circumstances said: Let there be extension of the suffrage; let the great Doctor's nostrum, the patient's old passionate prayer be fulfilled!

Parliamentary Radicalism, while it gave articulate utterance to the discontent of the English people, could not by its worst enemy be said to be without a function. If it is in the natural order of things that there must be discontent, no less so is it that such discontent should have an outlet, a Parliamentary voice. Here the matter is debated of, demonstrated, contradicted, qualified, reduced to feasibility; – can at least solace itself with hope, and die gently, convinced of *un*feasibility. The New, Untried ascertains how it will fit itself into the arrangements of the Old; whether the Old can be compelled to admit it; how in that case it may, with the minimum of violence, be admitted. Nor let us count it an easy one, this function of Radicalism; it was one of the most difficult. The pain-stricken patient does, indeed, without effort groan and complain; but not without effort does the physician ascertain what it is that has gone wrong with him, how some remedy may be devised for him. And above all, if your patient is not one sick man, but a whole sick nation! Dingy dumb millions, grimed with dust and sweat, with darkness, rage and sorrow, stood round these men, saying, or struggling as they could to say: 'Behold, our lot is unfair; our life is not whole but sick; we cannot live under injustice; go ye and get us justice!' For whether the poor operative clamoured for Time-bill, Factory-bill, Corn-bill, for or against whatever bill, this was what he meant. All bills plausibly presented might have some look of hope in them, might get some clamour of approval from him; as, for the man wholly sick, there is no disease in the Nosology[72] but he can trace in himself some symptoms of it. Such was the mission of Parliamentary Radicalism.

How Parliamentary Radicalism has fulfilled this mission, intrusted to its management these eight years now, is known to all men. The expectant millions have sat at a feast of the Barmecide;[73] been bidden fill themselves with the imagination of meat. What thing has Radicalism obtained for them; what other than shadows of things has it so much as asked for them? Cheap Justice, Justice to Ireland, Irish Appropriation-Clause, Ratepaying Clause, Poor-Rate, Church-Rate, Household Suffrage, Ballot-Question 'open' or shut: not things but shadows of things; Benthamee formulas; barren as the east-wind! An Ultra-radical, not seemingly of the Benthamee species, is forced to exclaim: 'The people are at last wearied. They say, Why should we be ruined in our shops, thrown out of our farms, voting for these men? Ministerial majorities decline; this Ministry has become impotent, had it even the will to do good. They have called long to us, "We are a Reform Ministry; will ye not support *us*?"[74] We have supported them; borne them forward indignantly on our shoulders, time after time, fall after fall, when they had been hurled out into the street; and lay prostrate, helpless, like dead luggage. It is the fact of a Reform

Ministry, not the name of one that we would support! Languor, sickness of hope deferred pervades the public mind; the public mind says at last, Why all this struggle for the *name* of a Reform Ministry? Let the Tories be Ministry if they will; let at least some living reality be Ministry! A rearing horse that will only run backward, he is not the horse one would choose to travel on: yet of all conceivable horses the worst is the dead horse. Mounted on a rearing horse, you may back him, spur him, check him, make a little way even backwards: but seated astride of your dead horse, what chance is there for you in the chapter of possibilities? You sit motionless, hopeless, a spectacle to gods and men.'

There is a class of revolutionists named *Girondins*, whose fate in history is remarkable enough! Men who rebel, and urge the Lower Classes to rebel, ought to have other than Formulas to go upon. Men who discern in the misery of the toiling complaining millions not misery, but only a raw-material which can be wrought upon and traded in, for one's own poor hidebound theories and egoisms; to whom millions of living fellow-creatures, with beating hearts in their bosoms, beating, suffering, hoping, are 'masses,' mere 'explosive masses for blowing-down Bastilles with,' for voting at hustings for *us*: such men are of the questionable species! No man is justified in resisting by word or deed the Authority he lives under, for a light cause, be such Authority what it may. Obedience, little as many may consider that side of the matter, is the primary duty of man. No man but is bound indefeasibly, with all force of obligation, to obey. Parents, teachers, superiors, leaders, these all creatures recognise as deserving obedience. Recognised or not recognised, a man *has* his superiors, a regular hierarchy above him; extending up, degree above degree, to Heaven itself and God the Maker, who made His world not for anarchy but for rule and order! It is not a light matter when the just man can recognise in the powers set over him no longer anything that is divine; when resistance against such becomes a deeper law of order than obedience to them; when the just man sees himself in the tragical position of a stirrer-up of strife! Rebel without due and most due cause, is the ugliest of words; the first rebel was Satan. –

But now in these circumstances shall we blame the unvoting disappointed millions that they turn away with horror from this name of a Reform Ministry, name of a Parliamentary Radicalism, and demand a fact and reality thereof? That they too, having still faith in what so many had faith in, still count 'extension of the suffrage' the one thing needful; and say, in such manner as they can, Let the suffrage be still extended, *then* all will be well? It is the ancient British faith; promulgated in these ages by prophets and evangelists; preached forth from barrel-heads by all manner of men. He who is free and blessed has his twenty-thousandth part of a master of tongue-fence in National Palaver; whosoever is not blessed but unhappy, the ailment of him is that he has it not. Ought he not to have it, then? By the law of God and of men, yea; – and will have it withal! Chartism, with its 'five points,' borne aloft on pike-heads and torchlight meetings, is there. Chartism is one of the most natural phenomena in England. Not that Chartism now exists should provoke wonder; but that the invited hungry people should have sat eight years at such table of the Barmecide, patiently expecting somewhat from the Name of a Reform Ministry, and not till after eight years have grown hopeless, this is the respectable side of the miracle.

10. Impossible

'But what are we to do?' exclaims the practical man, impatiently on every side: 'Descend from speculation and the safe pulpit, down into the rough market-place, and say what can be done!' – O practical man, there seem very many things which practice and true manlike effort, in Parliament and out of it, might actually avail to do. But the first of all things, as already said, is to gird thyself up for actual doing; to know that thou actually either must do, or, as the Irish say, 'come out of that!'

It is not a lucky word this same *impossible*: no good comes of those that have it so often in their mouth. Who is he that says always, There is a lion in the way? Sluggard, thou must slay the lion, then; the way has to be travelled! In Art, in Practice, innumerable critics will demonstrate that most things are henceforth impossible; that we are got, once for all, into the region of perennial commonplace, and must contentedly continue there. Let such critics demonstrate; it is the nature of them: what harm is in it? Poetry once well demonstrated to be impossible, arises the Burns, arises the Goethe. Unheroic commonplace being now clearly all we have to look for, comes the Napoleon, comes the conquest of the world. It was proved by fluxionary calculus,[75] that steamships could never get across from the farthest point of Ireland to the nearest of Newfoundland: impelling force, resisting force, maximum here, minimum there; by law of Nature, and geometric demonstration: – what could be done? The Great Western could weigh anchor from Bristol Port;[76] that could be done. The Great Western, bounding safe through the gullets of the Hudson, threw her cable out on the capstan of New York, and left our still moist paper-demonstration to dry itself at leisure. 'Impossible?' cried Mirabeau to his secretary, '*Ne me dites jamais ce bête de mot*, Never name to me that blockhead of a word!'

There is a phenomenon which one might call Paralytic Radicalism, in these days; which gauges with Statistic measuring-reed, sounds with Philosophic Politico-Economic plummet the deep dark sea of troubles; and having taught us rightly what an infinite sea of troubles it is, sums-up with the practical inference, and use of consolation, That nothing whatever can be done in it by man, who has simply to sit still, and look wistfully to 'time and general laws:' and thereupon, without so much as recommending suicide, coldly takes its leave of us. Most paralytic, uninstructive; unproductive of any comfort to one! They are an unreasonable class who cry, 'Peace, peace,' when there *is* no peace. But what kind of class are they who cry, 'Peace, peace, have I not *told you* that there is no peace!' Paralytic Radicalism, frequent among those Statistic friends of ours, is one of the most afflictive phenomena the mind of man can be called to contemplate. One prays that *it* at least might cease. Let Paralysis retire into secret places, and dormitories proper for it; the public highways ought not to be occupied by people demonstrating that motion is impossible. Paralytic; – and also, thank Heaven, entirely false! Listen to a thinker of another sort: 'All evil, and this evil too, is as a nightmare; the instant you begin to *stir* under it, the *evil* is, properly speaking, gone.' Consider, O reader, whether it be not actually so? Evil, once manfully fronted, ceases to be evil; there is generous battle-hope in place of dead passive misery; the evil itself has become a kind of good.

To the practical man, therefore, we will repeat that he has, as the first thing he can 'do,' to gird himself up for actual doing; to know well that he is either there to do, or not there at all. Once rightly girded up, how many things will present themselves as doable which now are not attemptable! Two things, great things, dwell, for the last ten years, in all thinking heads in England; and are hovering, of late, even on the tongues of not a few. With a word on each of these, we will dismiss the practical

man, and right gladly take ourselves into obscurity and silence
again. Universal Education is the first great thing we mean;
general Emigration is the second.

Who would suppose that Education were a thing which had to
be advocated on the ground of local expediency, or indeed on
any ground? As if it stood not on the basis of everlasting duty,
as a prime necessity of man. It is a thing that should need no
advocating; much as it does actually need. To impart the gift of
thinking to those who cannot think, and yet who could in that
case think: this, one would imagine, was the first function a
government had to set about discharging. Were it not a cruel
thing to see, in any province of an empire, the inhabitants living all mutilated in their limbs, each strong man with his right
arm lamed? How much crueler to find the strong soul, with its
eyes still sealed, its eyes extinct so that it sees not! Light has
come into the world, but to this poor peasant it has come in
vain. For six thousand years the Sons of Adam, in sleepless effort,
have been devising, doing, discovering; in mysterious infinite
indissoluble communion, warring, a little band of brothers,
against the great black empire of Necessity and Night; they
have accomplished such a conquest and conquests: and to this
man it is all as if it had not been. The four-and-twenty letters of
the Alphabet are still Runic enigmas to him. He passes by on
the other side; and that great Spiritual Kingdom, the toilwon
conquest of his own brothers, all that his brothers have conquered, is a thing non-extant for him. An invisible empire; he
knows it not, suspects it not. And is it not his withal; the conquest of his own brothers, the lawfully acquired possession of
all men? Baleful enchantment lies over him, from generation to
generation; he knows not that such an empire is his, that such
an empire is at all. O, what are bills of rights, emancipations of
black slaves into black apprentices, lawsuits in chancery for
some short usufruct of a bit of land? The grand 'seedfield of
Time' is this man's, and you give it him not. Time's seedfield,
which includes the Earth and all her seedfields and pearl-oceans,
nay her sowers too and pearl-divers, all that was wise and heroic
and victorious here below; of which the Earth's centuries are

but as furrows, for it stretches forth from the Beginning onward even into this Day!

> 'My inheritance, how lordly wide and fair;
> Time is my fair seedfield, to Time I'm heir!' –[77]

Heavier wrong is not done under the sun. It lasts from year to year, from century to century; the blinded sire slaves himself out, and leaves a blinded son; and men, made in the image of God, continue as two-legged beasts of labour; – and in the largest empire of the world, it is a debate whether a small fraction of the Revenue of one Day[78] (30,000*l.* is but that) shall, after Thirteen Centuries, be laid out on it, or not laid out on it. Have we Governors, have we Teachers; have we had a Church these thirteen hundred years? What is an Overseer of souls, an Archoverseer, Archiepiscopus? Is he something? If so, let him lay his hand on his heart, and say what thing!

But quitting all that, of which the human soul cannot well speak in terms of civility, let us observe now that Education is not only an eternal duty, but has at length become even a temporary and ephemeral one, which the necessities of the hour will oblige us to look after. These Twenty-four million labouring men, if their affairs remain unregulated, chaotic, will burn ricks and mills; reduce us, themselves and the world into ashes and ruin. Simply their affairs cannot remain unregulated, chaotic; but must be regulated, brought into some kind of order. What intellect were able to regulate them? The intellect of a Bacon, the energy of a Luther, if left to their own strength, might pause in dismay before such a task; a Bacon and Luther added together, to be perpetual prime minister over us, could not do it. No one great and greatest intellect can do it. What can? Only Twenty-four million ordinary intellects, once awakened into action; these, well presided over, may. Intellect, insight, is the discernment of order in disorder; it is the discovery of the will of Nature, of God's will; the beginning of the capability to walk according to that. With perfect intellect, were such possible without perfect morality, the world would be perfect; its efforts unerringly correct, its results continually successful, its condition faultless. Intellect is like light; the Chaos becomes a World under it: *fiat lux*. These Twenty-four million intellects are but common intellects; but they are intellects; in earnest about the matter, instructed each about his own province of it; labouring each perpetually, with what partial light can be attained, to bring such province into rationality. From the partial determinations and their conflict springs the universal. Precisely what quantity of intellect was in the Twenty-four millions will be exhibited by the result they arrive at; that quantity and no more. According as there was intellect or no intellect in the individuals, will the general conclusion they make-out embody itself as a world-healing Truth and Wisdom, or as a baseless fateful Hallucination, a Chimæra breathing *not* fabulous fire!

Dissenters call for one scheme of Education, the Church objects;[79] this party objects, and that; there is endless objection, by him and by her and by it: a subject encumbered with difficulties on every side! Pity that difficulties exist; that Religion, of all things, should occasion difficulties. We do not extenuate them: in their reality they are considerable; in their appearance and pretension, they are insuperable, heart-appalling to all Secretaries of the Home Department. For, in very truth, how can Religion be divorced from Education? An irreverent knowledge is no knowledge; may be a development of the logical or other handicraft faculty inward or outward; but is no culture of the soul of a man. A knowledge that ends in barren self-worship, comparative indifference or contempt for all God's Universe except one insignificant item thereof, what is it? Handicraft development, and even shallow as handicraft. Nevertheless is handicraft itself, and the habit of the merest logic, nothing? It is already something; it is the indispensable beginning of everything! Wise men know it to be an indispensable something; not yet much; and would so gladly superadd to it the element whereby it may become all. Wise men would not quarrel in attempting this; they would lovingly cooperate in attempting it.

'And now how teach religion?' so asks the indignant Ultra-radical, cited above; an Ultra-radical seemingly not of the

Benthamee species, with whom, though his dialect is far different, there are sound Churchmen, we hope, who have some fellow-feeling: 'How teach religion? By plying with liturgies, catechisms, credos; droning thirty-nine or other articles incessantly into the infant ear? Friends! In that case, why not apply to Birmingham, and have Machines made, and set-up at all street-corners, in highways and byways, to repeat and vociferate the same, not ceasing night or day? The genius of Birmingham is adequate to that. Albertus Magnus had a leather man that could articulate; not to speak of Martinus Scriblerus' Nürnberg man[80] that could reason as well as we know who! Depend upon it, Birmingham can make machines to repeat liturgies and articles; to do whatsoever feat is mechanical. And what were all schoolmasters, nay all priests and churches, compared with this Birmingham Iron Church! Votes of two millions in aid of the Church were then something. You order, at so many pounds a-head, so many thousand iron parsons as your grant covers; and fix them by satisfactory masonry in all quarters wheresoever wanted, to preach there independent of the world. In loud thoroughfares, still more in unawakened districts, troubled with argumentative infidelity, you make the windpipes wider, strengthen the main steam-cylinder; your parson preaches, to the due pitch, while you give him coal; and fears no man or thing. Here *were* a 'Church-extension;' to which I, with my last penny, did I believe in it, would subscribe.–

'Ye blind leaders of the blind! Are we Calmucks, that pray by turning of a rotatory calabash with written prayers in it? Is Mammon and machinery the means of converting human souls, as of spinning cotton? Is God, as Jean Paul[81] predicted it would be, become verily a Force; the Æther too a Gas! Alas, that Atheism should have got the length of putting on priests' vestments, and penetrating into the sanctuary itself! Can dronings of articles, repetitions of liturgies, and all the cash and contrivance of Birmingham and the Bank of England united bring ethereal fire into a human soul, quicken it out of earthly darkness into heavenly wisdom? Soul is kindled only by soul. To "teach" religion, the first thing needful, and also the last and the only thing, is finding of a man who *has* religion. All else follows from this, church-building, church-extension, what-ever else is needful follows; without this nothing will follow.'

From which we for our part conclude that the method of teaching religion to the English people is still far behind-hand; that the wise and pious may well ask themselves in silence wist-fully, 'How *is* that last priceless element, by which education becomes perfect, to be superadded?' and the unwise who think themselves pious, answering aloud, 'By this method, By that method,' long argue of it to small purpose.

But now, in the mean time, could not, by some fit official person, some fit announcement be made, in words well-weighed, in plan well-schemed, adequately representing the facts of the thing, That after thirteen centuries of waiting, he the official person, and England with him, was minded now to have the mystery of the Alphabetic Letters imparted to all human souls in this realm? Teaching of religion was a thing he could not undertake to settle this day; it would be work for a day after this; the work of this day was teaching of the alphabet to all people. The miraculous art of reading and writing, such seemed to him the needful preliminary of all teaching, the first corner-stone of what foundation soever could be laid for what edifice soever, in the teaching kind. Let pious Churchism make haste, let pious Dissenterism make haste, let all pious preach-ers and missionaries make haste, bestir themselves according to their zeal and skill: he the official person stood up for the Alphabet; and was even impatient for it, having waited thirteen centuries now. He insisted, and would take no denial, post-ponement, promise, excuse or subterfuge, That all English persons should be taught to read. He appealed to all rational Englishmen, of all creeds, classes and colours, Whether this was not a fair demand; nay whether it was not an indispensable one in these days, Swing and Chartism having risen? For a choice of inoffensive Hornbooks, and Schoolmasters able to teach reading, he trusted the mere secular sagacity of a National Collective Wisdom, in proper committee, might be found suffi-cient. He purposed to appoint such Schoolmasters, to venture on the choice of such Hornbooks; to send a Schoolmaster and Hornbook into every township, parish and hamlet of England;

so that, in ten years hence, an Englishman who could not read might be acknowledged as the monster, which he really is!

This official person's plan we do not give. The *thing* lies there, with the facts of it, and with the appearances or sham-facts of it; a plan adequately representing the facts of the thing could by human energy be struck out, does lie there for discovery and striking out. It is his, the official person's duty, not ours, to mature a plan. We can believe that Churchism and Dissenterism would clamour aloud; but yet that in the mere secular Wisdom of Parliament a perspicacity equal to the choice of Hornbooks might, in very deed, be found to reside. England we believe would, if consulted, resolve to that effect. Alas, grants of a half-day's revenue once in the thirteen centuries for such an object, do not call-out the voice of England, only the superficial clamour of England! Hornbooks unexceptionable to the candid portion of England, we will believe, might be selected. Nay, we can conceive that Schoolmasters fit to teach reading might, by a board of rational men, whether from Oxford or Hoxton,[82] or from both or neither of these places, be pitched upon. We can conceive even, as in Prussia, that a penalty, civil disabilities, that penalties and disabilities till they were found effectual, might be by law inflicted on every parent who did not teach his children to read, on every man who had not been taught to read. We can conceive, in fine, such is the vigour of our imagination, there might be found in England, at a dead-lift, strength enough to perform this miracle, and produce it henceforth as a miracle done: the teaching of England to read! Harder things, we do know, have been performed by nations before now, not abler-looking than England.

Ah me! if, by some beneficent chance, there should be an official man found in England who could and would, with deliberate courage, after ripe counsel, with candid insight, with patience, practical sense, knowing realities to be real, knowing clamours to be clamorous and to seem real, propose this thing, and the innumerable things springing from it, – woe to any Churchism or any Dissenterism that cast itself athwart the path of that man! Avaunt, ye gainsayers! is darkness and ignorance of the Alphabet necessary for you? Reconcile yourselves to the

Alphabet, or depart elsewhither! – Would not all that has genu-
ineness in England gradually rally round such a man; all that
has strength in England? For realities alone have strength;
wind-bags are wind; cant is cant, leave it alone there. Nor are
all clamours momentous; among living creatures, we find, the
loudest is the longest-eared; among lifeless things, the loudest is
the drum, the emptiest. Alas, that official persons, and all of us,
had not eyes to see what was real, what was merely chimerical,
and thought or called itself real! How many dread minatory
Castle-spectres should we leave there, with their admonishing
right-hand and ghastly-burning saucer-eyes, to do simply whatsoever they might find themselves able to do! Alas, that we
were not real ourselves; we should otherwise have surer vision
for the real. Castle-spectres, in their utmost terror, are but poor
mimicries of that real and most real terror which lies in the Life
of every Man: that, thou coward, is the thing to be afraid of, if
thou wilt live in fear. It is but the scratch of a bare bodkin; it is
but the flight of a few days of time; and even thou, poor palpi-
tating featherbrain, wilt find how real it is. ETERNITY: hast
thou heard of that? Is that a fact, or is it no fact? Are Bucking-
ham House and St Stephen's *in* that, or not in that?

But now we have to speak of the second great thing: Emigration. It was said above, all new epochs, so convulsed and
tumultuous to look upon, are 'expansions,' increase of faculty
not yet organised. It is eminently true of the confusions of this
time of ours. Disorganic Manchester afflicts us with its Chartisms; yet is not spinning of clothes for the naked intrinsically a
most blessed thing? Manchester once organic will bless and not
afflict. The confusions, if we would understand them, are at
bottom mere increase which we know not yet how to manage;
'new wealth which the old coffers will not hold.' How true is this,
above all, of the strange phenomenon called 'over-population'!
Over-population is the grand anomaly, which is bringing all
other anomalies to a crisis. Now once more, as at the end of the
Roman Empire, a most confused epoch and yet one of the
greatest, the Teutonic Countries find themselves too full. On a
certain western rim of our small Europe, there are more men

than were expected. Heaped up against the western shore there, and for a couple of hundred miles inward, the 'tide of population' swells too high, and confuses itself somewhat! Over-population? And yet, if this small western rim of Europe is overpeopled, does not everywhere else a whole vacant Earth, as it were, call to us, Come and till me, come and reap me! Can it be an evil that in an Earth such as ours there should be new Men? Considered as mercantile commodities, as working machines, is there in Birmingham or out of it a machine of such value? 'Good Heavens! a white European Man, standing on his two legs, with his two five-fingered Hands at his shackle-bones, and miraculous Head on his shoulders, is worth something considerable, one would say!' The stupid black African man brings money in the market; the much stupider four-footed horse brings money; – it is we that have not yet learned the art of managing our white European man!

The controversies on Malthus and the 'Population Principle,'[83] 'Preventive check' and so forth, with which the public ear has been deafened for a long while, are indeed sufficiently mournful. Dreary, stolid, dismal, without hope for this world or the next, is all that of the preventive check and the denial of the preventive check. Anti-Malthusians quoting their Bible against palpable facts are not a pleasant spectacle. On the other hand, how often have we read in Malthusian benefactors of the species: 'The working people have their condition in their own hands; let them diminish the supply of labourers, and of course the demand and the remuneration will increase!' Yes, let *them* diminish the supply: but who are they? They are twenty-four millions of human individuals, scattered over a hundred and eighteen thousand square miles of space and more; weaving, delving, hammering, joinering; each unknown to his neighbour; each distinct within his own skin. *They* are not a kind of character that can take a resolution, and act on it, very readily. Smart Sally in our alley proves all-too fascinating to brisk Tom in yours: can Tom be called on to make pause, and calculate the demand for labour in the British Empire first? Nay, if Tom did renounce his highest blessedness of life, and struggle and conquer like a Saint Francis of Assisi,[84] what would it profit him or us? Seven millions of the finest peasantry do not renounce, but proceed all the more briskly; and with blue-visaged Hibernians instead of fair Saxon Tomsons and Sallysons, the latter end of that country is worse than the beginning. O wonderful Malthusian prophets! Millenniums are undoubtedly coming, must come one way or the other: but will it be, think you, by twenty millions of working people simultaneously striking work in that department; passing, in universal trades-union, a resolution not to beget any more till the labour-market become satisfactory? By Day and Night! they were indeed irresistible so; not to be compelled by law or war; might make their own terms with the richer classes, and defy the world!

A shade more rational is that of those other benefactors of the species, who counsel that in each parish, in some central locality, instead of the Parish Clergyman, there might be established some Parish Exterminator; or say a Reservoir of Arsenic, kept up at the public expense, free to all parishioners; for *which* Church the rates probably would not be grudged. – Ah, it is bitter jesting on such a subject. One's heart is sick to look at the dreary chaos, and valley of Jehosaphat,[85] scattered with the limbs and souls of one's fellow-men; and no divine voice, only creaking of hungry vultures, inarticulate bodeful ravens, horn-eyed parrots that do articulate, proclaiming, Let these bones live!

Dante's *Divina Commedia* is called the mournfulest of books: transcendent mistemper of the noblest soul; utterance of a boundless, godlike, unspeakable, implacable sorrow and protest against the world. But in Holywell Street, not long ago, we bought, for three-pence, a book still mournfuler: the Pamphlet of one 'Marcus,' whom his poor Chartist editor and republisher calls the 'Demon Author.' This *Marcus* Pamphlet was the book alluded to by Stephens the Preacher Chartist,[86] in one of his harangues: it proves to be no fable that such a book existed; here it lies, 'Printed by John Hill, Black-horse Court, Fleet Street, and now reprinted for the instruction of the labourer, by William Dugdale, Holywell street, Strand,' the exasperated Chartist editor who sells it you for three-pence. We have read Marcus; but his sorrow is not divine. We hoped he would turn out to have been in sport: ah no, it is grim earnest with him; grim as very death. Marcus is not a demon author at all: he is a benefactor of the species in his own kind; has looked intensely on the world's woes, from a Benthamee-Malthusian watch-tower, under a Heaven dead as iron; and does now, with much longwindedness, in a drawling, snuffling, circuitous, extremely dull, yet at bottom handfast and positive manner, recommend that all children of working people, after the third, be disposed of by 'painless extinction.' Charcoal-vapour and other methods exist. The mothers would consent, might be made to consent. Three children might be left living; or perhaps, for Marcus's calculations are not yet perfect, two and a half. There might be 'beautiful cemeteries with colonnades and flower-plots,' in which the patriot infanticide matrons might delight to take their evening walk of contemplation; and reflect what patriotesses they were, what a cheerful flowery world it was.

Such is the scheme of Marcus; this is what he, for his share, could devise to heal the world's woes. A benefactor of the species, clearly recognisable as such: the saddest scientific mortal we have ever in this world fallen in with; sadder even than poetic Dante. His is a *no*-godlike sorrow; sadder than the god-like. The Chartist editor, dull as he, calls him demon author, and a man set-on by the Poor-Law Commissioners. What a black, godless, waste-struggling world, in this once merry England of ours, do such pamphlets and such editors betoken! *Laissez-faire* and Malthus, Malthus and *Laissez-faire*: ought not *these* two at length to part company? Might we not hope that both of them had as good as delivered their message now, and were about to go their ways?

For all this of the 'painless extinction,' and the rest is in a world where Canadian Forests stand unfelled, boundless Plains and Prairies unbroken with the plough; on the west and on the east green desert spaces never yet made white with corn; and to the overcrowded little western nook of Europe, our Terrestrial Planet, nine-tenths of it yet vacant or tenanted by nomades, is still crying, Come and till me, come and reap me! And in an England with wealth, and means for moving, such as no nation ever before had. With ships; with war-ships rotting idle, which, but bidden move and not rot, might bridge all oceans. With trained men, educated to pen and practise, to administer and act; briefless Barristers, chargeless Clergy, taskless Scholars, languishing in all court-houses, hiding in obscure garrets, besieging all antechambers, in passionate want of simply one thing, Work; – with as many Half-pay Officers of both Services, wearing themselves down in wretched tedium, as might lead an Emigrant host larger than Xerxes' was![87] *Laissez-faire* and Malthus positively must part company. Is it not as if this swelling, simmering, never-resting Europe of ours stood, once more, on the verge of an expansion without parallel; struggling, struggling like a mighty tree again about to burst in the embrace of summer, and shoot forth broad frondent boughs which would fill the whole earth? A disease; but the noblest of all – as of her who is in pain and sore travail, but travails that she may be a mother, and say, Behold, there is a new Man born!

'True thou Gold-Hofrath,' exclaims an eloquent satirical German of our acquaintance, in that strange Book of his,[88] 'True thou Gold-Hofrath: too crowded indeed! Meanwhile what portion of this inconsiderable Terraqueous Globe have ye actually tilled and delved, till it will grow no more? How thick stands your population in the Pampas and Savannas of America; round ancient Carthage, and in the interior of Africa; on both slopes of the Altaic chain, in the central Platform of Asia; in Spain, Greece, Turkey, Crim Tartary, the Curragh of Kildare? One man, in one year, as I have understood it, if you lend him earth, will feed himself and nine others. Alas, where now are the Hengsts and Alarics[89] of our still-glowing, still-expanding Europe; who, when their home is grown too narrow, will enlist and, like fire-pillars, guide onwards those superfluous masses of indomitable living Valour; equipped, not now with the battle-axe and war-chariot, but with the steam engine and ploughshare? Where are they? – Preserving their Game!'

from Heroes and Hero-Worship

In May 1840 Carlyle delivered a course of six lectures which were published in 1841 under the title *On Heroes, Hero-Worship, and the Heroic in History*. Although Carlyle's public lectures attracted considerable attention, and his rhetorical style seems well suited to such a medium, he disliked lecturing intensely because of the mental stress it caused him. *Heroes and Hero-Worship* was in fact his last course of public lectures, and the only one to appear in print.

The theme of *Heroes and Hero-Worship* is defined at the outset: 'Universal History, the history of what man has accomplished in this world, is at bottom the History of the Great Men who have worked here.' According to Carlyle, belief in utilitarianism has led to 'A bewildering, inextricable jungle of delusions, confusions, falsehoods and absurdities' which only a new 'Hero' can resolve. The lectures themselves are devoted to the heroes of the past, who are classified into six different kinds, and form an interesting, if somewhat random, indication of Carlyle's predilections – Odin, Mahomet, Dante, Shakespeare, Luther, John Knox, Johnson, Rousseau, Burns, Cromwell and Napoleon. The passage reprinted here is the first part of the fifth lecture, 'The Hero as Man of Letters'.

from The Hero as Man of Letters*

Hero-Gods, Prophets, Poets, Priests are forms of Heroism that belong to the old ages, make their appearance in the remotest times; some of them have ceased to be possible long since, and cannot any more show themselves in this world. The Hero as *Man of Letters*, again, of which class we are to speak today, is altogether a product of these new ages; and so long as the wondrous art of *Writing*, or of Ready-writing, which we call *Printing*, subsists, he may be expected to continue, as one of the main forms of Heroism for all future ages. He is, in various respects, a very singular phenomenon.

He is new, I say; he has hardly lasted above a century in the world yet. Never, till about a hundred years ago, was there seen any figure of a Great Soul living apart in that anomalous manner; endeavouring to speak-forth the inspiration that was in him by Printed Books, and find place and subsistence by what the world would please to give him for doing that. Much had been sold and bought, and left to make its own bargain in the marketplace; but the inspired wisdom of a Heroic Soul never till then, in that naked manner. He, with his copy-rights and copy-wrongs, in his squalid garret, in his rusty coat; ruling (for this is what he does), from his grave, after death, whole nations and generations who would, or would not, give him bread while living, – is a rather curious spectacle! Few shapes of Heroism can be more unexpected.

Alas, the Hero from of old has had to cramp himself into strange shapes: the world knows not well at any time what to

* Lecture 5.

do with him, so foreign is his aspect in the world! It seemed absurd to us, that men, in their rude admiration, should take some wise great Odin for a god, and worship him as such; some wise great Mahomet for one god-inspired, and religiously follow his Law for twelve centuries: but that a wise great Johnson, a Burns, a Rousseau, should be taken for some idle nondescript, extant in the world to amuse idleness, and have a few coins and applauses thrown him, that he might live thereby; *this* perhaps, as before hinted, will one day seem a still absurder phasis of things! – Meanwhile, since it is the spiritual always that determines the material, this same Man-of-Letters Hero must be regarded as our most important modern person. He, such as he may be, is the soul of all. What he teaches, the whole world will do and make. The world's manner of dealing with him is the most significant feature of the world's general position. Looking well at his life, we may get a glance, as deep as is readily possible for us, into the life of those singular centuries which have produced him, in which we ourselves live and work.

There are genuine Men of Letters, and not genuine; as in every kind there is a genuine and a spurious. If *Hero* be taken to mean genuine, then I say the Hero as Man of Letters will be found discharging a function for us which is ever honourable, ever the highest; and was once well known to be the highest. He is uttering-forth, in such way as he has, the inspired soul of him; all that a man, in any case, can do. I say *inspired*; for what we call 'originality,' 'sincerity,' 'genius,' the heroic quality we have no good name for, signifies that. The Hero is he who lives in the inward sphere of things, in the True, Divine and Eternal, which exists always, unseen to most, under the Temporary, Trivial: his being is in that; he declares that abroad, by act or speech as it may be, in declaring himself abroad. His life, as we said before, is a piece of the everlasting heart of Nature herself: all men's life is, – but the weak many know not the fact, and are untrue to it, in most times; the strong few are strong, heroic, perennial, because it cannot be hidden from them. The Man of Letters, like every Hero, is there to proclaim this in such sort as he can. Intrinsically it is the same function which the old generations named a man Prophet, Priest, Divinity for doing; which all manner of Heroes, by speech or by act, are sent into the world to do.

Fichte the German Philosopher delivered, some forty years ago at Erlangen, a highly remarkable Course of Lectures on this subject: '*Ueber das Wessen des Gelehrten*, On the Nature of the Literary Man.' Fichte, in conformity with the Transcendental Philosophy, of which he was a distinguished teacher, declares first: That all things which we see or work with in this Earth, especially we ourselves and all persons, are as a kind of vesture or sensuous Appearance: that under all there lies, as the essence of them, what he calls the 'Divine Idea of the World;' this is the Reality which 'lies at the bottom of all Appearance.' To the mass of men no such Divine Idea is recognisable in the world; they live merely, says Fichte, among the superficialities, practicalities and shows of the world, not dreaming that there is anything divine under them. But the Man of Letters is sent hither specially that he may discern for himself, and make manifest to us, this same Divine Idea: in every new generation it will manifest itself in a new dialect; and he is there for the purpose of doing that. Such is Fichte's phraseology; with which we need not quarrel. It is his way of naming what I here, by other words, am striving imperfectly to name; what there is at present no name for: The unspeakable Divine Significance, full of splendour, of wonder and terror, that lies in the being of every man, of every thing, – the Presence of the God who made every man and thing. Mahomet taught this in his dialect; Odin in his: it is the thing which all thinking hearts, in one dialect or another, are here to teach.

Fichte calls the Man of Letters, therefore, a Prophet, or as he prefers to phrase it, a Priest, continually unfolding the Godlike to men: Men of Letters are a perpetual Priesthood, from age to age, teaching all men that a God is still present in their life; that all 'Appearance,' whatsoever we see in the world, is but as a vesture for the 'Divine Idea of the World,' for 'that which lies at the bottom of Appearance.' In the true Literary Man there is thus ever, acknowledged or not by the world, a sacredness: he is the light of the world; the world's Priest; – guiding it, like a sacred Pillar of Fire, in its dark pilgrimage through the waste of Time. Fichte discriminates with sharp zeal the *true* Literary Man, what we here call the *Hero* as Man of Letters, from multitudes of false unheroic. Whoever lives not wholly in this Divine Idea, or living partially in it, struggles not, as for the one good, to live wholly in it, – he is, let him live where else he like, in what pomps and prosperities he like, no Literary Man; he is, says Fichte, a 'Bungler, *Stümper*.' Or at best, if he belong to the prosaic provinces, he may be a 'Hodman;' Fichte even calls him elsewhere a 'Nonentity,' and has in short no mercy for him, no wish that *he* should continue happy among us! This is Fichte's notion of the Man of Letters. It means, in its own form, precisely what we here mean.

In this point of view, I consider that, for the last hundred years, by far the notablest of all Literary Men is Fichte's countryman, Goethe. To that man too, in a strange way, there was given what we may call a life in the Divine Idea of the World; vision of the inward divine mystery: and strangely, out of his Books, the world rises imaged once more as godlike, the workmanship and temple of a God. Illuminated all, not in fierce impure fire-splendour as of Mahomet,[1] but in mild celestial radiance; – really a Prophecy in these most unprophetic times; to my mind, by far the greatest, though one of the quietest, among all the great things that have come to pass in them. Our chosen specimen of the Hero as Literary Man would be this Goethe. And it were a very pleasant plan for me here to discourse of his heroism: for I consider him to be a true Hero; heroic in what he said and did, and perhaps still more in what he did not say and did not do; to me a noble spectacle: a great heroic ancient man, speaking and keeping silence as an ancient Hero, in the guise of a most modern, high-bred, high-cultivated Man of Letters! We have had no such spectacle; no man capable of affording such, for the last hundred-and-fifty years.

But at present, such is the general state of knowledge about Goethe, it were worse than useless to attempt speaking of him in this case. Speak as I might, Goethe, to the great majority of you, would remain problematic, vague; no impression but a false one could be realised. Him we must leave to future times.

Johnson, Burns, Rousseau, three great figures from a prior time, from a far inferior state of circumstances, will suit us better here. Three men of the Eighteenth Century; the conditions of their life far more resemble what those of ours still are in England, than what Goethe's in Germany were. Alas, these men did not conquer like him; they fought bravely, and fell. They were not heroic bringers of the light, but heroic seekers of it. They lived under galling conditions; struggling as under mountains of impediment, and could not unfold themselves into clearness, or victorious interpretation of that 'Divine Idea.' It is rather the *Tombs* of three Literary Heroes that I have to show you. There are the monumental heaps, under which three spiritual giants lie buried. Very mournful, but also great and full of interest for us. We will linger by them for a while.

Complaint is often made, in these times, of what we call the disorganised condition of society: how ill many arranged forces of society fulfil their work; how many powerful forces are seen working in a wasteful, chaotic, altogether unarranged manner. It is too just a complaint, as we all know. But perhaps if we look at this of Books and the Writers of Books, we shall find here, as it were, the summary of all other disorganisation; – a sort of *heart*, from which, and to which, all other confusion circulates in the world! Considering what Book-writers do in the world, and what the world does with Book-writers, I should say, It is the most anomalous thing the world at present has to show. – We should get into a sea far beyond sounding, did we attempt to give account of this: but we must glance at it for the sake of our subject. The worst element in the life of these three Literary Heroes was, that they found their business and position such a chaos. On the beaten road there is tolerable travelling; but it is sore work, and many have to perish, fashioning a path through the impassable!

Our pious Fathers, feeling well what importance lay in the speaking of man to men, founded churches, made endowments, regulations; everywhere in the civilised world there is a Pulpit, environed with all manner of complex dignified appurtenances and furtherances, that therefrom a man with the tongue may, to best advantage, address his fellow-men. They felt that this was the most important thing; that without this there was no good thing. It is a right pious work, that of theirs; beautiful to behold! But now with the art of Writing, with the art of Printing, a total change has come over that business. The Writer of a Book, is not he a Preacher preaching not to this parish or that, on this day or that, but to all men in all times and places? Surely it is of the last importance that *he* do his work right, whoever do it wrong; – that the *eye* report not falsely, for then all the other members are astray! Well; how he may do his work, whether he do it right or wrong, or do it at all, is a point which no man in the world has taken the pains to think of. To a certain shopkeeper, trying to get some money for his books, if lucky, he is of some importance; to no other man of any. Whence he came, whither he is bound, by what ways he arrived, by what he might be furthered on his course, no one asks. He is an accident in society. He wanders like a wild Ishmaelite, in a world of which he is as the spiritual light, either the guidance or the misguidance!

Certainly the Art of Writing is the most miraculous of all things man has devised. Odin's *Runes* were the first form of the work of a Hero;[2] *Books*, written words, are still miraculous *Runes*, the latest form! In Books lies the *soul* of the whole Past Time; the articulate audible voice of the Past, when the body and material substance of it has altogether vanished like a dream. Mighty fleets and armies, harbours and arsenals, vast cities, high-domed, many-engined, – they are precious, great: but what do they become? Agamemnon, the many Agamemnons, Pericleses, and their Greece; all is gone now to some ruined fragments, dumb mournful wrecks and blocks: but the Books of Greece! There Greece, to every thinker, still very literally lives; can be called-up again into life. No magic *Rune* is stranger than a Book. All that Mankind has done, thought, gained or been: it is lying as in magic preservation in the pages of Books. They are the chosen possession of men.

Do not Books still accomplish *miracles*, as *Runes* were fabled to do? They persuade men. Not the wretchedest circulating-library novel, which foolish girls thumb and con in remote villages, but will help to regulate the actual practical weddings and households of those foolish girls. So 'Celia' felt, so 'Clifford' acted: the foolish Theorem of Life, stamped into those young brains, comes out as a solid Practice one day. Consider whether any *Rune* in the wildest imagination of Mythologist ever did such wonders as, on the actual firm Earth, some Books have done! What built St Paul's Cathedral? Look at the heart of the matter, it was that divine Hebrew BOOK, – the word partly of the man Moses, an outlaw tending his Midianitish herds, four thousand years ago, in the wilderness of Sinai! It is the strangest of things, yet nothing is truer. With the art of Writing, of which Printing is a simple, an inevitable and comparatively insignificant corollary, the true reign of miracles for mankind commenced. It related, with a wondrous new contiguity and perpetual closeness, the Past and Distant with the Present in time and place; all times and all places with this our actual Here and Now. All things were altered for men; all modes of important work of men: teaching, preaching, governing, and all else.

To look at Teaching, for instance. Universities are a notable, respectable product of the modern ages. Their existence too is modified, to the very basis of it, by the existence of Books. Universities arose while there were yet no Books procurable; while a man, for a single Book, had to give an estate of land. That, in those circumstances, when a man had some knowledge to communicate, he should do it by gathering the learners round him, face to face, was a necessity for him. If you wanted to know what Abelard[3] knew, you must go and listen to Abelard. Thousands, as many as thirty-thousand, went to hear Abelard and that metaphysical theology of his. And now for any other teacher who had also something of his own to teach, there was a great convenience opened: so many thousands eager to learn were already assembled yonder; of all places the best place for him was that. For any third teacher it was better still; and grew ever the better, the more teachers there came. It only neded now that the King took notice of this new phenomenon; combined or agglomerated the various schools into one school; gave it edifices, privileges, encouragements, and named it *Universitas*,

or School of all Sciences: the University of Paris, in its essential
characters, was there. The model of all subsequent Universities;
which down even to these days, for six centuries now, have
gone on to found themselves. Such, I conceive, was the origin
of Universities.

It is clear, however, that with this simple circumstance, facil-
ity of getting Books, the whole conditions of the business from
top to bottom were changed. Once invent Printing, you meta-
morphosed all Universities, or superseded them! The Teacher
needed not now to gather men personally round him, that he
might *speak* to them what he knew: print it in a Book, and all
learners far and wide, for a trifle, had it each at his own fire-
side, much more effectually to learn it! – Doubtless there is still
peculiar virtue in Speech; even writers of Books may still, in
some circumstances, find it convenient to speak also, – witness
our present meeting here! There is, one would say, and must
ever remain while man has a tongue, a distinct province for
Speech as well as for Writing and Printing. In regard to all
things this must remain; to Universities among others. But the
limits of the two have nowhere yet been pointed out, ascertained; much less put in practice: the University which would
completely take-in that great new fact, of the existence of
Printed Books, and stand on a clear footing for the Nineteenth
Century as the Paris one did for the Thirteenth, has not yet
come into existence. If we think of it, all that a University, or
final highest School can do for us, is still but what the first
School began doing, – teach us to *read*. We learn to *read*, in
various languages, in various sciences; we learn the alphabet
and letters of all manner of Books. But the place where we
are to get knowledge, even theoretic knowledge, is the Books
themselves! It depends on what we read, after all manner of
Professors have done their best for us. The true University of
these days is a Collection of Books.

But to the Church itself, as I hinted already, all is changed,
in its preaching, in its working, by the introduction of Books.
The Church is the working recognised Union of our Priests
or Prophets, of those who by wise teaching guide the souls of
men. While there was no Writing, even while there was no

Easy-writing, or *Printing*, the preaching of the voice was the natural sole method of performing this. But now with Books! – He that can write a true Book, to persuade England, is not he the Bishop and Archbishop, the Primate of England and of All England? I many a time say, the writers of Newspapers, Pamphlets, Poems, Books, these *are* the real working effective Church of a modern country. Nay not only our preaching, but even our worship, is not it too accomplished by means of Printed Books? The noble sentiment which a gifted soul has clothed for us in melodious words, which brings melody into our hearts, – is not this essentially, if we will understand it, of the nature of worship? There are many, in all countries, who, in this confused time, have no other method of worship. He who, in any way, shows us better than we knew before that a lily of the fields is beautiful, does he not show it us as effluence of the Fountain of all Beauty; as the *handwriting*, made visible there, of the great Maker of the Universe? He has sung for us, made us sing with him, a little verse of a sacred Psalm. Essentially so. How much more he who sings, who says, or in any way brings home to our heart the noble doings, feelings, darings and endurances of a brother man! He has verily touched our hearts as with a live coal *from the altar*. Perhaps there is no worship more authentic.

Literature, so far as it is Literature, is an 'apocalypse of Nature,' a revealing of the 'open secret.' It may well enough be named, in Fichte's style, a 'continuous revelation' of the Godlike in the Terrestrial and Common. The Godlike does ever, in very truth, endure there; is brought out, now in this dialect, now in that, with various degrees of clearness: all true gifted Singers and Speakers are, consciously or unconsciously, doing so. The dark stormful indignation of a Byron, so wayward and perverse, may have touches of it; nay the withered mockery of a French sceptic, – his mockery of the False, a love and worship of the True. How much more the sphere-harmony of a Shakspeare, of a Goethe; the cathedral-music of a Milton! They are something too, those humble genuine lark-notes of a Burns, – skylark, starting from the humble furrow, far overhead into the blue depths, and singing to us so genuinely there! For all true singing is of the nature of worship; as indeed all true *working* may be said to be, – whereof such *singing* is but the record, and fit melodious representation, to us. Fragments of a real 'Church Liturgy' and 'Body of Homilies,' strangely disguised from the common eye, are to be found weltering in that huge froth-ocean of Printed Speech we loosely call Literature! Books are our Church too.

On turning now to the Government of men. Witenagemote,[4] old Parliament, was a great thing. The affairs of the nation were there deliberated and decided; what we were to *do* as a nation. But does not, though the name Parliament subsists, the parliamentary debate go on now, everywhere and at all times, in a far more comprehensive way, *out* of Parliament altogether? Burke said there were Three Estates in Parliament; but, in the Reporters' Gallery yonder, there sat a *Fourth Estate* more important far than them all.[5] It is not a figure of speech, or a witty saying; it is a literal fact, – very momentous to us in these times. Literature is our Parliament too. Printing, which comes necessarily out of Writing, I say often, is equivalent to Democracy: invent Writing, Democracy is inevitable. Writing brings Printing; brings universal every-day extempore Printing, as we see at present. Whoever can speak, speaking now to the whole nation, becomes a power, a branch of government, with inalienable weight in law-making, in all acts of authority. It matters not what rank he has, what revenues or garnitures: the requisite thing is, that he have a tongue which others will listen to; this and nothing more is requisite. The nation is governed by all that has tongue in the nation: Democracy is virtually *there*. Add only, that whatsoever power exists will have itself, by and by, organised; working secretly under bandages, obscurations, obstructions, it will never rest till it get to work free, unencumbered, visible to all. Democracy virtually extant will insist on becoming palpably extant. –

On all sides, are we not driven to the conclusion that, of the things which man can do or make here below, by far the most momentous, wonderful and worthy are the things we call Books! Those poor bits of rag-paper with black ink on them; – from the Daily Newspaper to the sacred Hebrew BOOK, what have they not done, what are they not doing! – For indeed, whatever be the outward form of the thing (bits of paper, as we say, and black ink), is it not verily, at bottom, the highest act of man's faculty that produces a Book? It is the *Thought* of man; the true thaumaturgic virtue; by which man works all things whatsoever. All that he does, and brings to pass, is the vesture of a Thought. This London City, with all its houses, palaces, steamengines, cathedrals, and huge immeasurable traffic and tumult, what is it but a Thought, but millions of Thoughts made into One; – a huge immeasurable Spirit of a THOUGHT, embodied in brick, in iron, smoke, dust, Palaces, Parliaments, Hackney Coaches, Katherine Docks, and the rest of it! Not a brick was made but some man had to *think* of the making of that brick. – The thing we called 'bits of paper with traces of black ink,' is the *purest* embodiment a Thought of man can have. No wonder it is, in all ways, the activest and noblest.

All this, of the importance and supreme importance of the Man of Letters in modern Society, and how the Press is to such a degree superseding the Pulpit, the Senate, the *Senatus Academicus* and much else, has been admitted for a good while; and recognised often enough, in late times, with a sort of sentimental triumph and wonderment. It seems to me, the Sentimental by and by will have to give place to the Practical. If Men of Letters *are* so incalculably influential, actually performing such work for us from age to age, and even from day to day, then I think we may conclude that Men of Letters will not always wander like unrecognised unregulated Ishmaelites among us! Whatsoever thing, as I said above, has virtual unnoticed power will cast-off its wrappages, bandages, and step-forth one day with palpably articulated, universally visible power. That one man wear the clothes, and take the wages, of a function which is done by quite another: there can be no profit in this; this is not right, it is wrong. And yet, alas, the *making* of it right, – what a business, for long times to come! Sure enough, this that we call Organisation of the Literary Guild is still a great way off, encumbered with all manner of complexities. If you asked me what were the best possible organisation for the Men of Letters in modern society; the arrangement of furtherance and regulation, grounded the most accurately on the actual facts of their position and of the world's position, – I should beg to say that the problem far exceeded my faculty! It is not one man's faculty; it is that of many successive men turned earnestly upon it, that will bring-out even an approximate solution. What the best arrangement were, none of us could say. But if you ask, Which is the worst? I answer: This which we now have, that Chaos should sit umpire in it; this is the worst. To the best, or any good one, there is yet a long way.

One remark I must not omit. That royal or parliamentary grants of money are by no means the chief thing wanted! To give our Men of Letters stipends, endowments and all furtherance of cash, will do little towards the business. On the whole, one is weary of hearing about the omnipotence of money. I will say rather that, for a genuine man, it is no evil to be poor; that there ought to be Literary Men poor, – to show whether they are genuine or not! Mendicant Orders, bodies of good men doomed to *beg* were instituted in the Christian Church; a most natural and even necessary development of the spirit of Christianity. It was itself founded on Poverty, on Sorrow, Contradiction, Crucifixion, every species of worldly Distress and Degradation. We may say, that he who has not known those things, and learned from them the priceless lessons they have to teach, has missed a good opportunity of schooling. To beg, and go barefoot, in coarse woollen cloak with a rope round your loins, and be despised of all the world, was no beautiful business; – nor an honourable one in any eye, till the nobleness of those who did so had made it honoured of some!

Begging is not in our course at the present time: but for the rest of it, who will say that a Johnson is not perhaps the better for being poor? It is needful for him, at all rates, to know that outward profit, that success of any kind is *not* the goal he has to aim at. Pride, vanity, ill-conditioned egoism of all sorts, are bred in his heart, as in every heart; need, above all, to be cast-out of his heart, – to be, with whatever pangs, torn-out of it, cast-forth from it, as a thing worthless. Byron, born rich and noble, made-out even less than Burns, poor and plebeian. Who knows but, in that same 'best possible organisation' as yet far off, Poverty may still enter as an important element? What if our Men of Letters, men setting-up to be Spiritual Heroes, were still *then*, as they now are, a kind of 'involuntary monastic order;' bound still to this same ugly Poverty, – till they had tried what was in it too, till they had learned to make it too do for them! Money, in truth, can do much, but it cannot do all. We must know the province of it, and confine it there; and even spurn it back, when it wishes to get farther.

Besides, were the money-furtherances, the proper season for them, the fit assigner of them, all settled, – how is the Burns to be recognised that merits these? He must pass through the ordeal, and prove himself. *This* ordeal; this wild welter of a chaos which is called Literary Life: this too is a kind of ordeal! There is clear truth in the idea that a struggle from the lower classes of society, towards the upper regions and rewards of society, must ever continue. Strong men are born there, who ought to stand elsewhere than there. The manifold, inextricably complex, universal struggle of these constitutes, and must constitute, what is called the progress of society. For Men of Letters, as for all other sorts of men. How to regulate that struggle? There is the whole question. To leave it as it is, at the mercy of blind Chance; a whirl of distracted atoms, one cancelling the other; one of the thousand arriving saved, nine-hundred-and-ninety-nine lost by the way; your royal Johnson languishing inactive in garrets, or harnessed to the yoke of Printer Cave;[6] your Burns dying broken-hearted as a Gauger; your Rousseau driven into mad exasperation, kindling French Revolutions by his paradoxes: this, as we said, is clearly enough the *worst* regulation. The *best*, alas, is far from us!

And yet there can be no doubt but it is coming; advancing on us, as yet hidden in the bosom of centuries: this is a prophecy one can risk. For so soon as men get to discern the importance of a thing, they do infallibly set about arranging it, facilitating, forwarding it; and rest not till, in some approximate degree, they have accomplished that. I say, of all Priesthoods, Aristocracies, Governing Classes at present extant in the world, there is no class comparable for importance to that Priesthood of the Writers of Books. This is a fact which he who runs may read, – and draw inferences from. 'Literature will take care of itself,' answered Mr Pitt, when applied-to for some help for Burns. 'Yes,' adds Mr Southey, 'it will take care of itself; *and of you too*, if you do not look into it!'

The result to individual Men of Letters is not the momentous one; they are but individuals, an infinitesimal fraction of the great body; they can struggle on, and live or else die, as they have been wont. But it deeply concerns the whole society, whether it will set its *light* on high places, to walk thereby; or trample it under foot, and scatter it in all ways of wild waste (not without conflagration), as heretofore! Light is the one thing wanted for the world. Put wisdom in the head of the world, the world will fight its battle victoriously, and be the best world man can make it. I called this anomaly of a disorganic Literary Class the heart of all other anomalies, at once product and parent; some good arrangement for that would be as the *punctum saliens*[7] of a new vitality and just arrangement for all. Already, in some European countries, in France, in Prussia, one traces some beginnings of an arrangement for the Literary Class; indicating the gradual possibility of such. I believe that it is possible; that it will have to be possible.

By far the most interesting fact I hear about the Chinese is one on which we cannot arrive at clearness, but which excites endless curiosity even in the dim state: this namely, that they do attempt to make their Men of Letters their Governors! It would be rash to say, one understood how this was done, or with what degree of success it was done. All such things must be very *un*successful; yet a small degree of success is precious; the very attempt how precious! There does seem to be, all over China, a more or less active search everywhere to discover the men of talent that grow up in the young generation. Schools there are for every one: a foolish sort of training, yet still a sort. The youths who distinguish themselves in the lower school are promoted into favourable stations in the higher, that they may still more distinguish themselves, – forward and forward: it appears to be out of these that the Official Persons, and incipient Governors, are taken. These are they whom they *try* first, whether they can govern or not. And surely with the best hope: for they are the men that have already shown intellect. Try them: they have not governed or administered as yet; perhaps they cannot; but there is no doubt they have *some* Understanding, – without which no man can! Neither is Understanding a *tool*, as we are too apt to figure; 'it is a *hand* which can handle any tool.' Try these men: they are of all others the best worth trying. – Surely there is no kind of government, constitution, revolution, social apparatus or arrangement, that I know of in this world, so promising to one's scientific curiosity as this. The man of intellect at the top of affairs: this is the aim of all constitutions and revolutions, if they have any aim. For the man of true intellect, as I assert and believe always, is the noblehearted man withal, the true, just, humane and valiant man. Get *him* for governor, all is got; fail to get him, though you had Constitutions plentiful as blackberries, and a Parliament in every village, there is nothing yet got!

These things look strange, truly; and are not such as we commonly speculate upon. But we are fallen into strange times; these things will require to be speculated upon; to be rendered practicable, to be in some way put in practice. These, and many others. On all hands of us, there is the announcement, audible enough, that the old Empire of Routine has ended; that to say a thing has long been, is no reason for its continuing to be. The things which have been are fallen into decay, are fallen into incompetence; large masses of mankind, in every society of our Europe, are no longer capable of living at all by the things which have been. When millions of men can no longer by their utmost exertion gain food for themselves, and 'the third man for thirty-six weeks each year is short of third-rate potatoes,'[8] the things which have been must decidedly prepare to alter themselves! – I will now quit this of the organisation of Men of Letters.

Alas, the evil that pressed heaviest on those Literary Heroes of ours was not the want of organisation for Men of Letters, but a far deeper one; out of which, indeed, this and so many other evils for the Literary Man, and for all men, had, as from their fountain, taken rise. That our Hero as Man of Letters had to travel without highway, companionless, through an inorganic chaos, – and to leave his own life and faculty lying there, as a partial contribution towards *pushing* some highway through it: this, had not his faculty itself been so perverted and paralysed, he might have put up with, might have considered to be but the common lot of Heroes. His fatal misery was the *spiritual paralysis*, so we may name it, of the Age in which his life lay; whereby his life too, do what he might, was half-paralysed! The Eighteenth was a *Sceptical* Century; in which little word there is a whole Pandora's Box[9] of miseries. Scepticism means not intellectual Doubt alone, but moral Doubt; all sorts of *in*fidelity, insincerity, spiritual paralysis. Perhaps, in few centuries that one could specify since the world began, was a life of Heroism more difficult for a man. That was not an age of Faith, – an age of Heroes! The very possibility of Heroism had been, as it were, formally abnegated in the minds of all. Heroism was gone forever; Triviality, Formulism and Commonplace were come forever. The 'age of miracles' had been, or perhaps had not been; but it was not any longer. An effete world; wherein Wonder, Greatness, Godhood could not now dwell; – in one word, a godless world!

How mean, dwarfish are their ways of thinking, in this time, – compared not with the Christian Shakspeares and Miltons, but with the old Pagan Skalds, with any species of believing men! The living TREE Igdrasil, with the melodious prophetic waving of its world-wide boughs, deep-rooted as Hela,[10] has died-out into the clanking of a World-MACHINE. 'Tree' and 'Machine:' contrast these two things. I, for my share, declare the world to be no machine! I say that it does *not* go by wheel-and-pinion 'motives,' self-interests, checks, balances; that there is something far other in it than the clank of spinning-jennies, and parliamentary majorities; and, on the whole, that it is not a machine at all! – The old Norse Heathen had a truer notion of God's-world than these poor Machine-Sceptics: the old Heathen Norse were *sincere* men. But for these poor Sceptics there was no sincerity, no truth. Half-truth and hearsay was called truth. Truth, for most men, meant plausibility; to be measured by the number of votes you could get. They had lost any notion that sincerity was possible, or of what sincerity was. How many Plausibilities asking, with unaffected surprise and the air of offended virtue, What! am not I sincere? Spiritual Paralysis, I say, nothing left but a Mechanical life, was the characteristic of that century. For the common man, unless happily he stood *below* his century and belonged to another prior one, it was impossible to be a Believer, a Hero; he lay buried, unconscious, under these baleful influences. To the strongest man, only with infinite struggle and confusion was it possible to work himself half-loose; and lead as it were, in an enchanted, most tragical way, a spiritual death-in-life, and be a Half-Hero!

Scepticism is the name we give to all this; as the chief symptom, as the chief origin of all this. Concerning which so much were to be said! It would take many Discourses, not a small fraction of one Discourse, to state what one feels about that Eighteenth Century and its ways. As indeed this, and the like of this, which we now call Scepticism, is precisely the black malady and life-foe, against which all teaching and discoursing since man's life began has directed itself: the battle of Belief against Unbelief is the never-ending battle! Neither is it in the way of crimination that one would wish to speak. Scepticism, for that century, we must consider as the decay of old ways of believing, the preparation afar off for new better and wider ways, – an inevitable thing. We will not blame men for it; we will lament their hard fate. We will understand that destruction of old *forms* is not destruction of everlasting *substances*; that Scepticism, as sorrowful and hateful as we see it, is not an end but a beginning.

The other day speaking, without prior purpose that way, of Bentham's theory of man and man's life, I chanced to call it a more beggarly one than Mahomet's.[11] I am bound to say, now when it is once uttered, that such is my deliberate opinion. Not that one would mean offence against the man Jeremy Bentham, or those who respect and believe him. Bentham himself, and even the creed of Bentham, seems to me comparatively worthy of praise. It is a determinate *being* what all the world, in a cowardly half-and-half manner, was tending to be. Let us have the crisis; we shall either have death or the cure. I call this gross,

steamengine Utilitarianism an approach towards new Faith. It
was a laying-down of cant; a saying to oneself: 'Well then, this
world is a dead iron machine, the god of it Gravitation and
selfish Hunger; let us see what, by checking and balancing, and
good adjustment of tooth and pinion, can be made of it!'
Benthamism has something complete, manful, in such fearless
committal of itself to what it finds true; you may call it Heroic,
though a Heroism with its *eyes* put out! It is the culminating
point, and fearless ultimatum, of what lay in the half-and-half
state, pervading man's whole existence in that Eighteenth Century. It seems to me, all deniers of Godhood, and all lip-believers
of it, are bound to be Benthamites, if they have courage and
honesty. Benthamism is an *eyeless* Heroism: the Human Species, like a hapless blinded Samson grinding in the Philistine
Mill, clasps convulsively the pillars of its Mill; brings huge ruin
down, but ultimately deliverance withal. Of Bentham I meant
to say no harm.

But this I do say, and would wish all men to know and lay to
heart, that he who discerns nothing but Mechanism in the Universe has in the fatalest way missed the secret of the Universe
altogether. That all Godhood should vanish out of men's conception of this Universe seems to me precisely the most brutal
error, – I will not disparage Heathenism by calling it a Heathen
error, – that men could fall into. It is not true; it is false at the
very heart of it. A man who thinks so will think *wrong* about
all things in the world; this original sin will vitiate all other
conclusions he can form. One might call it the most lamentable
of Delusions, – not forgetting Witchcraft itself! Witchcraft
worshipped at least a living Devil; but this worships a dead
iron Devil; no God, not even a Devil! – Whatsoever is noble,
divine, inspired, drops thereby out of life. There remains everywhere in life a despicable *caput-mortuum*;[12] the mechanical
hull, all soul fled out of it. How can a man act heroically? The
'Doctrine of Motives'[13] will teach him that it is, under more or
less disguise, nothing but a wretched love of Pleasure, fear of
Pain; that Hunger, of applause, of cash, of whatsoever victual
it may be, is the ultimate fact of man's life. Atheism, in brief; –
which does indeed frightfully punish itself. The man, I say, is

become spiritually a paralytic man; this godlike Universe a dead mechanical steamengine, all working by motives, checks, balances, and I know not what; wherein, as in the detestable belly of some Phalaris-Bull[14] of his own contriving, he the poor Phalaris sits miserably dying!

Belief I define to be the healthy act of a man's mind. It is a mysterious indescribable process, that of getting to believe; – indescribable, as all vital acts are. We have our mind given us, not that it may cavil and argue, but that it may see into something, give us clear belief and understanding about something, whereon we are then to proceed to act. Doubt, truly, is not itself a crime. Certainly we do not rush out, clutch-up the first thing we find, and straightway believe that! All manner of doubt, inquiry, σχέψις[15] as it is named, about all manner of objects, dwells in every reasonable mind. It is the mystic working of the mind, on the object it is *getting* to know and believe. Belief comes out of all this, above ground, like the tree from its hidden *roots*. But now if, even on common things, we require that a man keep his doubts *silent*, and not babble of them till they in some measure become affirmations or denials; how much more in regard to the highest things, impossible to speak-of in words at all! That a man parade his doubt, and get to imagine that debating and logic (which means at best only the manner of *telling* us your thought, your belief or disbelief, about a thing) is the triumph and true work of what intellect he has: alas, this is as if you should *overturn* the tree, and instead of green boughs, leaves and fruits, show us ugly taloned roots turned-up into the air, – and no growth, only death and misery going-on!

For the Scepticism, as I said, is not intellectual only; it is moral also; a chronic atrophy and disease of the whole soul. A man lives by believing something; not by debating and arguing about many things. A sad case for him when all that he can manage to believe is something he can button in his pocket, and with one or the other organ eat and digest! Lower than that he will not get. We call those ages in which he gets so low the mournfulest, sickest and meanest of all ages. The world's heart is palsied, sick: how can any limb of it be whole? Genuine

Acting ceases in all departments of the world's work; dextrous
Similitude of Acting begins. The world's wages are pocketed,
the world's work is not done. Heroes have gone-out; Quacks
have come-in. Accordingly, what Century, since the end of
the Roman world, which also was a time of scepticism, simulacra and universal decadence, so abounds with Quacks as
that Eighteenth? Consider them, with their tumid sentimental
vapouring about virtue, benevolence, – the wretched Quack-
squadron, Cagliostro[16] at the head of them! Few men were
without quackery; they had got to consider it a necessary ingre-
dient and amalgam for truth. Chatham, our brave Chatham
himself, comes down to the House, all wrapt and bandaged;[17]
he 'has crawled out in great bodily suffering,' and so on; –
forgets, says Walpole, that he is acting the sick man; in the fire
of debate, snatches his arm from the sling, and oratorically swings
and brandishes it! Chatham himself lives the strangest mimetic
life, half-hero, half-quack, all along. For indeed the world is
full of dupes; and you have to gain the *world's* suffrage! How
the duties of the world will be done in that case, what quantities of error, which means failure, which means sorrow and
misery, to some and to many, will gradually accumulate in all
provinces of the world's business, we need not compute.

It seems to me, you lay your finger here on the heart of the
world's maladies, when you call it a Sceptical World. An insincere world; a godless untruth of a world! It is out of this, as I
consider, that the whole tribe of social pestilences, French Revolutions, Chartisms, and what not, have derived their being, –
their chief necessity to be. This must alter. Till this alter, nothing
can beneficially alter. My one hope of the world, my inexpug-
nable consolation in looking at the miseries of the world, is
that this is altering. Here and there one does now find a man
who knows, as of old, that this world is a Truth, and no Plausibility and Falsity; that he himself is alive, not dead or paralytic;
and that the world is alive, instinct with Godhood, beautiful
and awful, even as in the beginning of days! One man once
knowing this, many men, all men, must by and by come to
know it. It lies there clear, for whosoever will take the *spectacles* off his eyes and honestly look, to know! For such a man

the Unbelieving Century, with its unblessed Products, is already past; a new century is already come. The old unblessed Products and Performances, as solid as they look, are Phantasms, preparing speedily to vanish. To this and the other noisy, very great-looking Simulacrum with the whole world huzzahing at its heels, he can say, composedly stepping aside: Thou art not *true*; thou art not extant, only semblant; go thy way! – Yes, hollow Formulism, gross Benthamism, and other unheroic atheistic Insincerity is visibly and even rapidly declining. An unbelieving Eighteenth Century is but an exception, – such as now and then occurs. I prophesy that the world will once more become *sincere*; a believing world; with *many* Heroes in it, a heroic world! It will then be a victorious world; never till then.

Or indeed what of the world and its victories? Men speak too much about the world. Each one of us here, let the world go how it will, and be victorious or not victorious, has he not a Life of his own to lead? One Life; a little gleam of Time between two Eternities; no second chance to us forevermore! It were well for *us* to live not as fools and simulacra, but as wise and realities. The world's being saved will not save us; nor the world's being lost destroy us. We should look to ourselves: there is great merit here in the 'duty of staying at home'! And, on the whole, to say truth, I never heard of 'worlds' being 'saved' in any other way. That mania of saving worlds is itself a piece of the Eighteenth Century with its windy sentimentalism. Let us not follow it too far. For the saving of the *world* I will trust confidently to the Maker of the world; and look a little to my own saving, which I am more competent to! – In brief, for the 'world's' sake, and for our own, we will rejoice greatly that Scepticism, Insincerity, Mechanical Atheism, with all their poison-dews, are going, and as good as gone. –

Now it was under such conditions, in those times of Johnson, that our Men of Letters had to live. Times in which there was properly no truth in life. Old truths had fallen nigh dumb; the new lay yet hidden, not trying to speak. That Man's Life here below was a Sincerity and Fact, and would forever continue such, no new intimation, in that dusk of the world, had

yet dawned. No intimation; not even any French Revolution, –
which we define to be a Truth once more, though a Truth
clad in hellfire! How different was the Luther's pilgrimage,
with its assured goal, from the Johnson's, girt with mere traditions, suppositions, grown now incredible, unintelligible!
Mahomet's Formulas were of 'wood waxed and oiled,'[18] and
could be *burnt* out of one's way: poor Johnson's were far more
difficult to burn. – The strong man will ever find *work*, which
means difficulty, pain, to the full measure of his strength. But
to make-out a victory, in those circumstances of our poor
Hero as Man of Letters, was perhaps more difficult than in any.
Not obstruction, disorganisation, Bookseller Osborne and
Fourpence-halfpenny a day;[19] not this alone; but the light of his
own soul was taken from him. No landmark on the Earth; and,
alas, what is that to having no load-star in the Heaven! We
need not wonder that none of those Three men rose to victory.
That they fought truly is the highest praise. With a mournful
sympathy we will contemplate, if not three living victorious
Heroes, as I said, the Tombs of three fallen Heroes! They fell
for us too; making a way for us. There are the mountains which
they hurled abroad in their confused War of the Giants; under
which, their strength and life spent, they now lie buried . . .

Past and Present

Past and Present was written in 1843 as a consequence of a visit by Carlyle to Suffolk, during the course of which he saw the ruined abbey at Bury St Edmunds. He had earlier seen the workhouse at St Ives in Huntingdonshire, and been appalled at the wastage of human potential which it represented. In *Past and Present* Carlyle analyses the condition of his own society, and compares it with that of the mediaeval monastic community memorialized by the abbey, a contemporary account of which he found in the twelfth-century *Chronicle* of Jocelin, a monk of St Edmundsbury. The hero of the *Chronicle*, and of *Past and Present*, is the Abbot Sampson, whom Carlyle presents as a true leader in a time of social insecurity.

Past and Present is divided into four books, 'Proem', 'The Ancient Monk', 'The Modern Worker', and 'Horoscope', of which the second is devoted to an account of St Edmundsbury and its abbot, while the first, third and fourth consist of social analysis and prophecy. Four separate passages have been selected for inclusion here, in an attempt to indicate the technique that Carlyle adopted in this very unusual book.

(The text of the *Chronicle* used by Carlyle was that published for the Camden Society in 1840: his page references to this edition have been retained.)

Midas*

The condition of England, on which many pamphlets are now in the course of publication, and many thoughts unpublished are going on in every reflective head, is justly regarded as one of the most ominous, and withal one of the strangest, ever seen in this world. England is full of wealth, of multifarious produce, supply for human want in every kind; yet England is dying of inanition. With unabated bounty the land of England blooms and grows; waving with yellow harvests; thick-studded with workshops, industrial implements, with fifteen millions of workers, understood to be the strongest, the cunningest and the willingest our Earth ever had; these men are here; the work they have done, the fruit they have realised is here, abundant, exuberant on every hand of us: and behold, some baleful fiat as of Enchantment has gone forth, saying, 'Touch it not, ye workers, ye master-workers, ye master-idlers; none of you can touch it, no man of you shall be the better for it; this is enchanted fruit!' On the poor workers such fiat falls first, in its rudest shape; but on the rich master-workers too it falls; neither can the rich master-idlers, nor any richest or highest man escape, but all are like to be brought low with it, and made 'poor' enough in the money sense or a far fataler one.

Of these successful skilful workers some two millions, it is now counted, sit in Workhouses, Poor-law Prisons; or have 'out-door relief' flung over the wall to them, – the workhouse Bastille being filled to bursting,[1] and the strong Poor-law broken

* Book One, Chapter 1.

asunder by a stronger.* They sit there, these many months
now; their hope of deliverance as yet small. In workhouses,
pleasantly so-named, because work cannot be done in them.
Twelve-hundred-thousand workers in England alone; their
cunning right-hand lamed, lying idle in their sorrowful bosom;
their hopes, outlooks, share of this fair world, shut-in by
narrow walls. They sit there, pent up, as in a kind of horrid
enchantment; glad to be imprisoned and enchanted, that they
may not perish starved. The picturesque Tourist, in a sunny
autumn day, through this bounteous realm of England,
describes the Union Workhouse on his path. 'Passing by the
Workhouse of St Ives in Huntingdonshire, on a bright day last
autumn,' says the picturesque Tourist, 'I saw sitting on wooden
benches, in front of their Bastille and within their ring-wall
and its railings, some half-hundred or more of these men. Tall
robust figures, young mostly or of middle age; of honest coun-
tenance, many of them thoughtful and even intelligent-looking
men. They sat there, near by one another; but in a kind of tor-
por, especially in a silence, which was very striking. In silence:
for, alas, what word was to be said? An Earth all lying round,
crying, Come and till me, come and reap me; – yet we here sit
enchanted! In the eyes and brows of these men hung the
gloomiest expression, not of anger, but of grief and shame and
manifold inarticulate distress and weariness; they returned my
glance, with a glance that seemed to say, "Do not look at us.
We sit enchanted here, we know not why. The Sun shines and
the Earth calls; and, by the governing Powers and Impotences
of this England, we are forbidden to obey. It is impossible, they
tell us!" There was something that reminded me of Dante's
Hell in the look of all this; and I rode swiftly away.'

So many hundred thousands sit in workhouses: and other
hundred thousands have not yet got even workhouses; and in
thrifty Scotland itself, in Glasgow or Edinburgh City, in their
dark lanes, hidden from all but the eye of God, and of rare
Benevolence the minister of God, there are scenes of woe and

* The Return of Paupers for England and Wales, at Ladyday 1842, is, 'In-door
221,687, Out-door 1,207,402. Total 1,429,089.' *Official Report.*

destitution and desolation, such as, one may hope, the Sun never saw before in the most barbarous regions where men dwelt. Competent witnesses, the brave and humane Dr Alison,[2] who speaks what he knows, whose noble Healing Art in his charitable hands becomes once more a truly sacred one, report these things for us: these things are not of this year, or of last year, have no reference to our present state of commercial stagnation, but only to the common state. Not in sharp fever-fits, but in chronic gangrene of this kind is Scotland suffering. A Poor-law, any and every Poor-law, it may be observed, is but a temporary measure; an anodyne, not a remedy: Rich and Poor, when once the naked facts of their condition have come into collision, cannot long subsist together on a mere Poor-law. True enough: – and yet, human beings cannot be left to die! Scotland too, till something better come, must have a Poor-law,[3] if Scotland is not to be a byword among the nations. O, what a waste is there; of noble and thrice-noble national virtues; peasant Stoicisms, Heroisms; valiant manful habits, soul of a Nation's worth, – which all the metal of Potosi[4] cannot purchase back; to which the metal of Potosi, and all you can buy with *it*, is dross and dust!

Why dwell on this aspect of the matter? It is too indisputable, not doubtful now to any one. Descend where you will into the lower class, in Town or Country, by what avenue you will, by Factory Inquiries, Agricultural Inquiries, by Revenue Returns, by Mining-Labourer Committees, by opening your own eyes and looking, the same sorrowful result discloses itself: you have to admit that the working body of this rich English Nation has sunk or is fast sinking into a state, to which, all sides of it considered, there was literally never any parallel. At Stockport Assizes, – and this too has no reference to the present state of trade, being of date prior to that, – a Mother and a Father are arraigned and found guilty of poisoning three of their children, to defraud a 'burial-society' of some 3*l.* 8*s.* due on the death of each child: they are arraigned, found guilty; and the official authorities, it is whispered, hint that perhaps the case is not solitary, that perhaps you had better not probe farther into that department of things. This is in the autumn of 1841;

the crime itself is of the previous year or season. 'Brutal savages, degraded Irish,' mutters the idle reader of Newspapers;
hardly lingering on this incident. Yet it is an incident worth
lingering on; the depravity, savagery and degraded Irishism
being never so well admitted. In the British land, a human
Mother and Father, of white skin and professing the Christian
religion, had done this thing; they, with their Irishism and
necessity and savagery, had been driven to do it. Such instances
are like the highest mountain apex emerged into view; under
which lies a whole mountain region and land, not yet emerged.
A human Mother and Father had said to themselves, What
shall we do to escape starvation? We are deep sunk here, in our
dark cellar; and help is far. – Yes, in the Ugolino Hunger-tower[5]
stern things happen; best-loved little Gaddo fallen dead on his
Father's knees! – The Stockport Mother and Father think and
hint: Our poor little starveling Tom, who cries all day for victuals, who will see only evil and not good in this world: if he
were out of misery at once; he well dead, and the rest of us
perhaps kept alive? It is thought, and hinted; at last it is done.
And now Tom being killed, and all spent and eaten, Is it poor
little starveling Jack that must go, or poor little starveling
Will? – What a committee of ways and means![6]

In starved sieged cities, in the uttermost doomed ruin of old
Jerusalem fallen under the wrath of God, it was prophesied and
said, 'The hands of the pitiful women have sodden their own
children.' The stern Hebrew imagination could conceive no
blacker gulf of wretchedness; that was the ultimatum of degraded
god-punished man. And we here, in modern England, exuberant
with supply of all kinds, besieged by nothing if it be not by invisible Enchantments, are we reaching that? – How come these
things? Wherefore are they, wherefore should they be?

Nor are they of the St Ives workhouses, of the Glasgow lanes,
and Stockport cellars, the only unblessed among us. This successful industry of England, with its plethoric wealth, has as
yet made nobody rich; it is an enchanted wealth, and belongs
yet to nobody. We might ask, Which of us has it enriched? We
can spend thousands where we once spent hundreds; but can

purchase nothing good with them. In Poor and Rich, instead of
noble thrift and plenty, there is idle luxury alternating with
mean scarcity and inability. We have sumptuous garnitures for
our Life, but have forgotten to *live* in the middle of them. It is
an enchanted wealth; no man of us can yet touch it. The class
of men who feel that they are truly better off by means of it, let
them give us their name!

Many men eat finer cookery, drink dearer liquors, – with
what advantage they can report, and their Doctors can: but in
the heart of them, if we go out of the dyspeptic stomach, what
increase of blessedness is there? Are they better, beautifuler,
stronger, braver? Are they even what they call 'happier'? Do
they look with satisfaction on more things and human faces in
this God's-Earth; do more things and human faces look with
satisfaction on them? Not so. Human faces gloom discordantly,
disloyally on one another. Things, if it be not mere cotton and
iron things, are growing disobedient to man. The Master
Worker is enchanted, for the present, like his Workhouse Workman, clamours, in vain hitherto, for a very simple sort of
'Liberty:' the liberty 'to buy where he finds it cheapest, to sell
where he finds it dearest.' With guineas jingling in every pocket,
he was no whit richer; but now, the very guineas threatening to
vanish, he feels that he is poor indeed. Poor Master Worker!
And the Master Unworker, is not he in a still fataler situation?
Pausing amid his game-preserves, with awful eye, – as he well
may! Coercing fifty-pounds tenants;[7] coercing, bribing, cajol-
ing; 'doing what he likes with his own.' His mouth full of loud
futilities, and arguments to prove the excellence of his Corn-
law;[8] and in his heart the blackest misgiving, a desperate
half-consciousness that his excellent Corn-law is *in*defensible,
that his loud arguments for it are of a kind to strike men too
literally *dumb*.

To whom, then, is this wealth of England wealth? Who is it
that it blesses; makes happier, wiser, beautifuler, in any way
better? Who has got hold of it, to make it fetch and carry for
him, like a true servant, not like a false mock-servant; to do
him any real service whatsoever? As yet no one. We have more
riches than any Nation ever had before; we have less good of

them than any Nation ever had before. Our successful industry is hitherto unsuccessful; a strange success, if we stop here! In the midst of plethoric plenty, the people perish; with gold walls, and full barns, no man feels himself safe or satisfied. Workers, Master Workers, Unworkers, all men, come to a pause; stand fixed, and cannot farther. Fatal paralysis spreading inwards, from the extremities, in St Ives workhouses, in Stockport cellars, through all limbs, as if towards the heart itself. Have we actually got enchanted, then; accursed by some god?

Midas longed for gold, and insulted the Olympians.[9] He got gold, so that whatsoever he touched became gold, – and he, with his long ears, was little the better for it. Midas had misjudged the celestial music-tones; Midas had insulted Apollo and the gods: the gods gave him his wish, and a pair of long ears, which also were a good appendage to it. What a truth in these old Fables!

St Edmundsbury*

The *Burg*, Bury, or 'Berry' as they call it, of St Edmund is still a
prosperous brisk Town; beautifully diversifying, with its clear
brick houses, ancient clean streets, and twenty or fifteen thousand busy souls, the general grassy face of Suffolk; looking
out right pleasantly, from its hill-slope, towards the rising Sun:
and on the eastern edge of it, still runs, long, black and massive, a range of monastic ruins; into the wide internal spaces
of which the stranger is admitted on payment of one shilling.
Internal spaces laid out, at present, as a botanic garden. Here
stranger or townsman, sauntering at his leisure amid these vast
grim venerable ruins, may persuade himself that an Abbey of
St Edmundsbury did once exist; nay there is no doubt of it: see
here the ancient massive Gateway, of architecture interesting to
the eye of Dilettantism;[10] and farther on, that other ancient
Gateway, now about to tumble, unless Dilettantism, in these
very months, can subscribe money to cramp it and prop it!

Here, sure enough, is an Abbey; beautiful in the eye of Dilettantism. Giant pedantry also will step in, with its huge *Dugdale*
and other enormous *Monasticons*[11] under its arm, and cheerfully
apprise you, That this was a very great Abbey, owner and indeed
creator of St Edmund's Town itself, owner of wide lands and
revenues; nay that its lands were once a county of themselves;
that indeed King Canute or Knut was very kind to it, and gave
St Edmund his own gold crown off his head, on one occasion:
for the rest, that the Monks were of such and such a genus,
such and such a number; that they had so many carucates[12] of

* Book Two, Chapter 2.

land in this hundred, and so many in that; and then farther that the large Tower or Belfry was built by such a one, and the smaller Belfry was built by &c. &c. – Till human nature can stand no more of it; till human nature desperately take refuge in forgetfulness, almost in flat disbelief of the whole business, Monks, Monastery, Belfries, Carucates and all! Alas, what mountains of dead ashes, wreck and burnt bones, does assiduous Pedantry dig up from the Past Time, and name it History, and Philosophy of History; till, as we say, the human soul sinks wearied and bewildered; till the Past Time seems all one infinite incredible gray void, without sun, stars, hearth-fires, or candlelight; dim offensive dust-whirlwinds filling universal Nature; and over your Historical Library, it is as if all the Titans had written for themselves: DRY RUBBISH SHOT HERE!

And yet these grim old walls are not a dilettantism and dubiety; they are an earnest fact. It was a most real and serious purpose they were built for! Yes, another world it was, when these black ruins, white in their new mortar and fresh chiselling, first saw the sun as walls, long ago. Gauge not, with thy dilettante compasses, with that placid dilettante simper, the Heaven's-Watchtower of our Fathers, the fallen God's-Houses, the Golgotha of true Souls departed!

Their architecture, belfries, land-carucates? Yes, – and that is but a small item of the matter. Does it never give thee pause, this other strange item of it, that men then had a *soul*, – not by hearsay alone, and as a figure of speech; but as a truth that they *knew*, and practically went upon! Verily it was another world then. Their Missals have become incredible, a sheer platitude, sayest thou? Yes, a most poor platitude; and even, if thou wilt, an idolatry and blasphemy, should any one persuade *thee* to believe them, to pretend praying by them. But yet it is pity we had lost tiding of our souls: – actually we shall have to go in quest of them again, or worse in all ways will befall! A certain degree of soul, as Ben Jonson reminds us,[13] is indispensable to keep the very body from destruction of the frightfulest sort; to 'save us,' says he, 'the expense of *salt*.' Ben has known men who had soul enough to keep their body and five senses from becoming carrion, and save salt: – men, and also Nations. You may look in Manchester Hunger-mobs and Corn-law Commons Houses, and various other quarters, and say whether either soul or else salt is not somewhat wanted at present!

Another world, truly: and this present poor distressed world might get some profit by looking wisely into it, instead of foolishly. But at lowest, O dilettante friend, let us know always that it *was* a world, and not a void infinite of gray haze with fantasms swimming in it. These old St Edmundsbury walls, I say, were not peopled with fantasms; but with men of flesh and blood, made altogether as we are. Had thou and I then been, who knows but we ourselves had taken refuge from an evil Time, and fled to dwell here, and meditate on an Eternity, in such fashion as we could? Alas, how like an old osseous fragment, a broken blackened shin-bone of the old dead Ages, this black ruin looks out, not yet covered by the soil; still indicating what a once gigantic Life lies buried there! It is dead now, and dumb; but was alive once, and spake. For twenty generations, here was the earthly arena where painful living men worked out their life-wrestle, – looked at by Earth, by Heaven and Hell. Bells tolled to prayers; and men, of many humours, various thoughts, chanted vespers, matins; – and round the little islet of their life rolled forever (as round ours still rolls, though we are blind and deaf) the illimitable Ocean, tinting all things with its eternal hues and reflexes; making strange prophetic music! How silent now; all departed, clean gone. The World-Dramaturgist has written: *Exeunt.* The devouring Time-Demons have made away with it all: and in its stead, there is either nothing; or what is worse, offensive universal dust-clouds, and gray eclipse of Earth and Heaven, from 'dry rubbish shot here!'

Truly it is no easy matter to get across the chasm of Seven Centuries, filled with such material. But here, of all helps, is not a Boswell the welcomest; even a small Boswell? Veracity, true simplicity of heart, how valuable are these always! He that speaks what *is* really in him, will find men to listen, though under never such impediments. Even gossip, springing free and cheery from a human heart, this too is a kind of veracity and *speech*; – much preferable to pedantry and inane gray haze!

Jocelin is weak and garrulous, but he is human. Through the
thin watery gossip of our Jocelin, we do get some glimpses of
that deep-buried Time; discern veritably, though in a fitful
intermittent manner, these antique figures and their life-method,
face to face! Beautifully, in our earnest loving glance, the old
centuries melt from opaque to partially translucent, transparent here and there; and the void black Night, one finds, is
but the summing-up of innumerable peopled luminous *Days*.
Not parchment Chartularies,[14] Doctrines of the Constitution,
O Dryasdust; not altogether, my erudite friend!

Readers who please to go along with us into this poor
Jocelini Chronica shall wander inconveniently enough, as in
wintry twilight, through some poor stript hazel-grove, rustling
with foolish noises, and perpetually hindering the eyesight; but
across which, here and there, some real human figure is seen
moving: very strange; whom we could hail if he would answer; –
and we look into a pair of eyes deep as our own, *imaging* our
own, but all unconscious of us; to whom we, for the time, are
become as spirits and invisible!

Practical-Devotional*

Here indeed, by rule of antagonisms, may be the place to mention that, after King Richard's return, there was a liberty of
tourneying given to the fighting-men of England: that a Tour-
nament was proclaimed in the Abbot's domain, 'between
Thetford and St Edmundsbury,' – perhaps in the Euston region,
on Fakenham Heights, midway between these two localities:
that it was publicly prohibited by our Lord Abbot; and nevertheless was held in spite of him, – and by the parties, as would
seem, considered 'a gentle and free passage of arms.'

Nay, next year, there came to the same spot four-and-twenty
young men, sons of Nobles, for another passage of arms; who,
having completed the same, all rode into St Edmundsbury to
lodge for the night. Here is modesty! Our Lord Abbot, being
instructed of it, ordered the Gates to be closed; the whole party
shut in. The morrow was the Vigil of the Apostles Peter and
Paul; no outgate on the morrow. Giving their promise not
to depart without permission, those four-and-twenty young
bloods dieted all that day (*manducaverunt*) with the Lord
Abbot, waiting for trial on the morrow. 'But after dinner,' –
mark it, posterity! – 'the Lord Abbot retiring into his *Talamus*,[15]
they all started up, and began carolling and singing (*carolare
et cantare*); sending into the Town for wine; drinking, and
afterwards howling (*ululantes*); – totally depriving the Abbot
and Convent of their afternoon's nap; doing all this in derision of the Lord Abbot, and spending in such fashion the
whole day till evening, nor would they desist at the Lord

* Book Two, Chapter 15.

Abbot's order! Night coming on, they broke the bolts of the Town-Gates, and went off by violence!'* Was the like ever heard of? The roysterous young dogs; carolling, howling, breaking the Lord Abbot's sleep, – after that sinful chivalry cockfight of theirs! They too are a feature of distant centuries, as of near ones. St Edmund on the edge of your horizon, or whatever else there, young scamps, in the dandy state, whether cased in iron or in whalebone, begin to caper and carol on the green Earth! Our Lord Abbot excommunicated most of them; and they gradually came in for repentance.

Excommunication is a great recipe with our Lord Abbot; the prevailing purifier in those ages. Thus when the Townsfolk and Monks' menials quarrelled once at the Christmas Mysteries in St Edmund's Churchyard, and 'from words it came to cuffs, and from cuffs to cutting and the effusion of blood,' – our Lord Abbot excommunicates sixty of the rioters with bell, book and candle (*accensis candelis*), at one stroke.† Whereupon they all come suppliant, indeed nearly naked, 'nothing on but their breeches, *omnino nudi præter femoralia*, and prostrate themselves at the Church-door.' Figure that!

In fact, by excommunication or persuasion, by impetuosity of driving or adroitness in leading, this Abbot, it is now becoming plain everywhere, is a man that generally remains master at last. He tempers his medicine to the malady, now hot, now cool; prudent though fiery, an eminently practical man. Nay sometimes in his adroit practice there are swift turns almost of a surprising nature! Once, for example, it chanced that Geoffrey Riddell Bishop of Ely, a Prelate rather troublesome to our Abbot, made a request of him for timber from his wood towards certain edifices going on at Glemsford. The Abbot, a great builder himself, disliked the request; could not, however, give it a negative. While he lay, therefore, at his Manorhouse of Melford not long after, there comes to him one of the Lord Bishop's men or monks, with a message from his Lordship, 'That he now begged permission to cut down the requisite

* *Jocelini Chronica*, p. 40.
† ibid., p. 68.

trees in Elmswell Wood,' – so said the monk: Elms*well*, where
there are no trees but scrubs and shrubs, instead of Elms*et*, our
true nemus[16] and high-towering oak-wood, here on Melford
Manor! Elmswell? The Lord Abbot, in surprise, inquires priv-
ily of Richard his Forester; Richard answers that my Lord of
Ely has already had his *carpentarii* in Elms*et*, and marked out
for his own use all the best trees in the compass of it. Abbot
Samson thereupon answers the monk: 'Elmswell? Yes surely,
be it as my Lord Bishop wishes. The successful monk, on the
morrow morning, hastens home to Ely; but, on the morrow
morning, 'directly after mass,' Abbot Samson too was busy!
The successful monk, arriving at Ely, is rated for a goose and an
owl; is ordered back to say that Elmset was the place meant.
Alas, on arriving at Elmset, he finds the Bishop's trees, they
'and a hundred more,' all felled and piled, and the stamp of St
Edmund's Monastery burnt into them, – for roofing of the
great tower we are building there! Your importunate Bishop
must seek wood from Glemsford edifices in some other *nemus*
than this. A practical Abbot!

We said withal there was a terrible flash of anger in him: witness his address to old Herbert the Dean, who in a too thrifty
manner had erected a windmill for himself on his glebe-lands at
Haberdon. On the morrow, after mass, our Lord Abbot orders
the Cellerarius[17] to send off his carpenters to demolish the said
structure *brevi manu*, and lay up the wood in safe keeping. Old
Dean Herbert, hearing what was toward, comes tottering along
hither, to plead humbly for himself and his mill. The Abbot
answers: I am obliged to thee as if thou hadst cut off both my
feet! By God's face, *per os Dei*, I will not eat bread till that fabric be torn in pieces. Thou art an old man, and shouldst have
known that neither the King nor his Justiciary dare change
aught within the Liberties[18] without consent of Abbot and
Convent: and thou hast presumed on such a thing? I tell thee,
it will *not* be without damage to my mills; for the Townsfolk
will go to thy mill, and grind their corn (*bladum suum*) at their
own good pleasure; nor can I hinder them, since they are free
men. I will allow no new mills on such principle. Away, away:
before thou gettest home again, thou shalt see what thy mill

has grown to!'* – The very reverend the old Dean totters home
again, in all haste; tears the mill in pieces by his own *carpentarii*, to save at least the timber; and Abbot Samson's workmen,
coming up, find the ground already clear of it.

Easy to bully-down poor old rural Deans, and blow their
windmills away: but who is the man that dare abide King Richard's anger; cross the Lion in his path, and take him by the
whiskers! Abbot Samson too; he is that man, with justice on his
side. The case was this. Adam de Cokefield, one of the chief
feudatories of St Edmund, and a principal man in the Eastern
Counties, died, leaving large possessions, and for heiress a
daughter of three months; who by clear law, as all men know,
became thus Abbot Samson's ward; whom accordingly he proceeded to dispose of to such person as seemed fittest. But now
King Richard has another person in view, to whom the little
ward and her great possessions were a suitable thing. He, by
letter, requests that Abbot Samson will have the goodness to
give her to this person. Abbot Samson, with deep humility,
replies that she is already given. New letters from Richard, of
severer tenor; answered with new deep humilities, with gifts
and entreaties, with no promise of obedience. King Richard's
ire is kindled; messengers arrive at St Edmundsbury, with
emphatic message to obey or tremble! Abbot Samson, wisely
silent as to the King's threats, makes answer: 'The King can
send if he will, and seize the ward: force and power he has to
do his pleasure, and abolish the whole Abbey. But I, for my
part, never can be bent to wish this that he seeks, nor shall it by
me be ever done. For there is danger lest such things be made a
precedent of, to the prejudice of my successors. *Videat Altissimus*, Let the Most High look on it. Whatsoever thing shall
befall I will patiently endure.'

Such was Abbot Samson's deliberate decision. Why not?
Cœur-de-Lion is very dreadful, but not the dreadfulest. *Videat
Altissimus*. I reverence Cœur-de-Lion to the marrow of my
bones, and will in all right things be *homo suus*; but it is not,
properly speaking, with terror, with any fear at all. On the

* *Jocelini Chronica*, p. 43.

whole have I not looked on the face of 'Satan with outspread wings;'[19] steadily into Hellfire these seven-and-forty years; – and was not melted into terror even at that, such the Lord's goodness to me? Cœur-de-Lion!

Richard swore tornado oaths, worse than our armies in Flanders,[20] To be revenged on that proud Priest. But in the end he discovered that the Priest was right; and forgave him, and even loved him. 'King Richard wrote, soon after, to Abbot Samson, That he wanted one or two of the St Edmundsbury dogs, which he heard were good.' Abbot Samson sent him dogs of the best; Richard replied by the present of a ring, which Pope Innocent the Third had given him. Thou brave Richard, thou brave Samson! Richard too, I suppose, 'loved a man,' and knew one when he saw him.

No one will accuse our Lord Abbot of wanting worldly wisdom, due interest in worldly things. A skilful man; full of cunning insight, lively interests; always discerning the road to his object, be it circuit, be it short-cut, and victoriously travelling forward thereon. Nay rather it might seem, from Jocelin's Narrative, as if he had his eye all but exclusively directed on terrestrial matters, and was much too secular for a devout man. But this too, if we examine it, was right. For it is in the world that a man, devout or other, has his life to lead, his work waiting to be done. The basis of Abbot Samson's, we shall discover, was truly religion, after all. Returning from his dusty pilgrimage, with such welcome as we saw, 'he sat down at the foot of St Edmund's Shrine.' Not a talking theory, that; no, a silent practice: Thou, St Edmund, with what lies in thee, thou now must help me, or none will!

This also is a significant fact: the zealous interest our Abbot took in the Crusades. To all noble Christian hearts of that era, what earthly enterprise so noble? 'When Henry II., having taken the cross, came to St Edmund's, to pay his devotions before setting out, the Abbot secretly made for himself a cross of linen cloth: and, holding this in one hand and a threaded needle in the other, asked leave of the King to assume it.' The King could not spare Samson out of England; – the King

himself indeed never went. But the Abbot's eye was set on the
Holy Sepulchre, as on the spot of this Earth where the true
cause of Heaven was deciding itself. 'At the retaking of Jerusalem by the Pagans, Abbot Samson put on a cilice and hair-shirt,
and wore under-garments of hair-cloth ever after; he abstained
also from flesh and flesh-meats (*carne et carneis*) thenceforth
to the end of his life.' Like a dark cloud eclipsing the hopes of
Christendom, those tidings cast their shadow over St Edmundsbury too: Shall Samson Abbas take pleasure while Christ's Tomb
is in the hands of the Infidel? Samson, in pain of body, shall daily
be reminded of it, daily be admonished to grieve for it.

The great antique heart: how like a child's in its simplicity,
like a man's in its earnest solemnity and depth! Heaven lies
over him wheresoever he goes or stands on the Earth; making
all the Earth a mystic Temple to him, the Earth's business all a
kind of worship. Glimpses of bright creatures flash in the common sunlight; angels yet hover doing God's messages among
men: that rainbow was set in the clouds by the hand of God!
Wonder, miracle encompass the man; he lives in an element of
miracle; Heaven's splendour over his head, Hell's darkness
under his feet. A great Law of Duty, high as these two Infinitudes, dwarfing all else, annihilating all else, – making royal
Richard as small as peasant Samson, smaller if need be! – The
'imaginative faculties?' 'Rude poetic ages?' The 'primeval
poetic element?' Oh, for God's sake, good reader, talk no more
of all that![21] It was not a Dilettantism this of Abbot Samson. It
was a Reality, and it is one. The garment only of it is dead; the
essence of it lives through all Time and all Eternity!

And truly, as we said above, is not this comparative silence of
Abbot Samson as to his religion precisely the healthiest sign of
him and of it? 'The Unconscious is the alone Complete.' Abbot
Samson all along a busy working man, as all men are bound to
be, his religion, his worship was like his daily bread to him; –
which he did not take the trouble to talk much about; which he
merely ate at stated intervals, and lived and did his work upon!
This is Abbot Samson's Catholicism of the Twelfth Century; –
something like the *Ism* of all true men in all true centuries,

I fancy! Alas, compared with any of the *Isms* current in these poor days, what a thing! Compared with the respectablest, morbid, struggling Methodism, never so earnest; with the respectablest, ghastly, dead or galvanised Dilettantism, never so spasmodic!

Methodism with its eye forever turned on its own navel; asking itself with torturing anxiety of Hope and Fear, 'Am I right? am I wrong? Shall I be saved? shall I not be damned?' – what is this, at bottom, but a new phasis of *Egoism*, stretched out into the Infinite; not always the heavenlier for its infinitude! Brother, so soon as possible, endeavour to rise above all that. 'Thou *art* wrong; thou art like to be damned:' consider that as the fact, reconcile thyself even to that, if thou be a man; – then first is the devouring Universe subdued under thee, and from the black murk of midnight and noise of greedy Acheron, dawn as of an ever-lasting morning, how far above all Hope and all Fear, springs for thee, enlightening thy steep path, awakening in thy heart celestial Memnon's music!

But of our Dilettantisms, and galvanised Dilettantisms; of Puseyism[22] – O Heavens, what shall we say of Puseyism, in comparison to Twelfth-Century Catholicism? Little or nothing; for indeed it is a matter to strike one dumb.

> The Builder of this Universe was wise,
> He plann'd all souls, all systems, planets, particles:
> The Plan He shap'd all Worlds and Æons by,
> Was – Heavens! – Was thy small Nine-and-thirty Articles?

That certain human souls, living on this practical Earth, should think to save themselves and a ruined world by noisy theoretic demonstrations and laudations of *the* Church, instead of some unnoisy, unconscious, but *practical*, total, heart-and-soul demonstration of *a* Church: this, in the circle of revolving ages, this also was a thing we were to see. A kind of penultimate thing, precursor of very strange consummations; last thing but one? If there is no atmosphere, what will it serve a man to demonstrate the excellence of lungs? How much profitabler, when you can, like Abbot Samson, breathe; and go along your way!

Gospel of Mammonism*

Reader, even Christian Reader as thy title goes, hast thou any notion of Heaven and Hell? I rather apprehend, not. Often as the words are on our tongue, they have got a fabulous or semi-fabulous character for most of us, and pass on like a kind of transient similitude, like a sound signifying little.

Yet it is well worth while for us to know, once and always, that they are not a similitude, nor a fable nor semi-fable; that they are an everlasting highest fact! 'No Lake of Sicilian or other sulphur burns now anywhere in these ages,' sayest thou? Well, and if there did not! Believe that there does not; believe it if thou wilt, nay hold it by as a real increase, a rise to higher stages, to wider horizons and empires. All this has vanished, or has not vanished; believe as thou wilt as to all this. But that an Infinite of Practical Importance, speaking with strict arithmetical exactness, an *Infinite*, has vanished or can vanish from the Life of any Man: this thou shalt not believe! O brother, the Infinite of Terror, of Hope, of Pity, did it not at any moment disclose itself to thee, indubitable, unnameable? Came it never, like the gleam of *preter*natural eternal Oceans, like the voice of old Eternities, far-sounding through thy heart of hearts? Never? Alas, it was not thy Liberalism, then; it was thy Animalism! The Infinite is more sure than any other fact. But only men can discern it; mere building beavers, spinning arachnes, much more the predatory vulturous and vulpine species, do not discern it well!

* Book Three, Chapter 2.

'The word Hell,' says Sauerteig,[23] 'is still frequently in use among the English people: but I could not without difficulty ascertain what they meant by it. Hell generally signifies the Infinite Terror, the thing a man *is* infinitely afraid of, and shudders and shrinks from, struggling with his whole soul to escape from it. There is a Hell therefore, if you will consider, which accompanies man, in all stages of his history, and religious or other development: but the Hells of men and Peoples differ notably. With Christians it is the infinite terror of being found guilty before the Just Judge. With old Romans, I conjecture, it was the terror not of Pluto,[24] for whom probably they cared little, but of doing unworthily, doing unvirtuously, which was their word for un*man*fully. And now what is it, if you pierce through his Cants, his oft-repeated Hearsays, what he calls his Worships and so forth, – what is it that the modern English soul does, in very truth, dread infinitely, and contemplates with entire despair? What *is* his Hell, after all these reputable, oft-repeated Hearsays, what is it? With hesitation, with astonishment, I pronounce it to me: The terror of "Not succeeding;" of not making money, fame, or some other figure in the world, – chiefly of not making money! Is not that a somewhat singular Hell?'

Yes, O Sauerteig, it is very singular. If we do not 'succeed,' where is the use of us? We had better never have been born. 'Tremble intensely,' as our friend the Emperor of China says: *there* is the black Bottomless of Terror; what Sauerteig calls the 'Hell of the English'! – But indeed this Hell belongs naturally to the Gospel of Mammonism, which also has its corresponding Heaven. For there *is* one Reality among so many Phantasms; about one thing we are entirely in earnest: The making of money. Working Mammonism does divide the world with idle game-preserving Dilettantism: – thank Heaven that there is even a Mammonism, *any*thing we are in earnest about! Idleness is worst, Idleness alone is without hope: work earnestly at anything, you will by degrees learn to work at almost all things. There is endless hope in work, were it even work at making money.

True, it must be owned, we for the present, with our Mammon-Gospel, have come to strange conclusions. We call it a Society; and go about professing openly the totalest separation, isolation. Our life is not a mutual helpfulness; but rather, cloaked under due laws-of-war, named 'fair competition' and so forth, it is a mutual hostility. We have profoundly forgotten everywhere that *Cash-payment* is not the sole relation of human beings; we think, nothing doubting, that *it* absolves and liquidates all engagements of man. 'My starving workers?' answers the rich mill-owner: 'Did not I hire them fairly in the market? Did I not pay them, to the last sixpence, the sum covenanted for? What have I to do with them more?' – Verily Mammon-worship is a melancholy creed. When Cain, for his own behoof, had killed Abel, and was questioned, 'Where is thy brother?' he too made answer, 'Am I my brother's keeper?' Did I not pay my brother *his* wages, the thing he had merited from me?

O sumptous Merchant-Prince, illustrious game-preserving Duke, is there no way of 'killing' thy brother but Cain's rude way! 'A good man by the very look of him, by his very presence with us as a fellow wayfarer in this Life-pilgrimage, *promises* so much:' woe to him if he forget all such promises, if he never know that they were given! To a deadened soul, seared with the brute Idolatry of Sense, to whom going to Hell is equivalent to not making money, all 'promises,' and moral duties, that cannot be pleaded for in Courts of Requests,[25] address themselves in vain. Money he can be ordered to pay, but nothing more. I have not heard in all Past History, and expect not to hear in all Future History, of any Society anywhere under God's Heaven supporting itself on such Philosophy. The Universe is not made so; it is made otherwise than so. The man or nation of men that thinks it is made so, marches forward nothing doubting, step after step; but marches – whither we know! In these last two centuries of Atheistic Government (near two centuries now, since the blessed restoration of his Sacred Majesty, and Defender of the Faith, Charles Second), I reckon that we have pretty well exhausted what of 'firm earth' there was for us to march on; – and are now, very ominously, shuddering, reeling, and let us hope trying to recoil, on the cliff's edge!

For out of this that we call Atheism come so many other *isms* and falsities, each falsity with its misery at its heels! – A SOUL is not like wind (*spiritus*, or breath) contained within a capsule; the ALMIGHTY MAKER is not like a Clockmaker[26] that once, in old immemorial ages, having *made* his Horologe of a Universe, sits ever since and sees it go! Not at all. Hence comes Atheism; come, as we say, many other *isms*; and as the sum of all, comes *Valetism*,[27] the *reverse* of Heroism; sad root of all woes whatsoever. For indeed, as no man ever saw the above-said wind-element enclosed within its capsule, and finds it at bottom more deniable than conceivable; so too he finds, in spite of Bridgwater Bequests,[28] your Clockmaker Almighty an entirely questionable affair, a deniable affair; – and accordingly denies it, and along with it so much else. Alas, one knows not what and how much else! For the faith in an Invisible, Unnameable Godlike, present everywhere in all that we see and work and suffer, is the essence of all faith whatsoever; and that once denied, or still worse, asserted with lips only, and out of bound prayerbooks only, what other thing remains believable? That Cant well-ordered is marketable Cant; that Heroism means gas-lighted Histrionism; that seen with 'clear eyes' (as they call Valet-eyes), no man is a Hero, or ever was a Hero, but all men are Valets and Varlets. The accursed practical quintessence of all sorts of Unbelief! For if there be now no Hero, and the Histrio himself begin to be seen into, what hope is there for the seed of Adam here below? We are the doomed ever-lasting prey of the Quack; who, now in this guise, now in that, is to filch us, to pluck and eat us, by such modes as are convenient for him. For the modes and guises I care little. The Quack once inevitable, let him come swiftly, let him pluck and eat me; – swiftly, that I may at least have done with him; for in his Quack-world I can have no wish to linger. Though he slay me, yet will I *not* trust in him. Though he conquer nations, and have all the Flunkies of the Universe shouting at his heels, yet will I know well that *he* is an Inanity; that for him and his there is no continuance appointed, save only in Gehenna and the

Pool. Alas, the Atheist world, from its utmost summits of Heaven and Westminster-Hall, downwards through poor seven-feet Hats and 'Unveracities fallen hungry,' down to the lowest cellars and neglected hunger-dens of it, is very wretched.

One of Dr Alison's Scotch facts[29] struck us much.* A poor Irish Widow, her husband having died in one of the Lanes of Edinburgh, went forth with her three children, bare of all resource, to solicit help from the Charitable Establishments of that City. At this Charitable Establishment and then at that she was refused; referred from one to the other, helped by none; – till she had exhausted them all; till her strength and heart failed her: she sank down in typhus-fever; died, and infected her Lane with fever, so that 'seventeen other persons' died of fever there in consequence. The humane Physician asks thereupon, as with a heart too full for speaking, Would it not have been *economy* to help this poor Widow? She took typhus-fever, and killed seventeen of you! – Very curious. The forlorn Irish Widow applies to her fellow-creatures, as if saying, 'Behold I am sinking, bare of help: ye must help me! I am your sister, bone of your bone; one God made us: ye must help me!' They answer, 'No, impossible; thou art no sister of ours.' But she proves her sisterhood; her typhus-fever kills *them*: they actually were her brothers, though denying it! Had human creature ever to go lower for a proof?

For, as indeed was very natural in such case, all government of the Poor by the Rich has long ago been given over to Supply-and-demand, *Laissez-faire* and suchlike, and universally declared to be 'impossible.' 'You are no sister of ours; what shadow of proof is there? Here are our parchments, our padlocks, proving indisputably our money-safes to be *ours*, and you to have no business with them. Depart! It is impossible!' – Nay, what wouldst thou thyself have us do? cry indignant readers. Nothing, my friends, – till you have got a soul for yourselves again. Till then all things are 'impossible.' Till then I cannot even bid you buy, as the old Spartans would have

* *Observations on the Management of the Poor in Scotland*: by William Pulteney Alison, M.D. (Edinburgh, 1840).

done, two-pence worth of powder and lead, and compendi-
ously shoot to death this poor Irish Widow: even that is
'impossible,' for you. Nothing is left but that she prove her sisterhood by dying, and infecting you with typhus. Seventeen of
you lying dead will not deny such proof that she *was* flesh of
your flesh; and perhaps some of the living may lay it to heart.

'Impossible:' of a certain two-legged animal with feathers it is
said, if you draw a distinct chalk-circle round him, he sits
imprisoned, as if girt with the iron ring of Fate; and will die
there, though within sight of victuals, – or sit in sick misery
there, and be fatted to death. The name of this poor two-legged
animal is – Goose; and they make of him, when well fattened,
Pâté de foie gras, much prized by some!

Latter-Day Pamphlets

The Latter-Day Pamphlets were published over a period of seven months from February to August 1850. They had been preceded by an essay entitled 'Occasional Discourse on the Nigger Question' which appeared in *Fraser's Magazine* in December 1849, in which Carlyle berated philanthropic attitudes towards the West Indian Negroes. According to Froude, 'The Article on the "Nigger Question" gave universal offence. Many of his old admirers drew back after this.' In particular the article brought about the final break with Mill and its reception may have accounted for the publication of *Latter-Day Pamphlets* in pamphlet form, for Froude claims that no journal would accept them. The eight pamphlets, which present a highly emotional attack on various manifestations of philanthropy and democracy, are a clear expression of the extent of Carlyle's sense of social frustration. A latent sadism underlies much of his comment, and it is accompanied on occasion by a Swiftian use of the imagery of filth. Nevertheless, behind the rhetoric and the distortions lie important questions about the nature and function of democracy in a modern state, about the techniques of mass persuasion, and about the morality of political behaviour. Extracts from three of the pamphlets are reprinted here.

from No. 2: Model Prisons

... Several months ago, some friends took me with them to see one of the London Prisons; a Prison of the exemplary or model kind.[1] An immense circuit of buildings; cut-out, girt with a high ring-wall, from the lanes and streets of the quarter, which is a dim and crowded one. Gateway as to a fortified place; then a spacious court, like the square of a city; broad staircases, passages to interior courts; fronts of stately architecture all round. It lodges some Thousand or Twelve-hundred prisoners, besides the officers of the establishment. Surely one of the most perfect buildings, within the compass of London. We looked at the apartments, sleeping-cells, dining-rooms, working-rooms, general courts or special and private: excellent all, the ne-plus-ultra of human care and ingenuity; in my life I never saw so clean a building; probably no Duke in England lives in a mansion of such perfect and thorough cleanness.

The bread, the cocoa, soup, meat, all the various sorts of food, in their respective cooking-places, we tasted: found them of excellence superlative. The prisoners sat at work, light work, picking oakum, and the like, in airy apartments with glass-roofs, of agreeable temperature and perfect ventilation; silent, or at least conversing only by secret signs: others were out, taking their hour of promenade in clean flagged courts: methodic composure, cleanliness, peace, substantial wholesome comfort reigned everywhere supreme. The women in other apartments, some notable murderesses among them, all in the like state of methodic composure and substantial wholesome comfort, sat sewing: in long ranges of wash-houses, drying-houses and whatever pertains to the getting-up of clean linen, were certain

others, with all conceivable mechanical furtherances, not too
arduously working. The notable murderesses were, though with
great precautions of privacy, pointed out to us; and we were
requested not to look openly at them, or seem to notice them at
all, as it was found to 'cherish their vanity' when visitors looked
at them. Schools too were there; intelligent teachers of both
sexes, studiously instructing the still ignorant of these thieves.

From an inner room or gallery, we looked down into a range
of private courts, where certain Chartist Notabilities were
undergoing their term. Chartist Notability First struck me very
much: I had seen him about a year before, by involuntary accident and much to my disgust, magnetising a silly young person;
and had noted well the unlovely voracious look of him, his
thick oily skin, his heavy dull-burning eyes, his greedy mouth,
the dusky potent insatiable *animalism* that looked out of every
feature of him: a fellow adequate to animal-magnetise most
things, I did suppose; – and here was the post I now found him
arrived at. Next neighbour to him was Notability Second, a
philosophic or literary Chartist; walking rapidly to and fro in
his private court, a clean, high-walled place; the world and its
cares quite excluded, for some months to come: master of his
own time and spiritual resources to, as I supposed, a really
enviable extent. What 'literary man' to an equal extent! I fancied I, for my own part, so left with paper and ink, and all taxes
and botherations shut-out from me, could have written such a
Book as no reader will here ever get of me. Never, O reader,
never here in a mere house with taxes and botherations. Here,
alas, one has to snatch one's poor Book, bit by bit, as from a
conflagration; and to think and live, comparatively, as if the
house were not one's own, but mainly the world's and the devil's. Notability Second might have filled one with envy.

The Captain of the place, a gentleman of ancient Military
or Royal-Navy habits, was one of the most perfect governors;
professionally and by nature zealous for cleanliness, punc-
tuality, good order of every kind; a humane heart and yet a strong
one; soft of speech and manner, yet with an inflexible rigour of
command, so far as his limits went: 'iron hand in a velvet glove,'
as Napoleon defined it. A man of real worth, challenging at once

love and respect: the light of those mild bright eyes seemed to per-
meate the place as with an all-pervading vigilance, and kindly
yet victorious illumination; in the soft definite voice it was as if
Nature herself were promulgating her orders, gentlest mildest
orders, which however, in the end, there would be no disobeying,
which in the end there would be no living without fulfilment of.
A true *'aristos,'* and commander of men. A man worthy to have
commanded and guided forward, in good ways, Twelve-hundred
of the best commonpeople in London or the world: he was here,
for many years past, giving all his care and faculty to command,
and guide forward in such ways as there were, Twelve-hundred
of the worst. I looked with considerable admiration on this
gentleman; and with considerable astonishment, the reverse of
admiration, on the work he had here been set upon.

   This excellent Captain was too old a Commander to complain of anything; indeed he struggled visibly the other way, to
find in his own mind that all here was best; but I could sufficiently discern that, in his natural instincts, if not mounting
up to the region of his thoughts, there was a continual protest
going on against much of it; that nature and all his inarticulate
persuasion (however much forbidden to articulate itself) taught
him the futility and unfeasibility of the system followed here.
The Visiting Magistrates, he gently regretted rather than complained, had lately taken his treadwheel from him, men were
just now pulling it down; and how he was henceforth to enforce
discipline on these bad subjects, was much a difficulty with
him. 'They cared for nothing but the treadwheel, and for having their rations cut short;' of the two sole penalties, hard
work and occasional hunger, there remained now only one, and
that by no means the better one, as he thought. The 'sympathy'
of visitors, too, their 'pity' for his interesting scoundrel-subjects,
though he tried to like it, was evidently no joy to this practical
mind. Pity, yes; – but pity for the scoundrel-species? For those
who will not have pity on themselves, and will force the Universe and the Laws of Nature to have no 'pity' on them?
Meseems I could discover fitter objects of pity!

   In fact it was too clear, this excellent man had got a field for
his faculties which, in several respects, was by no means the

suitable one. To drill Twelve-hundred scoundrels by 'the
method of kindness,' and of abolishing your very treadwheel, –
how could any commander rejoice to have such a work cut-out
for him? You had but to look in the faces of these Twelve-
hundred, and despair, for most part, of ever 'commanding' them
at all. Miserable distorted block-heads, the generality; ape-faces,
imp-faces, angry dog-faces, heavy sullen ox-faces; degraded
underfoot perverse creatures, sons of *in*docility, greedy mutinous darkness, and in one word, of STUPIDITY, which is the
general mother of such. Stupidity intellectual and stupidity
moral (for the one always means the other, as you will, with
surprise or not, discover if you look) had born this progeny:
base-natured beings, on whom in the course of a maleficent subterranean life of London Scoundrelism, the Genius of Darkness
(called Satan, Devil, and other names) had now visibly impressed
his seal, and had marked them out as soldiers of Chaos and of
him, – appointed to serve in *his* Regiments, First of the line,
Second ditto, and so on in their order. Him, you could perceive,
they would serve; but not easily another than him. These were
the subjects whom our brave Captain and Prison-Governor was
appointed to command, and reclaim to *other* service, by 'the
method of love,' with a treadwheel abolished.

Hopeless forevermore such a project. These abject, ape,
wolf, ox, imp and other diabolic-animal specimens of humanity, who of the very gods could ever have commanded them by
love? A collar round the neck, and a cartwhip flourished over
the back; these, in a just and steady human hand, were what
the gods would have appointed them; and now when, by long
misconduct and neglect, they had sworn themselves into the
Devil's regiments of the line, and got the seal of Chaos impressed
on their visage, it was very doubtful whether even these would
be of avail for the unfortunate commander of Twelve-hundred
men! By 'love,' without hope except of peaceably teasing
oakum, or fear except of a temporary loss of dinner, he was to
guide these men, and wisely constrain them, – whitherward?
No-whither: that was his goal, if you will think well of it; that
was a second fundamental falsity in his problem. False in the
warp and false in the woof, thought one of us; about as false a

problem as any I have seen a good man set upon lately! To
guide scoundrels by 'love;' that is a false woof, I take it, a
method that will not hold together; hardly for the flower of
men will love alone do; and for the sediment and scoundrelism
of men it has not even a chance to do. And then to guide any
class of men, scoundrel or other, *No-whither*, which was this
poor Captain's problem, in this Prison with oakum for its one
element of hope or outlook, how can that prosper by 'love' or by
any conceivable method? That is a warp wholly false. Out of
which false warp, or originally false condition to start from, combined and daily woven into by your false woof, or methods of
'love' and suchlike, there arises for our poor Captain the falsest of
problems, and for a man of his faculty the unfairest of situations.
His problem was, not to command good men to do something,
but bad men to do (with superficial disguises) nothing.

On the whole, what a beautiful Establishment here fitted-up for
the accommodation of the scoundrel-world, male and female! As
I said, no Duke in England is, for all rational purposes which a
human being can or ought to aim at, lodged, fed, tended, taken
care of, with such perfection. Of poor craftsmen that pay rates
and taxes from their day's wages, of the dim millions that toil
and moil continually under the sun, we know what is the lodging and the tending. Of the Johnsons, Goldsmiths, lodged in
their squalid garrets; working often enough amid famine, darkness, tumult, dust and desolation, what work *they* have to
do: – of these as of 'spiritual backwoodsmen,' understood to be
preappointed to such a life, and like the pigs to killing, 'quite
used to it,' I say nothing. But of Dukes, which Duke, I could
ask, has cocoa, soup, meat, and food in general made ready, so
fit for keeping him in health, in ability to do and to enjoy?
Which Duke has a house so thoroughly clean, pure and airy;
lives in an element so wholesome, and perfectly adapted to the
use of soul and body as this same, which is provided here for
the Devil's regiments of the line? No Duke that I have ever
known. Dukes are waited-on by deleterious French cooks, by
perfunctory grooms of the chambers, and expensive crowds of
eye-servants, more imaginary than real: while here, Science,

Human Intellect and Beneficence have searched and sat studious, eager to do their very best; they have chosen a real Artist in Governing to see their best, in all details of it, done. Happy regiments of the line, what soldier to any earthly or celestial Power has such a lodging and attendance as you here? No soldier or servant direct or indirect of God or of man, in this England at present. Joy to you, regiments of the line. Your Master, I am told, has his Elect, and professes to be 'Prince of the Kingdoms of this World;' and truly I see he has power to do a good turn to those he loves, in England at least. Shall we say, May *he*, may the Devil give you good of it, ye Elect of Scoundrelism? I will rather pass by, uttering no prayer at all; musing rather in silence on the singular 'worship of God,' or practical 'reverence done to Human Worth' (which is the outcome and essence of all real 'worship' whatsoever) among the Posterity of Adam at this day.

For all round this beautiful Establishment, or Oasis of Purity, intended for the Devil's regiments of the line, lay continents of dingy poor and dirty dwellings, where the unfortunate not *yet* enlisted into that Force were struggling manifoldly, – in their workshops, in their marble-yards and timber-yards and tan-yards, in their close cellars, cobbler-stalls, hungry garrets, and poor dark trade-shops with red-herrings and tobacco-pipes crossed in the window, – to keep the Devil out-of-doors, and *not* enlist with him. And it was by a tax on these that the Barracks for the regiments of the line were kept up. Visiting Magistrates, impelled by Exeter Hall,[2] by Able-Editors, and the Philanthropic Movement of the Age, had given orders to that effect. Rates on the poor servant of God and of her Majesty, who still serves both in his way, painfully selling red-herrings; rates on him and his red-herrings to boil right soup for the Devil's declared Elect! Never in my travels, in any age or clime, had I fallen-in with such Visiting Magistrates before. Reserved they, I should suppose, for these ultimate or penultimate ages of the world, rich in all prodigies, political, spiritual, – ages surely with such a length of ears as was never paralleled before.

If I had a commonwealth to reform or to govern, certainly it should not be the Devil's regiments of the line that I would first of all concentrate my attention on! With them I should be apt to make rather brief work; to them one would apply the besom, try to sweep *them* with some rapidity into the dust-bin, and well out of one's road, I should rather say. Fill your thrashing-floor with docks, ragweeds, mugworths, and ply your flail upon them, – that is not the method to obtain sacks of wheat. Away, you: begone swiftly, *ye* regiments of the line: in the name of God and of His poor struggling servants, sore put to it to live in these bad days, I mean to rid myself of you with some degree of brevity. To feed you in palaces, to hire captains and school-masters and the choicest spiritual and material artificers to expend their industries on you, – No, by the Eternal! I have quite other work for that class of artists; Seven-and-twenty Millions of neglected mortals who have not yet quite declared for the Devil. Mark it, my diabolic friends, I mean to lay lea-ther on the backs of you, collars round the necks of you: and will teach you, after the examples of the gods, that this world is *not* your inheritance, or glad to see you in it. You, ye diabolic canaille, what has a Governor much to do with you? You, I think, he will rather swiftly dismiss from his thoughts, – which have the whole celestial and terrestrial for their scope, and not the subterranean of scoundreldom alone. You, I consider, he will sweep pretty rapidly into some Norfolk Island,[3] into some special Convict Colony or remote domestic Moorland, into some stone-walled Silent-System, under hard drill-sergeants, just as Rhadamanthus,[4] and inflexible as he, and there leave you to reap what you have sown; he meanwhile turning his endeavours to the thousandfold immeasurable interests of men and gods, – dismissing the one extremely contemptible interest of scoundrels; sweeping that into the cesspool, tumbling that over London Bridge, in a very brief manner, if needful! Who are you, ye thriftless sweepings of Creation, that we should for-ever be pestered with you? Have we no work to do but drilling Devil's regiments of the line?

If I had schoolmasters, my benevolent friend, do you imagine I would set them on teaching a set of unteachables, who as you perceive have already made up their mind that black *is* white, – that the Devil namely is the advantageous Master to serve in this world? My esteemed Benefactor of Humanity, it shall be

far from me. Minds open to that particular conviction are not
the material I like to work upon. When once my schoolmasters
have gone over all the other classes of society from top to bottom; and have no other soul to try with teaching, all being
thoroughly taught, – I will then send them to operate on *these*
regiments of the line: then, and, assure yourself, never till then.
The truth is, I am sick of scoundreldom, my esteemed Benefactor; it always was detestable to me; and here where I find it
lodged in palaces and waited on by the benevolent of the world,
it is more detestable, not to say insufferable to me than ever.

Of Beneficence, Benevolence, and the people that come
together to talk on platforms and subscribe five pounds, I will
say nothing here; indeed there is not room here for the twentieth
part of what were to be said of them. The beneficence, benevolence, and sublime virtue which issues in eloquent talk reported
in the Newspapers, with the subscription of five pounds, and
the feeling that one is a good citizen and ornament to society, –
concerning this, there were a great many unexpected remarks to
be made; but let this one, for the present occasion, suffice:

My sublime benevolent friends, don't you perceive, for one
thing, that here is a shockingly unfruitful investment for your
capital of Benevolence; precisely the *worst*, indeed, which
human ingenuity could select for you? 'Laws are unjust, temptations great,' &c. &c.: alas, I know it, and mourn for it, and
passionately call on all men to help in altering it. But according
to every hypothesis as to the law, and the temptations and pres-
sures towards vice, here are the individuals who, of all the
society, have yielded to said pressure. These are of the worst
substance for enduring pressure! The others yet stand and
make resistance to temptation, to the law's injustice; under all
the perversities and strangling impediments there are, the rest of
the society still keep their feet, and struggle forward, marching
under the banner of *Cosmos*, of God and Human Virtue; these
select Few, as I explain to you, are they who have fallen to
Chaos, and are sworn into certain regiments of the line. A
superior proclivity to Chaos is declared in these, by the very fact
of their being here! Of all the generation we live in, these are the
worst stuff. These, I say, are the Elixir of the Infatuated among

living mortals: if you want the *worst* investment for your Benevolence, here you accurately have it. O my surprising friends! Nowhere so as here can you be certain that a given quantity of wise teaching bestowed, of benevolent trouble taken, will yield *zero*, or the net *minimum* of return. It is sowing of your wheat upon Irish quagmires; laboriously harrowing it in upon the sand of the sea-shore. O my astonishing benevolent friends!

Yonder, in those dingy habitations, and shops of red-herring and tobacco-pipes, where men have not yet quite declared for the Devil; there, I say, is land: here is mere sea-beach. Thither go with your benevolence, thither to those dingy caverns of the poor; and there instruct and drill and manage, there where some fruit may come from it. And, above all and inclusive of all, cannot you go to those Solemn human Shams, Phantasm Captains, and Supreme Quacks that ride prosperously in every thoroughfare; and with severe benevolence, ask them, What they are doing here? They are the men whom it would behove you to drill a little, and tie to the halberts in a benevolent manner, if you could! 'We cannot,' say you? Yes, my friends, to a certain extent you can. By many well-known active methods, and by all manner of passive methods, you can. Strive thitherward, I advise you! thither, with whatever social effort there may lie in you! The well-head and 'consecrated' thrice-accursed chief fountain of all those waters of bitterness, – it is they, those Solemn Shams and Supreme Quacks of yours, little as they or you imagine it! Them, with severe benevolence, put a stop to; them send to their Father, far from the sight of the true and just, – if you would ever see a just world here!

What sort of reformers and workers are you, that work only on the rotten material? That never think of meddling with the material while it continues sound; that stress it and strain it with new rates and assessments, till once it has given way and declared itself rotten; whereupon you snatch greedily at it, and say, Now let us try to do some good upon it! You mistake in every way, my friends: the fact is, you fancy yourselves men of virtue, benevolence, what not; and you are not even men of sincerity and honest sense. I grieve to say it; but it is true. Good from you, and your operations, is not to be expected. You may go down! . . .

from No. 3: Downing Street

From all corners of the wide British Dominion there rises one complaint against the ineffectuality of what are nick-named our 'redtape' establishments, our Government Offices, Colonial Office, Foreign Office and the others, in Downing Street and the neighbourhood. To me individually these branches of human business are little known; but every British citizen and reflective passer-by has occasion to wonder much, and inquire earnestly, concerning them. To all men it is evident that the social interests of One-hundred and fifty Millions of us depend on the mysterious industry there carried on; and likewise that the dissatisfaction with it is great, universal, and continually increasing in intensity, – in fact, mounting, we might say, to the pitch of settled despair.

Every colony, every agent for a matter colonial, has his tragic tale to tell you of his sad experiences in the Colonial Office; what blind obstructions, fatal indolences, pedantries, stupidities, on the right and on the left, he had to do battle with; what a worldwide jungle of redtape, inhabited by doleful creatures, deaf or nearly so to human reason or entreaty, he had entered on; and how he paused in amazement, almost in despair; passionately appealed now to this doleful creature, now to that, and to the dead redtape jungle, and to the living Universe itself, and to the Voices and to the Silences; – and, on the whole, found that it was an adventure, in sorrowful fact, equal to the fabulous ones by old knights-errant against dragons and wizards in enchanted wildernesses and waste howling solitudes; not achievable except by nearly superhuman exercise of all the four cardinal virtues, and unexpected favour of the special

blessing of Heaven. His adventure achieved or found unachiev-
able, he has returned with experiences new to him in the affairs
of men. What this Colonial Office, inhabiting the head of
Downing Street, really *was*, and had to do, or try doing, in
God's practical Earth, he could not by any means precisely get
to know; believes that it does not itself in the least precisely
know. Believes that nobody knows; – that it is a mystery, a kind
of Heathen myth; – and stranger than any piece of the old
mythological Pantheon; for *it* practically presides over the destinies of many millions of living men.

Such is his report of the Colonial Office: and if we oftener
hear such a report of that than we do of the Home Office, Foreign Office or the rest, – the reason probably is, that Colonies
excite more attention at present than any of our other interests.
The Forty Colonies, it appears, are all pretty like rebelling just
now; and are to be pacified with constitutions; – luckier constitutions, let us hope, than some late ones have been. Loyal
Canada, for instance, had to quench a rebellion the other year;
and this year; in virtue of its constitution, it is called upon to
pay the rebels their damages;[5] which surely is a rather surprising result, however constitutional! – Men have rents and
moneys dependent in the Colonies; Emigration schemes, Black
Emancipations, New-Zealand and other schemes; and feel and
publish more emphatically what their Downing-Street woes in
these respects have been.

Were the state of poor *sallow* English ploughers and weavers,
what we may call the Sallow or Yellow Emancipation interest,
as much an object with Exeter-Hall Philanthropists as that of
the Black blockheads now all emancipated, and going at large
without work, or need of working, in West-India clover (and
fattening very much in it, one delights to hear), – then perhaps
the Home Office, its huge virtual task better understood, and
its small actual performance better seen into, might be found
still more deficient, and behind the wants of the age, than the
Colonial itself is.

How it stands with the Foreign Office, again, one still less
knows. Seizures of Sapienza, and the like sudden appearances
of Britain in the character of Hercules-Harlequin, waving, with

big bully-voice, her huge sword-of-sharpness over field-mice,
and in the air making horrid circles (horrid catherine-wheels
and death-disks of metallic terror from said huge sword), to see
how they will like it, – do from time to time astonish the world,
in a not pleasant manner. Hercules-Harlequin, the Attorney
Triumphant, the World's Busybody: none of these are parts this
Nation has a turn for; she, if you consulted her, would rather
not play these parts, but another! Seizures of Sapienza, correspondences with Sotomayor, remonstrances to Otho King of
Athens,[6] fleets hanging by their anchor in behalf of the Majesty of Portugal; and in short the whole, or at present very
nearly the whole, of that industry of protocolling, diplomatis-
ing, remonstrating, admonishing, and 'having the honour to
be,' – has sunk justly in public estimation to a very low figure.

For in fact, it is reasonably asked, What vital interest has
England in any cause now deciding itself in foreign parts? Once
there was a Papistry and Protestantism, important as life eternal and death eternal; more lately there was an interest of Civil
Order and Horrors of the French Revolution, important at
least as rent-roll and preservation of the game; but now what is
there? No cause in which any god or man of this British Nation
can be thought to be concerned. Sham-kingship, now recognised and even self-recognised everywhere to be sham, wrestles
and struggles with mere ballot-box Anarchy: not a pleasant
spectacle to British minds. Both parties in the wrestle professing earnest wishes of peace to us, what have we to do with it
except answer earnestly, 'Peace, yes certainly,' and mind our
affairs elsewhere. The British Nation has no concern with that
indispensable sorrowful and shameful wrestle now going on
everywhere in foreign parts. The British Nation already, by
self-experience centuries old, understands all that; was lucky
enough to transact the greater part of that, in noble ancient
ages, while the wrestle had not yet become a shameful one, but
on *both* sides of it there was wisdom, virtue, heroic nobleness
fruitful to all time, – thrice-lucky British Nation! The British
Nation, I say, has nothing to learn there; has now quite another
set of lessons to learn, far ahead of what is going on there. Sad

example there, of what the issue is, and how inevitable and how imminent, might admonish the British Nation to be speedy with its new lessons; to bestir itself, as men in peril of conflagration do, with the neighbouring houses all on fire! To obtain, for its own very pressing behoof, if by possibility it could, some real Captaincy instead of an imaginary one: to remove resolutely, and replace by a better sort, its own peculiar species of teaching and guiding histrios of various name, who here too are numerous exceedingly, and much in need of gentle removal, while the play is still good, and the comedy has not yet become *tragic*; – and to be a little swift about it withal; and so to escape the otherwise inevitable evil day! This Britain might learn: but she does not need a protocolling establishment, with much 'having the honour to be,' to teach it her.

No: – she has in fact certain cottons, hardwares and suchlike to sell in foreign parts, and certain wines, Portugal oranges, Baltic tar and other products to buy; and does need, I suppose, some kind of Consul, or accredited agent, accessible to British voyagers, here and there, in the chief cities of the Continent: through which functionary, or through the penny-post, if she had any specific message to foreign courts, it would be easy and proper to transmit the same. Special message-carriers, to be still called Ambassadors, if the name gratified them, could be sent when occasion great enough demanded; not sent when it did not. But for all purposes of a resident ambassador, I hear persons extensively and well acquainted among our foreign embassies at this date declare, That a well-selected *Times* reporter or 'own correspondent' ordered to reside in foreign capitals, and keep his eyes open, and (though sparingly) his pen going, would in reality be much more effective; – and surely we see well, he would come a good deal cheaper! Considerably cheaper in expense of money; and in expense of falsity and grimacing hypocrisy (of which no human arithmetic can count the ultimate *cost*) incalculably cheaper! If this is the fact, why not treat it as such? If this is so in any measure, we had better in that measure admit it to be so! The time, I believe, has come for asking with considerable severity, How far is it so?

Nay there are men now current in political society, men of weight though also of wit, who have been heard to say, 'That there was but one reform for the Foreign Office, – to set a live coal under it,' and with, of course, a fire-brigade which could prevent the undue spread of the devouring element into neighbouring houses, let that reform it! In such odour is the Foreign Office too, if it were not that the Public, oppressed and nearly stifled with a mere infinitude of bad odours, neglects this one, – in fact, being able nearly always to avoid the street where it is, *escapes* this one, and (except a passing curse, once in the quarter or so) as good as forgets the existence of it.

Such, from sad personal experience and credited prevailing rumour, is the exoteric public conviction about these sublime establishments in Downing Street and the neighbourhood, – the esoteric mysteries of which are indeed still held sacred by the initiated, but believed by the world to be mere Dalai-Lama pills,[7] manufactured let not refined lips hint how, and quite *un*salvatory to mankind. Every one may remark what a hope animates the eyes of any circle, when it is reported or even confidently asserted, that Sir Robert Peel has in his mind privately resolved to go, one day, into that stable of King Augias,[8] which appals human hearts, so rich is it, high-piled with the droppings of two hundred years; and Hercules-like to load a thousand night-wagons from it, and turn running water into it, and swash and shovel at it, and never leave it till the antique pavement, and real basis of the matter, show itself clean again! In any intelligent circle such a rumour, like the first break of day to men in darkness, enlightens all eyes; and each says devoutly, '*Faxitis*, O ye righteous Powers that have pity on us! All England grateful, with kindling looks, will rise in the rear of him, and from its deepest heart bid him good speed!'

For it is universally felt that some *esoteric* man, well acquainted with the mysteries and properties good and evil of the administrative stable, is the fittest to reform it, nay can alone reform it otherwise than by sheer violence and destruction, which is a way we would avoid; that in fact Sir Robert Peel is, at present, the one likely or possible man to reform it. And secondly it is felt that 'reform' in that Downing-Street department of affairs is precisely the reform which were worth all others; that those administrative establishments in Downing Street are really the Government of this huge ungoverned Empire; that to clean-out the dead pedantries, unveracities, indolent somnolent impotences, and accumulated dung-mountains there, is the beginning of all practical good whatsoever. Yes, get down once again to the actual *pavement* of that; ascertain what the thing is, and was before dung accumulated in it; and what it should and may, and must, for the life's sake of this Empire, henceforth become: here clearly lies the heart of the whole matter. Political reform, if this be not reformed, is naught and a mere mockery.

What England wants, and will require to have, or sink in nameless anarchies, is not a Reformed Parliament, meaning thereby a Parliament elected according to the six or the four or any other number of 'points'[9] and cunningly-devised improvements in hustings mechanism, but a Reformed Executive or Sovereign Body of Rulers and Administrators, – some improved method, innumerable improvements in our poor blind methods, of getting hold of these. Not a better Talking-Apparatus, the best conceivable Talking-Apparatus would do very little for us at present; – but an infinitely better Acting-Apparatus, the benefits of which would be invaluable now and henceforth. The practical question puts itself with ever-increasing stringency to all English minds: Can we, by no industry, energy, utmost expenditure of human ingenuity, and passionate invocation of the Heavens and the Earth, get to attain some twelve or ten or six men to manage the affairs of this nation in Downing Street and the chief posts elsewhere, who are abler for the work than those we have been used to, this long while? For it is really a heroic work, and cannot be done by histrios, and dextrous talkers having the honour to be: it is a heavy and appalling work; and, at the starting of it especially, will require Herculean men; such mountains of pedant exuviæ and obscene owl-droppings have accumulated in those regions, long the habitation of doleful creatures; the old *pavements*, the natural facts and real essential functions of those establishments, have not been seen by eyes for these two-hundred years last past! Herculean men acquainted with the virtues of running water, and with the divine necessity of getting down to the clear pavements and old veracities; who tremble before no amount of pedant exuviæ, no loudest shrieking of doleful creatures; who tremble only to live, themselves, like inane phantasms, and to leave their life as a paltry *contribution* to the guano mountains,[10] and not as a divine eternal protest against them!

These are the kind of men we want; these, the nearest possible approximation to these, are the men we must find and have, or go bankrupt altogether; for the concern as it is will evidently not hold long together. How true is this of Crabbe:[11] 'Men sit in Parliament eighty-three hours per week, debating about many things. Men sit in Downing Street, doing protocols, Syrian treaties, Greek questions, Portuguese, Spanish, French, Egyptian and Æthiopian questions; dextrously writing despatches, and having the honour to be. Not a question of them is at all pressing in comparison with the English question. Pacifico the miraculous Gibraltar Jew[12] has been hustled by some populace in Greece: upon him let the British Lion drop, very rapidly indeed, a constitutional tear. Radetzky is said to be advancing upon Milan;[13] – I am sorry to hear it, and perhaps it does deserve a despatch, or friendly letter, once and away: but the Irish Giant, named of Despair, is advancing upon London itself, laying waste all English cities, towns and villages; that is the interesting Government-despatch of the day! I notice him in Piccadilly, blue-visaged, thatched in rags, a blue child on each arm; hunger-driven, wide-mouthed, seeking whom he may devour: he, missioned by the just Heavens, too truly and too sadly their "divine missionary" come at last in *this* authoritative manner, will throw us all into Doubting Castle, I perceive! That is the phenomenon worth protocolling about, and writing despatches upon, and thinking of with all one's faculty day and night, if one wishes to have the honour to be – anything but a Phantasm Governor of England just now! I entreat your Lordship's all-but undivided attention to that Domestic Irish Giant, named of Despair, for a great many

years to come. Prophecy of him there has long been; but now
by the rot of the potato (blessed be the just gods, who send us
either swift death or some beginning of cure at last!), he is here
in person, and there is no denying him, or disregarding him
any more; and woe to the public watchman that ignores *him*,
and sees Pacifico the Gibraltar Jew instead!' ...

from No. 6: Parliaments

... But as to universal suffrage, again, – can it be proved that, since the beginning of the world, there was ever given a universal vote in favour of the worthiest man or thing? I have always understood that true worth, in any department, was difficult to recognise; that the worthiest, if he appealed to universal suffrage, would have but a poor chance. John Milton, inquiring of universal England what the worth of *Paradise Lost* was, received for answer, Five Pounds Sterling.[14] George Hudson,[15] inquiring in like manner what his services on the railways might be worth, received for answer (prompt temporary answer), Fifteen Hundred Thousand ditto. Alas, Jesus Christ asking the Jews what *he* deserved, was not the answer, Death on the gallows! – Will your Lordship believe me, I feel it almost a shame to insist on such truisms. Surely the doctrine of judgment by vote of hustings has sunk now, or should be fast sinking, to the condition of obsolete with all but the commonest of human intelligences. With me, I must own, it has never had any existence. The mass of men consulted at hustings, upon any high matter whatsoever, is as ugly an exhibition of human stupidity as this world sees.

Universal suffrage assembled at hustings, – I will consult it about the quality of New-Orleans pork, or the coarser kinds of Irish butter; but as to the character of men, I will if possible ask it no question: or if the question be asked and the answer given, I will generally consider, in cases of any importance, that the said answer is likely to be wrong, – that I have to listen to the said answer and receive it as authentic, and for my own share to go, and with whatever strength may lie in me, do the reverse of the same. Even so, your Lordship; for how should I follow a multitude to do evil? There are such things as multitudes all full of beer and nonsense, even of insincere factitious nonsense, who by hypothesis cannot but be wrong. Or what safety will there be in a thousand or ten thousand brawling potwallopers, or blockheads of any rank whatever, if the Fact, namely the whole Universe and the Eternal Destinies, be against me? These latter I for my share will try to follow, even if alone in doing so. It will be better for me.

Your Lordship, there are fools, cowards, knaves, and gluttonous traitors true only to their own appetite, in immense majority, in every rank of life; and there is nothing frightfuler than to see these voting and deciding! 'Not your way, my unhappy brothers, shall it be decided; no, not while I, and a company of poor men you may have heard of, live in this world. Vote it as you please," my friend Oliver[16] was wont to say or intimate; "vote it so, if you like; there is a company of poor men that will spend all their blood before they see it settled so!' – Who, in such sad moments, but has to *hate* the profane vulgar, and feel that he must and will debar it from him! And alas, the vulgarest vulgar, I often find, are not those in ragged coats at this day; but those in fine, superfine, and superfinest; – the more is the pity! Superfine coat symbolically indicates, like official stamp and signature, *Bank-of-England Thousand-Pound Note*; and blinkard owls, in city and country, accept it cheerfully as such: but look closer, you may find it mere *Bank of Elegance*; a flashnote travelling towards the eternal Fire; – and will have nothing to do with it, you, I hope!

Clearly enough, the King in constitutional countries would wish to ascertain all men's votes, their opinions, volitions on all manner of matters; that so his whole scene of operations, to the last cranny of it, might be illuminated for him, and he, wherever he were working, might work with perfect knowledge of the circumstances and materials. But the King, New Downing Street,[17] or whatever the Sovereign's name is, will be a very poor King indeed if he *admit* all these votes into his system of procedure, and transform them into acts; – indeed I think, in that case, he will not be long for this world as a King! No: though immense acclamation attend him at the first outset in that course, every volition and opinion finding itself admitted into the poor King's procedure, – yet unless the volitions and opinions are wise and not foolish, not the smallest ultimate prosperity can attend him; and all the acclamations of the world will not save him from the ignominious lot which Nature herself has appointed for all creatures that do *not* follow the Law which Nature has laid down.

You ask this and the other man what is his opinion, his notion, about varieties of things: and having ascertained what his notion is, and carried it off as a piece of information, – surely you are bound, many times, most times if you are a wise man, to go directly in the teeth of it, and for his sake and for yours to do directly the contrary of it. Any man's opinion one would accept; all men's opinion, could it be had absolutely without trouble, might be worth accepting. Nay on certain points I even ask my horse's opinion: – as to whether beans will suit him at this juncture, or a truss of tares; on this and the like points I carefully consult my horse; gather, by such language as he has, what my horse's candid opinion as to beans or the truss of tares is, and unhesitatingly follow the same. As what prudent rider would not? There is no foolishest man but knows one and the other thing more clearly than any the wisest man does; no glimmer of human or equine intelligence but can disclose something which even the intelligence of a Newton, *not* present in that exact juncture of circumstances, would not otherwise have ascertained. To such length you would gladly consult all equine, and much more all human intelligences: – to such length; and, strictly speaking, not any farther.

Of what use towards the general result of finding out what it is wise to do, – which is the one thing needful to all men and nations, – can the fool's vote be? It is either coincident with the wise man's vote, throwing no new light on the matter, and therefore superfluous; or else it is contradictory, and therefore still more superfluous, throwing mere darkness on the matter, and imperatively demanding to be annihilated, and returned to the giver with protest. Woe to you if you leave that valid!

There are expressions of volition too, as well as of opinion, which you collect from foolish men, and even from inferior creatures: these can do you no harm, these it may be very beneficial for you to have and know; – but these also, surely it is often imperative on you to contradict, and would be ruinous and baleful for you to *follow*. You have to apprise the unwise man, even as you do the unwise horse: 'On the truss of tares I took your vote, and have cheerfully fulfilled it; but in regard to choice of roads and the like, I regret to say you have no competency whatever. No, my unwise friend, we are for Hammersmith and the West, not for Highgate and the Northern parts, on this occasion: not by that left turn, by this turn to the right runs our road; thither, for reasons too intricate to explain at this moment, it will behove thee and me to go: Along, therefore!'

'But how?' your Lordship asks, and all the world with you: 'Are not two men stronger than one; must not two votes carry it over one?' I answer: No, nor two thousand nor two million. Many men vote; but in the end, you will infallibly find, none counts except the few who were *in the right*. Unit of that class, against as many zeros as you like! If the King's thought is according to the will of God, or to the law appointed for this Universe, I can assure your Lordship the King will ultimately carry that, were he but one in it against the whole world.

It is not by rude force, either of muscle or of will, that one man can govern twenty men, much more twenty millions of men. For the moment, if all the twenty are stark against his resolution never so wise, the twenty for the moment must have their foolish way; the wise resolution, for the moment, cannot be carried. Let their votes be taken, or known (as is often possible) without taking; and once well taken, let them be weighed, – which latter operation, also an essential one for the King or Governor, is very difficult. If the weight be in favour of the Governor, let him in general proceed; cheerfully accepting adverse account of heads, and dealing wisely with that according to his means; – often enough, in pressing cases, flatly disregarding that, and walking through the heart of it; for in general it is but frothy folly and loud-blustering rant and wind.

I have known minorities, and even small ones by the account of heads, do grand national feats long memorable to all the world, in these circumstances. Witness Cromwell and his Puritans; a minority at all times, by account of heads; yet the authors or saviours, as it ultimately proved, of whatsoever is divinest in the things we can still reckon ours in England. Minority by tale of heads; but weighed in Heaven's balances, a most clear majority: this 'company of poor men that will spend their blood rather,' on occasion shown, – it has now become a noble army of heroes, whose conquests were appointed to endure forever. Indeed it is on such terms that grand national and other feats, by the sons of Adam, are generally done. Not without risk and labour to the doers of them; no surely, for it never was an easy matter to do the real will of a Nation, much more the real will of this Universe in respect to a Nation. No, that is difficult and heroic; easy as it is to count the voting heads of a Nation at any time, and do the behests of their beer and balderdash; empty behests, very different from even their 'will,' poor blockheads, to say nothing of the Nation's will and the Universe's will! Which two, especially which latter, are alone worth doing.

But if not only the number but the weight of votes preponderate against your Governor, he, never so much in the right, will find it wise to hold his hand; to delay, for a time, this his beneficent execution, which is ultimately inevitable and indispensable, of Heaven's Decrees; the Nation being still unprepared. He will leave the bedarkened Nation yet a while alone. What can he do for it, if not even a small minority will stand by him? Let him strive to enlighten the Nation; let him pray, and in all ways endeavour, that the Nation be enlightened, – that a small minority may open their eyes and hearts to the message of Heaven, which he, heavy-laden man and governor, *has* been commissioned to see done in this transitory earth, at his peril! Heaven's message, sure enough, if it be true; and Hell's if it be not, though voted for by innumerable two-legged animals without feathers or with!

On the whole, honour to small minorities, when they are genuine ones. Severe is their battle sometimes, but it is victorious always like that of gods. Tancred of Hauteville's sons, some eight centuries ago, conquered all Italy;[18] bound it up into organic masses, of vital order after a sort; founded thrones and principalities upon the same, which have not yet entirely vanished, – which, the last dying wrecks of which, still wait for some worthier successor, it would appear. The Tancred Normans were some Four Thousand strong; the Italy they conquered in open fight, and bound up into masses at their ordering will, might count Eight Millions, all as large of bone, as eupeptic and black-whiskered as they. How came the small minority of Normans to prevail in this so hopeless-looking debate? Intrinsically, doubt it not, because they were in the right; because, in a dim, instinctive, but most genuine manner, they were doing the commandment of Heaven, and so Heaven had decided that they were to prevail. But extrinsically also, I can see, it was because the Normans were *not* afraid to have their skin scratched; and were prepared to die in their quarrel where needful. One man of that humour among a thousand of the other, consider it! Let the small minority, backed by the whole Universe, and looked on by such a cloud of invisible witnesses, fall into no despair.

What is to become of Parliament in the New Era, is less a question with me than what is to become of Downing Street. With a Reformed Downing Street strenuously bent on real and not imaginary management of our affairs, I could foresee all manner of reform to England and its Parliament; and at length in the gradual course of years, that highest acme of reform to Parliament and to England, a New Governing Authority, a real and not imaginary King set to preside there. With that, to my view, comes all blessedness whatsoever; without that comes, and can come, nothing but, with ever-accelerated pace, ANARCHY; or the *declaration* of the fact that we have no Governor, and have long had none.

For the rest, Anarchy advances as with seven-league boots, in these years. Either some New Downing Street and Incipiency of a real Hero-Kingship again, or else Chartist Parliament, with Apotheosis of Attorneyism; and Anarchy very undeniable to all the world: one or else the other, it seems to me, we shall soon have. Under a real Kingship the Parliament, we may rest satisfied, would gradually, with whatever difficulty, get itself inducted to its real function, and restricted to that, and moulded to the form fittest for that. If there can be no reform of Downing Street, I care not much for the reform of Parliament. Our doom, I perceive, is the Apotheosis of Attorneyism; into that blackest of terrestrial curses we must plunge, and take our fate there like the others.

For the sake both of the New Downing Street and of whatever its New Parliament may be, let us add here, what will vitally concern both these Institutions, a few facts, much forgotten at present, on the general question of Enfranchisement; – and therewith end. Who is slave, and eternally appointed to be governed; who free, and eternally appointed to govern? It would much avail us all to settle this question.

Slave or free is settled in Heaven for a man; acts of parliament attempting to settle it on earth for him, sometimes make sad work of it. Now and then they correctly copy Heaven's settlement in regard to it; proclaim audibly what is the silent fact, 'Here is a free man, let him be honoured!' – and so are of the nature of a God's Gospel to other men concerned. Far oftenest they quite miscopy Heaven's settlement, and copy merely the account of the Ledger, or some quite other settlement in regard to it; proclaiming with an air of discovery, 'Here is a Ten-pounder; here is a Thousand-pounder; Heavens, here is a Three-million-pounder, – is not he free?' Nay they are wont, here in England for some time back, to proclaim in the gross, as if it had become credible lately, all two-legged animals without feathers to be 'free.' 'Here is a distressed Nigger,' they proclaim, 'who much prefers idleness to work, – should not he be free to choose which? Is not he a man and brother? Clearly here are two legs and no feathers: let us vote him Twenty millions for enfranchisement, and so secure the blessing of the gods!' –

My friends, I grieve to remind you, but it is eternally the fact: Whom Heaven has made a slave, no parliament of men nor

power that exists on Earth can render free. No; he is chained by
fetters which parliaments with their millions cannot reach. You
can label him free; yes, and it is but labelling him a solecism, –
bidding him be the parent of solecisms wheresoever he goes.
You can give him pumpkins, houses of tenpound rent, houses
of ten-thousand pound: the bigger candle you light within the
slave-image of him, it will but show his slave-features on the
larger and more hideous scale. Heroism, manful wisdom is not
his: many things you can give him, but that thing never. Him
the Supreme Powers marked in the making of him, *slave*;
appointed him, at his and our peril, not to command but to
obey, in this world. Him you cannot enfranchise, not him; to
proclaim this man free is not a God's Gospel to other men; it is
an alarming Devil's Gospel to himself and to us all. Devil's Gospel little feared in these days; but brewing for the whole of us
its big oceans of destruction all the same. States are to be called
happy and noble in so far as they settle rightly who is slave and
who free; unhappy, ignoble, and doomed to destruction, as
they settle it wrong.

   We may depend on it, Heaven in the most constitutional countries knows well who is slave, who is not. And with regard to
voting, I lay it down as a rule, No real *slave's* vote is other than
a nuisance, whensoever or wheresoever or in what manner
soever it be given. That is a truth, No slave's vote; – and, alas,
here is another not quite so plain, though equally certain. That
as Nature and severe Destiny, not mere act of Parliament and
possession of money-capital, determine a man's slavehood, – so,
by these latter, it has been, in innumerable instances, determined
wrong just at present! Instances evident to everybody, and
instances suspected by nobody but the more discerning: – the
fact is, slaves are in a tremendous majority everywhere; and the
voting of them (not to be got rid of just yet) is a nuisance in
proportion. Nuisance of proportionally tremendous magnitude, properly indeed the grand fountain of all other nuisances
whatsoever.

   For it is evident, could you entirely exclude the slave's vote,
and admit only the heroic free man's vote, – folly, knavery, falsity, gluttonous imbecility, lowmindedness and cowardice had,

if not disappeared from the earth, reduced themselves to a rigorous minimum in human affairs; the ultimate New Era, and
best possible condition of human affairs, had actually come.
This is what I always pray for; rejoicing in everything that furthers it, sorrowing for everything that furthers the reverse of it.
And though I know it is yet a great way off, I know also either
that it is inevitably coming, or that human society, and the possibility of man's living on this earth, has ended. And so for
England too, may I think for England most and soonest of all,
it will be behooveful that we attain some rectification, innumerable rectifications, in regard to this essential matter; and
contrive to bid our Heaven's free men vote, and our Heaven's
slaves be silent, with infinitely more correctness than at present. Either on the hither brink of that black sea of Anarchy,
wherein other Nations at present lie drowning and plunging, or
after weltering through the same, if we can welter, – it will have
to be attained. In some measure, in some manner, attained: life
depends on that, death on the missing of that.

New definitions of slavery are pressingly wanted just now. The
definition of a free man is difficult to find, so that all men could
distinguish slave from free; found, it would be invaluable!
The free man once universally recognised, we should know
him who had the privilege to vote and assist in commanding,
at least to go himself uncommanded. Men do not know his
definition well at present; never knew it worse; – hence these
innumerable sorrows.

The free man is he who is *loyal* to the Laws of this Universe; who in his heart sees and knows, across all contradictions,
that injustice *cannot* befall him here; that except by sloth
and cowardly falsity evil is not possible here. The first symptom of such a man is not that he resists and rebels, but that
he obeys. As poor Henry Marten wrote in Chepstow Castle
long ago,[19]

> Reader, if thou an oft-told tale wilt trust,
> Thou'lt gladly do and suffer what thou must.

Gladly; he that will go gladly to his labour and his suffering, it is to him alone that the Upper Powers are favourable and the Field of Time will yield fruit. 'An oft-told tale,' friend Harry; all the noble of this world have known it, and in various dialects have striven to let us know it! The essence of all 'religion' that was and that will be, is to make men *free*. Who is he that, in this Life-pilgrimage, will consecrate himself at all hazards to obey God and God's servants, and to disobey the Devil and his? With pious valour this free man walks through the roaring tumults, invincibly the way whither he is bound. To him in the waste Saharas, through the grim solitudes peopled by galvanised corpses and doleful creatures, there is a loadstar; and his path, whatever those of others be, is towards the Eternal. A man well worth consulting, and taking the vote of, about matters temporal; and properly the only kind of man. Though always an exceptional, this was once a well-known man. He has become one of the rarest now; – but is not yet entirely extinct; and will become more plentiful, if the Gods intend to keep this Planet habitable long.

Him it were vain to try to find always without mistake; alas, if he were in the majority, this world would be all 'a school of virtue,' which it is far from being. Nevertheless to him, and in all times to him alone, belongs the rule of this world: that he be got to rule, that he be forbidden to rule and not got, means salvation or destruction to the world. Friend Peter, I am perfectly deliberate in calling this the truest doctrine of the constitution you have ever heard. And I recommend you to learn it gradually, and to lay it well to heart; for without it there is no salvation, and all other doctrines of the constitution are leather and prunella. Will any mass of Chancery parchments, think you, of respectablest traditions and Delolme philosophies,[20] save a man or People that forgets this, from the eternal fire? There does burn such a *fire* everywhere under this green earth-rind of ours, and London pavements themselves (as Paris pavements have done) can start up into sea-ridges, with a horrible 'trough of the sea,' if the fire-flood urge!

To this man, I say, belongs eternally the government of the world. Where he reigns, all is blessed; and the gods rejoice, and only the wicked make wail. Where the contrary of him reigns, all is accursed; and the gods lament, – and will, by terrible methods, rectify the matter by and by! Have you forbidden this man to rule? Obey he cannot where the Devil and his servants rule; how can he? He must die thrice ruined, damned by the gods, if he do. He will retire rather, into deserts and rocky inaccessibilities, companion to wild-beasts, to the dumb granites and the eternal stars, far from you and your affairs. You and your affairs, once well quit of him, go by a swift and ever swifter road! ...

The Life of John Sterling

Carlyle first met John Sterling in 1835, during his own early days in London, and a friendship developed which lasted for the remaining years of Sterling's life. Sterling was in many ways a typical representative of the intellectual climate of the 1830s and '40s. One of the 'Apostles' group of Cambridge undergraduates, he had been unable to find a satisfactory outlet for his talents in the world at large. In 1834 he took orders, only to resign his curacy eight months later, giving as his reason his proneness to tuberculosis. According to Carlyle, Sterling's real misgivings were intellectual, and he spent the rest of his life involved in various literary activities, achieving distinction as a contributor to the reviews. Shortly before his death in 1844 Sterling appointed Carlyle, together with his theological patron, Archdeacon Hare, as his literary executors. Hare produced a collection of Sterling's writings, together with a biographical account, in 1848, but Carlyle felt that this account was prejudiced by Hare's clerical position and he thus published his own *Life* in 1851.

The Life of John Sterling is hardly one of Carlyle's major works, but it is one of his most attractive. His account of his friend is warmly sympathetic and he particularly stresses his intellectual honesty and generosity of spirit. Sterling's brief spell as a curate is seen as a misguided attempt to impose unnatural constraints on these qualities, and is attributed to the unfortunate influence of Coleridge, whom Carlyle had himself met during his first visit to London in 1824. Coleridge's emphasis on the distinction to be drawn between the material and the spiritual has much in common with positions which

Carlyle held himself; Carlyle, however, regarded Coleridge's reformulation of the role of the established church as a delusion that evaded a more valid solution to the problems of the time. On a more personal level he objected to the mystique that surrounded Coleridge in his later years and his account of him in *The Life of John Sterling*, which is reprinted here, is a vivid expression of these misgivings. It is interesting to compare it with those of Hazlitt (in *The Spirit of the Age*, and elsewhere) and of John Stuart Mill, in his celebrated essay, first published in 1840.

Coleridge*

Coleridge sat on the brow of Highgate Hill, in those years, looking down on London and its smoke-tumult, like a sage escaped from the inanity of life's battle; attracting towards him the thoughts of innumerable brave souls still engaged there. His express contributions to poetry, philosophy, or any specific province of human literature or enlightenment, had been small and sadly intermittent; but he had, especially among young inquiring men, a higher than literary, a kind of prophetic or magician character. He was thought to hold, he alone in England, the key of German and other Transcendentalisms; knew the sublime secret of believing by 'the reason' what 'the understanding' had been obliged to fling out as incredible; and could still, after Hume and Voltaire had done their best and worst with him, profess himself an orthodox Christian, and say and print to the Church of England, with its singular old rubrics and surplices at Allhallow-tide, *Esto perpetua*. A sublime man; who, alone in those dark days, had saved his crown of spiritual manhood; escaping from the black materialisms, and revolutionary deluges, with 'God, Freedom, Immortality' still his: a king of men. The practical intellects of the world did not much heed him, or carelessly reckoned him a metaphysical dreamer: but to the rising spirits of the young generation he had this dusky sublime character; and sat there as a kind of *Magus*, girt in mystery and enigma; his Dodona oak-grove (Mr Gilman's house at Highgate)[1] whispering strange things, uncertain whether oracles or jargon.

* Part One, Chapter 8.

The Gilmans did not encourage much company, or excitation of any sort, round their sage; nevertheless access to him, if a youth did reverently wish it, was not difficult. He would stroll about the pleasant garden with you, sit in the pleasant rooms of the place, – perhaps take you to his own peculiar room, high up, with a rearward view, which was the chief view of all. A really charming outlook, in fine weather. Close at hand, wide sweep of flowery leafy gardens, their few houses mostly hidden, the very chimney-pots veiled under blossomy umbrage, flowed gloriously down hill; gloriously issuing in wide-tufted undulating plain-country, rich in all charms of field and town. Waving blooming country of the brightest green; dotted all over with handsome villas, handsome groves; crossed by roads and human traffic, here inaudible or heard only as a musical hum: and behind all swam, under olive-tinted haze, the illimitable limitary ocean of London, with its domes and steeples definite in the sun, big Paul's and the many memories attached to it hanging high over all. Nowhere, of its kind, could you see a grander prospect on a bright summer day, with the set of the air going southward, – southward, and so draping with the city-smoke not *you* but the city. Here for hours would Coleridge talk, concerning all conceivable or inconceivable things; and liked nothing better than to have an intelligent, or failing that, even a silent and patient human listener. He distinguished himself to all that ever heard him as at least the most surprising talker extant in this world, – and to some small minority, by no means to all, as the most excellent.

The good man, he was now getting old, towards sixty perhaps; and gave you the idea of a life that had been full of sufferings; a life heavy-laden, half-vanquished, still swimming painfully in seas of manifold physical and other bewilderment. Brow and head were round, and of massive weight, but the face was flabby and irresolute. The deep eyes, of a light hazel, were as full of sorrow as of inspiration; confused pain looked mildly from them, as in a kind of mild astonishment. The whole figure and air, good and amiable otherwise, might be called flabby and irresolute; expressive of weakness under possibility of strength. He hung loosely on his limbs, with knees bent, and stooping attitude; in walking, he rather shuffled than decisively stept; and a lady once remarked, he never could fix which side of the garden walk would suit him best, but continually shifted, in corkscrew fashion, and kept trying both. A heavy-laden, high-aspiring and surely much-suffering man. His voice, naturally soft and good, had contracted itself into a plaintive snuffle and singsong; he spoke as if preaching, – you would have said, preaching earnestly and also hopelessly the weightiest things. I still recollect his 'object' and 'subject,' terms of continual recurrence in the Kantean province; and how he sang and snuffled them into 'om-m-mject' and 'sum-m-mject,' with a kind of solemn shake or quaver, as he rolled along. No talk, in his century or in any other, could be more surprising.

Sterling, who assiduously attended him, with profound reverence, and was often with him by himself, for a good many months, gives a record of their first colloquy.* Their colloquies were numerous, and he had taken note of many; but they are all gone to the fire, except this first, which Mr Hare has printed, – unluckily without date. It contains a number of ingenious, true and half-true observations, and is of course a faithful epitome of the things said; but it gives small idea of Coleridge's way of talking; – this one feature is perhaps the most recognisable. 'Our interview lasted for three hours, during which he talked two hours and three quarters.' Nothing could be more copious than his talk; and furthermore it was always, virtually or literally, of the nature of a monologue; suffering no interruption, however reverent; hastily putting aside all foreign additions, annotations, or most ingenious desires for elucidation, as well-meant superfluities which would never do. Besides, it was talk not flowing anywhither like a river, but spreading everywhither in extricable currents and regurgitations like a lake or sea; terribly deficient in definite goal or aim, nay often in logical intelligibility; *what* you were to believe or do, on any earthly or heavenly thing, obstinately refusing to appear from it. So that, most times, you felt logically lost;

* *Biography*, by Hare, pp. xvi–xxvi.

swamped near to drowning in this tide of ingenious vocables, spreading out boundless as if to submerge the world.

To sit as a passive bucket and be pumped into, whether you consent or not, can in the long-run be exhilarating to no creature; how eloquent soever the flood of utterance that is descending. But if it be withal a confused unintelligible flood of utterance, threatening to submerge all known landmarks of thought, and drown the world and you! – I have heard Coleridge talk, with eager musical energy, two stricken hours, his face radiant and moist, and communicate no meaning whatsoever to any individual of his hearers, – certain of whom, I for one, still kept eagerly listening in hope; the most had long before given up, and formed (if the room were large enough) secondary humming groups of their own. He began anywhere: you put some question to him, made some suggestive observation: instead of answering this, or decidedly setting out towards answer of it, he would accumulate formidable apparatus, logical swim-bladders, transcendental life-preservers and other precautionary and vehiculatory gear, for setting out; perhaps did at last get under way, – but was swiftly solicited, turned aside by the glance of some radiant new game on this hand or that, into new courses; and ever into new; and before long into all the Universe, where it was uncertain what game you would catch, or whether any.

His talk, alas, was distinguished, like himself, by irresolution: it disliked to be troubled with conditions, abstinences, definite fulfilments; – loved to wander at its own sweet will, and make its auditor and his claims and humble wishes a mere passive bucket for itself! He had knowledge about many things and topics, much curious reading; but generally all topics led him, after a pass or two, into the high seas of theosophic philosophy, the hazy infinitude of Kantean transcendentalism, with its 'sum-m-mjects' and 'om-m-mjects.' Sad enough; for with such indolent impatience of the claims and ignorances of others, he had not the least talent for explaining this or anything unknown to them; and you swam and fluttered in the mistiest wide unintelligible deluge of things, for most part in a rather profitless uncomfortable manner.

Glorious islets, too, I have seen rise out of the haze; but they were few, and soon swallowed in the general element again. Balmy sunny islets, islets of the blest and the intelligible: – on which occasions those secondary humming groups would all cease humming, and hang breathless upon the eloquent words; till once your islet got wrapt in the mist again, and they could recommence humming. Eloquent artistically expressive words you always had; piercing radiances of a most subtle insight came at intervals; tones of noble pious sympathy, recognisable as pious though strangely coloured, were never wanting long: but in general you could not call this aimless, cloudcapt, cloud-based, lawlessly meandering human discourse of reason by the name of 'excellent talk,' but only of 'surprising;' and were reminded bitterly of Hazlitt's account of it: 'Excellent talker, very – if you let him start from no premises and come to no conclusion.' Coleridge was not without what talkers call wit, and there were touches of prickly sarcasm in him, contemptuous enough of the world and its idols and popular dignitaries; he had traits even of poetic humour: but in general he seemed deficient in laughter; or indeed in sympathy for concrete human things either on the sunny or on the stormy side. One right peal of concrete laughter at some convicted flesh-and-blood absurdity, one burst of noble indignation at some injustice or depravity, rubbing elbows with us on this solid Earth, how strange would it have been in that Kantean haze-world, and how infinitely cheering amid its vacant air-castles and dim-melting ghosts and shadows! None such ever came. His life had been an abstract thinking and dreaming, idealistic, passed amid the ghosts of defunct bodies and of unborn ones. The moaning singsong of that theosophico-metaphysical monotony left on you, at last, a very dreary feeling.

In close colloquy, flowing within narrower banks, I suppose he was more definite and apprehensible; Sterling in aftertimes did not complain of his unintelligibility, or imputed it only to the abstruse high nature of the topics handled. Let us hope so, let us try to believe so! There is no doubt but Coleridge could speak plain words on things plain: his observations and responses on the trivial matters that occurred were as simple as the commonest man's, or were even distinguished by superior simplicity as well as pertinency. 'Ah, your tea is too cold, Mr Coleridge!' mourned the good Mrs Gilman once, in her kind, reverential and yet protective manner, handing him a very tolerable though belated cup. – 'It's better than I deserve!' snuffled he, in a low hoarse murmur, partly courteous, chiefly pious, the tone of which still abides with me: 'It's better than I deserve!'

But indeed, to the young ardent mind, instinct with pious nobleness, yet driven to the grim deserts of Radicalism for a faith, his speculations had a charm much more than literary, a charm almost religious and prophetic. The constant gist of his discourse was lamentation over the sunk condition of the world; which he recognised to be given-up to Atheism and Materialism, full of mere sordid misbeliefs, mispursuits and misresults. All Science had become mechanical; the science not of men, but of a kind of human beavers. Churches themselves had died away into a godless mechanical condition; and stood there as mere Cases of Articles, mere Forms of Churches; like the dried carcasses of once-swift camels, which you find left withering in the thirst of the universal desert, – ghastly portents for the present, beneficent ships of the desert no more. Men's souls were blinded, hebetated; and sunk under the influence of Atheism and Materialism, and Hume and Voltaire: the world for the present was as an extinct world, deserted of God, and incapable of welldoing till it changed its heart and spirit. This, expressed I think with less of indignation and with more of long-drawn querulousness, was always recognisable as the ground-tone: – in which truly a pious young heart, driven into Radicalism and the opposition party, could not but recognise a too sorrowful truth; and ask of the Oracle, with all earnestness, What remedy, then?

The remedy, though Coleridge himself professed to see it as in sunbeams, could not, except by processes unspeakably diffi-cult, be described to you at all. On the whole, those dead Churches, this dead English Church especially, must be brought to life again. Why not? It was not dead; the soul of it, in this parched-up body, was tragically asleep only. Atheistic Philosophy

was true on its side, and Hume and Voltaire could on their own
ground speak irrefragably for themselves against any Church:
but lift the Church and them into a higher sphere of argument,
they died into inanition, the Church revivified itself into pristine
florid vigour, – became once more a living ship of the desert,
and invincibly bore you over stock and stone, But how, but
how! By attending to the 'reason' of man, said Coleridge, and
duly chaining-up the 'understanding' of man:[2] the *Vernunft*
(Reason) and *Verstand* (Understanding) of the Germans, it all
turned upon these, if you could well understand them, – which
you couldn't. For the rest, Mr Coleridge had on the anvil various Books, especially was about to write one grand Book *On
the Logos*,[3] which would help to bridge the chasm for us. So
much appeared, however: Churches, though proved false (as
you had imagined), were still true (as you were to imagine):
here was an Artist who could burn you up an old Church, root
and branch; and then as the Alchymists professed to do with
organic substances in general, distil you an 'Astral Spirit' from
the ashes, which was the very image of the old burnt article, its
airdrawn counterpart, – this you still had, or might get, and
draw uses from, if you could. Wait till the Book on the Logos
were done; – alas, till your own terrene eyes, blind with conceit
and the dust of logic, were purged, subtilised and spiritualised
into the sharpness of vision requisite for discerning such an
'om-m-mject.' – The ingenuous young English head, of those
days, stood strangely puzzled by such revelations; uncertain
whether it were getting inspired or getting infatuated into flat
imbecility; and strange effulgence, of new day or else of deeper
meteoric night, coloured the horizon of the future for it.

Let me not be unjust to this memorable man. Surely there
was here, in his pious, ever-labouring, subtle mind, a precious
truth, or prefigurement of truth; and yet a fatal delusion withal.
Prefigurement that, in spite of beaver sciences and temporary
spiritual hebetude and cecity, man and his Universe were eternally divine; and that no past nobleness, or revelation of the
divine, could or would ever be lost to him. Most true, surely,
and worthy of all acceptance. Good also to do what you can
with old Churches and practical Symbols of the Noble: may

quit not the burnt ruins of them while you find there is still gold
to be dug there. But, on the whole, do not think you can, by
logical alchymy, distil astral spirits from them; or if you could,
that said astral spirits, or defunct logical phantasms, could
serve you in anything. What the light of your mind, which is
the direct inspiration of the Almighty, pronounces incredible, –
that, in God's name, leave uncredited; at your peril do not try
believing that. No subtlest hocus-pocus of 'reason' *versus*
'understanding' will avail for that feat; – and it is terribly perilous to try it in these provinces!

The truth is, I now see, Coleridge's talk and speculation was
the emblem of himself: in it as in him, a ray of heavenly inspiration struggled, in a tragically ineffectual degree, with the
weakness of flesh and blood. He says once, he 'had skirted the
howling deserts of Infidelity;' this was evident enough: but he
had not had the courage, in defiance of pain and terror, to press
resolutely across said deserts to the new firm lands of Faith
beyond; he preferred to create logical fatamorganas[4] for himself on this hither side, and laboriously solace himself with
these.

To the man himself Nature had given, in high measure, the
seeds of a noble endowment; and to unfold it had been forbidden him. A subtle lynx-eyed intellect, tremulous pious sensibility
to all good and all beautiful; truly a ray of empyrean light; –
but imbedded in such weak laxity of character, in such
indolences and esuriences as had made strange work with it.
Once more, the tragic story of a high endowment with an insufficient will. An eye to discern the divineness of the Heaven's
splendours and lightnings, the insatiable wish to revel in their
godlike radiances and brilliances; but no heart to front the
scathing terrors of them, which is the first condition of your
conquering an abiding place there. The courage necessary for
him, above all things, had been denied this man. His life, with
such ray of the empyrean in it, was great and terrible to him;
and he had not valiantly grappled with it, he had fled from it;
sought refuge in vague day-dreams, hollow compromises, in
opium, in theosophic metaphysics. Harsh pain, danger, necessity, slavish harnessed toil, were of all things abhorrent to him.

And so the empyrean element, lying smothered under the terrene, and yet inextinguishable there, made sad writhings. For pain, danger, difficulty, steady slaving toil, and other highly disagreeable behests of destiny, shall in no wise be shirked by any brightest mortal that will approve himself loyal to his mission in this world; nay precisely the higher he is, the deeper will be the disagreeableness, and the detestability to flesh and blood, of the tasks laid on him; and the heavier too, and more tragic, his penalties if he neglect them.

For the old Eternal Powers do live forever; nor do their laws know any change, however we in our poor wigs and church-tippets may attempt to read their laws. To *steal* into Heaven, – by the modern method, of sticking ostrich-like your head into fallacies on Earth, equally as by the ancient and by all conceivable methods, – is forever forbidden. High-treason is the name of that attempt; and it continues to be punished as such. Strange enough: here once more was a kind of Heaven-scaling Ixion;[5] and to him, as to the old one, the just gods were very stern! The ever-revolving, never-advancing Wheel (of a kind) was his, through life; and from his Cloud-Juno did not he too procreate strange Centaurs, spectral Puseyisms,[6] monstrous illusory Hybrids, and ecclesiastical Chimeras, – which now roam the earth in a very lamentable manner!

History of Friedrich II of Prussia, called Frederick the Great

Carlyle devoted the latter part of his active life to *Frederick the Great*. According to Froude, he first expressed interest in the subject as early as 1845, after reading a life of Frederick by the German historian, Preuss. In 1852 he started serious preparatory reading and undertook the first of two visits to Germany to familiarize himself with the actual locations of the events of Frederick's life, and of his military campaigns. Carlyle started writing in 1853, but progress was slow and the first two volumes of the work did not appear until 1858. A third volume was published in 1863, a fourth in 1864, and two final volumes in 1865. Froude records Carlyle's comment on the completion of the work: 'The dreary task, and the sorrows and obstructions attending it . . . [are] . . . now happily over. No sympathy could be found on earth for those horrid struggles of twelve years.'

As John Holloway has pointed out in *The Victorian Sage*, *Frederick the Great* differs in important respects from Carlyle's previous historical works. Frederick himself is a figure distinguished not so much by obviously heroic virtues as by the single-minded persistence, and indeed the deviousness, which enabled him to establish the nationhood of Prussia against apparently insuperable odds. Carlyle conceals the deviousness, but if Frederick's military campaigns are emphasized they are predominantly the successes of a strategist and tactician. The period covered by the work is far longer than that of *The French Revolution*, and Carlyle concerns himself more than ever before with the accumulation of detail. Carlyle, as ever, uses history to demonstrate his personal beliefs, but there is little sense of an overall thematic structure and it is impossible at times to avoid the feeling that Carlyle has lost control of his material.

Frederick the Great is represented here by its opening pages, in which Carlyle indicates the motivation behind his choice of subject, rather than by passages from the main body of the work, which in this case would make little sense divorced from their immediate context. I have retained Carlyle's footnotes identifying his sources.

Proem; Friedrich's History
From the Distance We Are At*

About fourscore years ago, there used to be seen sauntering on the terraces of Sans Souci,[1] for a short time in the afternoon, or you might have met him elsewhere at an earlier hour, riding or driving in a rapid business manner on the open roads or through the scraggy woods and avenues of that intricate amphibious Potsdam region, a highly interesting lean little old man, of alert though slightly stooping figure; whose name among strangers was King *Friedrich the Second*, or Frederick the Great of Prussia, and at home among the common people, who much loved and esteemed him, was *Vater Fritz*, – Father Fred, – a name of familiarity which had not bred contempt in that instance. He is a King every inch of him, though without the trappings of a King. Presents himself in a Spartan simplicity of vesture: no crown but an old military cocked-hat, – generally old, or trampled and kneaded into absolute *softness*, if new; – no sceptre but one like Agamemnon's,[2] a walking-stick cut from the woods, which serves also as a riding-stick (with which he hits the horse 'between the ears,' say authors); – and for royal robes, a mere soldier's blue coat with red facings, coat likely to be old, and sure to have a good deal of Spanish snuff on the breast of it; rest of the apparel dim, unobtrusive in colour or cut, ending in high over-knee military boots, which may be brushed (and, I hope, kept soft with an underhand suspicion of oil), but are not permitted to be blackened or varnished; Day and Martin[3] with their soot-pots forbidden to approach.

* Book One, Chapter 1.

The man is not of godlike physiognomy, any more than of imposing stature or costume: close-shut mouth with thin lips, prominent jaws and nose, receding brow, by no means of Olympian height; head, however, is of long form, and has superlative gray eyes in it. Not what is called a beautiful man; nor yet, by all appearance, what is called a happy. On the contrary, the face bears evidence of many sorrows, as they are termed, of much hard labour done in this world; and seems to anticipate nothing but more still coming. Quiet stoicism, capable enough of what joy there were, but not expecting any worth mention; great unconscious and some conscious pride, well tempered with a cheery mockery of humour, – are written on that old face; which carries its chin well forward, in spite of the slight stoop about the neck; snuffy nose rather flung into the air, under its old cocked-hat, – like an old snuffy lion on the watch; and such a pair of eyes as no man or lion or lynx of that Century bore elsewhere, according to all the testimony we have. 'Those eyes,' says Mirabeau, 'which, at the bidding of his great soul, fascinated you with seduction or with terror (*portaient, au gré de son âme héroïque, la séduction ou la terreur*).'* Most excellent potent brilliant eyes, swift-darting as the stars, stedfast as the sun; gray, we said, of the azure-gray colour; large enough, not of glaring size; the habitual expression of them vigilance and penetrating sense, rapidly resting on depth. Which is an excellent combination; and gives us the notion of a lambent outer radiance springing from some great inner sea of light and fire in the man. The voice, if he speak to you, is of similar physiognomy: clear, melodious and sonorous; all tones are in it, from that of ingenuous inquiry, graceful sociality, light-flowing banter (rather prickly for most part), up to definite word of command, up to desolating word of rebuke and reprobation; a voice 'the clearest and most agreeable in conversation I ever heard,' says witty Dr Moore.† 'He speaks a

---

* Mirabeau, *Histoire Secrète de la Cour de Berlin*, Lettre 28ᵐᵉ (24 Septembre 1786), p. 128 (in edition of Paris, 1821).
† Moore, *View of Society and Manners in France, Switzerland and Germany* (London, 1779), ii. 246.

great deal,' continues the doctor; 'yet those who near him, regret that he does not speak a good deal more. His observations are always lively, very often just; and few men possess the talent of repartee in greater perfection.'

Just about threescore and ten years ago* his speakings and his workings came to finis in this World of Time; and he vanished from all eyes into other worlds, leaving much inquiry about him in the minds of men; – which, as my readers and I may feel too well, is yet by no means satisfied. As to his speech, indeed, though it had the worth just ascribed to it and more, and though masses of it were deliberately put on paper by himself, in prose and verse, and continue to be printed and kept legible, what he spoke has pretty much vanished into the inane; and except as record or document of what he did, hardly now concerns mankind. But the things he did were extremely remarkable; and cannot be forgotten by mankind. Indeed, they bear such fruit to the present hour as all the Newspapers are obliged to be taking note of, sometimes to an unpleasant degree. Editors vaguely account this man the 'Creator of the Prussian Monarchy;' which has since grown so large in the world, and troublesome to the Editorial mind in this and other countries. He was indeed the first who, in a highly public manner, notified its creation; announced to all men that it was, in very deed, created; standing on its feet there, and would go a great way, on the impulse it had got from him and others. As it has accordingly done; and may still keep doing to lengths little dreamt of by the British Editor in our time; whose prophesyings upon Prussia, and insights into Prussia, in its past, or present or future, are truly as yet inconsiderable, in proportion to the noise he makes with them! The more is the pity for him, – and for myself too in the Enterprise now on hand.

It is of this Figure, whom we see by the mind's eye in those Potsdam regions, visible for the last time seventy years ago, that we are now to treat, in the way of solacing ingenuous human curiosity. We are to try for some Historical Conception

---

* A.D. 1856 – 17th August 1786.

of this Man and King; some answer to the questions, 'What was he, then? Whence, how? And what did he achieve and suffer in the world?' – such answer as may prove admissible to ingenuous mankind, especially such as may correspond to the Fact (which stands there, abstruse indeed, but actual and unalterable), and so be sure of admissibility one day.

An Enterprise which turns out to be, the longer one looks at it, the more of a formidable, not to say unmanageable nature! Concerning which, on one or two points, it were good, if conveniently possible, to come to some preliminary understanding with the reader. Here, flying on loose leaves, are certain incidental utterances, of various date: these, as the topic is difficult, I will merely label and insert, instead of a formal Discourse, which were too apt to slide into something of a Lamentation, or otherwise take an unpleasant turn.

1. FRIEDRICH THEN, AND
FRIEDRICH NOW

This was a man of infinite mark to his contemporaries; who had witnessed surprising feats from him in the world; very questionable notions and ways, which he had contrived to maintain against the world and its criticisms. As an original man has always to do; much more an original ruler of men. The world, in fact, had tried hard to put him down, as it does, unconsciously or consciously, with all such; and after the most conscious exertions, and at one time a dead-lift spasm of all its energies for Seven Years,[4] had not been able. Principalities and powers, Imperial, Royal, Czarish, Papal, enemies innumerable as the sea-sand, had risen against him, only one helper left among the world's Potentates (and that one only while there should be help rendered in return); and he led them all such a dance as had astonished mankind and them.

No wonder they thought him worthy of notice. Every original man of any magnitude is; – nay, in the longrun, who or what else is? But how much more if your original man was a king over men; whose movements were polar, and carried from day to day those of the world along with them. The Samson Agonistes, – were his life passed like that of Samuel Johnson in dirty garrets, and the produce of it only some bits of written paper, – the Agonistes, and how he will comport himself in the Philistine mill; this is always a spectacle of truly epic and tragic nature. The rather, if your Samson, royal or other, is not yet blinded or subdued to the wheel; much more if he vanquish his enemies, *not* by suicidal methods, but march out at last flourishing his miraculous fighting implement, and leaving their mill and them in quite ruinous circumstances. As this King Friedrich fairly managed to do.

For he left the world all bankrupt, we may say; fallen into bottomless abysses of destruction; he still in a paying condition, and with footing capable to carry his affairs and him. When he died, in 1786, the enormous Phenomenon since called FRENCH REVOLUTION was already growling audibly in the depths of the world; meteoric-electric coruscations heralding it, all round the horizon. Strange enough to note, one of Friedrich's last visitors was Gabriel Honoré Riquetti, Comte de Mirabeau. These two saw one another; twice, for half an hour each time. The last of the old Gods and the first of the modern Titans;[5] – before Pelion leapt on Ossa;[6] and the foul Earth taking fire at last, its vile mephitic elements went up in volcanic thunder. This also is one of the peculiarities of Friedrich, that he is hitherto the last of the Kings; that he ushers-in the French Revolution, and closes an Epoch of World-History. Finishing-off forever the trade of King, think many; who have grown profoundly dark as to Kingship and him.

The French Revolution may be said to have, for about half a century, quite submerged Friedrich, abolished him from the memories of men; and now on coming to light again, he is found defaced under strange mud-incrustations, and the eyes of mankind look at him from a singularly changed, what we must call oblique and perverse point of vision. This is one of the difficulties in dealing with his History; – especially if you happen to believe both in the French Revolution and in him;

that is to say, both that Real Kingship is eternally indispensable, and also that the destruction of Sham Kingship (a frightful
process) is occasionally so.

On the breaking-out of that formidable Explosion, and Suicide of his Century, Friedrich sank into comparative obscurity;
eclipsed amid the ruins of that universal earthquake, the very
dust of which darkened all the air, and made of day a disastrous midnight. Black midnight, broken only by the blaze of
conflagrations; – wherein, to our terrified imaginations, were
seen, not men, French and other, but ghastly portents, stalking
wrathful, and shapes of avenging gods. It must be owned the
figure of Napoleon was titanic; especially to the generation that
looked on him, and that waited shuddering to be devoured by
him. In general, in that French Revolution, all was on a huge
scale; if not greater than anything in human experience, at least
more grandiose. All was recorded in bulletins, too, addressed
to the shilling-gallery; and there were fellows on the stage with
such a breadth of sabre, extent of whiskerage, strength of
windpipe, and command of men and gunpowder, as had never
been seen before. How they bellowed, stalked and flourished
about; counterfeiting Jove's thunder to an amazing degree! Terrific Drawcansir figures,[7] of enormous whiskerage, unlimited
command of gunpowder; not without sufficient ferocity, and
even a certain heroism, stage-heroism, in them; compared with
whom, to the shilling-gallery, and frightened excited theatre
at large, it seemed as if there had been no generals or sover-
eigns before; as if Friedrich, Gustavus, Cromwell, William
Conqueror and Alexander the Great were not worth speaking
of henceforth.

All this, however, in half a century is considerably altered.
The Drawcansir equipments getting gradually torn off, the natural size is seen better; translated from the bulletin style into
that of fact and history, miracles, even to the shilling-gallery,
are not so miraculous. It begins to be apparent that there lived
great men before the era of bulletins and Agamemnon.[8] Austerlitz and Wagram shot away more gunpowder, – gunpowder
probably in the proportion of ten to one, or a hundred to one;
but neither of them was tenth-part such a beating to your

enemy as that of Rossbach, brought about by strategic art, human ingenuity and intrepidity, and the loss of 165 men. Leuthen,[9] too, the battle of Leuthen (though so few English readers ever heard of it) may very well hold up its head beside any victory gained by Napoleon or another. For the odds were not far from three to one; the soldiers were of not far from equal quality; and only the General was consummately superior, and the defeat a destruction. Napoleon did indeed, by immense expenditure of men and gunpowder, overrun Europe for a time: but Napoleon never, by husbanding and wisely expending his men and gunpowder, defended a little Prussia against all Europe, year after year for seven years long, till Europe had enough, and gave-up the enterprise as one it could not manage. So soon as the Drawcansir equipments are well torn off, and the shilling-gallery got to silence, it will be found that there were great kings before Napoleon, – and likewise an Art of War, grounded on veracity and human courage and insight, not upon Drawcansir rodomontade, grandiose Dick-Turpinism, revolutionary madness, and unlimited expenditure of men and gunpowder. 'You may paint with a very big brush, and yet not be a great painter,' says a satirical friend of mine! This is becoming more and more apparent, as the dust-whirlwind, and huge uproar of the last generation, gradually dies away again.

2. EIGHTEENTH CENTURY

One of the grand difficulties in a History of Friedrich is, all along this same, That he lived in a Century which has no History and can have little or none. A Century so opulent in accumulated falsities, – sad opulence descending on it by inheritance, always at compound interest, and always largely increased by fresh acquirement on such immensity of standing capital; – opulent in that bad way as never Century before was! Which had no longer the consciousness of being false, so false had it grown; and was so steeped in falsity, and impregnated with it to the very bone, that – in fact the measure of the thing was full, and a French Revolution had to end it. To maintain much veracity in such an element, especially for a king, was no doubt doubly remarkable. But now, how extricate the man from his Century? How show the man, who is a Reality worthy of being seen, and yet keep his Century, as a Hypocrisy worthy of being hidden and forgotten, in the due abeyance?

To resuscitate the Eighteenth Century, or call into men's view, beyond what is necessary, the poor and sordid personages and transactions of an epoch so related to us, can be no purpose of mine on this occasion. The Eighteenth Century, it is well known, does not figure to me as a lovely one; needing to be kept in mind, or spoken of unnecessarily. To me the Eighteenth Century has nothing grand in it, except that grand universal Suicide, named French Revolution, by which it terminated its otherwise most worthless existence with at least one worthy act; – setting fire to its old home and self; and going up in flames and volcanic explosions, in a truly memorable and important manner. A very fit termination, as I thankfully feel, for such a Century. Century spendthrift, fraudulent-bankrupt; gone at length utterly insolvent, without real *money* of performance in its pocket, and the shops declining to take hypocrisies and speciosities any farther: – what could the poor Century do, but at length admit, 'Well, it is so. I am a swindler-century, and have long been; having learned the trick of it from my father and grandfather; knowing hardly any trade but that in false bills, which I thought foolishly might last forever, and still bring at least beef and pudding to the favoured of mankind. And behold it ends; and I am a detected swindler, and have nothing even to eat. What remains but that I blow my brains out, and do at length one true action?' Which the poor Century did; many thanks to it, in the circumstances.

For there was need once more of a Divine Revelation to the torpid frivolous children of men, if they were not to sink altogether into the ape condition. And in that whirlwind of the Universe, – lights obliterated, and the torn wrecks of Earth and Hell hurled aloft into the Empyrean; black whirlwind, which made even apes serious, and drove most of them mad, – there was, to men, a voice audible; voice from the heart of things once more, as if to say: 'Lying is not permitted in this Universe.

The wages of lying, you behold, are death. Lying means damnation in this Universe; and Beelzebub, never so elaborately decked in crowns and mitres, is *not* God! This was a revelation truly to be named of the Eternal, in our poor Eighteenth Century; and has greatly altered the complexion of said Century to the Historian ever since.

Whereby, in short, that Century is quite confiscate, fallen bankrupt, given up to the auctioneers; – Jew-brokers sorting out of it at this moment, in a confused distressing manner, what is still valuable or saleable. And, in fact, it lies massed up in our minds as a disastrous wrecked inanity, not useful to dwell upon; a kind of dusky chaotic background, on which the figures that had some veracity in them, – a small company, and ever growing smaller as our demands rise in strictness, – are delineated for us. – 'And yet it is the Century of our own Grandfathers?' cries the reader. Yes, reader! truly. It is the ground out of which we ourselves have sprung; whereon now we have our immediate footing, and first of all strike down our roots for nourishment; – and, alas, in large sections of the practical world, it (what we specially mean by *it*) still continues flourishing all round us! To forget it quite is not yet possible, nor would be profitable. What to do with it, and its forgotten fooleries and 'Histories,' worthy only of forgetting? – Well: so much of it as by nature *adheres*; what of it cannot be disengaged from our Hero and his operations: approximately so much, and no more! Let that be our bargain in regard to it.

3. ENGLISH PREPOSSESSIONS

With such wagonloads of Books and Printed Records as exist on the subject of Friedrich, it has always seemed possible, even for a stranger, to acquire some real understanding of him; – though practically, here and now, I have to own, it proves difficult beyond conception. Alas, the Books are not cosmic, they are chaotic; and turn out unexpectedly void of instruction to us. Small use in a talent of writing, if there be not first of all the talent of discerning, of loyally recognising; of discriminating

what is to be written! Books born mostly of Chaos, – which
want all things, even an *Index*, – are a painful object. In sorrow
and disgust, you wander over those multitudinous Books: you
dwell in endless regions of the superficial, of the nugatory: to
your bewildered sense it is as if no insight into the real heart of
Friedrich and his affairs were anywhere to be had. Truth is, the
Prussian Dryasdust, otherwise an honest fellow, and not afraid
of labour, excels all other Dryasdusts yet known; I have often
sorrowfully felt as if there were not in Nature, for darkness,
dreariness, immethodic platitude, anything comparable to him.
He writes big Books wanting in almost every quality; and does
not even give an *Index* to them. He has made of Friedrich's
History a wide-spread, inorganic, trackless matter; dismal to
your mind, and barren as a continent of Brandenburg sand![10] –
Enough, he could do no other: I have striven to forgive him. Let
the reader now forgive me; and think sometimes what probably my raw-material was! –

Curious enough, Friedrich lived in the Writing Era, – morning
of that strange Era which has grown to such a noon for us; – and
his favourite society, all his reign, was with the literary or writing
sort. Nor have they failed to write about him, they among the
others, about him and about him; and it is notable how little real
light, on any point of his existence or environment, they have
managed to communicate. Dim indeed, for most part a mere
epigrammatic sputter of darkness visible, is the 'picture' they
have fashioned to themselves of Friedrich and his Country and
his Century. Men not 'of genius,' apparently? Alas, no; men
fatally destitute of true eyesight, and of loyal heart first of all. So
far as I have noticed, there was not, with the single exception of
Mirabeau for one hour, any man to be called of genius, or with
an adequate power of human discernment, that ever personally
looked on Friedrich. Had many such men looked successively on
his History and him, we had not found it now in such a condition. Still altogether chaotic as a History; fatally destitute even of
the Indexes and mechanical appliances: Friedrich's self, and his
Country, and his Century, still undeciphered; very dark phenomena, all three, to the intelligent part of mankind.

*

In Prussia there has long been a certain stubborn though plan-less diligence in digging for the outward details of Friedrich's Life-History; though as to organising them, assorting them, or even putting labels on them; much more as to the least inter-pretation or human delineation of the man and his affairs, – you need not inquire in Prussia. In France, in England, it is still worse. There an immense ignorance prevails even as to the out-ward facts and phenomena of Friedrich's life; and instead of the Prussian no-interpretation, you find, in these vacant cir-cumstances, a great promptitude to interpret. Whereby judgments and prepossessions exist among us on that subject, especially on Friedrich's character, which are very ignorant indeed.

To Englishmen, the sources of knowledge or conviction about Friedrich, I have observed, are mainly these two. *First*, for his Public Character: it was an all-important fact, not to *it*, but to this country in regard to it, That George II., seeing good to plunge head-foremost into German Politics, and to take Maria Theresa's side in the Austrian-Succession War[11] of 1740–48, – needed to begin by assuring his Parliament and Newspapers, profoundly dark on the matter, that Friedrich was a robber and villain for taking the other side. Which assurance, resting on what basis we shall see by and by, George's Parliament and Newspapers cheerfully accepted, nothing doubting. And they have re-echoed and reverberated it, they and the rest of us, ever since, to all lengths, down to the present day; as a fact quite agreed upon, and the preliminary item in Friedrich's character. Robber and villain to begin with; that was one settled point.

Afterwards when George and Friedrich came to be allies, and the grand fightings of the Seven-Years War took place, George's Parliament and Newspapers settled a second point, in regard to Friedrich: 'One of the greatest soldiers ever born.' This second item the British Writer fully admits ever since: but he still adds to it the quality of robber, in a loose way; – and images to himself a royal Dick Turpin, of the kind known in Review-Articles, and Disquisitions on Progress of the Species, and labels it *Frederick*; very anxious to collect new babblement of lying Anecdotes, false Criticisms, hungry French Memoirs,

which will confirm him in that impossible idea. Had such
proved, on survey, to be the character of Friedrich, there is one
British Writer whose curiosity concerning him would pretty
soon have died away; nor could any amount of unwise desire
to satisfy that feeling in fellow-creatures less seriously disposed
have sustained him alive, in those baleful Historic Acherons
and Stygian Fens,[12] where he has had to dig and to fish so long,
far away from the upper light! – Let me request all readers to
blow that sorry chaff entirely out of their minds; and to believe
nothing on the subject except what they get some evidence for.

Second English source relates to the Private Character. Friedrich's Biography or Private Character, the English, like the
French, have gathered chiefly from a scandalous libel by Voltaire, which used to be called *Vie Privée du Roi de Prusse*
(Private Life of the King of Prussia):* libel undoubtedly written
by Voltaire, in a kind of fury; but not intended to be published
by him; nay burnt and annihilated, as he afterwards imagined.
No line of which, that cannot be otherwise proved, has a right
to be believed; and large portions of which *can* be proved to be
wild exaggerations and perversions, or even downright lies, –
written in a mood analogous to the Frenzy of John Dennis.[13]
This serves for the Biography or Private Character of Friedrich;
imputing all crimes to him, natural and unnatural; – offering
indeed, if combined with facts otherwise known, or even if well
considered by itself, a thoroughly flimsy, incredible and impossible image. Like that of some flaming Devil's Head, done in
phosphorus on the walls of the black-hole, by an Artist whom
you had locked-up there (not quite without reason) overnight.

Poor Voltaire wrote that *Vie Privée* in a state little inferior to
the Frenzy of John Dennis, – how brought about we shall see
by and by. And this is the Document which English readers are
surest to have read, and tried to credit as far as possible. Our

---

* First printed, from a stolen copy, at Geneva, 1784; first proved to be Voltaire's (which some of his admirers had striven to doubt), Paris, 1788; stands
avowed ever since, in all the Editions of his Works (ii. 9–113 of the Edition by
Baudouin Frères, 97 vols, Paris, 1825–1834), under the title *Mémoires pour
servir à la Vie de M. de Voltaire*, – with patches of repetition in the thing called
Commentaire Historique, which follows ibid. at great length.

counsel is, Out of window with it, he that would know Friedrich of Prussia! Keep it a while, he that would know François Arouet de Voltaire, and a certain numerous unfortunate class of mortals, whom Voltaire is sometimes capable of sinking to be spokesman for, in this world! – Alas, go where you will, especially in these irreverent ages, the noteworthy Dead is sure to be found lying under infinite dung, no end of calumnies and stupidities accumulated upon him. For the class we speak of, class of 'flunkies doing *saturnalia* below stairs,' is numerous, is innumerable; and can well remunerate a 'vocal flunky' that will serve their purposes on such an occasion! –

Friedrich is by no means one of the perfect demigods; and there are various things to be said against him with good ground. To the last, a questionable hero; with much in him which one could have wished not there, and much wanting which one could have wished. But there is one feature which strikes you at an early period of the inquiry, That in his way he is a Reality; that he always means what he speaks; grounds his actions, too, on what he recognises for the truth; and, in short, has nothing whatever of the Hypocrite or Phantasm. Which some readers will admit to be an extremely rare phenomenon.

We perceive that this man was far indeed from trying to deal swindler-like with the facts around him; that he honestly recognised said facts wherever they disclosed themselves, and was very anxious also to ascertain their existence where still hidden or dubious. For he knew well, to a quite uncommon degree, and with a merit all the higher as it was an unconscious one, how entirely inexorable is the nature of facts, whether recognised or not, ascertained or not; how vain all cunning of diplomacy, management and sophistry, to save any mortal who does *not* stand on the truth of things, from sinking, in the long-run. Sinking to the very Mudgods, with all his diplomacies, possessions, achievements; and becoming an unnameable object, hidden deep in the Cesspools of the Universe. This I hope to make manifest; this which I long ago discerned for myself, with pleasure, in the physiognomy of Friedrich and his life. Which indeed was the first real sanction, and has all along been my inducement and encouragement, to study his life and him. How this man, officially a King withal, comported himself in the Eighteenth Century, and managed *not* to be a Liar and Charlatan as his Century was, deserves to be seen a little by men and kings, and may silently have didactic meanings in it.

He that was honest with his existence has always meaning for us, be he king or peasant. He that merely shammed and grimaced with it, however much, and with whatever noise and trumpet-blowing, he may have cooked and eaten in this world, cannot long have any. Some men do *cook* enormously (let us call it *cooking*, what a man does in obedience to his *hunger* merely, to his desires and passions merely), – roasting whole continents and populations, in the flames of war or other discord; – witness the Napoleon above spoken of. For the appetite of man in that respect is unlimited; in truth, infinite; and the smallest of us could eat the entire Solar System, had we the chance given, and then cry, like Alexander of Macedon,[14] because we had no more Solar Systems to cook and eat. It is not the extent of the man's cookery that can much attach me to him; but only the man himself, and what of strength he had to wrestle with the mud-elements, and what of victory he got for his own benefit and mine.

4. ENCOURAGEMENTS, DISCOURAGEMENTS

French Revolution having spent itself, or sunk in France and elsewhere to what we see, a certain curiosity reawakens as to what of great or manful we can discover on the other side of that still troubled atmosphere of the Present and immediate Past. Curiosity quickened, or which should be quickened, by the great and all-absorbing question, How is that same exploded Past ever to settle down again? Not lost forever, it would appear: the New Era has not annihilated the old eras: New Era could by no means manage that; – never meant that, had it known its own mind (which it did not): its meaning was and is, to get its own well out of them; to readapt, in a purified shape, the old eras, and appropriate whatever was true and *not* combustible in them: that was the poor New Era's meaning, in the frightful explosion it made of itself and its possessions, to begin with!

And the question of questions now is: What part of that exploded Past, the ruins and dust of which still darken all the air, will continually gravitate back to us; be reshaped, transformed, readapted, that so, in new figures, under new conditions, it may enrich and nourish us again? What part of it, *not* being incombustible, has actually gone to flame and gas in the huge world-conflagration, and is now *gaseous*, mounting aloft; and will know no beneficence of gravitation, but mount, and roam upon the waste winds forever, – Nature so ordering it, in spite of any industry of Art? This is the universal question of afflicted mankind at present; and sure enough it will be long to settle.

On one point we can answer: Only what of the Past was *true* will come back to us. That is the one *asbestos* which survives all fire, and comes out purified; that is still ours, blessed be Heaven, and only that. By the law of Nature nothing more than that; and also, by the same law, nothing less than that. Let Art struggle how it may, for or against, – as foolish Art is seen extensively doing in our time, – there is where the limits of it will be. In which point of view, may not Friedrich, if he was a true man and King, justly excite some curiosity again; nay some quite peculiar curiosity, as the last Crowned Reality there was antecedent to that general outbreak and abolition? To many it appears certain there are to be no Kings of any sort, no Government more; less and less need of them henceforth, New Era having come. Which is a very wonderful notion; important if true; perhaps still more important, just at present, if untrue! My hopes of presenting, in this Last of the Kings, an exemplar to my contemporaries, I confess, are not high.

On the whole, it is evident the difficulties to a History of Friedrich are great and many: and the sad certainty is at last forced upon me that no good Book can, at this time, especially in this country, be written on the subject. Wherefore let the reader put up with an indifferent or bad one; he little knows how much worse it could easily have been! – Alas, the Ideal of History, as my friend Sauerteig knows, is very high; and it is not one serious man, but many successions of such, and whole serious generations of such, that can ever again build up History towards its old dignity. We must renounce ideals. We must sadly take up with the mournfulest barren realities; – dismal continents of Brandenburg sand, as in this instance; mere tumbled mountains of marine-stores, without so much as an Index to them!

Has the reader heard of Sauerteig's last batch of *Springwurzeln*,[15] a rather curious valedictory Piece? 'All History is an imprisoned Epic, nay an imprisoned Psalm and Prophecy,' says Sauerteig there. I wish, from my soul, he had *dis*imprisoned it in this instance! But he only says, in magniloquent language, how grand it would be if disimprisoned; – and hurls out, accidentally striking on this subject, the following rough sentences, suggestive though unpractical, with which I shall conclude:

'Schiller, it appears, at one time thought of writing an *Epic Poem upon Friedrich the Great*, "upon some action of Friedrich's," Schiller says. Happily Schiller did not do it. By oversetting fact, disregarding reality, and tumbling time and space topsyturvy, Schiller with his fine gifts might no doubt have written a temporary "epic poem," of the kind read and admired by many simple persons. But that would have helped little, and could not have lasted long. It is not the untrue imaginary Picture of a man and his life that I want from my Schiller, but the actual natural Likeness, true as the face itself, nay *truer*, in a sense. Which the Artist, if there is one, might help to give, and the Botcher (*Pfuscher*) never can! Alas, and the Artist does not even try it; leaves it altogether to the Botcher, being busy otherwise!

'Men surely will at length discover again, emerging from these dismal bewilderments in which the modern Ages reel and stagger this long while, that to them also, as to the most ancient men, all Pictures that cannot be credited are – Pictures of an idle nature; to be mostly swept out of doors. Such veritably, were it never so forgotten, is the law! Mistakes enough, lies enough will insinuate themselves into our most earnest portrayings of the True: but that we should, deliberately and of forethought, rake together what we know to be not true, and introduce that in the hope of doing good with it? I tell you, such practice was unknown in the ancient earnest times; and ought again to become unknown except to the more foolish classes!' That is Sauerteig's strange notion, not now of yesterday, as readers know: – and he goes then into 'Homer's Iliad,' the 'Hebrew Bible,' 'terrible Hebrew *veracity* of every line of it;' discovers an alarming 'kinship of Fiction to lying;' and asks, If anybody can compute 'the damage we poor moderns have got from our practices of fiction in Literature itself, not to speak of awfully higher provinces? Men will either see into all this by and by,' continues he; 'or plunge head foremost, in neglect of all this, whither they little dream as yet!

'But I think all real *Poets*, to this hour, are Psalmists and Iliadists after their sort; and have in them a divine impatience of lies, a divine incapacity of living among lies. Likewise, which is a corollary, that the highest Shakspeare producible is properly the fittest Historian producible; – and that it is frightful to see the *Gelehrte Dummkopf* (what we here may translate *Dryasdust*) 'doing the function of History, and the Shakspeare and the Goethe neglecting it. "Interpreting events;" interpreting the universally visible, entirely *in*dubitable Revelation of the Author of this Universe: how can Dryasdust interpret such things, the dark chaotic dullard, who knows the meaning of nothing cosmic or noble, nor ever will know? Poor wretch, one sees what kind of meaning *he* educes from Man's History, this long while past, and has got all the world to believe of it along with him. Unhappy Dryasdust, thrice-unhappy world that take Dryasdust's reading of the ways of God! But what else was possible? They that could have taught better were engaged in fiddling; for which there are good wages going. And our damage therefrom, our *damage*, – yes, if thou be still human and not cormorant, – perhaps it will transcend all Californias, English National Debts,[16] and show itself incomputable in continents of Bullion! –

'Believing that mankind are not doomed wholly to dog-like annihilation, I believe that much of this will mend. I believe

that the world will not always waste its inspired men in mere
fiddling to it. That the man of rhythmic nature will feel more
and more his vocation towards the Interpretation of Fact;
since only in the vital centre of that, could we once get thither,
lies all real melody; and that he will become, he, once again
the Historian of Events, – bewildered Dryasdust having at last
the happiness to be his servant, and to have some guidance
from him. Which will be blessed indeed. For the present, Dryasdust strikes me like a hapless Nigger gone masterless: Nigger
totally unfit for self-guidance; yet without master good or bad;
and whose feats in that capacity no god or man can rejoice in.

'History, with faithful Genius at the top and faithful Industry at the bottom, will then be capable of being written. History
will then actually *be* written, – the inspired gift of God
employing itself to illuminate the dark ways of God. A thing
thrice-pressingly needful to be done! Whereby the modern
Nations may again become a little less godless, and again have
their "epics" (of a different from the Schiller sort), and again
have several things they are still more fatally in want of at
present! – '

So that, it would seem, there *will* gradually among mankind,
if Friedrich last some centuries, be a real Epic made of his History? That is to say (presumably), it will become a perfected
Melodious Truth, and duly significant and duly beautiful bit of
Belief, to mankind; the essence of it fairly evolved from all the
chaff, the portrait of it actually given, and its real harmonies
with the laws of this Universe brought out, in bright and dark,
according to the God's Fact as it *was*; which poor Dryasdust
and the Newspapers never could get sight of, but were always
far from!

Well, if so, – and even if not quite *so*, – it is a comfort to
reflect that every true worker (who has blown away chaff &c.),
were his contribution no bigger than my own, may have
brought the good result *nearer* by a handbreadth or two. And
so we will end these preludings, and proceed upon our Problem, courteous reader.

Reminiscences

Carlyle's *Reminiscences* were first published in 1881, the year of his death, by the agency of his biographer, James Antony Froude. They contain a collection of often disjointed autobiographical material which, according to Froude's Preface, he had received from Carlyle in 1871, with instructions that it should be published, if he thought fit, after Carlyle's death. The publication of the *Reminiscences* led to considerable controversy, however, it being complained, with some justice, that Froude had disregarded explicit instructions that the manuscripts were to be destroyed.

There are four major sections in the *Reminiscences* as Froude reprinted them: a memoir of Carlyle's father, James Carlyle, written immediately after his death in 1832, sketches of Edward Irving, the close friend of his youth, and of Lord Jeffrey, both written 1866–7, and a memoir of Jane Welsh Carlyle, written on her death in 1866, and intended, according to Froude, as an introduction to a collection of her letters. The passage reprinted here is from the memoir of Jane Welsh Carlyle.

from Jane Welsh Carlyle

... My poor darling had, for constant accompaniment to all her bits of satisfactions, an altogether weak state of health, continually breaking down, into violent fits of headache in her best times, and in winter-season into cough etc. in lingering forms of a quite sad and exhausting sort. Wonderful to me how she, so sensitive a creature, maintained her hoping cheerful humour to such a degree, amidst all that; and, except the pain of inevitable sympathy, and vague fluttering fears, gave me no pain. Careful always to screen me from pain, as I by no means always reciprocally was; alas, no, miserable egoist in comparison. At this time I must have been in the thick of 'Cromwell;'[1] four years of abstruse toil, obscure speculations, futile wrestling, and misery, I used to count it had cost me, before I took to editing the 'Letters and Speeches' ('to have them out of my way'), which rapidly drained off the sour swamp water bodily, and left me, beyond all first expectation, quite free of the matter. Often I have thought how miserable my books must have been to her, and how, though they were none of her choosing, and had come upon her like ill weather or ill health, she at no instant, never once I do believe, made the least complaint of me or my behaviour (often bad, or at least thoughtless and weak) under them! Always some quizzing little lesson, the purport and effect of which was to encourage me; never once anything worse. Oh, it was noble, and I see it so well now, when it is gone from me, and no return possible.

'Cromwell' was by much the worst book-time, till this of 'Friedrich,' which indeed was infinitely worse; in the dregs of our strength too; – and lasted for about thirteen years. She was generally in quite weak health, too, and was often, for long weeks or months, miserably ill.

It was strange how she contrived to sift out of such a troublous forlorn day as hers, in each case, was, all the available little items, as she was sure to do, and used to have them ready for me in the evening when my work was done, in the prettiest little narrative anybody could have given of such things. Never again shall I have such melodious, humanly beautiful half-hours; they were the rainbow of my poor dripping day, and reminded me that there otherwise was a sun. At this time, and all along she 'did all the society;' was all brightness to the one or two (oftenest rather dull and prosaic fellows, for the better sort respected my seclusion, especially during that last 'Friedrich' time) whom I needed to see on my affairs in hand, or who, with more of brass than others, managed to intrude upon me. For these she did, in their several kinds, her very best. Her own people, whom I might be apt to feel wearisome (dislike any of them I never did, or his or her discharge from service would have swiftly followed), she kept beautifully out of my way, saving my 'politeness' withal; a very perfect skill she had in all this; and took my dark toiling periods, however long, sullen and severe they might be, with a loyalty and heart acquiescence that never failed, the heroic little soul!

'Latter-Day Pamphlet' time, and especially the time that preceded it (1848 etc.) must have been very sore and heavy. My heart was long overloaded with the meanings at length uttered there, and no way of getting them set forth would answer. I forget what ways I tried, or thought of. 'Times' newspaper was one (alert, airy, rather vacant editorial gentleman I remember going to once, in Printing House Square); but this, of course, proved hypothetical merely, as all others did, till we, as last shift, gave the rough MSS. to Chapman (in Forster's company one winter Sunday).[2] About half of those ultimately printed might be in Chapman's hands, but there was much manipulation as well as addition needed. Forster soon fell away, I could perceive, into terror and surprise, as indeed everybody did. 'A lost man!' thought everybody. Not she at any moment; much amused by the outside pother, she, and glad to see me getting delivered of my black electricities and consuming fires in that way. Strange letters came to us, during those nine months of pamphleteering, strange visitors (of moonstruck unprofitable type for most part), who had, for one reason or another, been each of them wearing himself half-mad on some one of the public scandals I was recognising and denouncing. I still remember some of their faces and the look their paper bundles had. She got a considerable entertainment out of all that, went along with me in everything (probably counselling a little here and there, a censorship well worth my regarding, and generally adoptable, here as everywhere), and minded no whit any results that might follow this evident speaking of the truth. Somebody, writing from India I think, and clearly meaning kindness, 'did hope' (some time afterwards) 'the tide would turn, and this lamentable hostility of the press die away into friendship again;' at which I remember our innocent laughter, ignorant till then what 'The Press's' feelings were, and leaving 'The Press' very welcome to them then. Neuberg[3] helped me zealously, as volunteer amanuensis etc., through all this business, but I know not that even he approved it all, or any of it to the bottom. In the whole world I had one complete approver; in that, as in other cases, one, and it was worth all.

On the back of 'Latter-Day Pamphlets' followed 'Life of Sterling;' a very quiet thing, but considerably disapproved of too, as I learned, and utterly revolting to the religious people in particular (to my surprise rather than otherwise). 'Doesn't believe in us, then, either?' Not he, for certain; can't, if you will know! Others urged disdainfully, 'What has Sterling done that he should have a Life!' 'Induced Carlyle somehow to write him one!' answered she once (to the Ferguses, I think) in an arch airy way which I can well fancy, and which shut up that question there. The book was afterwards greatly praised, again on rather weak terms I doubt. What now will please me best in it, and alone will, was then an accidental quality, the authentic light, under the due conditions, that is thrown by it on her. Oh, my dear one, sad is my soul for the loss of thee, and will to the end be, as I compute! Lonelier creature there is not henceforth in this world; neither person, work or thing going on in it that is of any value, in comparison, or even at all. Death I feel almost daily in express fact, death is the one haven; and have occasionally a kind of kingship, sorrowful, but sublime, almost godlike, in the feeling that that is nigh. Sometimes the image of her, gone in her car of victory (in that beautiful death), and as if nodding to me with a smile, 'I am gone, loved one; work a little longer, if thou still carest; if not, follow. There is no baseness, and no misery here. Courage, courage to the last!' that, sometimes, as in this moment, is inexpressibly beautiful to me, and comes nearer to bringing tears than it once did.

In 1852 had come the new modelling of our house, attended with infinite dusty confusion (headcarpenter, stupid though honest, fell ill, etc. etc.); confusion falling upon her more than me, and at length upon her altogether. She was the architect, guiding and directing and contriving genius, in all that enterprise, seemingly so foreign to her. But, indeed, she was ardent in it, and she had a talent that way which was altogether unique in my experience. An 'eye' first of all; equal in correctness to a joiner's square, this, up almost from her childhood, as I understood. Then a sense of order, sense of beauty, of wise and thrifty convenience; sense of wisdom altogether in fact, for that was it; a human intellect shining luminous in every direction, the highest and the lowest (as I remarked above). In childhood she used to be sent to seek when things fell lost; 'the best seeker of us all,' her father would say, or look (as she thought); for me also she sought everything, with such success as I never saw elsewhere. It was she who widened our drawing-room (as if by a stroke of genius) and made it zealously (at the partial expense of three feet from her own bedroom) into what it is, one of the prettiest little drawing-rooms I ever saw, and made the whole house into what it now is. How frugal, too, and how modest about it! House was hardly finished, when there arose that of the 'demon fowls,'[4] as she appropriately named them; macaws, Cochin-chinas, endless concert of crowing, cackling, shrieking roosters (from a bad or misled neighbour, next door) which cut us off from sleep or peace, at times altogether, and were like to drive me mad, and her through me, through sympathy with me. From which also she was my deliverer, had delivered and

contrived to deliver me from hundreds of such things (oh, my
beautiful little Alcides,[5] in the new days of anarchy and the
mud-gods, threatening to crush down a poor man, and kill him
with his work still on hand!) I remember well her setting off,
one winter morning, from the Grange on this enterprise, probably having thought of it most of the night (sleep denied). She
said to me next morning the first thing: 'Dear, we must extinguish those demon fowls, or they will extinguish us! Rent the
house (No.6, proprietor mad etc. etc.) ourselves! it is but some
40l. a year; pack away those vile people, and let it stand empty.
'I will go this very day upon it, if you assent;' and she went
accordingly, and slew altogether this Lerna hydra,[6] at far less
expense than taking the house, nay almost at no expense at all,
except by her fine intellect, taut, just discernment, swiftness of
decision, and general nobleness of mind (in short). Oh, my
bonny little woman, mine only in memory now!

I left the Grange two days after her, on this occasion, hasten-
ing through London, gloomy of mind, to see my dear old
mother yet once (if I might) before she died. She had, for many
months before, been evidently and painfully sinking away,
under no disease, but the ever-increasing infirmities of eighty-
three years of time. She had expressed no desire to see me, but
her love from my birth upwards, under all scenes and circumstances, I knew to be emphatically a mother's. I walked from
the Kirtlebridge Station[7] that dim winter morning; my one
thought 'Shall I see her yet alive?' She was still there; weary,
very weary, and wishing to be at rest. I think she only at times
knew me; so bewildering were her continual distresses; once
she entirely forgot me; then, in a minute or two, asked my pardon. Ah me! ah me! It was my mother and not my mother;
the last pale rim or sickle of the moon, which had once been
full, now sinking in the dark seas. This lasted only three days.
Saturday night she had her full faculties, but was in nearly
unendurable misery, not breath sufficient etc. etc. John[8] tried
various reliefs, had at last to give a few drops of laudanum,
which eased the misery, and in an hour or two brought sleep.
All next day she lay asleep, breathing equally but heavily, her
face grand and solemn, almost severe, like a marble statue;

about four P.M. the breathing suddenly halted, recommenced for half an instant, then fluttered, ceased. 'All the days of my appointed time,' she had often said, 'will I wait till my change come.' The most beautifully religious soul I ever knew. Proud enough she was too, though piously humble, and full of native intellect, humour, etc., though all undeveloped. On the religious side, looking into the very heart of the matter, I always reckon her rather superior to my Jane, who in other shapes and with far different exemplars and conditions, had a great deal of noble religion too. Her death filled me with a kind of dim amazement and crush of confused sorrows, which were very painful, but not so sharply pathetic as I might have expected. It was the earliest terror of my childhood 'that I might lose my mother;' and it had gone with me all my days. But and that is probably the whole account of it, I was then sunk in the miseries of 'Friedrich' etc. etc., in many miseries; and was then fifty-eight years of age. It is strange to me, in these very days, how peaceable, though still sacred and tender, the memory of my mother now lies in me. (This very morning, I got into dreaming confused nightmare stuff about some funeral and her; not hers, nor obviously my Jane's, seemingly my father's rather, and she sending me on it, – the saddest bewildered stuff. What a dismal debasing and confusing element is that of a sick body on the human soul or thinking part!)

It was in 1852 (September–October, for about a month) that I had first seen Germany, gone on my first errand as to 'Friedrich:' there was a second, five years afterwards; this time it was to enquire (of Preuss and Co.);[9] to look about me, search for books, portraits, etc. etc. I went from Scotsbrig (my dear old mother painfully weak, though I had no thought it would be the last time I should see her afoot); from Scotsbrig for Leith by Rotterdam, Köln, Bonn (Neuberg's); – and on the whole never had nearly so (outwardly) unpleasant a journey in my life; till the second and last I made thither. But the Chelsea establishment was under carpenters, painters; till those disappeared, no work possible, scarcely any living possible (though my brave woman did make it possible without complaint). 'Stay so many weeks, all painting at least shall then be off!' I returned, near broken-down utterly, at the set time; and alas, was met by a foul dabblement of paint oozing downstairs; the painters had proved treacherous to her; time could not be kept! It was the one instance of such a thing here: and, except the first sick surprise, I now recollect no more of it.

'Mamma, wine makes cosy!' said the bright little one, perhaps between two and three years old, her mother, after some walk with sprinkling of wet or the like, having given her a dram-glass of wine on their getting home: 'Mamma, wine makes cosy!' said the small silver voice, gaily sipping, getting its new bits of insight into natural philosophy! What 'pictures' has my beautiful one left me; what joys can surround every well-ordered human heart. I said long since, I never saw so beautiful a childhood. Her little bit of a first chair, its wee wee arms etc., visible to me in the closet at this moment, is still here, and always was. I have looked at it hundreds of times; from of old, with many thoughts. No daughter or son of hers was to sit there; so it had been appointed us, my darling. I have no book a thousandth-part so beautiful as thou; but these were our only 'children,' – and, in a true sense, these were verily ours; and will perhaps live some time in the world, after we are both gone; – and be of no damage to the poor brute chaos of a world, let us hope! The Will of the Supreme shall be accomplished. Amen. But to proceed.

Shortly after my return from Germany (next summer I think, while the Cochin-chinas were at work, and we could not quit the house, having spent so much on it, and got a long lease), there began a new still worse hurlyburly of the building kind, that of the new top-storey, – whole area of the house to be thrown into one sublime garret-room, lighted from above, thirty feet by thirty say, and at least eleven feet high, double-doored, double-windowed, impervious to sound, to – in short, to everything but self and work! I had my grave doubts about all this; but John Chorley,[10] in his friendly zeal, warmly urged it on, pushed, superintended; – and was a good deal disgusted with my dismal experience of the result. Something really good might have come of it in a scene where good and faithful work was to be had on the part of all, from architect downwards; but here, from all (except one good young man of the carpenter trade, whom I at length noticed thankfully in small matters), the 'work,' of planning to begin with, and then of executing, in all its details, was mere work of Belial, i.e. of the Father of lies; such 'work' as I had not conceived the possibility of among the sons of Adam till then. By degrees, I perceived it to be the ordinary English 'work' of this epoch; and, with manifold reflections, deep as Tophet,[11] on the outlooks this offered for us all, endeavoured to be silent as to my own little failure. My new illustrious 'study' was definable as the least inhabitable, and most entirely detestable and despicable bit of human workmanship in that kind, sad and odious to me very. But, by many and long-continued efforts, with endless botherations which lasted for two or three years after (one winter starved by 'Arnott's improved grate,' I recollect), I did get it patched together into something of supportability; and continued, though under protest, to inhabit it during all working hours, as I had indeed from the first done. The whole of the now printed 'Friedrich' was written there (or in summer in the back court and garden, when driven down by baking heat). Much rawer matter, I think, was tentatively on paper, before this sublime new 'study.' 'Friedrich' once done, I quitted the place for ever, and it is now a bedroom for the servants. The 'architect' for this beautiful bit of masonry and carpentry was one 'Parsons,' really a clever creature, I could see, but swimming as for dear life in a mere 'mother of dead dogs' (ultimately did become bankrupt). His men of all types, Irish hodmen and upwards, for real mendacity of hand, for drunkenness, greediness, mutinous nomadism, and anarchic malfeasance throughout, excelled all experience or conception. Shut the lid on their 'unexampled prosperity' and them, for evermore . . .

Notes

Carlyle's prose method involved a range of reference that often seems to have been as fortuitous as it was extensive. In particular he had an idiosyncratic technique of infiltrating minor details from his own reading into his work, and investing them with a rhetorical significance that depends very little on their specific meaning. Any attempt at a comprehensive treatment of these allusions would result in notes whose complexity would defeat their own ends, and in the interest of economy I have sometimes passed over references where explanation seemed unnecessary, or where it would seem to add little to Carlyle's immediate meaning. My omissions in many cases will inevitably seem arbitrary: it is hoped that they will not all be attributed to ignorance.

EARLY ESSAYS

1. *an Aeolian harp*: A musical instrument consisting of a wooden box over which strings were stretched. Exposed to the wind it produced harmonious sounds without human intervention: it has thus been frequently used as a symbol for inspiration in poetry.

2. *and this was he for whom the world found no fitter business than quarrelling with smugglers and vintners, computing excise-dues upon tallow, and gauging alebarrels!*: For a period towards the end of his life Burns held an official position as an exciseman, or 'gauger', as the post was called in Scotland. It compensated to some extent for his failure as a farmer.

3. *Horace's rule,* Si vis me flere: The full quotation, from the *Ars Poetica* is:

    > Si vis me flere, dolendum est
    > Primum ipsi tibi.
    > (If you wish to draw tears from
    > me, you must first feel pain yourself.

4. *his Harolds and Giaours*: Byron published *Childe Harold* from
    1812 to 1818 and *The Giaour* in 1813. Both poems were
    extremely successful and their Romantic heroes were instrumen-
    tal in the development of the Byronic myth.

5. *the Pasquinade*: A lampoon, often of political implications. The
    term derives from the custom, in sixteenth-century Rome, of
    affixing satirical verses to a statue commemorating Pasquin, a
    Roman cobbler notorious for his trenchant humour.

6. *a Concionator*: An elegant stylist, from the Latin 'concinno', to
    arrange appropriately, to join neatly together.

7. *a mere Dutch commentator*: It is possible that Carlyle may be
    thinking of the celebrated Dutch scholar Hugo Grotius (1583–
    1644), an English life of whom had appeared in 1826. Grotius
    wrote extensively on theology, history and law, and was one of
    the most distinguished products of a tradition of scholarship that
    flourished in the Low Countries after the Renaissance, notably at
    the University of Leyden. Whether or not Grotius is specifically
    implicated it is this tradition that Carlyle has in mind: his rhet-
    orical dismissal of it is, needless to say, scarcely deserved.

8. *From Newton's* Principia *to the* Shaster *and* Vedam: The *Shaster*
    and the *Vedam* are generic terms for the sacred writings of the
    Hindus. Carlyle here stresses that the extreme examples of sci-
    ence and of mysticism were all grist to Voltaire's intellectual mill.

9. *a discovery . . . rather of the Curtis than of the Columbus sort*:
    cf. *Signs of the Times*, p. 75, where Carlyle is more explicit about
    this comparison. Columbus he sees as an original genius; Cortes,
    or as he calls him here, Curtis, as a man who developed what
    was already known to exist.

10. *from eastern* Zends *and* Jewish Talmuds: The *Zend-Avesta* were
    the sacred writings of the Parsees; the *Talmud* is the body of Jew-
    ish traditional law and ceremonial.

11. *the* Henriade *. . . a geometrical diagram by Fermat*: Voltaire's
    Henriade, an epic poem on Henri IV of France, was printed in
    Rouen in 1723. Pierre de Fermat (1601–65) was a prominent
    French mathematician who was said to have been the first to hit
    upon the principle of the differential calculus.

12. *the logical terseness of a Hume or Robertson, the graceful ease
    and gay pictorial heartiness of a Herodotus or Froissart*: Wil-
    liam Robertson (1721–93) published *History of Scotland* (1759),
    History of Charles V (1769) and *History of America* (1779)
    while Hume's reputation as a historian rests on his *History of
    Great Britain* which appeared from 1754 to 1761. Both authors

adopted a rationalist attitude to their subject-matter, typical of their age. The *Histories* of Herodotus (5th century B.C.) and the *Chronicles* of Jean Froissart (*c.* 1337–1404) have always been admired for their narrative vividness and stylistic attractiveness.

13. *he who first led armies over the Alps, and gained the victories of Cannæ and Thrasymene*: i.e. Hannibal. The battles of Cannae and Thrasymene were two of the outstanding victories of his Roman campaign.

14. *except some few Marathons and Morgartens*: At the Battle of Marathon (490 B.C.) the Greeks, although heavily outnumbered, achieved a decisive victory over the Persians, thereby saving Athens from the consequences of a Persian invasion. At the Battle of Morgarten (1315) the Swiss, also outnumbered, defeated the ruling Austrian forces. The battle was a significant stage in the emancipation of Switzerland from the rule of the Habsburgs.

15. *a 'Crossing of the Rubicon', an 'Impeachment of Strafford', a 'Convocation of the Notables'*: Events which have traditionally been regarded as points of no return in Caesar's assumption of imperial power, the English Civil War, and the French Revolution respectively.

16. *a Palimpsest*: The name given to a manuscript from which the original writing has been partially erased to make room for a second entry. The scrutiny of Palimpsest manuscripts for their original contents was a significant development of eighteenth-century antiquarianism.

17. *and sails through whole untracked celestial spaces, between Aries and Libra*: Carlyle has involved himself in a complicated astronomical metaphor. Aries is the first of the signs of the Zodiac, Libra the seventh. The sun passes through Aries in the spring, Libra in the early autumn. The 'crop' of the 'husbandman' of History grows and ripens during this period independently of him, but he reassumes responsibility for it when 'he gathers it safe into his barn'.

SIGNS OF THE TIMES

1. *vaticination*: prophecy.

2. *Know'st thou* Yesterday . . . : The verse is Carlyle's rendering of a verse of Goethe's, which in its turn is a paraphrase of a French poem quoted by Voltaire. Froude records that Carlyle kept

Goethe's version appended to a portrait of Goethe which hung
on his wall.

3. *fatidical*: prophetic.

4. *deliration*: delirium.

5. *Aaron's-rod*: According to the Old Testament, Aaron was
divinely chosen amongst the Israelites to be their chief priest
after the journey out of Egypt when his rod blossomed in the
Tabernacle. Cf. *Numbers*, xvii, xviii.

6. *The repeal of the Test Acts . . . Catholic disabilities*: The Test and
Corporation Acts, which had the effect of limiting the activities
of Dissenters in public life, were finally repealed in 1828, while
the Roman Catholic Relief Act of 1829 extended similar freedom of conscience to Roman Catholics whose liberties had been
even more severely proscribed.

7. *The Fifth-monarchy men*: A radical millenarian sect of the seventeenth century who believed that Christ's reign on earth was
imminent. There was a resurgence of millenarianism at the time
of the industrial revolution, and in the lines that follow Carlyle
would seem to have in mind the followers of Joanna Southcott,
who died in 1814.

8. *the Birmingham Fire-king has visited the fabulous East*: The
implications of this reference are obvious enough; its source has
proved far more elusive. I am indebted to Mr Eugene Ferguson
of the University of Delaware for the suggestion that it refers to
the voyage of the Steamship *Enterprize* which sailed from
Gravesend to Calcutta in 1825, passing via the Cape of Good
Hope. There was considerable interest in the exploitation of
steam power on ocean routes at this time and the *Enterprize* was
the first steamship to travel from England to the Far East. Steam
engines would naturally be associated with Birmingham in the
public mind and the voyage of the *Enterprize*, which aroused
considerable public interest, could well have been regarded by
Carlyle as symbolic of the development of engineering science.

9. *Camoens*: The Portuguese poet Camoens, in his epic poem the
Lusiad (1572), celebrated the voyage of Vasco da Gama around
the Cape to India.

10. *Lancastrian machines; Hamiltonian machines*: Joseph Lancaster
(1778–1838) was a pioneer of primary education who outlined
his methods in *Improvements in Education* (1803). He was particularly noted for his advocacy of the monitorial system, by
which the elder pupils taught the younger in their turn. James
Hamilton (1769–1831) devised a system of language teaching

involving direct confrontation with inter-linear translations rather than a formal grammatical approach. This, he argued, led to earlier proficiency.

11. *the Bible-Society*: The British and Foreign Bible Society, founded by a group of Evangelicals in 1804 for the printing and free distribution of Bibles. It aroused considerable opposition from the Anglican establishment whose own society, the Society for the Propagation of Christian Knowledge, had lost its effectiveness.

12. *popularis aura*: Normally translated as 'the popular favour', more generally, 'public opinion'.

13. *The Bibliothèques, Glyptothèques, Technothèques, which front us in all capital cities*: Carlyle is ridiculing the numerous educational institutions that were springing up at this time as a consequence of utilitarian enthusiasm for the systematization and dissemination of knowledge. A 'Glyptothèque' is, literally, an institution devoted to the art of carving or engraving hence, presumably, an art-school.

14. *'Penny-a-week Purgatory Society'*: This sounds very like a hire-purchase arrangement for obtaining indulgences, but I have been unable to trace the reference.

15. *Malebranche, Pascal, Descartes and Fénelon ... Cousins and Villemains*: Carlyle is making a derogatory comparison between contemporary French intellectuals and the giants of the past. Victor Cousin (1792–1867) attempted a popularized synthesis of previous philosophic systems which he believed would provide a practical basis upon which life could be conducted. Abel-François Villemain (1790–1870) was an essayist whose open-mindedness on literary topics may have seemed to Carlyle undiscriminating.

16. *Professor Stewart*: See n. 19 below.

17. *a Lagrange or Laplace*: Joseph-Louis Lagrange (1736–1813) and Pierre-Simon Laplace (1749–1827) were French mathematicians who applied mathematics to the study of the solar system. Laplace was the more important of them and in his *Mécanique Céleste* he declared his aim to be 'to solve the great mechanical problems of the solar system and to bring theory to coincide so closely with observation that empirical equations should no longer be needed'. When asked by Napoleon where God fitted into his system he is reputed to have replied: 'I have no need of such an hypothesis.'

18. *his Essay*: i.e. Locke's *Essay concerning Human Understanding* (1690).

19. *The school of Reid*: This Scottish philosophical movement was popularly called the 'school of common sense' since, while it was based on the scientific study of human psychology, it attempted to evade the extreme scepticism of Hume, as revealed in his *Treatise of Human Nature* (1739–40), by asserting a practical attitude towards the problems of perception. Its chief exponent was Thomas Reid (1710–96, Professor of Moral Philosophy at the University of Glasgow; his disciple Dugald Stewart (1753–1828) held a similar post at Edinburgh.

20. *Hartley's, Darwin's, or Priestley's contemporaneous doings in England*: David Hartley (1705–57) developed the theory of the Association of Ideas by which he explained, in mechanistic terms, the development of the moral sense out of basic human sensations. He explained all mental phenomena by the existence of 'vibratiuncles' or minute nervous vibrations. His influence on Wordsworth, and more particularly Coleridge, was considerable. Erasmus Darwin (1731–1802) sought to demonstrate that living things become adapted to their environment, and Joseph Priestley (1733–1804) is noted for his investigations of the properties of gases and his scientific demonstration of the respiratory systems of plants.

21. *Dr Cabanis*: Pierre-Jean-Georges Cabanis (1757–1808), physiologist, psychologist and philosopher, argued for a physiological explanation of all mental processes: his dictum quoted here by Carlyle was famous and exemplifies the tendencies of his deductions. He went on to argue that the relationship between body and mind, properly developed, was reciprocal; thus as man's scientific knowledge developed, his passions might be more effectively controlled, a theory which had considerable appeal for French positivist philosophers like Saint-Simon and Comte. Cabanis's *Rapports du Physique et du Morale de l'Homme*, ridiculed here by Carlyle, was his most famous work and was published in 1802.

22. *Leuwenhoek microscopes*: The early nineteenth century saw a considerable improvement in the efficiency of microscopes, which contributed to the extensive interest in natural history at that time. Antony van Leuwenhoek (1632–1723), a Dutchman, was a pioneer in the field of microscopic investigation.

23. *Vauxhall*: At Vauxhall, on the south bank of the Thames, there were extensive pleasure-gardens 'where people might roam on a fine evening, eating, drinking, flirting, copulating, watching

fireworks or lantern displays' (Lewis Mumford *The City in History*). The gardens reached a peak of popularity in the late eighteenth and early nineteenth centuries.

24. *what in Martinus Scriblerus was still only an idea . . . Vaucanson did indeed make a wooden duck*: In Chapter 12 of the *Memoirs of Martinus Scriblerus*, a satirical pseudo-autobiography under the joint authorship of Arbuthnot, Pope, Swift and Gay, various free-thinking mechanistic theories of human nature were parodied. The culmination of the chapter describes how a 'Virtuoso at Nuremberg' plans to construct a robot which will be inspired with human consciousness, much as a spit, which is simply a machine, has within it the power to roast meat. Fantasy came close to fact when Jacques de Vaucanson (1709–82), a French inventor who applied himself to the construction of mechanical representations of living creatures, made a duck which paddled, pecked at grain and apparently digested it through a mechanical process imitative of the action of the digestive organs.

25. *a Smith, a De Lolme, a Bentham*: Adam Smith, the first systematic economist, John De Lolme, a constitutional theorist, and Jeremy Bentham, the founding father of English utilitarianism, are grouped together as representative of the general intellectual malaise. The reputations of Smith and Bentham have of course survived: that of De Lolme has not, although his *Constitution of England* (1771) enjoyed considerable contemporary success. Its basic thesis was that the freedom of the constitution depended on the balance of its different parts, a mechanistic argument that Carlyle would have certainly found objectionable.

26. *No dining at Freemasons' Tavern*: The Freemasons' Tavern was the meeting-place of a Debating Society organized by, among others, John Stuart Mill. The society's first meeting was in 1825 and it attracted many prominent intellectuals. Its activities are described in Mill's *Autobiography*, Ch. 4.

27. *cheap bread and a Habeas-corpus act*: The inflated price of bread, consequent upon the imposition of the Corn Laws, and the repeated suppression of Habeas Corpus were amongst the strongest grievances of Radical opinion in the early nineteenth century.

28. *taking the high* priori *road*: cf. Pope, *Dunciad*, Book IV, ll.471–2:

> We nobly take the high Priori road
> And reason downward, till we doubt of God.

An 'a priori' argument is an argument based on pure reason as distinct from one deduced from empirical observation.

29. *Epictetus was personally one*: The stoicism of Epictetus, who asserted the importance of the individual will and the irrelevance of external circumstances, would have had considerable attractions for Carlyle. Epictetus was originally a slave, although his master, an important Roman official, later set him free.

30. *What countries produced Columbus and Las Casas? Or ... Cortes, Pizarro, Alba, Ximenes?*: The answer in each case is either Portugal or Spain, although to be strictly accurate Columbus, of course, was Genoese.

31. *Sheridan Knowles and Beau Brummel*: James Sheridan Knowles was an Irish actor-dramatist who achieved considerable success in the 1820s, Hazlitt speaking of him as the first tragic author of the time. Carlyle, whose judgement in this instance seems to have been more acute, ironically compares him with Shakespeare, and Beau Brummel, the celebrated dandy, with Sir Philip Sidney.

32. *a Smith, a Hume or a Constant*: cf. notes 19 and 25 above. Benjamin Constant (1767–1830) was a politician and man of letters. His '*De la religion considérée dans sa source, ses formes et ses développements*' (1824–30) is probably the work which has called him to Carlyle's attention here.

33. *The* Euphuist *of our day*: i.e. the intellectual sophisticate. Lyly's *Euphues* (1578–80) is celebrated for its high-flown style.

34. *Like Sir Hudibras, for every Why we must have a Wherefore*: Sir Hudibras is the hero of a satirical poem by Samuel Butler (1612–80):

> He understood b'implicit faith
> Whatever Sceptic would enquire for
> For every WHY he had a WHEREFORE.

(Canto I, ll. 130–32) i.e. he answered one question by asking another and was thus involved in an endless chain of inquiry.

35. *Hume has written us a 'Natural History of Religion'*: In the work referred to, which was published in 1757, Hume subjected religion to his processes of sceptical historical analysis, remarking in the introduction that 'There is a great difference between historical facts and speculative opinions.'

36. *a tone of the Memnon statue*: The stones of the Colossi of Memnon at Abydos in ancient Egypt were reputed by the Romans to sing at dawn.

37. *as children pass through the fire to Moloch*: Moloch was a hea-
     then god referred to several times in the Old Testament whose
     rites involved the subjection of children to an ordeal by fire. Cf.
     particularly *Leviticus* xx, 2–5.

38. *Argus eyes*: Argus was a mythological monster who had numer-
     ous eyes, some of them in the back of his head, and thus could
     not be surprised.

39. *reckoning even from those of the Heraclides and the Pelasgi*:
     These two tribes are part of the pre-history of ancient Greece.
     The Heraclides were the mythological ancestors of the Dorian
     invaders of Greece and the Pelasgians were pre-Hellenic inhabit-
     ants of the country.

40. *Carbonari rebellions*: The Carbonari were members of a
     secret revolutionary movement which extended throughout
     Mediterranean Europe and was at its most powerful in 1820–21
     when a series of insurrections, unsuccessful in France, but tem-
     porarily successful in Spain, Greece and some Italian states,
     occurred.

SARTOR RESARTUS

1.   *'a Faust's mantle . . . the Sheet of clean and unclean beasts in the
     Apostle's Dream'*: In Goethe's *Faust*, Faust and Mephistopheles
     are carried across land and sea on a magic cloak; Acts x, describes
     how the apostle Peter, in a trance, saw a sheet descend from
     heaven bearing every kind of living creature.

2.   *a promise of new Fortunate Islands*: i.e. the *Fortunatae Insulae*,
     or 'Islands of the Blessed' of Greek mythology, to which heroes
     were said to pass without suffering death.

3.   Cogito, ergo sum: lit., 'I think, therefore I am', the famous pos-
     tulate on which Descartes founded his philosophy.

4.   *'In Being's floods, in Action's storm . . .'*: At the beginning of
     Goethe's *Faust*, Faust calls up the Earth-Spirit; the lines quoted
     are part of the Spirit's introductory speech.

5.   *Gouda*: A town in Holland, famous for its cheese.

6.   *as Swift has it, 'A forked straddling animal with bandy legs'*: The
     reference is to *Martinus Scriblerus* (see *Signs of the Times*, note
     24), Ch. 11; 'Let him surprise the Beauty he adores at a dis-
     advantage, survey himself naked, divested of artificial charms,
     and he will find himself a forked straddling animal with bandy
     legs, a short neck, a dun hide, and a pot belly.'

7. *a Sansculottist ... A new Adamite*: The Sansculottists were a group in the French Revolution who as a symbolic gesture gave up the traditional costume of knee-breeches for ordinary trousers; by extension the term came to mean anyone of extreme radical views. The Adamites were an early North African religious sect who sought to re-establish man's primeval innocence, going naked and rejecting marriage as part of their code.

8. *what he said lately about 'Aboriginal Savages'*: In Book I, Ch. 5 of *Sartor Resartus* the aborigines are given as the most primitive example of human life.

9. *Frankfort Coronations*: The German emperors were elected in Frankfurt, and afterwards crowned in the cathedral there.

10. *their high State Tragedy ... becomes a Pickleherring-Farce*: These are both types of traditional German drama, prominent in the seventeenth century.

11. *the tables (according to Horace) ... are dissolved*: cf. Horace, Satires, II, i, 86, 'Solventur risu tabulae'. In general terms the phrase means 'the case breaks down'.

12. *infandum! infandum!*: i.e. 'Unparalleled disaster!' From Virgil, *Aeneid*, I, 251.

13. *a forked Radish, with a head fantastically carved*: Falstaff's description of Justice Shallow, in Henry IV, Part Two, Act 3, Sc. ii.

14. *St Stephen's*: The Houses of Parliament.

15. *a Bed of Justice*: In the *ancien regime* the King of France was entitled to hold a 'Lit de Justice' at which his edicts to Parliament were absolute. The phrase itself describes the throne from which the commands were issued.

16. *in Yorick Sterne's words*: i.e. in *Tristram Shandy*, Vol. V, Ch. 7.

17. *the boundless Serbonian Bog of Sansculottism ... where ... whole nations might sink*: cf. *Paradise Lost*, Book II, ll, 592–4:

> A gulf profound as that Serbonian Bog
> Betwixt Damiata and mount Casius old
> Where armies whole have sunk.

Lake Serbonis is in Egypt, near the Suez Canal.

18. *Well said Saint Chrysostom, with his lips of gold, 'the true* SHEKINAH *is Man'*: Saint John Chrysostom, who was known by the epithet 'the golden-mouthed', was one of the great fathers of the early church. 'Shekinah' is a Talmudic word meaning literally 'dwelling-place'.

19. *the wisest of this age*: As always with Carlyle, Goethe, who makes the remark referred to in *Wilhelm Meister*.

20. *Arkwright looms . . . silent Arachnes*: Richard Arkwright (1732–92) was the inventor of the spinning frame, a major technological advance; Arachne was a maiden who in Greek mythology was turned into a spider.

21. *in partibus infidelium*: A term used by the Roman Catholic church meaning, literally, 'in the country of the heathen'.

22. *like the Doctor's in the Arabian Tale*: The reference is to a story in the *Arabian Nights* in which a learned doctor is maliciously slain by a king whom he had cured. After execution the doctor's head continued to give instructions to the king who himself died as a result of acting upon them.

23. *the Mechanics' Institute of Science*: An educational establishment for working men. The London Mechanics Institute was founded in 1823, after which the idea spread to the provinces, and particularly to Yorkshire and Lancashire. In their early days there was a strong bias towards science in the institutes, but they later changed in character.

24. *like true Old-Roman geese and goslings round their Capitol*: In 390 B.C., when the Gauls attempted to attack the Capitol, the alarm was supposed to have been given by sacred geese which were kept there.

25. *the whole* Mécanique Céleste *and* Hegel's Philosophy: For the *Mécanique Celeste* see *Signs of the Times*, note 17. The philosophy of Hegel, in that it asserted the inter-dependence of the 'real' and the 'rational', implied an emphasis on science and logic that would have been objectionable to Teufelsdröckh (and to Carlyle). The work which seems to be specifically referred to here is probably his *Encyclopædia of the Philosophical Sciences*.

26. *Armer Teufel!*: i.e. 'Poor Devil!'

27. *beatific Asphodel meadows, or the yellow-burning marl of a Hell-on-Earth?*: In Greek mythology the fields of Asphodel were the dwelling-places of the souls of departed heroes. The second half of the reference is taken from the description of Hell in *Paradise Lost* (Book I, ll, 295–301).

28. *Well sang the Hebrew Psalmist . . .* : cf. *Psalms* cxxxix, 9–10.

29. *the Schwarzwald*: i.e. the Black Forest.

30. *It is written, the Heavens and the Earth shall fade away like a Vesture*: cf. *Psalms* cii, 25–6.

31. *Hofrath Heuschrecke*: The name which Carlyle has earlier given to the colleague of Teufelsdröckh who has supplied the details of

his life and work. In the paragraphs which follow Carlyle makes
great play with the device on which *Sartor Resartus* is based, in
describing how the details of Teufelsdröckh's life came to light.

32. *The great Herr Minister Von Goethe has penetratingly
remarked* . . . : The quotation comes from *Wilhelm Meister*.

33. *steep Pisgah hills* . . . *this wonderful prophetic Hebron*: Mt Pisgah was the mountain from which Moses was shown the
promised land immediately before his death. Hebron was part of
the promised land, and the dwelling-place of Abraham.

34. *verehrtester Herr Herausgeber*: i.e. 'most esteemed Editor'.

35. *cursiv-schrift*: A particular style of small handwriting.

36. *like Sibylline leaves*: In Greek mythology the answers of the
Cumaean Sybil were given on leaves which were committed to
the wind.

37. *our first Bridge-builders, Sin and Death*: At the conclusion of
Paradise Lost, Book II, the figures of Sin and Death are shown
building a bridge across the abyss between Hell and 'th' utmost
Orb/Of this frail world'.

THE FRENCH REVOLUTION

1. *Astraea Redux*: Literally 'The Return of Justice', Astraea being
the Goddess of Justice. Dryden used the phrase as the title for his
poem on the Restoration of Charles II, and Carlyle uses it with
heavy irony to refer to the accession of Louis XVI. The classical
source of the theme is Virgil's Fourth Eclogue.

2. *these next Ten Years*: i.e. the first ten years of the reign of Louis
XVI.

3. *What wisest Philosophe* . . . *could prophesy* . . . *the event of
events?*: The 'philosophes' were a group of free-thinkers, inspired
primarily by Voltaire, who flourished in the intellectual climate
of eighteenth-century France. Predominantly optimistic and
anti-clerical, they asserted the supremacy of reason.

4. *On the Fifth of May, fifteen years hence* . . . *new Louis* . . . *will
be opening the States-General*: Organized into three 'estates', the
nobility, the clergy, and the 'third estate' or commons, the States-
General, whose powers were limited to those of petition, had not
been called since 1614.

5. *a sleepless Permanent Committee*: i.e. the Electors of Paris, who
had formed themselves into a 'Provisional Municipality', and
had decided to remain in permanent session during the crisis.

6. *Provost Flesselles ... may think of those Charleville Boxes*: Flesselles, chief magistrate of Paris, had earlier led the citizens to believe that arms were to be obtained from the arsenal at Charleville. When the cases arrived they were found to contain 'rags, foul-linen, candle-ends and bits of wood'. (Vol. I, Book Five, Ch. 5)

7. *National Guard*: The citizens of Paris had established a municipal militia for their own protection which became known as the Garde Nationale.

8. *Besenval's Camp is there*: Pierre Victor, Baron de Besenval, whose *Memoires* (1805) were one of Carlyle's sources, had been given the task of organizing the military resources around Paris. He made his headquarters at the Hotel des Invalides, the massive barracks for army veterans, which is one of the major monuments of Paris.

9. *such a figure drew Priam's curtains*: cf. Shakespeare, Henry IV, Part II, Act 1, Sc. ii:

> Even such a man, so faint, so spiritless,
> So dull, so dead in look, so woe-begone,
> Drew Priam's curtains in the dead of night
> And would have told him half his Troy was burnt.

10. *Gardes Françaises*: At the beginning of the uprising the Gardes Françaises, a section of the French army who had earlier been regarded by the authorities as suspect, and confined to their quarters, deserted in a body and joined the rioters.

11. *Old De Launay*: The Marquise de Launay, governor of the Bastille.

12. *Orcus*: In Latin mythology, one of the names of the nether world.

13. *the war of Pygmies and Cranes*: In the Iliad, Book III, Homer compares the advancing Trojan armies with the cranes, which, so he says, attack the African pygmies at the onset of every winter.

14. *the King of Siam's cannon*: Two silver-mounted cannon, a gift from the King of Siam to Louis XVI, which had been appropriated by the mob.

15. *the Brest Diligence*: i.e. the stagecoach from Brest.

16. *Tophet*: In the Old Testament the site of sacrifices to Moloch.

17. *Broglie is distant*: The Marechal de Broglie, Minister of War, who was in supreme command of the military forces, remained in Versailles throughout the riots.

18. *M. Marat*: Jean-Paul Marat, whose role of editor and journalist gave him great influence over the Paris mob, is one of the great character-studies of Carlyle's history. He is invariably represented as the epitome of malice, and his assassination by Charlotte Corday, which is foreshadowed here, is one of the high points of the third volume.

19. *The Ritter Gluck*: The composer Christophe Gluck (1714–87) is usually credited with having provided the foundation of important developments in romantic opera, and in particular with having intensified the dramatic potential of the medium. In 1756 he was awarded a Papal knighthood, and he made a point henceforth of referring to himself as Ritter ('Chevalier') von Gluck.

20. *the* chamade: The call to parley.

21. *Electoral Committee*: see note 5 above.

22. *It was the Titans warring with Olympus*: In Greek mythology the Titans were the children of Heaven and Earth. They rebelled against Zeus, and after being defeated were imprisoned in the nether world.

23. *It is one year and two months since these same men stood unparticipating with Brennus D'Agoust at the Palais de Justice, when Fate overtook D'Espréménil*: The incident referred to is described in Vol. I, Book Three, Ch. 8. In May 1788 Duval d'Espréménil, a member of the Parliament of Paris, was arrested while the Parliament was in session by a Captain D'Agoust, nicknamed 'Brennus' by Carlyle after the leader of the Gauls who dictated terms to the Roman senate in the fourth century B.C. The arrest of d'Espréménil contributed to the dissatisfaction that led eventually to the calling of the States-General.

24. *Friar Bacon's Brass Head*: Amongst the various legends surrounding the mediaeval philosopher Roger Bacon was one whereby he was credited with the possession of a head of brass which talked and prophesied the future. There is no authority for the legend in any of his extant works.

25. *Vice-President Lafayette*: The Marquise de Lafayette, Vice-President of the National Assembly, who during the Revolution attempted to maintain a conciliatory role. He had earlier distinguished himself in the American War of Independence, but his political career was less successful, and he eventually fled to Holland to escape the Jacobins.

26. *His Majesty ... perhaps dreams of double barrels and the Woods of Meudon*: The gardens and woods of Meudon, near

Versailles, were a favourite haunt of the Court. Louis XVI hunted there: hence, perhaps, the reference to 'double barrels.'

27. *'The gods themselves,' sings Pindar, 'cannot annihilate the action that is done'*: cf. Pindar, Olympian Odes, ii, l.16: 'Even Time, the father of all, cannot undo the past, whether right or wrong.'

28. *your Epimenides, your somnolent Peter Klaus, since named Rip Van Winkle*: Parallel references to celebrated sleepers. Epimenides was a largely legendary Cretan prophet of the sixth century B.C. who was reputed to have fallen asleep in a cave and slept for fifty-seven years. Peter Klaus was the hero of a German folk-legend which was the source of Washington Irving's *Rip Van Winkle*. In both versions of the story the hero sleeps in a cave for twenty years and returns to a new order of things.

29. *your miraculous Seven-sleeper*: The seven sleepers were the heroes of an early Christian story who, to avoid persecution, took refuge in a cave and, when it was blocked up, slept for 200 years.

30. *The cannonading of Nanci*: In September 1790 a mutiny at Nanci was put down with considerable bloodshed by the Marquise de Bouille, commander of the Metz garrison. The incident forms the substance of Vol. II, Book Two.

31. *the one sanguineous Drapeau Rouge*: At the Massacre of the Champ de Mars the imposition of martial law was indicated by the unfurling of a red flag.

32. *even as Hannibal's rock-rending vinegar lay in the sweet new wine*: According to the Roman historian Livy, Hannibal, during his crossing of the Alps, cut a passage through solid rock by first heating it and then pouring vinegar on it. The vinegar would have come from the wine which the soldiers carried with them.

33. *call him, for instance, Lafayette*: See note 25 above.

34. *the Gospel of Jean-Jacques*: i.e. Rousseau's *Social Contract*, which Carlyle refers to on several occasions in *The French Revolution* as the source-book for libertarian schemes of government.

35. *his Rozinante war-garron*: Rozinante was the steed of Don Quixote; the phrase implies the futility of the emigré's military activities.

36. *Can he bear to have a Distaff, a* Quenouille *sent to him . . . as if he were no Hercules, but an Omphale?*: A Distaff (Fr: quenouille) is a staff used in spinning, and thus traditionally a symbol of feminine pursuits. It would appear that these were

sent as an insult by those aristocrats who had emigrated to those who remained inactive in France. According to Greek legend Omphale was a Lydian queen who purchased Hercules as a slave and set him to women's work.

37. *Louis Capet*: The traditional family name of Louis XVI, under which, as an egalitarian gesture, he was charged.

38. *the Girondins*: In general terms the more moderate Republican party. Opposed by the Jacobins, they maintained the major influence in the Legislative Assembly. They were unable to sustain this power in the National Convention, however, and their leaders were expelled from that body in 1793, most of them perishing in the Reign of Terror.

39. *Danton, who has just got back from mission in the Netherlands*: Georges Jacques Danton, the most eloquent and powerful personality amongst the revolutionary leaders. An opponent of the Girondins, he voted for the death of Louis XVI, having returned to the trial from a visit to the Netherlands which had been overrun by the French army. (See note 50 below)

40. *Philippe Egalité*: Philippe, Duc D'Orleans, who opposed the King from the early days of the revolution, and took the name 'Egalité' to identify with the republican cause. Carlyle regards him at all times as a treacherous intriguer.

41. *Mère Duchesse*: A prominent mob orator, to whom Carlyle refers on several occasions as a representative of the female element in the revolutionary crowd.

42. *At Méot the Restaurateur's no Captain Dampmartin now dines*: Dampmartin, a royalist officer, produced a work entitled *Evènements qui se sont passés sous mes yeux pendant la Révolution Française* (1799) which Carlyle used as a source-book. This is a typical example of Carlyle's habit, throughout *The French Revolution*, of alluding to incidents about which he had read, but which he leaves unexplained in the work itself. Méot was a famous Parisian cook, and Carlyle has abstracted from Dampmartin's memoirs the suggestion that his restaurant was a centre of Royalist intrigue.

43. *their bones lie whitening Argonne Wood*: Many of the emigrés who had enlisted in the Prussian army lost their lives at the Battle of Valmy in the Argonne forest in September 1792, when the Prussians were turned back by the republican French under the command of Dumouriez.

44. *like a Phalaris shut in the belly of his own red-heated Brazen Bull*: Phalaris, a Sicilian tyrant of the sixth century B.C., was

reputed to roast his victims alive in a bronze bull. It is said that on his overthrow he himself was burned in the same bull.

45. *Lally went on his hurdle; his mouth filled with a gag*: The Comte de Lally commanded an unsuccessful French expedition to India. He was forced to surrender to the English in 1761, but was released on parole. After his return to France he was imprisoned in the Bastille, and then tried and executed. The humiliating nature of his death had earlier been instanced as an example of political malevolence (cf. Vol. I, Book Three, Ch. 5).

46. *Valet Cléry*: Jean Baptiste Cléry, Louis XVI's *valet de chambre* during his imprisonment, from whose memoirs the description that follows is taken.

47. *the Cerberus Municipals*: In Greek mythology Cerberus was the name of the dog that guarded the infernal regions.

48. *Roland ... sends in his demission*: Jean Marie Roland de la Platière, husband of the more famous Mme Roland, was appointed Minister of the Interior in 1792, but resigned his post immediately after the King's execution.

49. næniæ: Lamentations for the dead.

50. *Dumouriez, conquering Holland, growls ominous discontent*: Charles François Dumouriez, leader of the French army, after defeating the Prussians at Valmy (see note 43 above) led a campaign into the Low Countries. He had strong Royalist sympathies, however, and eventually went into exile.

51. *Deputy Fauchet*: The Abbé Fauchet, who after playing a prominent part in the early stages of the Revolution became disillusioned by its excesses. As a consequence of his opposition to the Jacobins he was arrested and executed in October 1793.

52. *that Iron Press of the Tuileries*: A crucial factor in the impeachment of Louis XVI was the discovery, in the Tuileries, of an iron chest containing letters and documents of a counter-revolutionary nature.

53. *England declares war ... being shocked principally, it would seem, at the condition of the River Scheldt*: A particular issue which led to war between England and France concerned navigation rights in the River Scheldt, which since the Treaty of Westphalia (1648) had been the prerogative of the Dutch. Carlyle goes on to correct his statement that England was the first to declare war: the manner in which he does so is a splendid demonstration of his sense of priorities as a historian.

CHARTISM

1. *when the 'National Petition' carts itself in wagons along the streets*: The National Petition for the enactment of the six points of the Charter – universal male suffrage, equal electoral districts, removal of members' property qualifications, payment of members of parliament, the secret ballot and annual general elections – was presented to Parliament in 1839, debated and rejected. Carlyle's description of the way in which the petition was carried to Parliament is literally accurate, so great was the number of signatures.

2. *a Reform ministry*: For a period of nine years after the Reform Bill of 1832 the Whigs held power, with the exception of a few months in 1834. Carlyle refers on several occasions to a 'Reform ministry': he would seem to apply the term to refer to this period of Whig domination, and in particular to Lord Melbourne's second cabinet, which governed from 1835 until 1841.

3. *'Glasgow Thuggery'*: Carlyle has in mind here the revelations about trade union practices which resulted from the Glasgow Cotton Spinners' strike of 1837. The strike led to a Select Committee on Combinations in 1838, which exposed numerous examples of clandestine intimidation by the union members.

4. *Chartist torch-meetings, Birmingham riots, Swing conflagrations*: Torch-light meetings and processions were a popular feature of the Chartist movement. On 4 July 1839, the Mayor of Birmingham, with the aid of a force of London policemen, attempted to disperse a Chartist meeting in the Bull Ring. Troops had to be called in to reinforce the civil powers. The 'Swing Riots' was the name given to the outbursts of machine-breaking and incendiarism by agricultural labourers in 1830, 'Captain Swing' being the signature frequently attached to the threatening letters which gave warning of these incidents.

5. *No African expedition now, as in the days of Herodotus, is fitted out* against the South-wind: Herodotus, in his *Histories*, Book IV, tells of an African tribe called the Psylli who held the south wind responsible for a drought and marched into the desert against it. Once in the desert they were caught in a sandstorm and buried in the sand.

6. *He were an Oedipus, and deliverer from sad social pestilence*: Oedipus exiled himself from Thebes to deliver his country from

the pestilence that was a consequence of his unwitting incest with Jocasta.

7. 'as the statist *thinks, the bell clinks*': Carlyle's adaptation of the proverb, 'as the fool thinks, the bell clinks'.

8. *the sieve of the Danaides*: In Greek legend the Danaides were the daughters of Danaus, who were condemned to fill bottomless vessels with water perpetually for killing their husbands, the sons of Aegyptus.

9. *Pactolus*: A brook in Asia Minor. Its sands were once famous for the gold to be found there: the wealth of Croesus traditionally had its origin there.

10. *a Pamphlet 'published by Charles Knight and Company,'* ... *Northampton Tables, compiled by Dr Price ... Carlisle Tables, collected by Dr Heysham*: Examples of the proliferation of statistical literature concerning living conditions at this time. Carlyle identifies the 'Pamphlet' in a footnote: '*An Essay on the Means of Insurance against the Casualties of &c. &c.* London, Charles Knight and Company, 1836. Price two shillings.' The Northampton tables, compiled by the distinguished statistician Richard Price, were based on the Bills of Mortality kept in the Parish of All Saints, Northampton, and established what was regarded as a fair average of longevity on which life insurance calculations could be based. Dr Heysham, a medical practitioner and philanthropist of Carlisle, kept statistical records of the annual births, marriages, diseases and deaths in Carlisle from 1779 to 1788. These statistics were first published in 1797.

11. *New Poor-Law Bill*: The Poor Law Amendment Act of 1834 provided that, except under special circumstances, the able-bodied should not receive outdoor relief. It instituted a new central authority, the Poor Law Commissioners, to whom newly elected boards of Guardians were responsible, thus removing responsibility from the parish officers with whom it had traditionally rested. The Commissioners produced a series of annual reports on their activities, but the advantages of a more consistent and centralized system were compromised by the indiscriminate application of the principles concerning the provision of relief, which led in many cases to the workhouses becoming little more than over-crowded prisons, referred to, by the occupants themselves, as 'Bastilles'.

12. *Hyperion*: In Greek mythology a Titan, son of Heaven and Earth, and the father of the sun, the moon and the dawn. The

name was also loosely used as a patronymic for the Sun God himself and it is in this sense that it appears here.

13. '*the widow picking nettles for her children's dinner; and the perfumed seigneur delicately lounging in the Oeil-du-Boeuf*': On several occasions in *Chartism* Carlyle uses as illustrations details from his reading for *The French Revolution*. The 'Oeil-du-Boeuf' was a gallery at Versailles, frequented by members of the court.

14. *Targum*: The Targums are Aramaic paraphrases of the Old Testament; Carlyle's reference is, of course, ironic.

15. '*Statute of the Forty-third of Elizabeth*': The statute on which the accumulation of Poor-Law which the 1834 act replaced was based. Its governing principle was the 'Right to Work', i.e. the entitlement to work, if necessary financed by a poor-rate, for the able-bodied unemployed. Only those who refused to work were to be institutionalized. Unfortunately the system had degenerated into a means of subsidizing the agricultural wages bill; furthermore the work provided was often a formality and the 'Right to Work' had become the 'Right to Relief'.

16. *Burns expresses feelingly what thoughts it gave him*: i.e. in his poem *Man Was Made to Mourn*:

> See yonder poor, o'erlabour'd wight,
> So abject, mean and vile,
> Who begs a brother of the earth
> To give him leave to toil;
> And see his lordly fellow-worm,
> The poor petition spurn,
> Unmindful, tho' a weeping wife,
> And helpless offspring mourn.

17. *a fact perhaps the most eloquent that was ever written down in any language*: Carlyle quotes this statistic on more than one occasion; see e.g. *The French Revolution*, Vol. III, Book Seven, Ch. 6, where its source is given as the *Report of the Irish Poor-Law Commission*, 1836.

18. *Strigul*: Richard Strongbow, 'Lord of Strigoil', who was invited to Ireland in 1170 by Dermot, King of Leinster. He was followed by Henry II in 1171, and English political involvement in Ireland can be said to date from these events.

19. *Crowds of miserable Irish darken all our towns*: Irish labourers, who at first came to England as seasonal immigrants, were becoming an increasingly common social phenomenon in the

1830s and '40s. They were often used as a source of cheap labour, particularly in the industrial towns, a situation which led to considerable working-class hostility against them.

20. *Dutch William*: i.e. William of Orange, whose difficulties in Ireland were a constant distraction throughout his reign.

21. *the giant Steamengine in a giant English Nation*: i.e. industrialization.

22. *Proteus*: A Greek sea-god, servant of Poseidon, who could assume all manner of terrifying shapes, but could be made to answer questions when forced to assume his true form.

23. *Mr Symmons*: Most probably Jelinger C. Symons, who in 1839 published a book entitled *Arts and Artisans: With Sketches of the Progress of Foreign Manufactures*, in which he discussed variations in wage-rates.

24. *Tophet*: See *The French Revolution*, note 16.

25. *Simooms*: Desert winds, sandstorms.

26. *Phalaris' Bull*: See *The French Revolution*, note 44.

27. *as Novalis says, by a 'simultaneous universal act of suicide'*: This is a paraphrase of a passage from Novalis's *Pupils at Sais* to which Carlyle had drawn attention in his essay on Novalis.

28. *The Romans conquered Mithridates*: Mithridates, King of Pontus (*c.* 120–65 B.C.), waged frequent wars against Rome in Asia Minor. He was finally defeated, and deserted in extremity by his people who had tired of his constant demands upon them.

29. *strong Teutonic men ... drilled this wild Teutonic people*: The anthropological paradox is explained in Chapter 8: 'Does the ... Physiologist reflect who those same Normans, Northmen, originally were? Baltic Saxons, and what other miscellany of Lurdanes, Jutes and Deutsch Pirates from the East-sea marshes would join them in plunder of France!' (this ed., p. 175).

30. *like your old Chivalry* Femgericht: A system of irregular and secret tribunals operating in Germany, and in particular in Westphalia, in the fourteenth and fifteenth centuries.

31. *The cunningest Mephistopheles cannot deceive a simple Margaret of honest heart*: At the climax of Goethe's *Faust*, Part One, Margareta rejects Mephistopheles's temptation to depart with Faust, preferring to face execution for the murder of the child she had borne Faust earlier in the drama.

32. *Domdaniel* Parcs-aux-cerfs *and 'Peasants living on meal-husks and boiled grass'*: see note 13 above. 'Domdaniel Parcs-aux-cerfs' is a contemptuous reference to the deer-parks of Versailles (cf. *French Revolution*, Vol. I, Book One, Ch. I).

33. *Diderot Atheisms*: Denys Diderot (1713–84) was one of the most prominent of the free-thinkers whose intellectual attitudes anticipated the French Revolution. His *Pensées Philosophiques* (1746) asserted an uncompromising atheism.

34. *Seven-years Silesian robber-wars*: i.e. the Seven Years War (1756–63). See *Frederick the Great*, note 4.

35. *Antæus-like*: Antæus, a giant, son of Poseidon and Earth, compelled all comers to wrestle with him and slew them when they were overthrown. He himself was reputed to obtain added strength from contact with his mother Earth.

36. *(if there be historical truth in Joseph Miller)*: The story is taken from one of the many versions of *Joe Miller's Jests*, a compilation of anecdotes first published in 1739 and frequently added to in various later editions.

37. *Deputy Lapoule, in the* Salle des Menus *at Versailles*: The incident is described in *French Revolution*, Vol. I, Book One, Ch. 2.

38. *'Use every man according to his* rights, *and who shall escape whipping?'*: Cf. *Hamlet*, Act 2, Sc. ii.

39. *Lyons fusilladings, Nantes noyadings*: Two famous incidents during the Reign of Terror, both of which are described by Carlyle in *French Revolution*, Vol. III, Book Five, Ch. 3. At Lyons, 'Two hundred and nine men are marched forth over the River, to be shot in mass, by musket and cannon.' At Nantes ninety priests were drowned in the Loire, the incident being known as the 'Noyade' of Nantes.

40. *Fact passionately joins Messiah Thom of Canterbury, and has himself shot for a new fifth-monarchy brought in by Bedlam*: In May 1838 a religious fanatic, J. N. Tom, or, as he preferred to be called, 'Sir William Courtenay, King of Jerusalem, Prince of Arabia, King of the Gypsies', attracted a following of Kentish labourers and, having shot a constable, engaged in battle with the militia near Canterbury. Tom and some dozen of his followers were killed. See *Signs of the Times*, note 7.

41. *universal suffrage and 'the five points'*: See note 1 above. Carlyle here has distinguished the major issue of universal suffrage from the other 'five points' of the Charter and he repeats the distinction later in the chapter, although by this time the phrase has assumed a predominantly rhetorical significance.

42. *a sardonic German writer*: i.e. Sauerteig, the fictitious Carlylean persona, whose version of English history forms the substance of Chapter 8.

43. *hungry Greeks throttling down hungry Greeks on the floor of a St Stephen's*: i.e. disputatious members of the House of Commons.

44. *Peterloo ... the Place-de-Grève*: Historic sites of social disturbance. The Peterloo massacre occurred in Manchester in 1819, when a crowd of over 50,000 people, who had assembled to listen to the radical orator, Henry Hunt, was broken up by the militia. There were eleven deaths and over four hundred wounded. The Place de Grève, originally the site of public executions in Paris, was a focal point for gatherings of the revolutionary crowd, particularly in the early stages of the Revolution.

45. *It had to purge out its argumentive Girondins, elect its Supreme Committee of Salut, guillotine into silence and extinction all that gainsaid it*: See *French Revolution*, note 38. The 'Comité de Salut' was established in 1793 by the Revolutionary Convention to take all measures of defence, external and internal. It thus became the effective government of France during the Reign of Terror.

46. *St-Simonisms, Robert-Macairisms, and the 'Literature of Desperation'*: Claud Henri, Comte de Saint-Simon (1760–1825) exercised considerable posthumous influence on the founders of the social sciences. His social philosophy was predominantly utilitarian and philanthropic, and a Saint-Simonian community was formed which attempted to live out his theories in practice. Robert Macaire was a fictitious confidence trickster made popular in the 1830s by the cartoons of Daumier. His name became synonymous with any form of roguery. The phrase 'Literature of Desperation' would seem to suggest one of the more extreme forms of Romanticism, but I have been unable to trace its origin.

47. *Belshazzar fire-letters*: The mysterious writing which appeared on the wall at Belshazzar's feast, warning him of his fate (*Daniel*, v, 5).

48. *A sooty African can become a Toussaint L'Ouverture, a murderous Three-fingered Jack, let the yellow West Indies say to it what they will*: Toussaint L'Ouverture, by birth a slave, became a distinguished Negro leader and liberator of Haiti. When Napoleon attempted to restore slavery in the French West Indies he led the Negro opposition and eventually died in a French prison in 1803. It was frequently assumed that the feverish climate of the West Indies destroyed the will, hence Carlyle's reference to 'the

yellow West Indies'. The point that he is making is that even there a man is master of his own fate.

49. *A Scottish Poet*: i.e. Burns. See *Early Essays*, note 2.

50. *these same* 'Memoires' *of Horace Walpole*: Horace Walpole was the son of Robert Walpole, the great eighteenth-century Prime Minister. Himself a member of parliament, he is most famous as an author. His *Castle of Otranto* established the vogue of the Gothic novel, while his memoirs and correspondence are an invaluable source for historians of eighteenth-century politics.

51. *Samuel Johnson, furnished with 'fourpence-halfpenny a-day'*: See *Heroes and Hero-worship*, note 19.

52. *Talfourd Copyright Bill*: A bill introduced to parliament in 1837 by Sir Thomas Talfourd, judge and author, and at that time member for Reading. Initially it was rejected, but it was passed in 1842. As an acknowledgement of Talfourd's efforts to secure copyright for authors Dickens dedicated *Pickwick Papers* to him.

53. *Philippe d'Orléans, not yet Egalité*: See *French Revolution*, note 40.

54. *a strange rhapsodic 'History of the Teuton Kindred'* (Geschichte der Teutschen Sippschaft)': An entirely imaginary work, as is indicated by its attribution to the mythical Sauerteig.

55. *Harzgebirge rock*: The rock of the Harz mountains. Carlyle is stressing the Teutonic origins of the Ancient Britons.

56. *the tribe of* Theuth: The Teutons, used loosely here as a generic term for the original inhabitants of Germany.

57. *its other Cassiterides* Tin-Islands: The islands mentioned by Herodotus as the place where the Phoenicians bartered for tin. They have been variously identified as the Scilly Isles, the Cornish coast, and Britain generally.

58. *the Heptarchy or Seven Kingdoms*: The seven Kingdoms (Kent, East Anglia, Sussex, Wessex, Northumbria, Mercia and Essex) which comprised Saxon England.

59. *Mr Thierry has written an ingenious book*: Histoire de la Conquête de l'Angleterre par les Normands (1825), by Jacques Thierry, the secretary of Saint-Simon. Thierry's romantic attitude towards history would have attracted Carlyle.

60. *the partial Delolmish, Benthamee, or other French or English answers*: See *Signs of the Times*, note 25.

61. *Sarmat*: Sarmatia was a region extending northwards from the Black Sea. Carlyle is aiming at a rhetorical anthropological inclusiveness.

62. *Prynne's bloody ears*: William Prynne, the seventeenth-century Puritan pamphleteer, was pilloried and lost his ears for his writings under Charles I. He successfully petitioned to the Long Parliament for redress.

63. *Hail to thee, poor little ship Mayflower . . . what ship Argo . . . was other than a foolish bumbarge in comparison!*: The *Mayflower* was the ship in which the Pilgrim Fathers sailed to New England in 1620. It is here compared with the Argo, in which Jason sailed in search of the Golden Fleece.

64. *like Saul the son of Kish, seeking a small thing, they found this unexpected great thing*: The reference is to the story told in 1 Samuel ix of Saul's search for his father's asses, which resulted in his finding the prophet Samuel who told him he was to be King of Israel.

65. *in England too since 1831*: i.e. since the first introduction of the Reform Bill, finally passed in 1832.

66. *Valmy*: See *The French Revolution*, note 43.

67. *The Prospero evoked the singing of Ariel, and took captive the world with those melodies*: i.e. in *The Tempest*. Carlyle equates industrial developments with Prospero's all-powerful magic.

68. *Prometheus, Tubalcain, Triptolemus*: Mythical figures representing fire, metalwork and farming respectively. Prometheus first stole fire from the gods; Tubalcain was 'an instructer of every artificer in brass and iron' (Genesis iv, 22); Triptolemus, according to Greek legend, was divinely gifted in the arts of husbandry.

69. *choragus*: choir-leader.

70. *When Arkwright shall have become mythic like Arachne*: See *Sartor Resartus*, note 22.

71. *an Enceladus*: In Greek mythology, a giant buried by Athene under the island of Sicily, to whose movements volcanic eruptions and earthquakes were attributed.

72. *the Nosology*: The whole catalogue of diseases.

73. *a feast of the Barmecide*: The story is told in the *Arabian Nights* of a sultan from the family of the Barmecides who placed a set of empty dishes before a beggar, telling him that they contained food. The beggar complied with the joke and pretended to eat the illusory meal.

74. *They have called long to us, 'We are a Reform Ministry; will ye not support us?'*: See note 2 above. In this instance Carlyle is clearly referring to Melbourne's second Whig administration, which was at the point of break-up at the time when *Chartism* was written.

75. *fluxionary calculus*: a rhetorical archaism; the name by which the differential calculus was originally known.

76. *The Great Western could weigh anchor from Bristol Port*: The *Great Western* crossed the Atlantic from Bristol to New York in fifteen days in April 1838, thus becoming the first full-scale steamship to achieve a passage from England to America.

77. '*My inheritance . . . I'm heir* ': The quotation is from a poem in Goethe's *West-östlicher Divan*; the translation is Carlyle's. A variation of the couplet appears at the head of *Wilhelm Meister's Travels*, and was quoted by Carlyle on several occasions, most notably as a motto for *Sartor Resartus*.

78. *a small fraction of the Revenue of one Day*: In 1833 the House of Commons gave a grant of £20,000 towards school building. The grant was repeated in 1834, and then raised to £30,000 to include the needs of Scotland.

79. *Dissenters call for one scheme of Education, the Church objects*: Popular education in England had its origin in the sectarian Sunday schools, and its advancement by State support, which was a matter of considerable debate at the time when Carlyle was writing *Chartism*, was hindered by dispute between the established church and the non-conformists.

80. *Albertus Magnus had a leather man that could articulate; not to speak of Martinus Scriblerus' Nürnberg man*: See *Signs of the Times*, note 24.

81. *Jean Paul*: Jean Paul Friedrich Richter (1763–1825), the German humorist, novelist and philosopher, whom Carlyle had translated and on whom he wrote two essays. Richter's transcendentalist philosophy, and in particular the mixture of whimsy and rhetoric in which it is presented, had considerable appeal for Carlyle.

82. *whether from Oxford or Hoxton*: i.e. whether backed by tradition or by dissent. The associations of Oxford are obvious, those of Hoxton less so. Situated in London, it was the site of a well-known Dissenting Academy in the eighteenth century, and although the Academy had been dispersed well before Carlyle came to write *Chartism* its reputation would seem to have endured.

83. *Malthus and the 'Population Principle'*: Put at its simplest the population theory of Malthus stated that population tends to increase beyond the means of subsistence. The theory was used by utilitarians both to assert the inevitability of poverty, and to hold the poor responsible for their own condition if they failed to limit their families.

84. *struggle and conquer like a Saint Francis of Assisi*: St Francis of Assisi, before his conversion, was reputed to have led a life of pleasure; his conversion itself was said to be the result of a protracted spiritual conflict.

85. *valley of Jehosaphat*: See 2 Chronicles xx, where the story is told of God's protection of the Israelites, led by Jehoshaphat, against overwhelming odds. The Israelites' enemies fell out amongst themselves, and when the Israelites arrived on the scene they found only their slaughtered bodies. The valley of Jehoshaphat thus came to signify the place where God would pronounce judgement on the enemies of Israel.

86. *This* Marcus *Pamphlet was the book alluded to by Stephens the Preacher Chartist*: The pamphlet concerned was entitled *The Possibility of Limiting Populousness* and advocated infanticide as a means of population control. The pseudonymous 'Marcus' was never identified, and it must be assumed that he was either a satirist or a Neo-Malthusian crank. The pamphlet was given considerable publicity by the Chartist activist J. R. Stephens, an expelled Wesleyan minister.

87. *an Emigrant host larger than Xerxes' was!*: The army led by Xerxes, King of Persia, when he invaded Greece. It was said to have been the greatest army ever known.

88. *'True thou Gold-Hofrath,' exclaims an eloquent satirical German of our acquaintance, in that strange Book of his*: Carlyle is in fact quoting himself: the reference is to *Sartor Resartus*, Book Three, Ch. 4, the last paragraph of which is repeated in its entirety here.

89. *the Hengsts and Alarics*: Hengist, with Horsa traditionally the first Saxon colonizer of Britain; Alaric, the Visigoth chief who, after invading Greece and Italy, sacked Rome in 410.

HEROES AND HERO-WORSHIP

1. *not in fierce impure fire-splendour as of Mahomet*: Carlyle frequently refers to points that he had made in the earlier lectures in the sequence. The second lecture, *The Hero as Prophet*, was devoted to Mahomet; describing his inspiration Carlyle had written: 'Such light had come, as it could, to illuminate the darkness of this wild Arab soul. A confused dazzling spendour as of life and Heaven, in the great darkness which threatened to be death: he called it revelation and the angel Gabriel; – who of us can yet know what to call it?'

2. *Odin's* Runes *were the first form of the work of a Hero*: In the first lecture, *The Hero as Divinity*, Carlyle attributes the invention of the Runic Alphabet to Odin, the chief of the Norse Gods: 'Runes are the Scandinavian alphabet; suppose Odin to have been the inventor of Letters, as well as "magic", among that people! It is the greatest invention man has ever made, this of marking-down the unseen thought that is in him by written characters.'

3. *Abelard*: Peter Abelard (1079–1142) was a French theologian and philosopher whose emphasis on logic was intended to provide, where possible, an intellectual justification for issues of faith. The foundation of the University of Paris, which developed from the cathedral school of Nôtre-Dame, was to a large extent the result of the impetus to learning which Abelard gave while teaching publicly in Paris, first at the cathedral school itself, and then at the schools on the Mont Saint-Geneviève of which he was the founder.

4. *Witenagemote*: The Anglo-Saxon national council.

5. *Burke said that there were Three Estates in Parliament; but, in the Reporters' Gallery yonder, there sat a* Fourth Estate *more important far than them all*: Carlyle's attribution to Burke of this usage of the expression 'Fourth Estate' has never been confirmed. It has also been attributed to Lord Brougham in a parliamentary speech in the 1820s and Carlyle is probably relying here on hearsay.

6. *harnessed to the yoke of Printer Cave*: Edward Cave, a London publisher, owned the *Gentleman's Magazine* for which Dr Johnson wrote his Parliamentary Debates in the early part of his career. Johnson did not feel the yoke to be as heavy as Carlyle implies: 'Of his friend Cave he always spoke with great affection. "Yet, (said he), Cave, (who never looked out of his window, but with a view to the Gentleman's Magazine,) was a penurious paymaster; he would contract for lines by the hundred, and expect the long hundred; but he was a good man and always delighted to have his friends at his table"' (Boswell, *Life of Johnson*).

7. punctum saliens: (Lat.) In traditional medical terminology, the first trace of the heart in an embryo.

8. '*the third man for thirty-six weeks each year is short of third-rate potatoes*': This statistic, which Carlyle was fond of quoting, refers to conditions in Ireland in times of famine. cf. *Chartism*. Ch. 4 (this edition p. 138) where it also appears, slightly altered.

9. *Pandora's Box*: According to Greek legend, Pandora, the first
    woman, was driven by curiosity to open a box containing all
    kinds of misery and evil, thus being responsible for their intro-
    duction on this earth.

10. *The living TREE Igdrasil ... deep-rooted as Hela*: Carlyle had
    described the Norse myth of the tree Igdrasil in the first lecture:
    'Igdrasil, the Ash-tree of Existence, has its roots deep-down in
    the kingdom of Hela or Death: its trunk reaches up heaven-high,
    spreads its boughs over the whole Universe: it is the Tree of
    Existence ... The rustle of it is the noise of Human Existence,
    onwards from of old.'

11. *The other day speaking ... of Bentham's theory of man and
    man's life, I chanced to call it a more beggarly one than Mahom-
    et's*: Carlyle made the comparison at the conclusion of his second
    lecture, and John Stuart Mill, who was among the audience, is
    reported to have called out 'No' in protest.

12. caput-mortuum: (Lat.) worthless residue.

13. *The 'Doctrine of Motives'*: i.e. Utilitarianism, which reduced all
    human motivation to the achievement of pleasure, and the mini-
    mization of pain.

14. *some Phalaris-Bull of his own contriving*: see *The French Revo-
    lution*, note 44.

15. σχέψις: (Gk.) speculation, consideration.

16. *Cagliostro*: The Count Cagliostro, a Sicilian charlatan who
    claimed to have magical powers and to be two thousand years
    old, travelled throughout Europe in the latter part of the eight-
    eenth century, practising hypnotism and pretended magic. Carlyle
    seized on him as a representative figure of the era he detested,
    and in two of his earlier essays, *Count Cagliostro* (1833) and
    The Diamond Necklace (1837), he gives highly dramatic accounts
    of his activities. *The Diamond Necklace*, which describes Cagli-
    ostro's most spectacular fraud, practised on the French Court,
    gives a foretaste of *The French Revolution*.

17. *Chatham ... comes down to the House, all wrapt and band-
    aged*: William Pitt, first Earl of Chatham, the great eighteenth-
    century statesman, was a powerful orator. Throughout his life he
    suffered severely from gout, which added a certain drama to his
    parliamentary appearances. Horace Walpole, to whom Carlyle
    attributes the story told here, frequently stresses his penchant for
    'acting the gout' in his *Memoirs*.

18. *Mahomet's Formulas were of 'wood waxed and oiled'*: In the
    second lecture Carlyle refers to Mahomet's rejection of the

'Wooden idols' of traditional Arab religion: 'this wild man of the Desert ... had seen into the kernel of the matter. Idolatry is nothing: these Wooden Idols of yours, "ye rub them with oil and wax, and the flies stick on them", – these are wood, I tell you!'

19. *Bookseller Osborne and Fourpence-halfpenny a day*: Thomas Osborne, a London bookseller and publisher, employed Johnson briefly to draw up a catalogue of the library of the Earl of Oxford. His chief claim to fame is that Johnson once struck him: 'Sir, he was impertinent to me, and I beat him' (Boswell, *Life of Johnson*). Johnson's financial circumstances were notoriously difficult in the early stages of his career, but it is not clear where Carlyle gets his precise figure from here.

PAST AND PRESENT

1. *the workhouse Bastille being filled to bursting*: See *Chartism*, note 11.

2. *Dr Alison*: William Pulteney Alison (1790–1859), an Edinburgh physician who, in a pamphlet entitled *Observations on the Management of the Poor in Scotland and its Effects on the Health of the Great Towns* (1840), revealed the disparity between minimum social conditions in England and in Scotland. He was able to show, for example, that the death-rate in Glasgow was twice as high as it was in London.

3. *Scotland ... must have a Poor-law*: In Scotland, until 1845, there was no legal claim to any kind of relief for any except the disabled.

4. *Potosi*: A South American province on the slopes of the Andes, famous for its silver-mines.

5. *Ugolino Hunger-tower*: The reference is to a story told by Dante, *Inferno*, xxxiii, concerning a Count Ugolino of Pisa who, together with his sons and grandsons, was incarcerated and starved as a consequence of a political feud. As Dante tells the story, the children beg the father to eat them.

6. *committee of ways and means*: ironically, a Parliamentary committee concerned with the raising of money.

7. *fifty-pounds tenants*: Tenants occupying lands or property liable to a yearly rent of not less than fifty pounds were enfranchised by the 1832 Reform Bill, and were thus exposed to the coercion of their landlords, which could be severe.

8. *the excellence of his Corn-Law*: The Corn-Laws, introduced in 1815 and revised in 1828, were a protectionist measure aimed at limiting the import of corn and were thus favoured by English land-owners. They ensured that the price of bread remained high and were a constant grievance during times of hardship. They were finally repealed in 1846.

9. *Midas longed for gold, and insulted the Olympians*: There are two legends about Midas: (i) that everything he touched turned to gold, as a result of a request he made to Dionysus, and (ii) that he 'insulted the Olympians' by preferring the music of Pan to that of Apollo, whereupon Apollo gave him the ears of an ass. Carlyle, not untypically, has confused the two stories.

10. *Dilletantism*: Throughout *Past and Present* Carlyle attacks those whose attitudes are dictated by taste and fashion. Here he refers to the attractions the ruins would have had for the proponents of the Gothic Revival and in particular to the fashion, at this time, for raising money to preserve ancient monuments.

11. Dugdale *and other enormous* Monasticons: The *Monasticon Anglicanum* of Sir William Dugdale (1605–86) is an invaluable source-book for the study of the English church before the Reformation.

12. *carucates*: A technical term, meaning the amount of land that can be ploughed in one year with a team of eight oxen.

13. *as Ben Jonson reminds us*: The reference is to *The Devil is an Ass*, I, vi:

> so much blasted flesh, as scarce hath soul
> In stead of salt to keep it sweet ...

and implies that self-preservation is as much a spiritual as a practical matter.

14. *Chartularies*: Collection of records.

15. Talamus: When referring directly to the *Chronicle*, Carlyle often introduces a latinism from the original to give an impression of authenticity. I have only provided translations where it seems genuinely necessary. The *Talamus* was the Abbot's private chamber.

16. *nemus*: Specifically, a wood with glades and pasture land for cattle.

17. *the Cellerarius*: the supervisor of the domestic arrangements of the Abbey.

18. *within the Liberties*: Monastic land was privileged and the temporal power was unable to interfere with its administration.

19. *'Satan with outspread wings'*: In an earlier chapter Carlyle gives an account of how the Abbot Samson, when a child, dreamt that he saw the Devil about to seize him and was only saved by the intervention of St Edmund.

20. *worse than our armies in Flanders*: The reference is to Sterne's *Tristram Shandy*, Book III, Ch. 11, where Dr Slop reads the order of excommunication: 'Our armies swore terribly in Flanders, cried my uncle Toby, – but nothing to this.'

21. *talk no more of all that!*: Carlyle is dismissing the clichés of neo-Gothic Romanticism.

22. *Puseyism*: Edward Bouverie Pusey (1800–82) was a leader of the Tractarian movement which laid particular emphasis on the importance of church ritual and culminated in the reception of John Henry Newman into the Roman Catholic church in 1845. Tractarianism was a live issue in the early 1840s when Carlyle was writing *Past and Present* and a particular point at issue was the correct interpretation of the thirty-nine articles. Carlyle clearly regards the movement's preoccupations as precious and irrelevant in the face of the issues that he believed confronted society.

23. *Sauerteig*: See *Chartism*, note 42.

24. *Pluto*: In Roman mythology the ruler of the underworld.

25. *Courts of Requests*: Courts for the recovery of small debts. In 1846 they were superseded by the County Courts.

26. *the ALMIGHTY MAKER is not like a Clockmaker*: William Paley, in his *Natural Theology* (1802), had argued that he was and the analogy became a cliché of rationalist theology.

27. *Valetism*: A term of Carlyle's own invention, implying an attitude of mind for which fashion rather than conviction is the motivating factor.

28. *Bridgwater Bequests*: A prize bequeathed by the eighth Earl of Bridgewater (1758–1829) for the best treatise on the 'Power, Wisdom and Goodness of God, as manifested in the Creation'.

29. *Dr Alison's Scotch facts*: See note 2 above.

LATTER-DAY PAMPHLETS

1. *a Prison of the exemplary or model kind*: Froude states specifically that the prison concerned was the Millbank Penitentiary, but

Philip Collins, in *Dickens and Crime*, London, 1962, has argued that the internal evidence suggests the Middlesex House of Correction at Coldbath Fields. Certainly Carlyle's description of 'The Captain of the place, a gentleman of ancient Military or Royal-Navy habits' would seem to fit Captain George Chesterton, Governor of Coldbath Fields from 1829 to 1854, while the regimen which Carlyle describes is similar to that in operation there in the 1840s and 1850s when his colouring of the details is discounted.

2. *Exeter Hall*: A large building, built in 1831 expressly for the use of charitable and religious institutions, which stood in the Strand.

3. *Norfolk Island*: A penal settlement in the Pacific Ocean to which were sent the most recalcitrant transported convicts.

4. *Rhadamanthus*: In Greek mythology the judge of departed souls, whose justice was rigorous and irrefutable.

5. *Loyal Canada, for instance, had to quench a rebellion the other year; and ... is called upon to pay the rebels their damages*: In 1837 a series of disturbances in the Canadian provinces led ultimately to the grant of responsible government to a united Canada in the late 1840s. One of the first acts of the Canadian ministers was to introduce a bill compensating those who had suffered damage in the 1837 disturbances.

6. *Seizures of Sapienza, correspondences with Sotomayor, remonstrances to Otho King of Athens ... etc.*: During the course of his isolationist argument Carlyle ridicules various issues in which the British Government, with Lord Palmerston as Foreign Secretary, had become involved. In 1850 King Otho of Athens became estranged from the British Government due to a series of petty incidents which included his annexation of the island of Sapienza, and the plundering of the house of Don Pacifico, a Gibralterian Jew and thus a British subject, who occupied the post of Portuguese consul at Piraeus. The British government blockaded the Greek ports to enforce acceptance of its terms for compensation. The Sotomayor correspondence involved a separate issue with the Spanish Government, the Duke of Sotomayor being Spanish Minister for Foreign Affairs in 1847. More important than the details of the incidents is Carlyle's belittling of them – in itself a jingoistic attack on gunboat diplomacy.

7. *mere Dalai-Lama pills*: i.e. quack remedies.

8. *that stable of King Augias*: The cleansing of the Augian stables was one of the labours of Hercules. They were occupied by an

immense herd of oxen and had never been cleaned before. Hercules accomplished the task by diverting the course of the River Alpheus, so that it ran through the stables.

9. *a Parliament elected according to the six or the four or any other number of 'points'*: See *Chartism*, note 1.

10. *the guano mountains*: Guano, a natural manure formed of the excrement of sea-fowl, was imported in large quantities to this country in the nineteenth century. It is mainly found in the islands off the coast of Peru.

11. *Crabbe*: Another of Carlyle's adopted personæ. He is introduced in the first pamphlet as a mythical journalist, editor of the equally mythical *Intermittent Radiator*.

12. *Pacifico the miraculous Gibraltar Jew*: See note 6 above.

13. *Radetzky is said to be advancing upon Milan*: In 1846 the aged Count Radetzky, an Austrian military hero, re-occupied Milan, which had temporarily achieved independence from Habsburg rule.

14. *John Milton ... received for answer, Five Pounds Sterling*: Milton sold the copyright of *Paradise Lost* for a basic payment of five pounds, with the stipulation that further payments were to be made according to the number of copies sold. He still only received a further five pounds in his own lifetime.

15. *George Hudson*: The famous Victorian railway promoter, whose career seemed to Carlyle symbolic of the delusions of the age. His speculations brought him an enormous fortune, but the railway crisis of 1847–8 brought about his downfall and in 1849, after being accused of fraud, he was ruined. The seventh *Latter-Day Pamphlet*, entitled 'Hudson's Statue' makes great play of his career.

16. *my friend Oliver*: i.e. Cromwell. Carlyle probably has in mind the dismissal of the Rump Parliament, described in *Oliver Cromwell*, Vol. III.

17. *New Downing Street*: The title Carlyle gives in the *Latter-Day Pamphlets* to his proposals for a reformed system of government.

18. *Tancred of Hauteville's sons ... conquered all Italy*: The conquest of south Italy and Sicily in the eleventh century was effected with a small army by the twelve sons of Tancred of Hauteville, a Norman nobleman.

19. *As poor Henry Marten wrote in Chepstow Castle long ago*: Henry Marten was a prominent supporter of the Puritan cause in the Civil War, and one of the judges of Charles I. After the

Restoration he was imprisoned for life; he died in Chepstow Castle in 1680. Carlyle described him, in *Oliver Cromwell's Letters and Speeches*, as 'a tight little fellow, though of somewhat loose life . . . a right hard-headed, stout-hearted little man, full of sharp fire and cheerful light'.

20. *Delolme philosophies*: See *Signs of the Times*, note 25.

THE LIFE OF JOHN STERLING

1. *a kind of* Magus . . . *his Dodona oak-grove (Mr Gilman's House at Highgate)*: The Magi were originally the ancient Persian priestly cast; Dodona was the seat of the oldest Greek oracle, dedicated to Zeus. Coleridge had lived at Highgate with the apothecary James Gilman since 1816, his addiction to opium having made it impossible for him to live alone.

2. *By attending to the 'reason' of man . . . and duly chaining-up the 'understanding' of man*: In his religious and ethical theorizing Coleridge posited a world divided between the observable processes of civilization, which were the province of the 'understanding', and abstract ethical values, which were the concern of 'reason'. 'Reason,' he wrote, 'is the Power of Universal and necessary Convictions, the Source and Substance of Truths above Sense', whereas 'the Judgements of the Understanding are binding only in relation to the objects of our Senses.' The two concepts are similar to the seminal concepts of 'Fancy' and 'Imagination' in Coleridge's literary theory.

3. *one grand book* On the Logos: In his later years Coleridge frequently referred to a projected *magnum opus* to be entitled 'Logosophia, or 'On the Logos', which would give a comprehensive account of his metaphysical theories. His various philosophical writings, as we have them, were conceived of only as incidental to this all-embracing design. In a letter of 1817 he refers to '20 years incessant thought and 10 years positive labour' devoted to 'the one in six volumes Logosophia . . . this work I cannot even get a Bookseller to print', but in fact nothing in publishable form was ever produced.

4. *fatamorganas*: Mirages attributable to fairy agency.

5. *a kind of Heaven-scaling Ixion*: According to Greek legend Ixion, who had murdered his father-in-law, was protected by Zeus. Notwithstanding, he attempted to seduce Hera (*Rom*: Juno), the wife of Zeus. By embracing a cloud which he believed

to be Hera he became father to various monstrous hybrids, most notably the Centaurs who were half man and half horse. Zeus then punished Ixion by binding him to a wheel of fire which turned for ever.

6. *Puseyisms*: See *Past and Present*, note 22.

HISTORY OF FREDERICK THE GREAT

1. *Sans Souci*: The palace built by Frederick the Great in Potsdam towards the end of his life. He died there in 1786.

2. *no sceptre but one like Agamemnon's*: On the face of it this seems a curious comparison, since the sceptre of Agamemnon was an heirloom of the house of Atreus, and originally made by Hephaestus, the divine metal-worker. (See *Iliad*, Book II, ll. 101 et seq.) Greek σχῆπτρον, a sceptre, however had the further meaning of a staff, and in the famous quarrel between Achilles and Agamemnon, with which the *Iliad* opens, the staff held by Achilles and passed from speaker to speaker is described as having been cut from a tree. This, I suspect, accounts for the apparent confusion in this case.

3. *Day and Martin*: Makers of a proprietary brand of boot-polish of proverbial popularity.

4. *a dead-lift spasm of all its energies for Seven Years*: i.e. the Seven Years War, during which Frederick faced a coalition of Austria, Russia, France, Sweden and Saxony. The conclusion of the war left Frederick in control of the disputed territories of Pomerania and Silesia and can be said to have established the nationhood of Prussia itself, thus laying the foundations of modern Germany.

5. *the first of the modern Titans*: Mirabeau is the one unqualified hero of *The French Revolution*: 'A man who had "swallowed all formulas", who in these strange times, felt called to live Titanically, and also to die so. As he, for his part, had swallowed all formulas, what Formula is there, never so comprehensive, that will express truly the *plus* and the *minus* of him; give us the accurate net-result of him? There is hitherto none such. Moralities not a few must shriek condemnatory over this Mirabeau; the Morality by which he could be judged has not yet been uttered in the speech of men' (Vol. II, Book Three, Ch. 8). Mirabeau returned to France after a period of secret service in Prussia and took a prominent part in the early stages of the Revolution,

aiming to reform the monarchy rather than to overthrow it. His premature death in 1791 undoubtedly affected the course of the Revolution, removing as it did a powerful influence for firm government.

6. *before Pelion leapt on Ossa*: In Greek mythology the Aloidae, two infant giants, threatened to beseige Olympus by piling Mt Pelion on Mt Ossa. The phrase 'Pelion upon Ossa' has become a proverbial expression of the escalation of disaster.

7. *Terrific Drawcansir figures*: Drawcansir is a character who appears in the last act of Villiers's burlesque, *The Rehearsal*, killing the various combatants on both sides of a mock-heroic stage battle. The play itself is a parody of the kind of heroic tragedy made popular by Dryden.

8. *before the era of bulletins and Agamemnon*: Carlyle suggests here that the French Revolution and the Napoleonic wars were the first great European events to be extensively reported in the press; 'Agamemnon' in this case would seem to refer to Napoleon himself.

9. *Austerlitz ... Wagram ... Rossbach ... Leuthen*: The battles of Austerlitz (1805) and Wagram (1809) were significant successes for Napoleon in his European campaign, bringing him victories against the Russians and the Austrians respectively. They are here contrasted with the Battles of Rossbach and Leuthen (1757) which were important victories for Frederick the Great in the Seven Years War. Both are vividly described in *Frederick the Great*, Book 28.

10. *Brandenburg sand*: The province of Brandenburg was notoriously low and flat, its soil consisting largely of sand.

11. *George II., seeing good ... to take Maria Theresa's side in the Austrian-Succession War*: The War of the Austrian Succession (1740–48) was a consequence of the death of Charles VI of Austria, the last male of the Habsburg line. The succession was invested in his daughter, Maria Theresa, who, supported only by England, faced a European alliance, including Frederick the Great, determined to exploit the apparent weakness of her position. Although she lost Silesia to Frederick, Maria Theresa held out for over seven years, and the Peace of Aix-la-Chapelle established her as the rightful ruler of Austria. In the Seven Years War England changed sides and supported Frederick against Austria.

12. *those baleful Historic Acherons and Stygian Fens*: In classical mythology the Rivers Acheron and Styx were both rivers of the underworld.

13.   *the Frenzy of John Dennis*: John Dennis (1657–1734) was the
      author of various tragedies and was satirized for his bombastic
      mode of expression by Pope (*Essay on Criticism*, iii, ll.585–7).
      Pope also attacked Dennis in a pamphlet entitled *The Narrative
      of Dr Robert Norris, concerning the strange and deplorable
      frenzy of Mr John Dennis* (1713).

14.   *and then cry, like Alexander of Macedon*: Alexander the Great
      was reputed to have wept at the realization that there were no
      more kingdoms to conquer.

15.   *Sauerteig's last batch of* Springwurzeln: Yet another work by
      Carlyle's mythical German historian. Translated, its title is
      the name of a plant of poisonous, but also medicinal qualities
      (the caper-spurge).

16.   *all Californias, English National Debts*: Carlyle is deriding the
      conventional historian's preoccupation with materialistic issues:
      these two examples are instances of wealth of mythic propor-
      tions. The example of California was probably suggested by the
      discovery of gold there in 1848.

REMINISCENCES

1.   '*Cromwell*': Carlyle's edition of *Oliver Cromwell's Letters and
      Speeches*, which was completed and first published in 1845.

2.   *till we, as last shift, gave the rough MSS. to Chapman* (*in For-
      ster's company one winter Sunday*): Carlyle's difficulties over the
      publication of *Latter-Day Pamphlets* arose from the contentious
      nature of their content, (see p. 253). Frederick Chapman was the
      head of the publishing house of Chapman and Hall, publishers
      of Carlyle's work from *Past and Present* onwards; John Forster,
      the biographer of Dickens, was a close friend of the Carlyles, and
      particularly of Jane.

3.   *Neuberg*: Joseph Neuberg, a German admirer of Carlyle, then
      resident in London, who accompanied him on his first visit to
      Germany and acted as his amanuensis during the writing of
      Frederick the Great.

4.   *that of the 'demon fowls'*: Both the Carlyles were poor sleepers,
      and Carlyle in particular was neurotic about noise. During the
      early stages of his work on *Frederick the Great* he was involved
      in a dispute with his neighbours over the noise made by their
      domestic fowls. Carlyle eventually tried to solve the problem by
      building a soundproof study, with scarcely successful results.

5. *Alcides*: i.e. Hercules.
6. *this Lerna hydra*: Lerna was the district where Hercules slew the Hydra, the many-headed monster.
7. *Kirtlebridge Station*: The Carlyle family home was at this time at Scotsbrig, a farm in Ecclefechan, Kirtlebridge being the nearest station.
8. *John*: Carlyle's younger brother, to whom Froude refers as 'his early friend, the brother of his heart'. He also aspired to a literary career but, save for a translation of Dante, achieved very little.
9. *Preuss and Co.*: i.e. the German historians who had written on Frederick the Great. Preuss's *Friedrich der Grosse, eine Lebensgeschichte* (1832-4) first inspired Carlyle's own interest in Frederick; Carlyle describes Preuss in *Frederick the Great* as, 'A meritoriously exact man; acquainted with the details of Friedrich's Biography ... as few men ever were' (Book IV, Ch. 1).
10. *John Chorley*: A friend and admirer of Carlyle, who appointed himself supervisor of the soundproof study project.
11. *Tophet*: See *French Revolution*, note 16.